ARCO

10,000 IDEAS

for term papers, projects, reports and speeches

5th edition

INTRIGUING, ORIGINAL RESEARCH
TOPICS FOR EVERY STUDENT'S NEED

KATHRYN LAMM

3704
$14.95

28219

Fifth Edition

MACMILLAN
A Simon & Schuster Macmillan Company
1633 Broadway
New York, NY 10019-6785

Macmillan Publishing books may be purchased for business or sales promtional
use. For information please write: Special Markets Department, Macmillan
Publishing USA, 1633 Broadway, New York, NY 10019.

An Arco Book

MACMILLAN is a registered trademark of Macmillan, Inc.
Arco is a registered trademark of Prentice-Hall, Inc.

Library of Congress Number: 97-81090
ISBN: 0-02-862512-9

Manufactured in the United States of America

1 2 3 4 5 6 7 8 9 10

CONTENTS

How to Use This Book

Here's the book every student has been waiting for. It is chock-full of timely, interesting topics suitable for almost any research assignment, from the junior high school through college years. The wide range of ideas suggested here is designed to plunge students into the research project process by helping them overcome the first problem students always have: What topic shall I choose? And it is indeed often a difficult choice, hampered by a lack of familiarity with the wide range of subjects available and an absence of suggestions from other sources. This book bridges these gaps by bringing to mind thought-provoking and stimulating subjects. There is something for everyone here; 10,000 choices, categorized by subject and designated by degree of difficulty. Once a topic is selected, the rest of the project will flow along smoothly.

Teachers may choose topics, using this book as a source of ideas, or students may be free to select their own. The virtue of this book is that all of its topics have been tested, all can be researched with relative ease in most libraries, and each will yield substantial and interesting information. This timely new edition has been updated to include current, relevant topics for today's students.

A research project can be a term paper, report, debate, speech or thesis. Each of these usually involves the selection of a topic, comprehensive research, a narrowing of the contents to a manageable level, and documentation of the resulting material. These steps are necessary regardless of what format the final product takes. The purpose is to find out what you don't know by using outside sources. Students are assigned research projects for all sorts of reasons: to learn how to use the library and all of its many reference sources, to organize the data they locate, to uncover information about an interesting subject, or to lead them into new areas of knowledge.

For whatever reason the assignment is made, or whatever its level, the basic research procedures are the same. And since you must start with a topic, you'll need to know how to use this book.

The Symbols

As you read through the different subject categories, you will notice that each topic has a small symbol in the left-hand margin. These symbols have been included to help you select a topic that is suitable for your particular assignment. Requirements vary, and so do libraries and other sources of information. Some topics are more suitable for research in large academic libraries, while information about others can be easily found in most public and high school libraries. The symbols that follow will help you find an ideal topic, one you can successfully research according to the conditions of your assignment. These symbols can also assist a teacher to make assignments at the correct level of difficulty.

●   This topic is of average difficulty and is usually suitable for high school and undergraduate level assignments.

§   Substitutions are possible for the underlined word(s) in this subject area. For example: "Migration patterns of the trumpeter swan" may be changed to some other bird or animal, provided the change is both interesting and appropriate. (Remember, some animals and birds don't migrate).

➤   This subject area is broad and may have to be narrowed down to accommodate a particular assignment. In general, the higher the grade level, the more detailed, complex, and narrow the subject coverage is expected to be.

★   Ample information should be available on this topic in most libraries.

○   This topic may require prior or specialized knowledge on the part of the researcher in order to read and understand the material well enough to use it wisely. If in doubt, test-read several articles in this subject area before making a final topic choice.

▲   This subject may require the information resources of a large public or academic library. Do not select it if you are in a lower grade or if your research options are limited.

↙   Not all communities have local information that is easily acces-
       sible. Check these source possibilities before selecting this topic.
       Bear in mind also that not all "local option" topics are applica-
       ble to every area; if they are not, they may well suggest a re-
       lated topic that will be more appropriate.

×   The use of examples and supporting evidence will enhance this
       topic.

The way to use this book effectively is to browse through it, especially
in those areas you think might be most interesting. Select a topic you would
enjoy learning about, and check the symbol in the left-hand margin to see
whether it is in your area of competency and within the means of your information sources. Take into account the type, size, and scope of your assignment, and if necessary, narrow or broaden the topic accordingly. Do
not choose a topic, for example, that requires extensive research when your
final product need only be a short 500 words.

You will notice that in almost every subject category the topics range
widely and often overlap other subject areas. They were compiled in this
manner in order to offer the widest range of suggestions, and to inspire as
many variations as possible. While many topics suggest a specific point of
view, you are free to select the most appealing aspect of any topic, including the opposing view. Once again, however, be sure to select an area
that will be interesting and fun to learn about.

Some Helpful Hints as You Go

- Select a topic that interests and intrigues you. You will be spending many intimate hours with this topic, and there is no rule against enjoying your research.

- Choose a topic that fits your educational background. You must be able to understand what you read, and be able to put it into your own words. If the topic is too complex, your data will be unmanageable. This is especially true of highly technical subjects.

- Choose a topic that fits your assignment. Questions about the suitability of a topic should be addressed to your instructor.

- Be sure the topic you select is one about which you can remain objective. Don't go into a project with preconceptions. Be prepared to change your opinion because of new evidence; the "open mind" is a distinct advantage in research.

- Consider the time schedule allowed for completion. Will it be sufficient to allow you to find the necessary information? Your preliminary search should give you an indication of how difficult it will be to locate the material.

- Do not expect to find a whole book on your topic. If you do, chances are the topic is too broad. A research project is usually an exercise in total coverage of a narrow subject area.

- Don't rely on your memory. Make thorough notes of all new information before you return the book or article to the library shelf. And make sure you know where all of the information came from (dates, title, author, etc.).

- Learn how indexes and other reference sources are arranged and what data you can expect to find in them. If you are in doubt about using an unfamiliar reference book, check the introductory pages explaining its coverage, arrangement, and uses. In this way you can teach yourself to be an independent and resourceful researcher.

- After becoming thoroughly knowledgeable about your selected subject, make an outline of what you will include in your final project. You will probably change it as you move along, but it will give your research more direction.

- Even with an outline, you will probably collect more information than you can use. Resist the temptation to include it in your final draft; it won't fit and will probably weaken your presentation.

- Don't give up too easily. Most research requires patience and persistence. Every so often, consult the research strategy outlined above and evaluate your tactics.

- The common problems with research projects are: failure to narrow the topic sufficiently, failure to use enough sources in the research, failure to assimilate and organize information from sources, and failure to document sources properly. These flaws are all easy to overcome, and should be caught at the topic selection and research stage, rather than at the writing stage. By the time you write, you're usually so committed to the topic that you can't change your approach. Avoid these late problems by following the tips and strategies above.

- *Above all, ask for assistance.* People in libraries want to help — that's why they are there. Complete as much of your research as possible independently, then approach the librarian with your remaining needs. Remember, it is a rare researcher — at any level — who doesn't need help sometimes.

Adolescents

See also: Children; Education; Family Life; Literature for Children; Marriage

- Common teenage stress factors
- The proper punishment of juvenile offenders is a contested issue. Discuss standard contemporary procedures and the suggested reforms.
★ A social and psychological profile of a typical teenage runaway
- What can be done to help prevent runaways? Examine some of the more successful programs.
○ Teenage schizophrenia
- Why have competency test scores of high school students consistently declined?
- What have studies proved to be the relationship between working parents and juvenile delinquency? Are there other relevant factors? What are some of them?
★ The problems of adolescent marriages
- The causes of teenage drug addiction
✕ How parents can improve communication with their teenager(s)
- Dietary deficiencies of American

teenagers. Detail these nutritional lacks. How do they affect health, both short- and long-term?
§ Adolescence in China
○ The teenager and peer group pressures. Characterize typical response patterns.
- Teenage alcoholism is increasing. To what do experts attribute this change?
- Teenagers and marijuana: short-term and long-range effects. Select some of the most recent and significant studies. Compare their conclusions.
▲ Many educators charge that students in American high schools are undisciplined. How widespread is the problem? In what ways has it affected learning?
- Psychological stresses of the overweight teenager
★ Study techniques that work for high school students
★ How to get into the college you want
- Changing attitudes toward mar-

6

riage and the family among America's youth

- ● A profile of the female juvenile offender
- ● Is college necessary? Should young people be allowed to make this choice?
- ● Problems of the married high school student
- ▲ Should the high school curriculum be expanded? How?
- ● Measures to rehabilitate the teenage dropout. Do the experts agree?
- ✔ Summer employment possibilities for teenagers. Investigate this on a local level or as a broad national overview.
- ● The increasing prevalence of teenage pregnancies. What are the socioeconomic factors involved?
- ● The stages and ages of adolescence in modern America
- ● Major causes of juvenile crime in urban centers
- ➡ Common psychological problems of adolescents
- ● Emotional aspects of teenage pregnancy for both of the potential parents
- ● Sexual behavior and the American teenager: Changing mores?
- ● Adolescent peer pressure and how it is used by advertisers
- ★ Typical problems of the high school dropout
- ★ How to talk about sex with your adolescent
- ● Adolescent suicide: its prevalence and possible causes
- ● The youth movement in Nazi Germany before World War II
- × How teenagers can best communicate with their parents
- ● Adolescence in America as described in *The Adventures of Tom Sawyer* (Mark Twain) and in *The Catcher in the Rye* (J.D. Salinger)
- ● Refute or defend this analysis: The American teenager has been portrayed as self-indulgent, self-centered, and immature as compared to his/her European counterpart.
- ● The relationship between juvenile delinquency and family instability
- ● How to talk to adolescents about love and marriage
- ● Adolescence and peer group pressures. What are some of the normal methods for dealing with them? What are some of the problems?
- ▲ What are some of the successful programs being utilized to improve parent-adolescent communication?
- ● What's wrong with America's high schools: a survey of current opinion
- ★ What are the television viewing habits of the average teenager?
- ● Typical attitudes of adolescents toward drug use and abuse
- ● "Teen Power" as a marketing and advertising concept. What

is the purchasing power of teenagers in terms of dollars? In
market segments?
- Levels of adolescent drug abuse:
1970 & 1990
- Adolescent health problems
★ Teenagers in China today. How
have their lives changed since
1930? 1950? Tienanmen Square?
× How teenage parents can cope
with adult responsibilities. Cite

the most common problems encountered by young mothers and
fathers and give examples of
helpful solutions.
★ The effects of crack/cocaine use on
adolescents. Consider physiological, emotional and social factors.
× Should contraceptive devices be
available to teenagers at high
school clinics?

Key to Symbols

•	average difficulty	◆	narrow down topic
§	substitutes possible	▲	large public or college library required
★	ample information in most libraries	✔	local option topic
○	specialized knowledge required	×	examples and supporting evidence needed

Advertising

See also: Journalism; Media; Television and Radio

× Why (or how) advertising pays

• Compare and contrast the depiction of women in the advertisements in women's magazines (*Ladies' Home Journal, Redbook, Woman's Day*) to those in men's magazines (*Playboy, Penthouse, Esquire*).

• The use of jingles in advertising and why they "sell"

§ Macho beer ads

• The responsible advertiser. What are the major ethical considerations?

→ The art of store window displays

• Why some professions do not advertise and what would happen if they did

• Color and its interrelationship with sales appeal

• How television commercial audiences are determined and selected by the advertiser

▲ Is advertising necessary? The Hershey Company: Survey the changes in policy and procedures. How have these changes affected profits?

▲ Defend or refute: "Advertising regulates discussion of public issues through its control of the news media." (K.A. Longman)

▲ Political advertising. Select a particular campaign and analyze the advertising components used. What were the effects?

• Advertising before 1500

• The origins of outdoor advertising

• How advertising rates are determined

★ How to complain about advertising

• A psychiatrist recently stated that advertising is permanently damaging to American society. Defend this thesis or prove it is unjustified.

• Subliminal advertising: Threat or gimmick?

★ Job opportunities in advertising

• The psychology of soap opera advertising. Analyze at least twenty samples selected by time-span (all-inclusive) or by type of product (selective).

× Does advertising create unnecessary needs?

• Advertising and the oil industry.

Has the industry changed its advertising approach? If so, why?

➤ What are the most effective advertising techniques? Select a medium.

✕ Analyze examples of deceptive television advertising.

○ Design an advertising campaign for a new product (soap, baby food, cosmetic, etc.).

● Fifty years of cigarette advertising: a historical overview

★ How some advertising manipulates consumer fears

➤ The effects of television advertising on children. Cite appropriate authorities and studies. (May be narrowed to one type of effect.)

● How to enforce the truth in advertising

● Consumer advocates and nutritionists have urged the promotion of unsugared products for children. Does advertising reflect these proposals? Why or why not?

● How advertising mailing lists are compiled. How are recipients targeted?

○ Describe the ways in which industrial development and advertising are interrelated. Why do some large corporations (General Foods, Proctor and Gamble) spend a great deal of money on advertising, and others (Mobil Corporation)

spend a relatively minor amount?

○ Many economists feel that advertising distorts the functioning of a truly competitive marketplace, while many businessmen view advertising as a prime instrument of competition. Discuss this paradox.

★ What are the traditional arguments against advertising? Consider both the social and the economic aspects.

● Formulate a complete creative advertising strategy for a product. Explain why your strategy is the best for the product.

● How to formulate realistic advertising goals

● How advertisers determine media budget allocations among newspapers, television, magazines, direct mail, etc.

● Compare and contrast publicity and public relations.

✕ Social class (as opposed to income and education) as a market determinant for advertisers

● Who uses advertising agencies?

✕ What were some of the advertising innovations of Francis Wayland Ayer? How did they affect the field as a whole?

● The roles and goals of the National Advertising Review Board. Should their power be expanded, decreased, or changed?

- What is the "public interest"? Does it have the same meaning in advertising that it does in medicine, government, and law?
- How should the fairness doctrine be interpreted and extended toward advertising for young children?
- The recent growth of social advertising. What factors are involved in this growth? Will expansions continue?
- How is advertising research used in modern advertising practice? What are some of the inherent shortcomings?
- ○ What are the benefits of multimedia advertising programs? Compare a typical ad campaign to one using a single medium.
- Examine various definitions of advertising. Are these sources objective? Are they from supporters or detractors? Include some from earlier times as well as from contemporary sources.
- ★ Regulations that monitor and control fraudulent advertising
- Compare and contrast the advertising in three women-oriented magazines (*Cosmopolitan, Ladies' Home Journal,* and *Ms.*) in terms of products, quality of advertising, consumer markets, etc.
- × Study twenty newspaper or magazine advertisements and analyze their differing approaches to the consumer.
- ▲ Posttesting versus pretesting of advertisements
- ○ Select ten television commercials and detail their marketing approaches and the competitive strategies involved. Similar products are preferable.
- How to plan an advertising budget for a small business. Select a hypothetical product or service if an actual business is not available.
- ▲ How to write television commercials
- Radio advertising, 1920–1940
- Should outdoor advertising be encouraged, regulated, or abolished? Include the views of business, consumer and environmentalist.
- Forms of advertising before the twentieth century
- ▲ Newspaper advertising in England in the seventeenth and eighteenth centuries
- Factors contributing to the rapid growth of advertising in the past century
- How to measure advertising success
- How advertisers locate, define, and forecast specific markets for their goods and services
- The pros and cons of federal legislation regulating advertising
- Compare the benefits and disadvantages of utilizing an in-house advertising department for a business concern versus the

use of an independent advertising agency.

★ Controls and regulation of advertising since 1925. Select one medium for this survey.

● Advertising in colonial America

● What an advertising agency can do for its clients

● Refute or defend: Advertising narrows the range of consumer choices.

× Compare and contrast: "created" need and "natural" need

● Select a large sample of television commercials and analyze them according to the standards of the National Association of Broadcasters and the Wheeler-Lea Amendment.

§ Changes in automotive advertising since 1915

➥ Discuss the relation between advertising and economic growth

● The advertising techniques and practices of P.T. Barnum

● Compare and contrast the advantages and disadvantages of radio and television advertising in terms of audience, costs, market potential, and other relevant issues.

● Advertising expenditures decline in economic recessions and depressions. Does advertising generate sales or do sales cause more advertising?

▲ Product posttesting procedures. How and when is each used?

Do advertising experts feel that some are more accurately valid and reliable than others?

● Advertisers know that middle- and upper-class consumers listen to and read more advertising than consumers in lower economic levels. What are the reasons for this differential? How does it affect advertising strategy?

● How advertisers select the appropriate television (or radio) time

● How contemporary advertising reflects the "me" generation market

● Advertising changed with the beginning of the Industrial Revolution. Describe these changes and long-range effects.

● Why advertising campaigns fail

★ Compare and contrast propaganda and advertising.

➥ How has advertising changed the attitudes and beliefs of America? Select a particular subject area.

✔ What makes a successful advertising person, according to the people who hire them? Conduct a variety of interviews to answer this question.

● Political advertising is demeaning both to the office and to the candidate. What are the issues involved in this statement? Are there two sides to the question?

★ The mail-order catalog business in America, past and present

○ An advertising executive said, "Consumers read ads, not creative strategies." What are the implications of this quotation?

× From magazines or newspapers, select a variety of advertisements which seem to be unethical or misleading. After thoughtful analysis, discuss the ads in terms of their source, audience objectives, and basic truth.

▲ American newspaper advertising started in *The Philadelphia Gazette*, Benjamin Franklin's paper. Analyze the ads which appeared during the first years. Were they original? Do we still employ these techniques today?

★ How consumers can fight back against misleading, deceptive, or fraudulent advertising

● How the Pure Food and Drug Act (1906) changed American advertising

● The first magazine advertisements

× How does print copywriting differ from broadcast copywriting? What are the advantages and disadvantages of each?

● Should advertising copy be oriented toward persuading the listener or reader, or should it be aimed only to inform? What are the ethical issues involved?

★ Has the current advertising trend of naming competitors been proven successful? Why or why not?

Key to Symbols

● **average difficulty**
§ **substitutes possible**
★ **ample information in most libraries**
○ **specialized knowledge required**

↙ **narrow down topic**
▲ **large public or college library required**
↙ **local option topic**
× **examples and supporting evidence needed**

African Americans

See also: Ethnic and Minority Groups

- Evaluate the relative successes and failures of the nonviolent boycotts and sit-ins in the South during the 1950's.
- ▲ Has the African American ghetto changed since 1950? Consider social, economic, and educational elements.
- The role of African Americans in professional sports. In what ways has this role changed? Construct an overview.
- ★ Slavery and emancipation as depicted in *Uncle Tom's Cabin* (Harriet Beecher Stowe)
- ➥ African Americans in today's labor market
- ★ Origins of the Black Muslim religion
- Compare and contrast: the 1965 Watts riots and the 1992 Los Angeles riots
- ▲ Social organization in the urban African-American ghetto
- ○ Political power and the African-American coalition, 1950 to present
- The use of black dialect by young schoolchildren and how it affects their learning abilities
- ○ Does using black English hamper the social and economic advancement of adults?
- ▲ Self-concept problems in African American ghetto children
- ★ The treatment and punishment of fugitive slaves before the Civil War
- ★ The achievements and failures of the NAACP (National Association for the Advancement of Colored People)
- The status of African Americans directly after the Civil War
- African American militancy, 1965–1990
- § Life as a poor black person in Kenya
- Implications of the Dred Scott Case
- James Meredith and desegregation of the University of Mississippi
- ✕ African Americans in American society as characterized in the fiction of Toni Morrison
- ○ African American voters in the South; their impact, past and present
- ▲ Compare and contrast the social connotations of the terms "negro," "colored," "black," "nigger," and others that are relevant.

14

- Measures to alleviate unemployment in the ghetto
- The recent successes of African Americans in Southern politics
- Racism in the O.J. Simpson trial. Examine both sides of this controversy.
- The prevalence of sickle-cell anemia among African American youth. What are the genetic factors?
- The Scottsboro case: a historical reevaluation
- African Americans and the military in modern America
- Television's images of African Americans
- African American participation in the Civil War
- African American attitudes in Ralph Ellison's *The Invisible Man*
- ★ Discuss the experiences and conclusions of John H. Griffin, the white writer who passed as a black and wrote *Black Like Me.*
- Common practices of early American slave traders
- ○ African American identity versus white ideals and standards
- ▲ The contemporary African American artists
- What happened in Little Rock from 1957 to 1959?
- Interracial marriages. Evaluate how well they tend to work. What are the major difficulties for husband, wife, and children? How has society traditionally viewed the union? Has this view changed?
- African American women in politics
- Civil rights advances, 1980–present
- Martin Luther King's Washington march, 1963
- ✕ The image of the alienated African American man in American literature, 1950–1990
- Organized labor and the African American worker
- What economic advances were made by African Americans during World War I? How was this progress eroded by postwar events?
- ✔ Social, economic, and political status and situation of African Americans in your local community
- Treatment of African Americans in Southern prisons. Have conditions improved? Are conditions different in state institutions and in local units?
- ○ Black music: an African heritage
- Black colleges in the United States: their status today
- Racism in the North before the Civil War
- The establishment of Harlem as an African American ghetto
- ★ Watts riot (1965)
- The origins of the Black Power movement in America
- ★ Racial balance through busing: Success or failure?
- Compare and contrast Martin Luther King and Malcolm X.

- The slave ship rebellion led by Cinque in 1839. Include in this coverage his eventual defense by John Quincy Adams.
- ✗ African American women as single parents: some typical problems
- ✗ Literary stereotypes of slavery
- Racism in children's literature

- ★ The Civil Rights Act and its immediate effects
- The racial undertones in *The Tales of Brer Rabbit*
- The verdict in the Rodney King case has been widely debated. Examine this debate and draw a conclusion.

Key to Symbols

- **average difficulty**
- § **substitutes possible**
- ★ **ample information in most libraries**
- ○ **specialized knowledge required**

- ☛ **narrow down topic**
- ▲ **large public or college library required**
- ↙ **local option topic**
- ✗ **examples and supporting evidence needed**

Aging

See also: Social Problems

- The issues involved in compulsory retirement
- Standards for nursing homes. Are they adequate? How is the industry monitored and regulated?
- ☛ Problems of the aged in the United States.
- ★ Medicare problems and prospects
- Stereotypes of the aged in children's books
- Home core vs. nursing home care for the infirm elderly
- § Life-styles in Sun City, Arizona (or in another retirement community)
- ★ Death: Hospital, hospice, or home?
- Financial problems of the ageing today
- ✔ Survey the nursing homes for the elderly in your area and compare them to state and national standards.
- ★ Early retirement: pros and cons
- In the past, Alzheimer's disease has been both progressive and incurable. Are recent findings more optimistic?
- Economic aspects of housing for the elderly
- ✔ Special accommodations for the elderly in your community. Include

social and cultural programs, recreation centers, special pricing, and privileges.
- The joys of being old. A number of books and essays have been written on this subject. Read some of them and discuss the views expressed.
- Crime rates and the elderly
- Retirement in the United States: the current economic outlook for those about to retire
- § Coping with a stroke
- Are retirement communities the answer for the aged? Why or why not?
- Social and psychological difficulties for the elderly hard-of-hearing
- ☛ How society views the elderly. Treat this subject either historically or on a contemporary basis
- Occupational discrimination against the older worker
- ▲ Issues involved in nursing home certification
- O Does the brain age? Myths and reality
- ★ Sex and the aging process
- Self-advocacy groups for older

people
- The case for subsidized housing for the aged
- Scientific relationships between nutrition and aging
★ How to mentally prepare for retirement
- Major factors influencing longevity. Cite informed opinion and the results of current research.
- Activities appropriate for senior citizen centers
- Alzheimer's disease: a silent epidemic
- How senior citizens can keep in shape through physical conditioning
- Independent living for the elderly
★ Are social security benefits adequate for the future? What changes have been proposed? Discuss their scope and practicality.
▲ Changing conceptions of senility. Examine both the medical and psychological advances.
- Occupations for those over sixty
- Discuss the reasons for the increase in mistreatment of the aged ("battered grandparents").
- Crime prevention measures for senior citizens
- Home food delivery for the aged and homebound
➥ Living conditions in nursing homes for the low-income elderly
- How aging affects personality
× Successful volunteer projects for senior citizens
- Healthy exercise programs for the aged
▲ Trends in geriatric research
○ Can we slow the aging process? What are the findings of recent studies?
- Medical care for the elderly in the United States: a historical overview
- Retirement and mental health
- The elderly widow in American society
- Sports for the elderly
★ How to choose a nursing home
★ Why Social Security will be insufficient for the retirement years of most older people today
× Myths of old age. Counter these myths with relevant scientific, psychological, and sociological data and findings.
- The Senior Olympics. What are the goals of this organization? Who participates?
▲ Senior day care: an idea whose time has come
- Many older citizens have participated in Elderhostel programs all over the world. Enlarge upon this program, its activities, goals, accomplishments and participants.
- Discuss the implications of this statement: Age is a social state, not a biological one.
- Identify the stereotypes of old people as generally portrayed on television. Are they valid? In what ways are they misleading?
○ Biological theories of aging

Agriculture

See also: Ecology; Environment; Gardening

- Why farmers do not readily accept alternative pest control measures
- § Environmental constraints for agriculture in the Great Plains area of the United States
- Describe and evaluate the economic and ecological pros and cons of crop monoculture.
- Examine Carl Sauer's theories on the origins of agriculture. Do modern authorities agree on these points?
- How is the federal government alleviating the major economic problems faced by the American farmer? Should other measures be initiated? Describe them.
- § The effects of mechanization on wheat (corn, etc.) production
- The Green Revolution: What were its origins and original goals?
- ➤ Select a recent innovation in agricultural technology and detail its characteristics, uses, and significance to the industry.
- Prospects for marine agriculture
- Rice farmers in Indonesia and

their ancient water-moving technology
- ★ The growth of agribusiness in the United States
- ★ Can the small farmer survive?
- Predator control measures. Discuss the controversy over methods commonly employed.
- ➤ Status of agricultural development in third world countries.
- ○ New innovations in farm machinery
- ★ Agricultural production problems in Russia. Consider the period from 1965 to the present.
- ➤ The economics of modern farm life. Select either the small family farm or a larger multiacre unit.
- ★ Crop subsidies: Boom or boondoggle?
- The migrant farm worker in the United States today
- ★ Pesticides and the agricultural community
- ➤ Agricultural legislation and treaties since 1900. Examine their range, import, and feasibility.
- Collective farms in Israel

§ Agricultural policies in Costa Rica, or select another developing nation. Include agrarian reform measures.

★ How inflation and high interest rates affect the small farmer

• Careers in agribusiness

✓ What life was like on a farm in your locality ninety or one hundred-and-ninety years ago

• Organizing the small farm for efficiency and productivity

• Tobacco production from the American colonies to the present day

• Cattle brands in the West

▲ Agricultural applications of current genetic engineering innovations and discoveries

• The utility of artificial insemination of livestock for the modern farmer

★ Twentieth-century cattle rustling

▲ The ancient Hohokam Indians' desert irrigation techniques in the Southwestern United States

• Chemical fertilizer hazards

○ The functions of animal castration in modern herd management

➧ How to operate a successful truck farm

• Hydroponic gardening

▲ Modern methods of crop rotation

• The United States' farm subsidy programs, past and present

★ How the spread of plow and draft animals altered early agricultural methods

• Fertilizers today: their chemical base, cost, utility, and benefits

▲ The culture of edible freshwater plants for human and animal consumption

• Advances in natural pest management. Discuss the most successful examples of biological control by beneficial insects, etc.

• Future prospects for food production in underdeveloped countries: a world view

• Large-scale fish farming in the United States. Has this been economically feasible in the past? Where and how?

▲ Prospects for agroforestry

• Compare and contrast monoculture and mixed culture farming

• Environmental damage caused by large-scale stock farming

★ Health factors of pesticide residues

▲ Wind protection measures for farmlands

• Agricultural cooperatives: Are they successful?

○ Ramifications of the introduction of antibiotics in animal feed

• Ecological weed control

§ Modern poultry management

• Agricultural-based pollution of water supplies

• The pineapple empire of Hawaii

➧ Food production in an overcrowded world: resources and technology

AIDS

See also: Health; Medicine

★ New drug applications have helped many AIDS patients. What are they and why do they work?

★ Evaluate and describe the ethical considerations of mandatory AIDS testing.

● AIDS and the blood supply. Consider past problems and today's safeguards.

● How have needle exchange programs been successful in decreasing the spread of AIDS?

● Is AIDS a true epidemic? Why or why not?

★ Is the public concern about school children with AIDS justified? Consider known modes of transmission and significant opinion of appropriate experts.

● Using the World Health Organization's statistics, debate the global estimates of HIV/AIDS incidence. Include projections of future infections.

▲ What are the legal protections for persons infected with AIDS and HIV?

○ Describe the use of the drug AZT (and others) for AIDS patients. What are the advantages and disadvantages?

✕ Special problems of infected children

○ How gene therapy is being used to treat AIDS and HIV

● Sexual attitudes and AIDS

● Discuss changing homosexual lifestyles since the increase in AIDS victims.

● Describe the development of HIV to full-blown AIDS.

✕ How HIV/AIDS has changed our behavior

★ Why the AIDS epidemic is no longer "someone else's problem"

○ Are we close to a cure? Evaluate the last few years of research.

● How AIDS is transmitted

● Who has the right to know about positive test results?

● AIDS babies: what is the incidence, treatment, and survival prognosis?

● Insurance providers have often proved adversarial in their relations with HIV/AIDS patients. Has this improved? Why or why not?

★ Doctors have often refused to treat HIV/AIDS patients. Is this justifiable?

✕ Has the governmental response to the epidemic been influenced by the fact that most of those originally afflicted were homosexuals and drug addicts?

● Mandatory AIDS testing is nothing more than the greatest good for the greatest number. True?

➤ Examine proposed policies of the United States and other nations in their fight to control the spread of AIDS.

✕ Knowingly infecting others with HIV has occurred. Examine several instances.

★ AIDS is particularly virulent in the African continent. Why has the spread been intensified there?

★ Detail the rise and spread of AIDS in the United States.

● Why free syringes are not readily available to drug users for AIDS prevention

● Mainstreaming the HIV/AIDS infected child

★ How AIDS spreads and contaminates

● Ethics, AIDS, and the unfaithful mate

● What do informed scientists project for the future spread of the virus?

★ Detail the common relationship between drug addiction and AIDS.

✕ There are many well publicized and widely believed myths about AIDS. What are they?

● Many feel AIDS testing should be mandatory. What are the potential problems this will cause?

American Scene

See also Contemporary Issues; Social Problems

- Historical review of social and political protest during the sixties. Discuss the issues, the participants, and the results.
- × The function of the American Civil Liberties Union as exemplified by several recent issues and cases
- Tradition in American life. Discuss customs and life-styles that are uniquely American.
- O Compare today's economic conditions in the United States with those before the Great Depression (1932–39).
- The plight of the modern Eskimo
- ★ The high cost of funerals. Do social pressures keep them high?
- ★ The spread in America of the "fortress mentality"
- ★ Marijuana as a U.S. cash crop
- ★ Effects of the "Sun Belt" migration on northern urban centers in the United States
- Functional illiteracy in the United States. What are current levels? What are the consequences and ramifications for society?

- Does the United States have pet overpopulation?
- O The myth of the frontier and contemporary American values
- Cultural diversity in the United States
- Are our current immigration quotas realistic? Examine several relevant factors.
- ★ Many states are considering and implementing privately controlled prisons. Examine this innovation.
- What are poverty levels in the US? Detail the statistical changes and the reasons for them.
- ★ Would mandatory AIDS testing for everyone constitute an invasion of privacy?
- It has been suggested that English-only laws are thinly veiled political attacks on immigrants. True?
- × Images of African Americans in American literature since 1950
- ★ HMOs (health maintenance organizations) have spread in the US. They are often criticized? Why?

- ● Compare and contrast conditions in United States coal mines, 1920–1990.
- ● The Amana Colonies of Iowa
- ● The harsh and unhappy life of the homeless
- ● Who really controls America's political parties?
- ★ America's shrinking farmland
- ● "In God we trust." Use examples and statistics to support or deny that America is "one nation under God."
- ➡ American prejudices: their origins and implications
- ▲ The influence of Eastern religions in America, 1960–1980
- ○ The "Jesus movement." Is America psychologically ready for a widespread religious revival?
- ● The Black Muslim, 1960–1975
- ● America's litigious society: causes and costs of this increasing trend to sue
- ● Consequences of increased geographic mobility in the United States
- ➡ The effects of Christianity on sex in America
- ○ Changing American attitudes toward success
- ● Consequences of the population shift from urban to suburban centers: 1950–1990
- ● What will the savings and loan cleanup cost Americans and how will it be paid?
- ● Should the United States have national health insurance? Examine the best methods of funding and the possible effects on the medical community.
- ● Detail the nature and scope of asbestos in public buildings and how it is being removed.
- ○ Why Star Wars was never feasible.
- ● Punk Rock as a social phenomenon
- ★ The origin of the Mardi Gras celebration in New Orleans
- ✔ Evaluate the efforts to preserve and commemorate historic sites in your local community or state.
- ● The Horatio Alger success story in modern America: Myth or reality?
- ● Busing for racial balance in American communities: a survey of current practices
- ★ The fast-food phenomenon in America
- ● The evolution of suburbia from "bedroom" community to independent entity
- ● Vietnam fallout — the veteran
- ● Sport as a social institution in America
- ● Compare and contrast the views of America as presented by Alexis de Tocqueville in *Democracy in America* (1840) and by Richard Reeves in *American Journey: Traveling with de Tocqueville in Search of Democracy in America* (1982).

- The growing acceptance and tolerance of homosexuals in American society. Discuss these attitudinal changes, geographically and socioeconomically.
- Defend or refute: The United States is not overpopulated.
★ Why the United States has not adopted the metric system
- The military versus the civilian life-style
- The museum boom
★ How the telephone changed American life
- The conscientious objector in America
- Experiments in integrated living — the commune today
- A thirties view: Swing music is ruining our youth.
- Abuses in the pet industry. Discuss "puppy mills," pet store conditions, smuggled and diseased animals, etc.
★ America's vanishing wilderness
- The blue laws in America, then and now
- "All men are created equal" is an American slogan. Discuss and analyze the varying interpretations of this motto.
- The revival of big band jazz
- How the supermarket has changed eating habits and social patterns in America
§ The current effects of religious right-wing pressure groups on schools (or libraries and other institutions)

- Violence in America. To what degree has it increased? What do experts feel are the determining factors influencing this growth?
- Changing cultural patterns and their effects on feminine and masculine roles in American society
➡ In what ways have computers changed American life?
✕ Drug use among professional athletes
- Whatever happened to the salmon?
✕ "Sun Belt" problems. Rapid expansion has caused many disruptions. What are the critical issues and what are communities doing to remedy them?
- Comic strips as a reflection of American values
- The impact of the gay community on American society and life
- Is a more self-service-oriented (do-it-yourself) economy a trend for the near future? Why?
○ How Americans have changed their attitudes toward the presidency since 1970
★ Is America in the 1990's a "permissive society"? What are the factors that substantiate your answer?
- The growing business of personal surveillance
➡ Discuss the changing American

political attitudes toward one of the following American subgroups: African Americans, welfare recipients, small businessmen, millionaires, teenagers.

- What bumper stickers tell us about America
- The traditional South: myths and realities
- The American national character as viewed from abroad. Cite and compare a number of recent observations from foreign visitors.
- Analyze the ethnic communities in your locality
- What happened at Woodstock? Was it a passing fad or a "new dawn"?
- Why America needs heroes
- The role of the policeman in modern American life
- Communism in the United States, 1920–1960
- Why the United States does not have adequate gun control laws and legislation
- Why Congress has not effected legislation to reduce acid rain
- What has caused the American "underclass"? Why have their numbers increased?
- How the states are benefitting from the lottery
- What the United States is doing to prevent terrorism at home
- Migration from the Frost Belt to the Sun Belt
- Our shrinking middle class
- United States spy scandals. Ex-

plain how security should be altered to forestall the leaking of classified material.

- What are the usual protectionist strategies employed by the United States to protect trade? Are they working? Are they fair? To whom?
- The Karen Ann Quinlan case (1975–1985) and the issues it raised about euthanasia
- The crackdown on drunken drivers: a survey of techniques and results on a national scale
- Why is abortion such a widespread and volatile issue in America?
- The changing scope of emergency room service. Consider patients, finances, insurance, staff and availability.
- What can be done to lessen airport congestion, both on the ground and in the air?
- Religious meetings in schools. Should they be allowed? Any religion or cult? Who should decide this issue?
- Is the United States still a world superpower?
- Should testing for AIDS be mandatory? If not, why and if so, under what conditions?
- Scientists predict a catastrophic loss of United States' plant species by the year 2000. Why?
- Overcrowding in American national parks
- Illegal crack houses have flourished. What are communities doing to combat them?

▲ What will happen when nuclear plants wear out? Detail several possible scenarios.

● The costs of illiteracy

★ Has the enforcement of seat-belt laws affected accident rates and fatalities?

● Motorcycle gangs yesterday and today

● Is old-fashioned American self-reliance coming back in style? How? Why?

● Walled communities are increasing across the United States. Why? What are their advantages and disadvantages?

● Is society growing impatient with having to support (through taxes) the homeless, food stamp recipients, addicts, and welfare mothers?

● Who was responsible for the Waco (Texas) cult compound fire and deaths?

✕ It has often been suggested that economic prosperity is more important to our country than the conservation of our natural resources. Is this true?

✕ How individual Americans are responding to increasing crime in their communities

★ Guns for everyone: the case for (or against) gun control

● Examine the events leading to the 1992 riots in Los Angeles

▲ Contemporary critics have stated that America is becoming a nation of rigid and permanent castes. Right or wrong? Or partly true?

● Are our nuclear power plants safe from terrorist attacks?

Key to Symbols

● average difficulty
§ substitutes possible
★ ample information in most libraries
○ specialized knowledge required

▾ narrow down topic
▲ large public or college library required
✓ local option topic
✕ examples and supporting evidence needed

Animal Behavior

See also: Biology; Evolution

▲ Primate intelligence: the state of the art

● Many laboratory experiments have found that high density populations produce behavioral abnormalities. What are some of the most universal and significant deviations?

● Are there any animals that fight to kill?

● Archie Carr and the sea turtles

○ Training the quarter horse

● How migrating birds navigate

✕ Training guard dogs

★ Using tidal rhythms: the mating behavior of the grunion

▲ New attempts at domestication of the musk-oxen or elands

● The assessment of dolphin intelligence: recent studies

▲ The baboon group as a mechanism for troop safety

➥ Investigate the findings of recent field studies on any one of the following: lions, hyenas, orangutangs, gorillas, elephants, wolves, howler monkeys, gelada baboons

▲ Coyote adaptions to the human urban environment. In what way has its traditional behavior altered? How has it affected health, food supply, mating, infant rearing, etc.

▲ Pair-bonding among primates

● The functions of peer-play among young monkeys

★ How Jane Van Lawick-Goodall established communication with the chimpanzees in her pioneering study

● Territorial imperatives of the Serengeti

● Compare and contrast the social organization of the hyena (Africa), the dingo (Australia), and the wolf (North America).

● Compare and contrast the learned "speech" of chimpanzees Washoe and Sarah.

● The chimpanzee mother

✕ Causes and scope of aggression in animals. Select several for examples: e.g., the domestic cat, baboon, honey bee, coral fish, etc.

● The function of grooming among primates

★ The dolphin in art, history, and mythology

- Sex among the stickleback
- The life cycle of the Emperor penguin: survival in a very cold climate
- Techniques of insect direction-finding
§ The social life of a group-oriented animal (select one)
- The life of temporary ponds
- The role of zoos in the preservation of endangered animals
- Functions of territory in the animal world
- The courting, mating, and nestbuilding of bowerbirds
- Social organization of prairie dogs
- Chimpanzee infant behavior
- The prosimians are an ancient type of primate. How have they adjusted to competition from more advanced anthropoids?
§ How macaques maintain group stability
- The training of Tennessee walking horses is very stringent. Some say it is cruel. Investigate this accusation and defend or refute it with credible evidence.
○ Variations in birdsong dialects
- How seeing-eye dogs are trained
× An evaluation of cooperative behavior among the ants
★ Chimpanzees and the use of tools
§ Social behavior of the mountain gorilla (or orangutan, chimpanzee, or gibbon)

× Darwin's principle of antithesis
- Courtship and breeding behavior among underwater animals
▲ Evidence of reasoning in animals. Use scientific data as a justification for your conclusions.
- Teaching human language to apes
- Instances of tool use by animals
§ Lion hunting behavior
- The fungus gardens of ants and termites
- Slave-making ants
★ Why wild animals make poor pets
- Cleaning symbiosis in fishes
- Maternal deprivation and behavioral abnormalities in young rhesus monkeys
§ Man's use of the elephant today and in the past
▲ Mountain gorilla life-patterns: recent observations
- Training carrier pigeons
- The outer limits of cat behavior modification
- The United States Navy's use of dolphins
○ Infanticide among the primates
- The suicidal migrations of lemmings
- Infant care among the primates
- The social dolphins: What are the usual social organizations and how do they interreact?
- The role of domestic animals in primitive cultures
★ Roman games and wild animals
- Use of dogs for narcotic

detection
★ What trapping does to animals
○ Do animals play?
● Why do birds sing?
● Alarm and danger signals among birds
● The advantages of a long infant-dependency period among primates
▲ The macaques (*Macaca fuscata*) of Japan. Concentrate on the Koshima and Takasakiyama colonies and investigate their recent behavioral adaptions.
★ The construction techniques of the beaver

● Seal hunting continues in Canada. What are the issues involved? In the face of world protest, explain why this practice continues.
➟ A significant number of studies have been completed on animal language. Select one and detail the study and conclusions. What new knowledge has resulted? Data may include information known from previous experimentation.
● How whales communicate
★ The increase in dolphin deaths. Will a solution arrive in time?

Key to Symbols

●	average difficulty	➟	narrow down topic
§	substitutes possible	▲	large public or college library required
★	ample information in most libraries	✔	local option topic
○	specialized knowledge required	×	examples and supporting evidence needed

Anthropology

See also: Archeology; Customs, Traditions, and Folkways; Evolution; Myth, Symbol, and Folklore

- What have been the varying definitions of "race" among anthropologists? Compare and contrast the most important of these definitions.
○ Compare brain sizes of early and modern humans. Discuss the correlation (or lack of) between brain size and cultural development.
§ Incan religion
- Man as a tool-making primate
○ The evolutionary changes of the first human skulls
- Aztec ceremonial rites
▲ Why civilization developed more slowly in the Americas than it did in Europe
- Primitive techniques for working stone. Compare the methods and show how each innovation fostered changes in lifeways.
★ How the discovery of fire changed the life of primitive man
- The effects of the end of the last ice age on nomadic cultures
- The significance of blood types of North and South American Indians
- Daily life in the Incan city of Machu Picchu
- Compare and contrast modern superstition and ancient myth
★ The culture of the Australian aborigines before the white man
- Neolithic cave art in Spain
➡ Funeral rites of Native Americans. Select a particular tribe.
○ Malinowski's views of religion and magic
- The place of the shaman in primitive cultures
- Fossil man in the Americas
○ Mendelian inheritance in man
- Early fossil man in Europe
§ The balsa raft in primitive societies. Or, select some other form of travel which may have influenced or changed that society's history.
▲ Current research on the origin of *Homo sapiens*. Select one or two recent finds and discuss the implications.
- Olmec heads: their origin and

31

significance
- The ground figures in the Nazca Desert. Evaluate the evidence and conclusions of scientific studies and investigations.
× The effects of the early missionaries on cultures in the South Pacific
☛ The facts behind evolutionary theories
- Characteristics of the Stone Age Magdalenian culture
- The domestication of animals during the Neolithic era
- Factors influencing the change from nomad to village agricultural life in early human history
- Mysteries of the Mayan civilization. What are the unanswered questions in anthropological research?
- Life in a Neanderthal cave
- The Aztec civilization after the Spanish Conquest
★ The monolithic stone heads of Easter Island
- Man and tools in prehistory
§ Hindu funeral and burial customs
- Compare and contrast the technological advances of the Mesolithic and Neolithic eras
- Uses of tattooing in primitive societies
- Zuñi (American Indian) fetishes
- The cultural conflicts of the modern American Eskimo
▲ Innovative field techniques of

Margaret Mead. What is the recent controversy surrounding the validity of her methodology?
- Social life and customs of the Bedouins before 1930
★ The Bering Strait and human migration
☛ Acculturation problems in underdeveloped countries. Or select one country and describe in detail its adjustment problems and prospects.
- Papago Indian baskets
§ Mayan myths
- Puberty rites: a comparison of three primitive tribes
- Cockfighting as local sport
- The modern Bedouin of Saudi Arabia: a culture in flux
★ The domestication of the dog
- The Hunzas
§ Family life in the Samoan Islands
- The significance of Louis Leakey's discoveries in the Olduvai Gorge
- Stonehenge theories
○ Compare and contrast the "territorial imperative" in animals and humans.
- Similarities between Christian and pagan rituals
- The myth of the cowboy
★ How man survived the Ice Age
- The culture of the Tasaday, a contemporary tribe of the Philippine Islands. Investigate recent hoax accusations.
- Early evidence of the domestica-

tion of the horse
- How family and kinship structures unified primitive societies
★ Life after death as viewed by several primitive cultures
§ Trace the development of a major primate adaptive process (cranial morphology, dentition, locomotion) in a primate.
▲ The Oligocene fossils of the Fayum: varying interpretations
○ Robert Ardrey has suggested that aggressive combat is built into human nature from our evolutionary past as hunters. What evidence is there to support (or refute) this hypothesis?
▲ Examine the anatomical variability of Australopithecine fossils from several sites in South and East Africa.
- Many insects have complex behavioral systems but cannot be said to have a culture. Man does. What is culture? What are the major definitions? Analyze the views of a variety of social scientists, both contemporary and in the past.
➥ Modern herding or pastoral societies
- Examine the historical foundations of racial typologies.
○ How culture affects human biology
- Compare the sexual behavior of the human female with that of the female chimpanzee. Relate the differences to the variants in

the basic social units of each.
- Compare the family structure and primary features of the following groups: the early Christians, colonial Americans, the Tasaday, the Hopi, and the contemporary American middle-class family.
- Polyandry exists in a number of societies. What are the benefits to the social systems? Are there disadvantages?
▲ Compare the upper Paleolithic subsistence patterns and general social organization in the Old and New Worlds.
- Compare and contrast the hunting and gathering methods of a primitive desert tribe with that of rain forest dwellers.
- How the races developed: theories and conjectures
- The role of symbolic behavior in culture
○ What evidence is there to support the hominid status of Ramapithecus?
- Milestones of Pleistocene cultural evolution
○ How does the process of specialization relate to adaptive radiation?
- Characteristics of early hominid tools
- Word formation patterns by chimpanzees who have been taught a language
▲ Why is kinship as a social mechanism decreasing in ur-

banized and industrialized societies?

- ▲ The Ngatatjara Tribe (Australia) and its Stone Age inheritance
- ● Characteristics of Bushman culture of the Kalahari Desert (Africa). What cultural changes have occurred in the last thirty years?
- ○ What cultural changes resulted from the following physical characteristics: the opposable thumb, bipedal locomotion, and fewer offspring (longer childhood)?
- ● Are there superior and inferior races? Consult leading authorities and compare and contrast their views.
- ● Influential factors in early hominid migrations
- ● The cargo cult of the South Pacific. How and why did it originate?
- ▲ Totemism in American culture
- ● Discuss the connections between human bipedal locomotion and the locomotive behavior of living primates.
- ● How anthropology uses primatological data
- ○ Examine Ruth Benedict's definition of "culture configuration" (*Patterns of Culture*) and discuss the relationship between these configurations. How do they affect individual variation and autonomy?
- ● Modern hunters and gatherers. Select several from Australian aborigines, Eskimo, or Bushmen and compare their social organization.
- ➧ Compare science, religion, and magic as institutions in modern industrialized societies.
- × Geographical isolation and speciation. Illustrate this relationship by some of the more outstanding examples.
- ● Significant excavations of Raymond Dart, Australian anthropologist
- ● Compare the early development of agriculture in Mesoamerica and the Near East. What accounts for the similarities?
- ▲ Compare the organization of the ancient cities of Uruk (Mesopotamian) and Teotihuacán (Mesoamerican), or select two other appropriate sites for comparison.
- ● The demographics of human skin color
- ○ The analytic tools of anthropology (for example, the cephalic index and blood-typing)
- ● Supernaturalism in American culture, past and present
- ● Compare the concepts of ownership among people in industrialized societies with those found among hunters and gatherers in agrarian cultures.
- ➧ The social functions of witchcraft in some societies. Select several for analysis.

- Use some contemporary urban examples to illustrate Oscar Lewis's concept of the "culture of poverty."
- x The results of rapid increases in cultural complexity and technology on primitive cultures. Select several as illustrations.
- The first wild wheat hybrids. What was the effect on human life patterns?
- ★ Thor Heyerdahl's transoceanic migration theories and how he has (or has not) proved them
- Distinguishing characteristics of the Bronze Age
- How Egyptian mummies were preserved
- Early Pacific migration theories, conjectures, and possibilities
- The medicine man in Navajo culture
- Religion in Bali and its integration into the social structure
- O The historical versus the functionalist theory of anthropological research
- Primate infant development and its human parallels
- ★ How man evolved from a hunter to a gatherer
- x Discuss and compare several contemporary nomadic cultures.
- ✔ Plan a field tour of your state which involves the major anthropological sites. Include museums if they house relevant collections.
- The practice of cannibalism in primitive cultures
- ★ Life in a prehistoric cliff dwelling
- ▲ Anthropological discoveries in Ethiopia's Omo River Valley
- Firewalkers of Fiji
- Hopi kachinas
- ▲ Evidence supporting the domestication of animals in the Paleolithic era
- § Maoris of New Zealand (or select another Pacific culture either from Micronesia, Melanesia or Polynesia). Examine their origins and the culture before the incursions of exploration and trade.
- How the discovery and utilization of rotary motion changed the course of early civilization
- O Compare and contrast lower and upper Paleolithic tools.
- x Human racial classifications: discuss criteria and significant examples
- Select a technological innovation (saddle, plow, weapon, etc.) and trace it back to its origin. Detail its evolution and historical significance to past cultures.
- Man's genetic adaptations to the environment
- The cultural diversity of food habits
- The Bushmen of the Kalahari Desert. Discuss their social organization and nomadic lifestyle.
- Detail the differing facial fea-

tures in human racial types.

→ Upper Pleistocene man in Europe.

• Explore the relationships between archeology and physical anthropology.

• Compare the findings from three anthropologists relating age status (children, infant, adolescent) in various societies.

▲ The field of anthropology has evolved to cover many diverse areas. Explore these new boundaries and discuss some of the research and findings that are the result of this expansion.

× Diffusion and cultural change

× The cultural dimensions of body contact

→ Early human skills: their evolution and implications

• Paleolithic art as key to man's earliest cultures

• A frozen 5,000 year old corpse was found (1991) in Austria's Tyrol. What has it told us about early Bronze Age Europe?

○ The remains of *Australopithecus ramidus*, the oldest (4.4 million years) hominid yet found in the human evolutionary family, was recently unearthed in Ethiopia. What is its significance?

• Paleolithic and Neolithic forms of transportation

• The polar Eskimo family

× Describe the practice of forensic anthropology. What major finds have been possible using this new technology?

• 20,000 year old paintings were recently discovered in the Chauvet Cave (France). Why are they important?

• Detail the race, language, or culture of one of the following historic peoples:

Afghans	Lombards
Angles	Manchus
Aryans	Maoris
Assyrians	Minoans
Aztecs	Mongols
Bantus	Negritos
Basques	Normans
Berbers	Picts
Bushmen	Saxons
Celts	Sumerians
Copts	Toltecs
Dorians	Vandals
Etruscans	Visigoths
Franks	Walloons
Kurds	

Archeology

See also: Anthropology; Evolution

- How do archeologists identify evidences of domestication of both plants and animals in excavation sites?
- § The excavation of Thebes. What were the major finds, sites, problems, current status, and any other factors unique to this site?
- ▲ America's first trade networks — the archeological evidence. What are the implications of these findings?
- ★ The great stone heads of Easter Island. Do anthropologists agree about their origins and meaning?
- ➥ How archeological discoveries have substantiated the Old Testament
- What attempts have been made to identify Mount Ararat and locate the remains of the Ark? What were the findings and conclusions?
- ▲ Frozen mammoths thus far discovered — how have they been excavated and preserved?
- Evidence supporting Norse occupation of the New World before 1492
- What the Koster Site (Illinois) has produced and what archeologists have theorized and learned
- Qin Dynasty warriors and horses (Xi'an, China)
- The bronze horses of eastern Han, China
- ○ How the electron microscope is used in archeological analysis techniques
- The discovery and excavation of Templo Mayor in downtown Mexico City
- How fossilized remains are reconstructed
- § Major archeological sites of Mexico
- ○ Tree ring dating techniques and technology
- Problems in the control of the plundering of archeological sites, particularly in the American Southwest
- § The excavation of the Roman forum. What problems were encountered? What were the primary discoveries? Has there been reconstruction? Are any

37

excavations current?

- The Elgin marbles and why they are in England
- The relocation of Abu-Simbel for the Aswan Dam
- Religious and social significance of Olmec sculpture
- Archeological evidence supporting the Theseus legend
○ The preservation of Paleolithic cave art: modern problems and technologies
- The discovery and restoration of the bronze Greek warriors at Reggio di Calabria, Italy
- Methods of archeological site preparation
§ Plan a tour of the principal Mayan archeological sites. Justify and explain your choices.
★ The discovery of Tutankhamen's tomb
- The earliest Paleolithic cultures as viewed through art from that era
- The arrival of humans in the New World: archeological evidence
★ The Piltdown man hoax
➳ Digging up Troy
- How archeologists date artifacts

➳ Deciphering the Dead Sea Scrolls
- Reconstruction of Knossos, Crete, by Sir Arthur J. Evans
× Advances in marine archeology
- Contrast and compare Mesolithic and Neolithic dwelling construction. Cover the materials used and techniques employed. Choose several Near East or European sites.
- Archeological evidences of fire-making among early Paleolithic and Neolithic cultures
▲ Similarities in the henges of England
▲ Who built Scotland's brocks?
- Air photography and archeological sites
§ The archeology of Jericho
- Uses of radio carbon dating
- Recent finds in Egypt (1970–1990)
★ The tomb of Philip II of Macedonia. How was it discovered and excavated? Describe its contents and their significance.
▲ The modern uses of chemistry in archeology
- Describe what urban archeologists have learned from our garbage.

Key to Symbols

- • average difficulty
- § substitutes possible
- ★ ample information in most libraries
- ○ specialized knowledge required

- ➳ narrow down topic
- ▲ large public or college library required
- ↙ local option topic
- × examples and supporting evidence needed

Architecture

See also: Art; Interior Design

○ Concrete and freeform house design

☛ Innovative changes in American home design

● Log house construction. Compare and contrast the methods used on the American frontier with those used in modern log construction.

☛ Skyscrapers

● The rise, zenith, and decline of Gothic architecture: an overview

● Colosseums, from Rome to Los Angeles

★ Compare and contrast the principal features of classical and medieval architecture.

● Islamic architecture in Spain and Portugal. What are the similarities? Are they typical of Islamic design and decoration?

● Can the Acropolis be saved from pollution, decay, and erosion?

☛ How Williamsburg, Virginia was authenticated and reconstructed. Select one structure.

▲ Building earthquake-proof structures

● Architectural styles in Pompeii, Italy

● Shopping center design

§ The architecture of ancient Corinth

● The lintel: its dynamics and historical significance

● Why vaulting developed

○ Egyptian and Persian contributions to Greek architecture

▲ The Dorian temples of Sicily

✕ Ancient instances of the use of the arch

● Compare and contrast the facades of the Cathedrals of Notre Dame, Amiens, and Reims.

● Compare and contrast the Egyptian Temple of Karnak and the Greek Parthenon.

● Predecessors of the skyscraper

○ Compare the Romanesque architecture of Ste. Madeline of Vezelay and St. Benoit-sur-Loire, France.

○ Design the details for the ideal subdivision. Select the lot size, costs, structure size, and plan.

● Gargoyles in Gothic cathedrals

● Compare and contrast Greek

and Roman housing.

× Successful inner city renovations, 1960 to present

★ The White House: design, original construction, and remodelings

• Underground houses

• Why every home builder should use an architect

➤ Building the Eiffel Tower

✔ Investigate three outstanding buildings in your town. Who designed and built them? Also cover style, materials, uses, etc.

• Baroque, Byzantine, and Gothic: Compare and contrast these artistic styles.

○ Designing structures to diminish noise

• How the Renaissance changed architecture

★ Insect architecture

• How safe are high-rise buildings in a fire?

• Characteristics and examples of the Beaux Arts style of architecture

• Roman triumphal arches

• The architectural evolution of the medieval castle

▲ What was the influence of Roman architecture on Thomas Jefferson?

▲ Contemporary evaluations of the architectural designs of Frank Lloyd Wright

★ The mosque in the Islamic world. What are its outstanding architectural characteristics?

• Building the Parthenon

• The architecture of Machu Picchu. How was construction accomplished?

× Barrier-free design factors

• The Seven Wonders of the World today

• Compare and contrast castles built as fortifications to those constructed for their aesthetics.

○ Trace the history of the medieval monastary design beginning with the Carolingian period. Include the practical as well as religious function of the structures.

• Postmodern architecture

× Design features of energy-efficient homes

• Playground design

• The use of the arch and dome in Islamic architecture

★ The amphitheater in ancient times and in the modern world

★ Important features of solar house design

▲ Built-in security features in new construction

§ The architecture of the ancient city of Angkor, Cambodia

• The ziggurats of Mesopotamia (c. 2000 B.C.)

➤ Renaissance country palaces

• "Falling Water" in Bear Run, Pennsylvania as an illustration of Frank Lloyd Wright's architectural philosophy

▲ The role of the architect during the Renaissance

▲ The influence of Brunelleschi on Renaissance architecture

● Examine the various methods by which communities and individuals can preserve and finance the salvage of architectural monuments.

§ Common elements of style, design, and decoration in art nouveau architecture

§ Women in architecture: the career of Julia Morgan

★ Discuss and compare the three Greek architectural orders.

● How the Egyptian pyramids were built

▲ Colonial church architecture

● The balloon-frame house on the frontier

☛ Construction of the Gothic cathedral. Select a cathedral, detail its design, construction problems, costs, etc. Or, analyze construction elements common to all cathedrals of this period.

★ Buckminster Fuller and the geodesic dome

● Development of the International Style

● The design and building of Brasilia, Brazil

★ How to build with adobe

✕ Origin and singular examples of the dome

§ The architecture of New Orleans (or, substitute another area with equally unique architecture)

✔ Survey and describe the architectural styles represented on your town or city's main street.

● Visionary architecture. Include designs by Bruce Goff, Louis Kahn, Buckminster Fuller, Paolo Soleri, among others.

▲ Eero Saarinen's design for and the construction of the St. Louis Arch (Jefferson National Expansion Memorial)

● Decorative details in the buildings of Louis Henry Sullivan

● Eminent examples of Palladian architecture in the United States

● Aztec architectural achievements at the time of Cortez

● Neoclassicism in American architecture, from Jefferson to the present

○ Should there be uniform architectural earthquake standards?

● Low-cost homes for the homeless

Architectural Wonders

The following constructions are both celebrated and unique. Select one and analyze its design, uses, construction, or influence as a model for later styles, trends, modifications, or innovations in architectural history.

- Temple of Edfu (Egypt)
- Madrasa and Mausoleum of Sultan Hasan (Cairo, Egypt)
- Church of San Vitale (Ravenna, Italy)
- St. Paul's-Outside-the-Walls (Rome, Italy)
- Alhambra (Granada, Spain)
- Summer palace (Beijing, China)
- Angkor Wat (Cambodia)
- Notre-Dame (Paris, France)
- Chartres Cathedral (Chartres, France)
- Blue Mosque (Istanbul, Turkey)
- Rockefeller Center (New York City)
- Arch of Constantine (Rome, Italy)
- Church of Il Gesu (Rome, Italy)
- Palace of Versailles (Versailles, France)
- Château de Chambord (Loire Valley, France)
- Temple of the Warriors (Chichén Itzá, Yucatan, Mexico)
- Temple of Todai-ji (Nara, Japan)
- The Dome of the Rock (Jerusalem, Israel)
- Palace of Minos (Crete, Greece)
- Tower of London (London, England)
- Palace of Diocletian (Split, Croatia)
- Trans World Air Terminal (Kennedy Airport, New York)
- Villa Savoie (Poissy-sur-Seine, France)
- Amalienburg lodge (Munich, Germany)
- Palladio's Villa Rotunda (Vicenza, Italy)
- Notre-Dame du Haut (Ronchamp, France)
- Bauhaus (Dessau, Germany)
- Eiffel Tower (Paris, France)
- Crystal Palace (London, England)
- Persepolis (Shiraz, Iran)
- "Falling Water" (Bear Run, Pennsylvania)
- Cathedral Church of St. John the Divine (New York City)
- Independence Hall (Philadelphia, Pennsylvania)

- Lincoln Memorial (Washington, D.C.)
- Great Pagoda of the Wild Geese (Xian, China)
- Great Temple of Amon at Karnak (Luxor, Egypt)
- Propylaea of the Acropolis (Athens, Greece)
- Hoover Dam (Black Canyon, Arizona—Nevada)
- Verrazano-Narrows Bridge (New York City)
- Great Wall of China
- Taj Mahal (Agra, India)
- Hagia Sophia (Istanbul, Turkey)
- Pantheon (Rome, Italy)
- Hadrian's Villa (Tivoli, Italy)
- World Trade Center (New York City)
- St. Paul's Cathedral (London, England)
- St. Peter's Basilica (Rome, Italy)
- Cathedral of St. Mark (Venice, Italy)
- Mont-Saint-Michel (Bay of Mont-Saint-Michel, France)
- Leaning Tower of Pisa (Pisa, Italy)
- Florence Cathedral (Florence, Italy)
- Opera House (Sydney, Australia)
- Church of the Holy Family (Barcelona, Spain)
- Royal Crescent (Bath, England)
- Great Sphinx (Cairo, Egypt)
- English Channel Tunnel ("Chunnel")

Key to Symbols

•	average difficulty	←	narrow down topic
§	substitutes possible	▲	large public or college library required
★	ample information in most libraries	↙	local option topic
○	specialized knowledge required	✗	examples and supporting evidence needed

Art

See also: Architecture; Film; Humanities; Interior Design; Photography

- Why did colonial America not produce artists comparable to its European counterparts? Consider the social, economic, educational, and political aspects of this situation.
- "Art is the most intense mode of individuation that the world has known." (Oscar Wilde) Collect examples to illustrate and justify this thesis.
○ Compare the techniques and some representative works of analytic and synthetic cubism.
- Women artists from the French impressionist period
× What is computer art? Include examples with your descriptions.
§ Techniques of engraving
- The basis of the controversy over Diego Rivera's artistic work in the United States
★ Ghiberti's creation of the baptistry doors of the Florence Cathedral ("The Gates of Paradise")
▲ The woodcuts of Albrecht Dürer and the northern European crafts tradition
- How has modern technology influenced styles of art?
➥ Levels of public support of the arts in the United States. Select one area of the arts and examine funding, etc. for the last twenty years.
➥ Art has often responded directly to current events, political, economic, and social. Select one of these areas and use relevant examples to illustrate this point.
○ Dadaism as a precursor of surrealism
- The relationship between the Barbizon school and impressionism
§ Birds in art
★ The scope and influence of the National Endowment for the Arts
- Should big business support the arts? Detail some successful instances of such funding. Was it on a local or national basis?
○ Design the perfect studio for the artist. Consider media used, lighting, storage, utility, esthetics, and other necessary factors.
- Cultural patronage in Elizabethan England. What were its

44

effects on the establishment and spread of the arts throughout society?

- Examine the relationship between German expressionist painting, theater, and film.
★ Compare and contrast Mayan and Olmec architecture, sculpture, and artistic artifacts.
▲ The invention of linear perspective and some of its earliest applications in fifteenth- and sixteenth-century art
- The influence of miniature design motifs on Islamic architecture and weaving
- The American western art market: its economics, works, and patrons
○ The New York art market today
• Artists as "Bohemians": the myths, the legends, and the grimmer realities
- Robert Smithson and environmental art
★ Chinoiserie in eighteenth-century Europe: its designs and applications
- The WPA (Work Projects Administration) in the Great Depression employed many artists and writers. Describe this program and some of the more successful results.
- American women art collectors (1890–1920)
★ How inflation has affected the arts
- Floral motifs in art noveau

⬦ Mythology in Florentine Renaissance art
- Art as an investment: past performance and future trends
- Describe the effects of streamlining on industrial design (cars, trains, etc.) in the 1930's.
- Gertrude Whitney and the beginnings of the Whitney Museum of American Art
- Discuss, using examples, a major influence on Renaissance art.
★ Compare and contrast the etching and engraving processes.
- Pros and cons of conceptual art
○ Realism in nineteenth-century French art: the artist as social radical
▲ The impact of "optimism" on the art and literature of the Enlightenment Age
- Pop art: Social commentary or put-on?
§ The critic's view of Claes Oldenburg. Survey some of the experts' analyses of this artist. Compare and evaluate these opinions.
⬦ Posters: old and new
✕ Famous art forgeries and how they were detected
- The art of Bali. The island artists have had increased tourism and attention. Has this influenced the quality and production?
- The Ghent altarpiece: "the Sistine Chapel of Northern Europe"

- William Blake: poet, painter, engraver
- Regional art in America
- ★ Etruscan tombs and the art inside them
- ★ Michelangelo's Sistine Chapel. Compare its visual components since the cleaning and restoration
- Symbols of birth in art
- The artisan and the medieval cathedral
- ○ The influence of Piet Mondrian on contemporary design
- Surrealism explained
- ★ Compare and contrast the stylistic elements of classicism and romanticism.
- Erotic art of the old masters
- ○ Parallels between creativity in art and science
- Art thefts. How are they being successfully prevented?
- ▲ Orders of angels in art
- The relationship between decoration and architecture in Islamic art
- × How the medium affects the message
- ○ Reality and the visual arts: distortion and abstraction
- The avant-garde at the end of World War II
- ▲ Ancient Egyptian dyes and pigments
- ▲ Coptic art and religion in Egypt
- The Amarna period in Egyptian art

- Egyptian art and architecture as a reflection of Egyptian religion
- The qualities and uses of Carrara marble. What famous pieces are of this stone? Why is it such a desirable medium?
- How does classical Greek art reflect the values of Classical Greece?
- ★ Geometric art in Ancient Greece
- ▲ Aphrodite in Greek Art
- ★ Art and architecture in Periclean Athens
- ▲ Caravaggio's influence on seventeenth-century Rome
- × Discuss several examples of a successful combination of art and contemporary technologies.
- The impact of the Armory Show in New York City (1913). What was the reaction in America by both art critics and the public to this introduction to abstract art?
- How optical illusions are constructed
- The Bauhaus school of art
- Dada: an international art movement
- Art censorship. Who should make the decision? Why?
- "I don't know anything about art but I know what I like." Is this an acceptable position? Support your conclusion with opinions from a variety of cultural spokespeople.
- Should art be subsidized?

Art — Decorative Arts and Crafts

See also: Interior Design

- Fibers for weaving. Compare and contrast the use of synthetic versus natural materials.
- Spinning in antiquity. What were the materials, tools, methods?
- ✗ Ancient pottery shaping techniques
- Classical Greek jewelry
- § Paper crafts for children
- Victorian beadwork
- The design and decoration of the Faberge egg
- ✔ Visit several traditional craft collections in your locality. Select one type (pottery, metalwork, woven fabrics, etc.) and describe the collection, its diversity, uses, historical precedents and origins, etc.)
- § American weathervane designs. Or, choose another common folk design.
- § Traditional Indonesian crafts
- § What are the materials and tools necessary for wood carving? (Select a craft.) What are the requisite skills?
- The art of store window display

- The Pueblo pottery of Maria Martinez
- § Religious art of Spain
- Metal craftsmanship of Celtic art. What were the tools employed? What were the unique features?
- Greek vase decoration: materials and techniques
- Early basket weaves
- Antique frauds. How are they perpetrated? What are some cautionary measures for the potential investor?
- ★ Dolls in America before 1900
- ➡ Select one method of textile design (batik, stencil, applique, etc.) and detail not only the methodology but also noteworthy examples and their historical contexts.
- Jewelry techniques of the Middle Ages
- ★ How to make natural dyes
- Classic and modern Japanese flower arranging. On what principles is it based?
- The nature of Celtic illuminated manuscripts as illustrated by the

Book of Kells and the *Lindisfarne Gospels*

× Byzantine *cloisonné*. Include descriptions of a number of outstanding examples.

● How to make jewelry by the lost wax process

➡ Navajo rugs

★ Marketing and selling handicrafts

● Decorated eggs through the years

● The art of handmade paper

§ Inca designs

● Enameling methods throughout the ages

● Babylonian crafts

§ Folk art of Mexico. Include a discussion of the outstanding or unusual, the materials used, religious significance, etc.

● Jewelry of the 1930's

➡ The antique business in America. Select one area (glass, toys, etc.) and survey trends and prices.

● Medieval tapestry motifs

● The Eskimo craft of scrimshaw. What have been the traditional designs? What was their purpose? Are they still produced?

§ Historic Wedgwood designs and decorations

▲ Molas (embroidery) of the Cuna Indians of Central America

★ Clown makeup: a traditional art

● Automated weaving with the jacquard loom (1801). How did this change the weaving industry?

● Minoan gold jewelry technology and design. What were its origins? In what ways was it unique?

● Carousel figures

● Factors which hindered the widespread use of pottery in early civilizations

● The English arts and crafts movement of the nineteenth century

---

Key to Symbols

●	average difficulty	➡	narrow down topic
§	substitutes possible	▲	large public or college library required
★	ample information in most libraries	✔	local option topic
○	specialized knowledge required	×	examples and supporting evidence needed

Art — Painting

See also: Photography

★ The new Giverny and the old Monet

● Children in Mary Cassatt's paintings

● Differing portrayals of the Virgin

○ Compare and contrast the works of Duccio and Cimabue.

➡ The rise and refinement of the Byzantine mosaic

● The nude in fifteenth-century painting

● The use of color in Egyptian decoration

● Techniques of Paleolithic cave paintings

● The contemporary relationship between photography and modern painting

▲ Interpretations of Botticelli's *Primavera*

○ The influence of Tolstoy on Vincent Van Gogh

● The mythological paintings of Rubens

● The Picasso exhibition (1980)

● Daily life in Greece as depicted by vase paintings

● Minoan frescos. Discuss their stylistic elements, colors, materials, and original sites. Which have survived? In what condition?

★ The formal elements of Chinese landscape painting

▲ Critical and public reaction to *The Surgical Clinic of Professor Gross* by Thomas Eakins

● Cubism in the works of Picasso and Braque

▲ Religious elements in the paintings of the Hudson River school

○ Music, oriental philosophy, and the art of Wassily Kandinsky

● The ashcan school ("the Eight") was regarded as a particularly American phenomenon. In what ways was it unique?

● Examine the ways in which modern technology has altered the artist's tools and physical product.

● John James Audubon: Artist or illustrator?

★ Discuss the role of "disguised symbolism" in late medieval Flemish painting.

★ Michelangelo's design of the

Sistine Chapel

§ The seascapes of Winslow Homer

● The use of perspective and color in Islamic miniatures

● Pablo Picasso: the cubist years

● Daily life as glimpsed in the interior scenes of Vermeer, Terborch, and De Hooch

● Characteristics of English romantic painters, 1750–1850

● Abstract expressionism after Jackson Pollock

▲ Why do the Genesis stories on the Sistine Chapel occur in reverse order as the viewer approaches the altar?

● Photorealism in painting: Why not photograph?

§ Giotto's use of color

● The influence of Pablo Picasso on abstract art

▲ Critical appraisals of *Les Demoiselles d'Avignon* (Picasso): then and now

● Enlarged-field painting: development, innovations, and trends

★ Materials, colors, and symbolism of Navajo sand paintings

★ Surrealism and Salvador Dali

● The Fauves of French painting

○ Color, line, subject, and value in Rembrandt's *Night Watch*

★ Techniques of fresco painting

● The lasting influence of Marcel Duchamp

● Compare and contrast the landscape paintings of Hobbema and van Ruysdael.

● Characteristic styles of Egyptian painting

● Paintings of the Last Supper. Discuss their variety, historical contexts, and compare critical opinions.

● The human figure in the paintings of El Greco

▲ The mosaics in San Vitale, Ravenna Italy

★ Rembrandt's self-portraits

● The social protest of Picasso's *Guernica*

● Da Vinci's *Mona Lisa*: the legend and the reality

● The human figure in the works of Andrew Wyeth

● Paul Gauguin in the South Pacific

➥ The early developments and uses of perspective in painting

§ The Barbizon school of painting

● The fantasy world of Hieronymus Bosch

● George Catlin's portrayal of the character and customs of American Indians

§ How to paint with watercolors. Examine some of the specialized techniques necessary to successfully master this medium.

● The invention of oil painting: When, where, why?

● Botticelli's women

Art — Sculpture

See also: Architecture; Humanities

- Compare the rendering of the face by the Greeks and by the Romans.
- The design and installation of the Statue of Liberty
★ Pietas in medieval and Renaissance art
- Alexander Calder's mobiles: their unique design and influence on later sculpture
- The story of the Parthenon's Elgin Marbles. Why is there still controversy surrounding them?
○ The seeming interrelationship between ancient Cycladic sculpture and many contemporary works
★ Compare archaic and classical Greek sculpture.
- How Michelangelo "freed" the statue from the marble
★ The carvings on the doors of the Sistine Chapel
- Compare the sculptures on the Arch of Titus with those on the Column of Trajan.
- The colossal sculptures of ancient Egypt. What were their similarities, purposes, and locations? What is extant?
- Mesopotamian animal sculpture

▲ American memorial sculpture of the nineteenth century
- The miniature sculptures of Japanese netsuke
- Gargoyles in Gothic architecture and their mythic origins
▲ How the sculptor Auguste Rodin anticipated the aims and styles of many twentieth-century sculptors
- Proportions in Greek sculpture
- The existentialist sculptures of Alberto Giacometti
- Earthwork sculpture: Is it art or a blighted landscape?
- Early Chinese bronzes: their craft and design
- The environmental sculptures of George Segal
○ The interrelation of sculpture and architecture in the works of Gianlorenzo Bernini
- Compare and contrast representation of the human figure by Aristide Maillol, Henry Moore, and Michelangelo.
§ Casting techniques used by _____ (Auguste Rodin, Henry Moore, etc.)
- Compare and contrast Rodin's

51

Thinker with Michelangelo's *David*.

▲ Analyze the influence of Egyptian sculpture on archaic Greek sculpture.

• Ghiberti's creation of the baptistry doors of the Florence Cathedral ("The Gates of Paradise")

Key to Symbols

•	average difficulty	↞	narrow down topic
§	substitutes possible	▲	large public or college
★	ample information in most		library required
	libraries	↙	local option topic
○	specialized knowledge	✕	examples and supporting
	required		evidence needed

Asia and the Pacific

See also: Foreign Policy; World Scene

▲ What was the role of American foreign policy in China during World War II?

○ China has always been a potential market for American goods and trade. In these terms, evaluate Hay's Open Door notes and Nixon's China policy. What is the policy of the current administration?

● What Asian issues were settled by the Korean War? Which by the Vietnam War?

○ What were the major effects of colonialism on the political geography of Southeast Asia?

● Chinese Nationalists on Taiwan — then and now. Assess their changed political status.

★ The post-Mao era in China. Select a facet of Chinese life and discuss it in detail. Choose from political, economic, educational, or social factors. Compare and contrast them.

● The causes, purges, and after-effects of the Great Proletarian Cultural Revolution.

● How China sees itself

★ The glorious reign of Kublai Khan

● The ancient oriental custom of footbinding

● Korea since World War II has been divided into two sections. What have been the major developments in each? What are the prospects for reunification?

● The rise of Mao and the Chinese Communist Party: the early years

● The Manchurian Incident (1931)

● The significance of Richard Nixon's 1972 China visit. What have been its effects on recent Sino-American relations?

● Describe the nature and the development of Southeast Asia's three main agricultural systems.

✕ The image of China in the words of Pearl Buck

★ The westernization of China, from 1970 to date

▲ Chinese nuclear explosions

★ The state of Chinese civilization in 2000 B.C. What were the major advances to that point?

● The arts in the T'ang Dynasty

(618–907)
- Why Mao's "Great Leap Forward" failed
§ Discuss the rise of China's <u>steel</u> industry.
- Chinese agriculture since the Revolution
★ Peasant life in Communist China today
- The rise of Singapore as a twentieth-century world trade center. Compare it to Hong Kong.
- Why China turned to communism
▲ Many historians have reevaluated the causes and effects of the Boxer Rebellion. Survey and compare these opinions.
- Artistic interpretations of the Buddha throughout history
- Traditional Chinese and Soviet/Russian hostilities. Narrate past problems and exchanges and survey the current conditions between the two nations. Why has there been a traditional hostility?
- Analyze the factors contributing to the successes or failures of the Chinese commune.
✕ The Japanese art of paper folding (origami)
- Post-war recovery in Vietnam. What has happened in the economy since the withdrawal of American forces?
★ The martial arts as practiced in Asian nations
- The complexity and diversity of

ancient Chinese picture writing
▲ The artistry of Ming dynasty vases
○ The relationship between Chinese calligraphy and painting
- Events leading to the fall of the Manchu dynasty. What were the immediate and long-range results of this government's reversal?
★ Life in a Buddhist monastery
- The role and relevance of Confucianism in modern China
▲ Healing by acupuncture as practiced in modern China
★ The techniques of Kabuki theater. Consider the actors, costumes, scenery, and makeup.
▲ The role of the government in Japan's industrial growth.
☛ The scope and dimensions of communism in the modern Asian world
★ The traditional geisha in Japan. What was her training and social function?
- The status of women in modern China. How have their roles changed from that of the traditional Chinese woman?
- Japan's remarkable postwar economic recovery and how it was accomplished
- Religion in China under Mao
- Discuss family planning in China in recent years. Evaluate the need for such a program. Has it been successful?
☛ Christianity in oriental societies

- Compare and contrast the role of the individual in Communist China and in the United States.
- Opium use in the Orient, then and now
- Recreation and sport in Communist China
- Japanese attitudes toward suicide
- The British presence in Asia during the days of the Empire. What were the immediate effects on the socio-economic system? Were these effects permanent?
- China's mass mentality psychological aspects
- Ancient Japanese Samurai
- The American postwar occupation of Japan
- The Chinese Opium War. What were the major issues? Were they resolved?
- Describe the nature of tropical ecosystems and detail some of the environmental problems as they relate to Southeast Asia.
- The rise and fall of the "Gang of Four" in China
- ▲ Investigate the life and times of Minamoto Yoritomo (1148-1199), who was a Japanese warrior chieftain and founder of the first shogunate.
- The poetic medium of Haiku. Discuss its form, styles, themes, and content.
- Aristocratic Japanese life as portrayed in "The Tale of Genji" by Murasaki Shikibu
- ➡ Attitudes toward marriage and divorce in the Asian world. Have traditional views changed in the twentieth century?
- ★ The Japanese blue-collar worker. Include a discussion of his or her relationship to employer, working schedules, salaries, benefits, and productivity levels.
- ➡ The South Pacific in World War II. Select an island.
- ★ Hong Kong as a Chinese territory. Examine the changes, both negative and positive.
- The composition and religious connotations of the formal oriental garden
- Compare Taiwan's recent economic growth with its recent political situation.
- O Compare and contrast Buddhism as practiced in Japan, China, Korea, and other Asian countries.
- ➡ How is China changing? Examine this question from economic, social, and political viewpoints. Or choose one area and present in-depth coverage.
- Comment on home ownership in China.
- O In the post-Mao period, China has been divided over its future direction. What are the basic issues?
- What have been the main factors in Hong Kong's recent economic development and

growth?

★ What effects has limited arable land had on the manner in which the Japanese utilize their environment?

• What have been the consequences of Japan's traditional insularity on its modern economic development?

• Contrast the social and cultural programs of the "Great Leap Forward" and the Cultural Revolution in China.

▲ The social, political, and economic accomplishments of the Meiji restoration (Japan)

★ China's emerging lifestyles: a change for the better—Refute or defend this contention.

▲ How China ended drug abuse

★ What factors have accounted for the remarkably rapid social and economic accomplishments of many recent Asian immigrants to the United States? Why have they excelled educationally as well?

▲ United States/China exchange programs

• How reforms in China's agricultural system have provided economic incentives for individual farmers

• Amerasian children in Vietnam: a continuing disgrace

▲ How has the failure of communism in Russia affected the political system in China?

• China since Tienanmen Square

• Analyze the major elements of the Japanese automobile industry. What accounts for their success?

× Trade barriers with Asian countries: should they be loosened or tightened?

▲ The siege of Singapore, 1941–1942

• What is being done to protect the orangutans in Sumatra and Borneo?

• American strategy in the South Pacific in World War II

• Why the Pacific Rim will be a natural trading area

• The long-ranging effects of the 1995 Kobe earthquake for Japan

---

Key to Symbols

•	average difficulty	↞	narrow down topic
§	substitutes possible	▲	large public or college
★	ample information in most		library required
	libraries	↙	local option topic
○	specialized knowledge	×	examples and supporting
	required		evidence needed

Astronomy

See also: Physics; Space

- The telescopes of Galileo: their design and construction
- What are the realistic possibilities for interstellar communication? Survey a sampling of informed scientific opinions and compare their conclusions.
- Water on Venus? What have been the results of the latest studies?
- The moons of Saturn
- The climate of Venus
- ★ The discovery of the galaxies
- The significance of the "expanding universe" concept
- The steady-state theory of continuous creation versus the big-bang theory
- Computers and the modern telescope
- The spectroscope: its design, history, and functions
- × Calendar reform: ancient and modern
- ▲ Is the modern observatory adequate? What are the current needs of the scientific community?
- The scientific knowledge of the first astronomers
- Moon myths throughout the ages
- Early nebular hypotheses
- The radio telescope
- Sun spot cycles and how they affect the earth
- How the pyramids and other ancient constructions were used for astronomical observations
- The origin of cosmic rays
- ★ The topography of the moon
- Technology of the early telescopes
- × Ancient theories of numerology
- Ancient and modern theories about meteors and comets
- ▲ Scientific data and findings from the comet Kohoutek
- The relationship between sun spots and the auroras
- Discuss the career of Maria Mitchell (1818–1889), America's first woman astronomer.
- The discovery and significance of the Van Allen radiation belts
- How modern astronomy evaluates the theories of Copernicus
- ▲ The measurement of red shifts in other galaxies
- ✔ Telescope lenses in modern observatories. If possible, visit an observatory and detail the tele-

scope in current use.
- What is the structure of stars?
- How old is the solar system? Survey and contrast a full range of recent scientific opinion.
- The Jupiter effect
- How to navigate by the stars
- The pros and cons of the big-bang theory of the earth's creation
○ The significance to science of the relationship between pulsars and supernovas
- Compare and contrast quasars and pulsars.
- Black holes: What are they? What is their significance to cosmology?
- Where is the origin of quasars?
- What we know about pulsars and what science would like to learn
- The "new" rings of Saturn: discoveries by Voyager II
- The critical issues involved in future space ventures
- New science of cosmology
★ The evolution of a star
➤ The findings of Voyager II
- How are solar phenomena produced?
- The formation of the moon
★ Constellation myths (Greek, Ro-

man, Chinese, Eskimo, etc.) Choose either one culture or one constellation.
▲ In the opinion of the astronomical scientists, were the Apollo moon missions justified?
- The ends of space: theories and speculations
○ Instrumentation in astronomy, from 1975 to date
▲ The rings of Saturn. Investigate recent findings.
★ Compare Halley's Comet to other important comets of the past.
- The Milky Way—how much do we really know?
★ The Hubble space telescope: its capacities, repair in space, and eventual discoveries
- What we know about supernovas. Has scientific opinion shifted? Analyze their place in the cosmos.
★ The discoveries of Voyager II
- How old is the universe? Examine and explain several contemporary theories.
○ How galaxies evolve: the great missing link of modern astrophysics
▲ Supernova 1987A, the nearest supernova explosion in modern times

---

Key to Symbols

•	average difficulty	➤	narrow down topic
§	substitutes possible	▲	large public or college
★	ample information in most		library required
	libraries	✔	local option topic
○	specialized knowledge	✗	examples and supporting
	required		evidence needed

Automotive

See also: Transportation

↙ Investigate automotive fatality and injury rates in your state. Have they increased or declined? Why? What safety measures and innovations have been instituted?

§ Past and present design characteristics of the Volkswagen automobile. Include illustrations of the features discussed.

● The economics of the antique car market in the United States

★ Why the American auto industry consistently makes the largest cars in the world

● Wankel engine: its development, utility, and flaws

● Defend: Motorcycles need not be dangerous.

● What makes a hot rod different?

● How to maintain a car at home. What functions should not be attempted by the owner and why?

★ No-fault automobile insurance: its advantages for the driver

● How cars are road-tested by automobile manufacturers

● How cars are road-tested by consumer organizations

● Women racing drivers

➥ Repairing diesel engines

★ The economic challenge of Japanese auto imports to the American automobile industry

▲ Police squad cars: specifications, design, and equipment

● How the Red Flag Act impeded the development of the automotive industry

▲ Survey the advertising used for the first Fords and compare it to modern Ford advertising.

▲ Compare and contrast the Daimler's Panhard of 1894 and the modern automobile.

★ Ralph Nader's effect on the auto industry

● Early steam-powered road carriages

● How General Motors designs and engineers new models

➥ Restoring old cars

● The jeep in World War II. What were its outstanding features? Why was it so consistently reliable?

● The efficient arrangement of tools in an auto body repair shop

- ● Off-road vehicle abuse of the landscape. What measures should be instituted to lessen the environmental damage?
- ● Design factors of the Apollo Lunar Roving Vehicle
- ▲ New racing car designs: 1980 to date
- ● Why the DeLorean automobile was a failure
- ➡ The effects of the automobile on the structure and evolution of American cities
- ● How the automobile changed American society
- ✓ Shop for automotive financing at several financial institutions (savings and loan, bank, credit union, etc.) and evaluate the advantages/disadvantages each offers the consumer. Compare these to a cash purchase.
- ▲ Before the Model T: Models A through S
- ○ An evaluation of the reliability of automotive EPA mileage ratings
- ● Converting gasoline-powered engines into butane. Include the advantages and disadvantages of this source of power.
- ● Compare and contrast the safety factors of compact versus large cars.
- ★ Alcohol versus gasoline as fuel
- ● Automotive crash protection technology. Which cars afford maximum protection? What improvements should be made?
- ● The advantages of the diesel engine
- ● Automotive unions: their origins and effects on the industry
- ★ The automobile as a status symbol in America
- ● The first Fords and their effects on American industry
- ● The economics of the automobile industry: 1980–present
- ● Compare and contrast the Cadillac, Mercedes-Benz, and Rolls-Royce automobiles.
- ● Compare and contrast the diesel and gasoline automotive engines.
- × "The American Dream" and automotive advertising
- ● The car as movie star
- ● Select one of the following cars, models, or makes, all of which were notable for their influence on automotive design, or their association with a person, era, or event:

  Cord
  Hitler's Mercedes
  Stutz Bearcat
  Chevrolet Corvette
  MG
  Volkswagen Beetle
  Henry Ford's Model T, the Tin Lizzy
  Lotus
  Dusenberg
  Rolls-Royce
  DeLorean
  Ford Thunderbird
  Ford Edsel

Stanley Steamer
Kaiser-Frazer
Studebaker
Jeep
Owen Magnetic
Pierce-Arrow
Marmon
Baker Electric
1907 Thomas Flyer
Bluebird of Sir Malcolm
 Campbell

- The role of the automobile industry in the United States economy: an overview
- How motor vehicle fatalities could be decreased
○ The determination of auto insurance rates
- How foreign competition has changed the United States auto industry
- Management of the Chrysler Corporation, 1975–1981
▲ Motor vehicle design in the year 2000
- Should the auto industry accept federal assistance?
- Should the federal government be responsible for automotive safety design?
- What factors contributed to the growth and wide use of the automobile in America?
★ How to buy a used car
★ Common auto repair scams and how to recognize and avoid them
↙ The plight of the local car dealer. If possible, interview

several.
- Should auto insurance be mandatory for all drivers?
- Gas rationing: how it worked in the past and how it would work in the future
- Auto emission controls. Discuss the events leading to their use; also the benefits, costs and what measures should be initiated, if any, to increase their utility.
- Odometer tampering by dishonest car dealers. How prevalent a practice? Is this detectable by the buyer? Can it be prevented?
★ Should the United States institute auto imports quotas in order to protect the automobile industry? Do other countries employ such protectionist measures?
★ How seatbelt laws, air bags, and stricter drunk-driving laws are altering accident statistics
★ The major causes of fatal auto accidents
★ Research airbags, their utility, cost and technology
- How to teach someone to drive
○ What are the problems, possibilities and future results of increasing automobile fuel efficiency?
- The modern automotive manufacturing plant
★ Big cars are generally safer than small cars. But big cars use more fuel and pollute more. Is there a middle ground?

Aviation

See also: Astronomy; Space; Transportation

★ Survival needs for small aircraft. Describe the equipment and materials necessary to help survive a crisis situation.
● How to fly a glider
○ Helicopter dynamics
● Problems of supersonic flight. Include some of the technology available to resolve these obstacles.
★ How successful is the *Concorde* supersonic jet?
★ The transatlantic flight of Charles Lindbergh
● The destruction of the *Hindenburg* dirigible. What effects did this have on future technological advances in this area?
● Night aerial operations in World War II
● Tactics used by Baron Manfred von Richthofen (the "Red Baron") in World War I
▲ Describe the flight of Amy Johnson, the first woman to fly solo from London to Australia.
● Airplane kits for home builders
○ Safe air traffic control
○ Are FAA regulations adequate?
● The role of women in the history of aviation
● Early balloon flights, 1782–1793. Include a discussion of successes and failures, heights, distances, and descriptions of some of the outstanding participants.
★ The design features of the *Kitty Hawk*
▲ The world's most dangerous airlines. Why? Who are the experts? Do they agree?
● Pilotless warplanes
✕ Airports of tomorrow
○ Evaluate "ultralight" aircraft kits
● Advances in ultralight flight
● Historical perspectives on the trial of Billy Mitchell (1925)
● What goes on at air traffic control
★ Are aircraft carriers obsolete?
● Further measures for airline safety
● Should the airlines be nationalized?
○ How to navigate by the stars
↜ Military air intelligence techniques
● Functions and possible changes in the Civil Aeronautics Board
★ Careers in aviation

62

- Japanese kamikaze missions during the course of World War II
▲ The use of air support in the landings at Normandy
▲ The future for robotic aircraft
- Unsafe airports in the United States
- The training of an airline pilot
- Should the federal government give economic assistance to airlines?
▲ Pilot error in recent airline accidents
▲ Airport security. Why is it necessary? What are the newest technological innovations?
- Aircraft design in World War I: the state of the art
- The use of gliders in military operations
○ The failure of the SST
- Allied aircraft versus Axis aircraft in World War I: a comparison
★ The development of the aircraft carrier
- Early balloons: specifications, construction, materials, and performance
- The early design and construction of rigid airships
★ Skyjacking: airline preventive and control measures
- Major causes of small plane crashes
- Major causes of commercial airliner crashes
- Safeguards and preventive measures for small plane safety
★ The aviation empire of Howard Hughes
- Early parachute construction
▲ The metal dirigible of David Schwarz (1897)
- The balloon flight to the stratosphere by Auguste Piccard in 1931
- Airplanes and maneuvers of the first aerial combat encounters
- The romance of flying as presented in the writings of Antoine de Saint Exupéry, the French aviator and writer
○ Experimental airplanes that didn't work
- The development of the Lear Jet
○ Storm hazards in aviation for light aircraft and how to avoid them
- The Curtiss-Wright patent controversy
- The design of the Wright Brothers' Flyers I, II, and III
× Some practical solutions to airport congestion
- Noise abatement options for airports
- Should airports be profitable?
➡ Modern American combat aircraft
★ Discuss the issues in the air controllers' strike and subsequent government and union actions.
- What happens when airlines are deregulated?
- The planes of *Luftwaffe* in World War II
★ Major factors affecting the growth of airline transportation

- Should the government build and control United States airports?
- New industries brought about by the advent of the air age
- Flight in mythology and legend
- ▲ The designs of Kelly Johnson
- ★ What are some of the proposals to remedy the heavy air traffic at major airports?
- What effects has aviation had on the management practices of corporations?
- The Stealth bomber
- The aeronautical drawings of Leonardo Da Vinci. How accurate were they in light of later developments? Why were they suppressed? What was their contribution to the knowledge of flight?
- The gliders of Otto Lilienthal
- Recent experimental airships. Select one or two for discussion.
- The future of the dirigible and other lighter-than-air craft. Examine also their use in conjunction with other machines, such as the helicopter.
- American military airpower: the state of the art
- ★ The helicopter and air mobility in the Vietnam War
- The autogiro rotary-wing aircraft
- Closed-course airplane racing
- ★ Examine and describe recent efforts by airlines to monitor and control hazardous cargo.

- ▲ Problems connected to manufacturer's liability for light aircraft
- Select one of the following airplanes, all of which were famous because of design, association with an important event or person, or their influence on aviation and on military history.

Spirit of St. Louis
Enola Gay
Ford Trimotor (4 AT)
Douglas DC 3 (from 1935)
Sopwith Camel
Spitfire
Junkers JU 87 Stuka
Messerschmitt Bf 109
Albatros D-Va
Boeing Model B14 Clipper Flying-Boat
Republic P-47D Thunderbolt
Focke-Wulf Fw 190
De Havilland Mosquito
Boeing B-17 Flying Fortress
Columbia
Lockheed Constellation
Flyer I
Vin-Fiz Flyer of 1911
Spad 1 3
Bristol F2 B
De Havilland Tiger Moth
Lockheed Vega
Junkers Ju 52/3m
Zero
Vought F4U Corsair
Dassault Mirage G8
MiG- 17 Fresco

Lockheed F-104
McDonnell Douglas F-4 *Phantom*
U.S. General Dynamics F-111
Tupolev TU-144
Anglo-French B.A.C. Aerospatiale *Concorde*

★ How airlines are trying to prevent acts of terrorism
○ The problems of "fatigued" air-

craft used by commercial airlines
● Examine several frequent flyer programs and evaluate the costs and the rewards
★ Is our current air traffic control system adequate? What improvements should be made?
● Do we need a faster plane than the Concorde? Is the technology available?

Key to Symbols

● average difficulty	➤ narrow down topic
§ substitutes possible	▲ large public or college
★ ample information in most	library required
libraries	↙ local option topic
○ specialized knowledge	× examples and supporting
required	evidence needed

Bioethics

See also: Biology; Health; Medicine; Genetics and Heredity; Religion

○ Should each state adopt a uniform program of funding for organ-transplant operations?

● Progress toward a "Bill of Rights" for patients

▲ What obstacles may prevent the increased use of frozen human embryos in scientific research?

★ Who may decide if a patient should be euthanized?

● Although fetal cell tissues are used in several areas of medicine, this practice is hotly contested. Why?

● When is a person dead so that organs can be harvested for transplantation to save another's life?

✕ Is there such a thing as a "rational" suicide?

★ Should there be more stringent curbs on the use of animals in research?

▲ Examine the relationship between genetically engineered products and owner patents.

● Should doctors assist patients who wish to commit suicide because of pain and terminal illness?

● Ethics in ancient medicine

★ Why have there always been universal bans on incest?

● Detail the ramifications of the Nancy Cruzan Supreme Court decision (1990).

★ Common and uncommon compli-

cations of surrogate motherhood

● Is it moral for doctors and scientists to alter human genetic inheritance?

● Defend or refute: All human life must be preserved, regardless of the suffering or cost involved.

● Since organ transplants are very expensive, often only wealthy people can afford them. What are the dynamics of this situation?

✕ The risks and perils of genetic engineering

★ Is it right to cause an infant pain and suffering in an attempt to save its life?

▲ Euthanasia in the Netherlands. Describe the parameters of an accepted practice.

● Many feel it is unethical to transplant kidneys from living donors even though such procedures are often successful. Examine this position.

● Should the federal government fund research using fetal cell transplants?

★ Severely defective newborns and the Baby Doe Rule

● The justifications for the Tuskegee syphilis experiment (1930) by the National Health Service

● Administering the death penalty by lethal injection is viewed by many health professionals as an

66

ethical issue. Why?

- Should individuals retain rights to tissues and cells removed from their body during surgery and subsequently used in scientific research?
- × The risks and benefits of human medical experimentation
- The use of animal organs as human transplants. Does the animal have any rights in these cases?
- ★ Who should decide the fate of handicapped newborns?
- ○ If a doctor withheld extraordinary treatment from a terminally ill patient, could a murder prosecution result?
- ★ Should those who test HIV positive or have AIDS be identified? Why or why not?
- ★ Why everyone should have a living will
- Should there be a top dollar for all medical expenses?
- Who should decide what death is?
- Describe the socioeconomic effects that would result if all pregnant women were required to undergo amniocentesis.
- Examine recent (last 15 years) right-to-die legislation.
- ○ Guidelines for genetic experimentation
- Does human life begin at conception or birth?
- It has been suggested that in vitro fertilization is a form of abortion since usually more than one egg is used. Defend or refute.

- ○ The bioethics of DNA
- In vitro fertilization is becoming more common. Are there ethical considerations involved?
- The "morning after" birth control pill destroys the fertilized egg. Is this abortion?
- ★ Evaluate the arguments in the Karen Quinlan right-to-die case.
- Do you own your own life or does society?
- When abortions are the result of a fetal abnormality diagnosis, should they be considered a form of genetic engineering?
- ➤ For-profit hospitals have flourished in the last decade. Detractors claim their goals are detrimental to quality patient care.
- Should there be a total ban on artificial genetic changes for humans?
- ★ Kidney dialysis is very expensive and not available to everyone. Who decides?
- Some contend that relaxed regulations on right-to-die issues will invite euthanasia and infanticide. Examine this premise.
- Should family members be allowed to select treatment for the mentally incompetent?
- Evaluate this statement: "Legalized euthanasia would be the denial of hope for further progress against presently incurable maladies."
- × The uses of in vitro fertilization for endangered animals

★ Mandatory AIDS testing is nothing more than the greatest good for the greatest number. True?

➤ Life, death, and medical ethics

✕ Humans have been used for medical experimentation. Examine the guidelines and special considerations involved.

• The pro-life view of abortion

• Surrogate mothers: examine the ethical considerations of the parents, the child, and society.

★ Should suicide be everyone's personal choice? Anyone's?

• Should the French abortion pill, RU 486, be available on demand in the United States? Expand on the controversy over its distribution.

• Who should receive life support? Who should make the decisions?

• What should be the legal status of a child conceived from banked sperm if that sperm donor dies?

• There have been several con-tested adoptions because an unmarried mother, lying to the father, put their baby up for adoption. Should the father have custody?

★ Heroic lifesaving measures in the nursery. To what degree should these procedures be employed for physically and mentally impaired infants?

• Should biogenetic researchers be allowed to tamper with human heredity?

• The future of personality change through chemistry. Consider drugs such as Prozac and the "rules" governing their use.

• Doctors are often selective of their clientele. Should they have the right to refuse treatment of AIDS patients, for example?

★ To what extent should technology be used to prolong a life?

• Ethical aspects of euthanasia.

Biology

See also: Animal Behavior; Bioethics; Ecology; Evolution; Genetics

- Compare and contrast a freshwater and a saltwater fish. Discuss their internal organs and life processes.
○ The functions of steroid hormones
○ Gas-exchange mechanisms. How do they differ in insects, humans, fish, and plants?
★ Gill variations and adaptions
- How have horses, jellyfish, earthworms, honeybees, and humans made successful adaptions for food procurement?
× Compare the following terms, using as examples a variety of life forms: saprophyte, parasite, herbivore, carnivore and omnivore.
- Early scientists generally espoused the process of spontaneous generation. When and how was it discredited and disproved? By what methods?
○ What was the contribution of Robert Hooke to our knowledge of cells and cell structure?
▲ If man and other higher animals were able to be cloned, what would be the effects on human

society? Consult authoritative sources to support your answers.
○ Some scientists now believe that symbiosis between primitive organisms in the distant past are responsible for much of the complexity of human cellular structure. What is the evidence to support this thesis?
- What characteristics are shared by all primates? Why is this significant?
× Insect sense organs
- Compare and contrast bacteria and virus. What is the significance of their differences?
- The role of Darwinism in contemporary biology
- Theories which explain the endogenous clock phenomenon
- Life in salt lakes. Include the Dead Sea in this survey.
§ History of the domestic cat
★ Compare and contrast Old World monkeys with those found in the New World.
- How snail shells develop. Compare varieties.
- The major characteristics of pri-

69

mates that set them apart from other mammals and from man
- DNA: the blueprint of life
× Sexual dimorphism
§ Life forms of the Sahara desert
★ Biological basis for the mermaid legend (manatees, dugong, etc.)
× Batesian mimicry
- Compare and contrast the social structure of the ant and the termite.
○ Recombinant DNA guidelines. Are they adequate? How do they function?
▲ What are the results of the latest bird navigation studies?
★ How did the advent of agriculture change human populations?
- Is there a "balance of nature"? Use scientific data and evidence to support your answer.
- Trace the evolution of learned behavior in primates.
➥ Select several birds on the endangered species list and detail their plight and possible corrective measures which may prevent their extinction.
○ The mechanics and diversity of bird flight
- Use of tools by the lower animals
- The ice fish
★ The bats of Carlsbad Caverns (New Mexico)
➥ Protective coloration in insects. Select one species.
- Fossils of Dinosaur National Monument. What have we learned from these excavations?
○ Industrial applications of microbiology
★ The mechanism of moth metamorphosis
- Endorphins: the painkillers within us
× Examples of insect architecture and biomechanics
- Social organization of the honeybee
▲ The life cycle of the queen polistes wasp
- The wonderful pituitary gland
○ Artificial methods of parthenogenesis
- The "electric" fishes
- Flight mechanisms among insects
§ Courtship among the bower birds, or select another species which has elaborate and unique mating behavior.
§ Special adaptions of the woodpecker
★ Life cycle of the butterfly
★ Adaptions to night vision among mammals
▲ The internal chronometer in animals. What have been the scientific findings from 1970 to present? Select several studies and compare and contrast them.
- How animals learn: recent experimental advances
- Our biological clock and its relationship to sleep
➥ Natural mutation
- Dolphins and intelligence. What

is the current level of scientific knowledge? Sum up the results of several of the most significant studies.

- Surrogate mothers for vanishing species? What are the issues involved?
▲ Ocean hot-vent life forms: new findings
○ How does DNA control cellular activity?
- Mechanisms of fish propulsion
× Eyes: Compare and contrast primitive and complex varieties.
- The near extinction and recent domestication of the musk ox
▲ Mutation from natural radiation
- Life under the arctic ice. Recent investigations have made many new discoveries. What are they and why are some particularly significant?
★ Compare and contrast the dentition of a predator, a ruminant, and a rodent.
- How to tell a bird by its nest
× Animals that utilize ultrasound
- The tides, the moon, and the horseshoe crab
§ Defense mechanisms of the termite
○ Morphological effects of animal domestication
- Biological effects of radiation
- The symbiotic relationship of Lomechusa beetle and the Formica ant: Who wins?
- How DDT affects wildlife

- Aristotle's biological classifications
➤ Primate territorial behavior
★ How coral atolls are formed
- Are zoos humane?
× Life in the ocean's deep
§ Compare and contrast four of the major bird identification books. Compare their coverage. Assess which is appropriate for the beginner and for the expert. Which is best for your area? Or, select butterfly, shell, or insect books for similar comparisons.
- How the invention of the microscope in the sixteenth century changed the scope of biological knowledge
- Why the Galapagos Islands are unique
▲ California's control measures for the Mediterranean fruit fly
- Caribou migration
- The Darwin/Wallace controversy in a nutshell
- The invasion of the fire ants in the United States. What are their origins and current range? What are future projections?
★ Salmon migration in Western rivers
§ The tiger: habitat, habits, and prospects
- Animal types of the coral reef
- The evolution of the human brain
- Biogenesis, the origin of life.

Cite scientific theories and supporting evidence of each.

★ Life cycle of the penguin

★ The unique primates of Madagascar

● Northern American game fish

✕ Protective mimicry in anthropods

● Biological pest control by natural enemies

● Why the rhinoceros cannot survive

★ Direction-finding in bees

● Why the platypus is an evolutionary paradox

▲ Measurements of octopus intelligence

● How bats navigate

● The function of antennae in insects

● The laws of natural selection

● Evidences of life in the Precambrian era

○ Errors in Carolus Linnaeus's *Systema naturae* (1735)

✕ Patterns of aggression among the apes

▲ Compare/contrast human and chimpanzee infant development.

● Evolutionary relationship between fish and reptiles

● Birds that cannot fly. Why?

○ The place of prosimians in primate evolution

● Natural habitat of the giant pandas

● Adaptions of the kangaroo rat to arid southwest deserts

▲ Odor perception in salmon

➜ Diversity in a tropical rain forest

✕ Bill adaptations in birds

● Compare and contrast examples of circadian and endogenous rhythms in the animal world.

★ Butterfly migration. Select several species.

● Clydesdale horses: a unique breed

● How do biologists account for the variety of life spans among the animals? What factors have influenced species variation?

▲ Bird banding techniques

● The use of echoes by animals

● Ultrasonic hearing in dolphins

✕ How animals use odors

§ The visual acuity of <u>cats</u> (dogs, eagles, horses, etc.)

● Bioluminescence in marine life

○ Time perception in the insect world

§ Niche diversity among the <u>storks</u>

● Discuss the physiological factors which alone and in combination contribute to insect survival.

● Dinosaurs: Hot- or cold-blooded?

● Darwin's finches and what they proved

★ Habits of the grizzly bear

● The effects of smog on plant life

● The first amphibians. Detail their structure, variety, origin, and adaptions.

● Gorillas: Ferocious aggressors

or benign giants? Consult current sources.

- The significance of primate eye placement and hand configuration
- Compare and contrast chicken and rat embryonic development (or any bird/mammal combination).
- Compare and contrast the embryonic development of humans and primates.
▲ Coloration as a factor of primate communication
- Cloning: the popular myths and the scientific facts
× Insect polymorphism
- The metabolism of hibernation
- The structure of blood groups
§ The ecological niche of the vervet monkey
§ Compare trout varieties and discuss their range and populations.
○ Scientists have now been able to reconstruct DNA from ancient insects trapped in amber. Why is this significant?
○ Categorize all the life on a square-yard area of ground.
- The digestive mechanism of grass-eating mammals
× Instances of parallel evolution
× Symbiotic plant systems
- How desert plants have adapted to aridity
- Ecology of the tropical rain forest
- Plant recolonization on Mount St. Helens since the eruptions

- Compare and contrast Old and New World succulents.
★ Compare and contrast succulents and cacti.
- How zoos will serve as "Noah's archives," collecting species and genetic material in order to prevent animal extinctions
➡ Plants used by the American Indians. Select a use, such as food, clothing, medicine, etc.
- The loss of genetic diversity among cereal crops. Why has this caused concern among biologists and other scientific experts?
× Vestigial structures in higher animals, including man
- Could life exist without the process of meiosis? How would it differ from present life? If it couldn't, why not?
- Secondary sexual characteristics of the human male and female
★ What are some of the adaptions of flowering plants which encourage cross-pollination?
○ The relationship between age and mutation rate in human populations
- The wonderful hemoglobin molecule
- Using pheromones for the control of insect pests
○ The structure of a horse's hoof
- Water conservation by desert animals
- Watson and Crick's hunt for the helix

- Animal extinctions in the Americas by early man
- Describe the characteristics of typical plants found in each biological life zone.
★ How flowers advertise
- Techniques of pollen transference
- The historic significance of the bristlecone pine
- Compare and contrast the sequoia and the redwood.
★ Insectivorous plants
- Plant adaptations to extreme cold (heat)
▲ Plants as indicators of pollution
★ Photosynthesis
✔ How to plant a backyard bird sanctuary for your locality. Consider both resident and migrant populations as well as plant suitability.
★ Hallucination-producing plants
- The hypotheses explaining the origin of viruses. Compare the evidence of each and its relative acceptance by the scientific community.
- Both vertebrates and anthropoids are highly evolved examples of their respective evolutionary lines. They have convergently evolved some similar solutions to problems of reproduction and survival. Compare these adaptions.
- Compare the embryonic similarities of fishes, turtles, frogs, chickens, rabbits, and humans.
- Certain bacteria are essential components of life. What are their functions?
○ Dentition in a prosimian, monkey, pongid, and human: a comparison
- High altitude environments and their effects on human populations. Consult the most recent biological and anthropological studies.
★ What are the environmental issues raised by the release of genetically engineered organisms? Do biologists agree on the effects?
○ Guidelines from the National Institutes of Health for human gene therapy. Are they adequate? What is the state of the art?
○ The giant panda is a bear and the lesser, or red panda, is a raccoon. Evaluate these facts in biological and evolutionary terms.
▲ Forensic applications of molecular biology
▲ Biology in the courtroom: DNA analysis as evidence
★ How oil spills damage wildlife
- New deep-sea life forms

Boats and Boating

See also: Oceans and Seas

- ★ Life on board with Columbus
- ★ The role of the river steamboat in American commerce, 1840–1870
- ● How to make a dugout canoe
- ▲ Economics of the modern merchant marine industry
- ● The first ironclad ships: their structure and design
- ● Viking ships. Examine their seaworthiness, design, materials, and unique features
- ● The first oceangoing steamships
- ● Wind-powered freighters for transoceanic travel: A ship of the future?
- ★ Nautical rules of the road
- ★ The naval battle of the *Monitor* and the *Merrimack*
- ○ The submarine of the future
- ● The German development of the U-Boat, 1943–1945
- × Historic designs of small sailboats
- ● The evolution of the submarine as a warship
- × Historic instances of naval blockades
- ● The role of the United States Navy in the Persian Gulf War
- ● Viking ships: recent archeological contributions. Select one excavation or discovery and discuss its significance.
- ● Prototype windships
- ➡ The colonial shipbuilding industry in America
- ● Could the *Titanic* disaster have been avoided?
- ● The early whaling fleets
- ● Reasons for the destruction of the Spanish Armada
- ➡ America's Cup
- ● The Age of Discovery and ship design (fifteenth and sixteenth centuries)
- ● Why the windjammers were the ultimate windships
- ★ The evolution of the rudder
- ● Life on a Chinese junk (or sampan)
- ● The fate of the *Endurance* and the men who sailed her
- ● The death of the German World War II battleship *Graf Spee*
- ▲ Clipper ship and windjammer figureheads
- ● The China trade. What were the routes and what were the major items of trade? In what

ways did it influence commerce?

○ What you should know before you buy a small sailboat

▲ In December 1944, the Third Fleet sustained tremendous typhoon damage in the Pacific. Could this encounter have been prevented? Who was responsible?

● The greatest sea fight in history: the battle of Leyte Gulf

○ The aerodynamics of iceboats

● The submarine *Nautilus* and its underwater travels at the North Pole

★ How factory ships changed the fishing industry in the twentieth century

● In what ways were both shipbuilding and navigational techniques improved in the eras directly preceding Columbus? How did this contribute to exploration in general?

× The wind is the same, the sails are different. Account for these distinctions in terms of material, currents, customs, and esthetics.

● The canoes of the South Pacific

§ Vessels of Dutch waterways

● Nautical knots and their uses

● Select one of the following ships or types of ship. All were notable because of their association with a historic event (or events), or represented an advance in ship design or construction. Concentrate on the most significant or unique aspects of one

of them.

Argonaut

Titanic

Santa Maria

Monitor

Gypsy Moth

Cutty Sark

U.S.S. *Arizona*

Old Ironsides

United States

America

Queen Elizabeth II

Constitution

Sutton Hoo

The Gokstad ship

The Oseberg ship

Delta Queen

Beagle

Trieste

Merrimack (Virginia)

Mauretania

Mary Rose

Container Ship

Aircraft carrier

Whale ship

Cargo ship

Cruiser

Destroyer

Ketch

Clipper

Italian carrack

Egyptian merchant ship

Venetian galley

English galleon

Brigantine

Chinese junk

Schooner

● How they found the *Titanic* and what they found

Business and Industry

See also Business and Industry — Small Business; Computers; Economics; Ethical Business Practices; Labor; Working World

§ The current president's attitude toward the business community

O Select, describe, and discuss instances from America's past in which social Darwinism has been used to justify business practices.

● Why business and industry want to change the Clean Air Act

● How business practices in the United States led to the rise of consumerism in modern America

● What are the relative merits of a centralized business organization, as opposed to one which is decentralized?

➤ Industrial recruitment practices

★ The advantages of profit sharing. Include both employer and employee viewpoints.

✕ Building a corporate image

● The responsibility of business and industry in the control of workplace-related injuries and diseases

O Examine and evaluate some of the current financing methods for real estate contracts.

➤ Business dealings in the late

1800's in the United States were notoriously unregulated and corrupt. Has government regulation effectively curtailed these practices in the twentieth century?

➤ The 1920's was an era of prosperity and growth in the American business community. Select one company which originated during this era and chart its economic course.

● Describe the traditional methods of market testing. What innovations have changed some of these practices?

▲ Why more than 80 percent of new products that reach the marketplace fail

✕ Examine the major federal acts that have attempted regulation of industry's anticompetitive activities. How have the regulations been enforced? Use actual cases as examples.

● Should the United States impose more trade barriers? On what products? What countries?

● What factors contributed to the

rapid growth of American industry after 1812?

- × How large corporations exercise political power at the national and international level
- • Will increased automation lead to increased unemployment in business and industry?
- • How do monopolies and oligopolies function in the American business community? Include natural monopolies.
- • Why was the Sherman Antitrust Act a failure?
- ★ The housing squeeze
- • The increase and extent of foreign investments in the United States economy
- • Preventing employee theft. What have been some of the most effective and innovative techniques used in recent years?
- ▲ Quality control in Japanese industry
- • Japanese-United States trade: 1975 to date
- ➧ Safety in industry. Discuss regulation, abuses, and proposed directions for change. Select one industrial area.
- • What is involved in the international sales contract?
- ★ How the metric system affects United States business and industry
- • Long distance moving
- ✓ Select several large business organizations in your area and compare the personnel selection policies of each. Use, for example, a hospital, a retailer, a manufacturer, and a bank.
- × Business ethics: practices and problems
- • Compare and contrast the structure of profit and nonprofit organizations. Include personnel and objectives.
- ▲ Several American companies have applied Japanese managerial methods to their companies. What have been the results?
- • Functions of the personnel manager in a large business complex
- • Factors that affect housing in today's real estate markets
- § The relationship between the federal government and the steel industry
- • How discount houses affect retail businesses
- • The voice of America's big business: the Business Roundtable
- • How business can protect itself against white collar crime
- ○ Development of the first computer languages
- • Justice Department antitrust actions against American Telephone & Telegraph. What were the essential issues involved? The outcome?
- ○ Sales forecasting using econometric models
- ➧ The relationship between governmental regulation and business risk and growth

- Advertising and the oil companies. In what ways do any changes in advertising methods and content reflect social and environmental issues? Economic problems?
§ Survey the investment potential of the beer industry and select the most profitable stock.
○ The function of corporate power in the United States
○ Why many corporations pay no federal taxes
☛ Job attrition or creation through automation
• How high interest rates affect capital expenditure
★ The organization and functions of the New York Stock Exchange
✕ Business cycles
• Competition and the soft drink companies: a case history
○ How to design a market survey
★ The rise of the supermarket
• Theories of business leadership
✕ Methods of worker motivation in industry
• The mail order wonder: Sears, Roebuck & Co., 1893 to the present
§ Advertising and marketing techniques of the manufactured home industry
☛ Nuclear power: the attitudes of the business community
• The decline of the American automotive industry. What factors explain this trend?

• The industrial recovery of postwar Germany
○ Recent antimonopoly legislation
★ Shoplifting: Who does it and why?
§ The economics of ski resorts (or other recreational facilities)
• How the Mafia has invaded legitimate business
• Twentieth-century horse traders: the American Arabian horse business
§ How the Industrial Revolution changed the steel industry
★ The advantages and disadvantages of the four-day work week
★ The video game business
☛ Past performance and future prospects for franchises. Select one or two large franchising concerns.
• Why price-fixing is unethical
• Should business have social responsibilities? What should they be? Survey a number of authoritative sources and consider their conclusions.
§ Sales strategies of Levi Strauss & Co.
• The growth of the multinational
○ The case against government regulation of securities
• Arab money and American business
§ Functions of a certified public accountant
★ What factors are contributing to the expanded use of credit

cards? Which might influence their decline?

§ World gold production. Chart and analyze for 1880, 1920, and 1990

● The use of lie detector testing in business and industry

● How postal rates influence direct mail sales

§ The McDonald's hamburger success story

↙ Inventory control, theories, and practices. Select a particular business and analyze in detail, preferably by visits and interviews.

● Does profit sharing increase worker productivity?

★ Arson: how the insurance industry combats it

● Why large corporations train their own employees

● The possibilities for paperless offices

○ Procedures for the prevention of embezzlement

● Oil industry profits: Who should benefit?

▲ The development and utilization of robots by Japanese industry

● How can the government promote more competition in business?

➥ The profit motive, free enterprise system, and America's natural resources. Select one segment of the economy, iron ore, coal, forest products, agriculture, etc., and discuss it in

the context of the above elements.

○ Antitrust and how it has changed the American business structure. Evaluate both the benefits and problems it has generated.

● Should government regulate industry? Justify your answer with expert opinions.

● The history of credit cards

➥ Declining productivity in the United States: trends, causes, and prospects

● Women as business executives. What characteristics have proved to be the most effective?

§ Economics of the American paper industry

➥ Manufacturing in colonial New England

● High technology industries and the Japanese threat

● The auto industry in Europe: a survey

★ The influence of the first railroads on American manufacturing

● The textile industry before and after the Industrial Revolution

▲ Successful practices used to diminish the depersonalization of the assembly line

★ Explain: In 1924 every other car in the world was a Model T.

● The economics of conventional coal mining versus strip mining

➥ American business involvement in

the Arab Gulf States

× How industry helps (or does not help) the third world nations

• Current federal regulation of American business

• What are the costs to the business community of white collar crime?

⇌ The history of antitrust laws in the United States

• Compare and contrast the structure and organization of modern industry in the United States and Japan.

• Is foreign investment in United States business beneficial to the economy on both a short-term and a long-range basis?

• China as a new market for the United States

• The organization of a Las Vegas gambling casino

★ The phenomenal rise and fall of "Silicon Valley," California

★ Functions and standards of the Better Business Bureau

○ The computation and significance of the Dow-Jones Industrial Average

§ The growth of and prospects for California wineries

• Foreign production capacities and American-made consumer goods: Is a balance possible?

⇌ Events leading to the stock market crash of October, 1929

• Physical fitness boom. A boom for new businesses?

★ The alcoholic executive

• Establishment and operations of the Trilateral Commission

• How to sell insurance

• Japan has implemented a high growth rate strategy since 1950. What have been the social and economic results?

✓ Interview at least three people engaged in the area of business that you wish to enter.

§ The development and marketing of digital recordings

• Compare industrialism in the United States and Japan in terms of government support, permanent employment, group solidarity, and the process of decision-making.

○ How the European Common Market affects the United States business economy

▴ How have marketing concepts changed the retailing industry? Chart these modifications since 1950.

• Publications every businessman should read: an annotated bibliography

× Characteristics of the global corporation

• American suburban lifestyles and the retail industry

• Public confidence in big business has been eroded in recent years. What are the primary reasons?

• Innovations and new characteristics of the business world in the year 2000

- The role of competition in a free enterprise economy
- The Savings and Loan failure. What were the reasons, who was responsible, and what were the implications to the financial community?
- The pros and cons of export/ import quotas
- × The evils of corporate gossip
- ▲ Potential markets in modern China
- ★ Should companies use polygraphs (lie-detectors) in the pre-employment screening of job applicants?
- ○ Why the savings and loan industry has encountered financial problems in recent years. How have their current operations differed from those in the past? How has the economy altered?

- Executives: the new unemployed
- ➤ Current industrial research in bio-technology
- ○ Strategies of programmed trading in the New York Stock Exchange
- ➤ Arbitrage and American business
- × Has government scrutiny of the marketplace been too relaxed over the last decade?
- ○ The ins and outs of the hostile takeover business
- ○ The failure of supply-side economics and how this affects today's economy
- The resurgence of the American automotive industry. Is this a long-range trend? What factors are involved?

Key to Symbols

•	average difficulty	➤	narrow down topic
§	substitutes possible	▲	large public or college
★	ample information in most		library required
	libraries	✔	local option topic
○	specialized knowledge required	×	examples and supporting evidence needed

Business and Industry — Small Business

See also: Business and Industry; Computers; Economics; Labor; Working World

- How to select a retail outlet for a product
- § Plan a complete advertising campaign for a small firm specializing in _____. Include media samples.
- § Describe the product, layout, equipment, and processing procedures for a <u>fast food</u> <u>restaurant</u>.
- Insurance for the small businessman — a survey of options
- ✔ Evaluate the advertising possibilities and potentials for a small business establishment in your locality.
- Accounting procedures for small businesses. Include a survey of typical expenses, cash requirements, etc.
- § Design an advertising campaign for your own small business of _____. Select a product or service and market area.
- ○ Tax advantages for small businesses
- How to market (your) crafts
- How to successfully initiate a sales promotion campaign. Se-

lect a product or service area.
- ✗ How the decline of small businessmen has changed the American business economy
- Select five books that deal with running your own small business. Compare and contrast them. Include the opinions of critics through book reviews if they are available.
- How to operate a successful mail-order business
- ★ How inflation affects the small businessman
- ★ Facilities and services of the Small Business Administration
- ✔ What services are available to local businesses from banks in your area?
- How to select and purchase a franchise
- ✔ The requirements for small businesses in your local community and state
- ➥ Select one franchise opportunity (from the *Wall Street Journal*, for example) and write to the company for information. Evaluate and compare it to similar

franchises. Research the company's background, financial status, size, etc.

- Credit and collection policies and operations. Choose three major credit companies and compare their regulations and procedures.
- Inventory management policies and procedures
- Employee benefits for small businesses
▲ How to market products overseas
- How to develop a business plan before starting a small business
○ Short-term financing for the small business organization
- Theft in retail outlets. How large is the problem? What are the remedies?
- How to evaluate marketing and advertising options for small businesses
- Accounting services for the small business. What is required?
▲ The independent sales agent and the small business
✔ Interview two small business owners (in similar or related areas) and compare their finance methods of record-keeping, production, advertising, sales strategy, marketing, etc.
§ Shopping center locations and how to evaluate them for a ready-to-wear business
★ Compare and contrast Individual

Retirement Accounts and Keogh Plans.
- Security measures for the small office
- What factors account for the increase in small business failures?
○ What a computer can and cannot do for a typical small business
✔ Visit several successful small businesses and discuss their start-up costs, overhead, personal inventory, and other financial details. Compare and contrast the results.
- How to display merchandise
- The economic plight of small businessmen in a high interest world
☛ Problems in small business management
- Compare and contrast the merits of solo versus partnership in a small business venture.
✔ Interview two small business owners and compare their educational and work backgrounds.
✔ Select the perfect location site for a hypothetical small business. Survey the market potential and population trends, consult the Chamber of Commerce, analyze traffic patterns, and any other relevant factors that might contribute to the success or failure of the venture.
- How to buy a small business
- Crime prevention for the small

business

- ○ Leasing versus purchase of equipment: an analysis of the factors
- • How to sell a small business
- ▲ How to analyze a market area for stability and growth potential
- • Techniques for telephone selling. What are the advantages and disadvantages of this method?
- • How to increase sales through effective interior displays
- • Building good customer relations
- • Preventing employee pilferage
- ▲ How to construct an effective market questionnaire
- ○ The attitude and role of the federal government has not traditionally served the needs of small business. Expand upon this statement.
- ★ Can the small businessman survive the crisis in liability insurance?

Key to Symbols

- • **average difficulty**
- § **substitutes possible**
- ★ **ample information in most libraries**
- ○ **specialized knowledge required**
- ➨ **narrow down topic**
- ▲ **large public or college library required**
- ✓ **local option topic**
- × **examples and supporting evidence needed**

Chemistry

See also: Physics

- Chemical uses of the laser
★ Toxic dumping: Who is responsible?
§ Discovery of penicillin
○ Are other biochemistries possible?
- The development of the periodic table
⬠ The discovery of the elements
○ The chemical composition of the moon
- What the ancients knew about the elements
- The consequences of the discovery of uranium
★ The ancient alchemists
- The chemistry of acid rain and its environmental effects on plant, animal, and ecological systems
○ Chemical measures to alleviate the detrimental effects of acid rain
○ Practical aspects of the production of methane from waste material
- Chemical carcinogens
- Chemical safety regulations
- "Primordial soup" — life's beginnings?

★ Possible methods of hazardous waste storage
○ Products from petroleum. Select a product area and describe the most important technologies and innovations.
▲ Detail the five most significant discoveries in chemistry, from 1980 to date.
- Drug industry testing and safety procedures
- Chemistry of food preservation
★ What excess sulfur dioxide does to plants, animals, and inorganic materials
- Chemical pollution from agricultural spraying
- The uses of animal and plant odor compounds in biological pest control
○ Primary and secondary reactions of photochemical smog
- Chemical knowledge and applications in preclassical antiquity
- Chemical hazards control
- Common chemical reactions in the kitchen
- How oil spills are neutralized
★ CFCs (chlorofluorocarbons) and the global ozone layer

- The safety hazards of synthetic building materials
▲ Scientific advances in the synthetic reproduction of the elements
- Prevention of corrosion in pipes (water, oil, gas)
○ The chemistry of lightning
★ Ozone: what it is, why we need it, and what may happen to it in the future
- Chemical composition of ocean water
○ Synthetic reproduction of natural foods (butter, milk, meat, etc.)
- Relate the processes involved in purification of water
- Emission control devices: pros and cons
- Fire dangers of synthetic materials
➥ Analyze the conditions in space which make possible the manufacturing of rare metals, crystals, and other new technologies that cannot be produced naturally.
§ Early development and uses of rubber
- How synthetic fibers were discovered, improved, and utilized
- How chemistry is used in the art world
- How archeologists use modern chemical technologies in excavations and historical dating
➥ Chemical additives in our foods

and how some may affect the human body
§ Pollution of _____ (water, air, soil) by the chemical industry
- Pheromones: chemical communicators
- Dioxin, the most dangerous chemical man has ever developed
- The chemical path from opium to heroin
▲ Recent advances in the manufacturing of synthetic penicillins
- How antibiotics work in the body
- Endorphins: the brain's own morphine
- How drugs are screened for human use by the drug industry and the federal government
▲ What are the possibilities for a new class of drugs based on the natural chemicals of the human brain?
- The chemical effects of marijuana
➥ Are industrial chemical plants safe or are we likely to have other accidents such as that in Bhopal, India (1984)?
▲ EDB (ethylene dibromide) and the Federal Drug Administration, the Environmental Protection Agency and the United States Department of Agriculture
- How to neutralize acid rain

Children

See also: Adolescents; Education; Family Life; Literature for Children; Marriage

▲ Recent research has shown human newborns to have more competencies than was previously believed. Focus on some of these studies and the surprising results.

○ Malnutrition and brain development in young children

● Why kidnapping by parents is increasing in the United States

★ Ethical issues involved in infant euthanasia for hopelessly deformed newborns

● Childbirth lore and folk wisdom

★ How to make reading a habit with children

● Psychological aspects of the young child's art. Select a short age-span.

● Cartoons and violence: how young children react

▲ Self-concept in the disadvantaged child

● Raising children in affluent America. Many critics claim that our young are soft, lazy, and self-indulgent. Discuss an aspect of this situation and cite a variety of opinions which either support or refute it.

★ The severely mentally retarded child: Home or institution? Consider the relevant emotional, economic, physical, and educational issues.

● Adjustment problems of the deaf child in the home and community

★ Preparing a child for a hospital experience

▲ How to increase licensed child care facilities in slum and ghetto areas. Survey some of the successful programs and include a discussion of standards, funding, demographics, etc.

● Hyperkinetic children and their problems

★ How to tell children about death (both before and after death occurs)

● Smoking and the unborn child. Survey the relevant literature from 1970 to date.

● Nightmares and sleepwalking in the young child

● The first three years: formative influences

- Should adopted children meet their natural parents?
- Helping children to adjust to a new parent
▲ The control of autism in children
§ Children in modern China
★ The pros and cons of marriage without children
- Watch, analyze, and discuss the commercials during one four-hour period on Saturday morning television. What are some possible effects on young viewers? What are the values projected?
☛ The television role-model and the child viewer
× Music for preschool children
- Noncompetitive games for children
- Childrearing among the Eskimos. How does it differ from the American norm?
★ Car safety for children
- Learning games for the preschooler
★ Musical instruments children can make and use
- Early kindergartens. How have they evolved and improved? Have their functions changed?
- Safety factors in children's play equipment both at home and at school
- How to instill in children a respect for the natural world
★ Breast feeding versus the bottle
- Shy children: causes, concerns, and corrections

- Causes and rates of infant mortality on a world basis
★ Preparing children for a new baby
- Children of alcoholics. What are their particular problems and what have been the significant and most damaging long-range effects?
- Pornography and the exploitation of children
- Treatment of abused children
- How to discipline children. There are many theories. Compare and contrast several major ones.
▲ Child geniuses: How smart are they?
- How to evaluate a preschool
★ How to train a babysitter
- How to help the hearing-impaired child
× Violence and aggression on television and the effect on young children. Use examples from acted dramas, not cartoons.
- How to help a child face the death of a parent
▲ Sudden Infant Death Syndrome: the latest findings
- Melodic and rhythmic games for children
- Children's environmentally induced handicaps
○ Identity and self-image of adopted children
★ Storytelling for children
○ Intelligence testing through the

young child's art: accuracy
and validity

▲ The facts about sibling rivalry

▲ Design the playground area of
a day-care center. Consider
size, funds, equipment, ages,
weather; use ratios.

● Legal rights of children

➥ Emotionally disturbed children: causes and treatments

§ Toys for the two-year-old

➥ Causes of mental retardation in
children

● Compare and contrast child
rearing principles and practices
in the USSR and America.

○ Aphasia in children: incidence,
causes, and treatments

§ Mozart as child prodigy

● Classic examples of racism in
children's literature

● How to allay and dispel anxiety
in children

● Common causes of brain
damage in children

● The children of separation and
divorce: their common problems

➥ Rearing a physically handicapped child

● Why some children do not learn
easily

● Origins of children's finger
games

● Maternal-infant bonding. What
have psychologists discovered
about this process? How does it
affect a child's growth and development?

✕ How to teach children nonsexist
values. Define these values. Use
several examples for each.

● How children develop a healthy
self-image

★ How children's eating preferences are influenced by television

● Discipline: What the psychologists say. Survey a variety of
authorities.

● Bed-wetting and the young child

● Long-term effects on children of
neglect and emotional deprivation

▲ Programs for foster child care.
What have been the critical
areas of concern? Have they
been remedied? How should
care be improved?

➥ Factors contributing to the emotional health of young children

○ The slow learner in the classroom

● How to raise a responsible child

● Babies: the first two weeks

● Problems of visually impaired
children

● Environmental hazards to children

● What children learn from their
playmates

✔ Day-care facilities for the un-
derprivileged in your locality.
Are they adequately staffed,
equipped, and funded? Visit
several.

▲ Educating a child at home:
strengths, weaknesses, and

variables

★ What children can gain from their grandparents

✔ Foster home care in your state. What are the regulations? What criticisms do local professionals have of existing facilities?

★ Causes and incidence of lead poisoning. What measures have been instituted for prevention?

● Etiquette for young children

● Incidence of drug use and addiction among school-age children in the United States

○ Why the gifted child should receive special education. Detail the specific areas and types of instruction which would be most beneficial.

● Adoption options in modern America

● Why fewer babies are available for adoption in the United States

★ Discuss events leading to the birth of Louise Joy Brown, the first test-tube baby (July 26, 1978).

● Children's attitudes towards death. How are they most often affected by the death of a family member or friend?

○ How do the children of a society learn their culture? Describe the primary institutions, the people involved, and the probable effects of each on the maturing child.

● The adverse effects of bottle-feeding in third world countries

▲ Why boys are customarily allowed less flexibility than girls throughout childhood in gender-role behavior.

● Causes of birth abnormalities

● The fairness in advertising claims doctrine and advertising for children on American television

● Examples of aggressive behavior in the first two years of life

○ Compare the learning and use of symbols for communication by chimpanzees and very young children. What are the most marked parallels? Where and when do their developments diverge?

● Methods and practices for the encouragement of infant motor development

★ Describe the television viewing habits of the average preschooler.

● Discuss the purposes of the Head Start Program, evaluate its effectiveness, and its current role in childhood education.

● How to tell when a child is depressed

✕ Recent advances in infertility treatment

★ Is public concern about school children with AIDS (Acquired Immune Deficiency Syndrome) justified? Consider known modes of transmission and significant opinion of appropriate authorities.

● How to help the abused child

- How to keep children safe in automobiles
★ In the past, severely deformed infants usually died at birth; now they are often saved by technologically advanced equipment and huge amounts of money. Same feel this technology and funding would be more appropriately applied elsewhere. Analyze these issues.
★ The alarming increase of AIDS babies. Survey the situation today and tomorrow.
- Many Amerasian children have come from Vietnam to the United States. How successful has this program been?
★ Sexual abuse in child care centers: fact or hysteria?
× Fetal diagnosis procedures: what they can find and how they find it
- Why the Uniform Adoption Act should be changed
- Fetal alcohol syndrome: its prevalence and effects
- Examine the ramifications of sperm

donor selection by prospective parents.
× The number of noncustodial parents abducting their own children has increased. What is the outcome in most cases?
★ Why many parents and educators support the growing "back to basics" movement
➥ Multiple births attained through fertility drugs have increased. What problems does this present to the individual and to society?
★ Attention Deficit Syndrome (ADS) and how children's learning suffers
- Should fetuses or infants be used as organ donors?
- Describe the characteristics likely to be exhibited by abused and/or neglected children.
- The pros and cons of corporal punishment of children
★ Pornography and the Internet: how to protect your children

Key to Symbols

- **average difficulty**
§ **substitutes possible**
★ **ample information in most libraries**
○ **specialized knowledge required**

➥ **narrow down topic**
▲ **large public or college library required**
✔ **local option topic**
× **examples and supporting evidence**

Community Concerns

See also: Urban Affairs

★ Should the federal government, the state, or the community control the food stamp program? Discuss the issues involved. What possible new problems could arise were the program to be changed?

▲ How communities can make low-income housing projects a successful and permanent addition to the local environment

✔ Analyze your community's emergency-preparedness. Include not only a nuclear disaster, but also other possibilities such as a flood, earthquake, hurricane, toxic wastes, etc.

● Burglar and fire alarms: a survey and ranking of existing systems

✔ What is the major economic problem in your local area?

● Advantages and disadvantages of cooperatives

★ How to grow your own food and save money

● Sex discrimination in housing

▲ Planning a community playground

§ How to prepare for an earthquake and what to do when one occurs

✔ Life in the early days of your town, city, or community

● Home owners' insurance. Contact five different companies and compare the costs, benefits, and services.

● How communities have successfully combated crime

● Do real estate sales restrictions in housing developments violate the United States *Constitution*, particularly the Fourteenth Amendment?

✔ What are the parameters of your local zoning laws? Are they adequate? If not, how should they be amended?

★ Should we have local registration of handguns?

● Should victims of crime be compensated?

● Factors influencing police and community relations. Are these factors constant or do they change in varying-sized communities?

- How communities can reestablish a sense of community, cohesion, and unity
- ★ Home ownership: America's fading dream?
- Practical aspects of "getting back to self-sufficiency"
- ★ The town meeting in America's past
- Retirement communities: Isolation or community? Discuss the psychological and social factors.
- Organization of the elderly as volunteers. What have been the most successful methods? What are some of the possibilities for the future?
- ✔ The pros and cons of home ownership. Relate these factors to your locality.
- ▲ Changing attitudes towards drug abuse. Discuss community programs and centers.
- ▲ Nursing home fires: prevalence and code reform proposals
- The consequences of the housing crunch in the American economy. Include the problems of builders, buyers, and sellers.
- ○ Home mortgages and creative financing today
- A new form of local government: community associations
- Should society allow the invasion of another's privacy? Include a definition of privacy.
- ▲ How apartment-to-condominium conversion affects the community. Include the impact on

various economic and age groups.
- Detail the feasibility of school vouchers, charter schools, and the private management of public schools
- Why small towns are/are not the best places to raise a family
- ○ Land schemes and scams and how to avoid them
- The development of retirement communities in America
- Should local communities have autonomy over such issues as gambling and prostitution?
- America's woodlands: What's happening to them?
- What can the individual do to protect the environment?
- ▲ Government housing versus private builders — the pros and cons for the community
- ▲ Trends in urban homesteading
- Characterize suburban life in the United States since 1950. You may choose to select one area or one latitudinal sample.
- Consumer co-ops around the world. Include those in Sweden, Canada, Holland, and England as examples.
- The increase in backyard farming in the United States since 1970. Compare to the "victory gardens" of the 1940's and to European traditions.
- ✔ If there is a functioning commune in your locality, visit it and analyze the participants'

economic and social situation. Also focus on family units, education, employment, and unified goals.

★ Community and family fire safety standards and practices

● The social patterns and structure of an Israeli kibbutz

● Functional considerations in park planning and design

● Should our post office be turned over to the private sector?

● Pornography by phone. What is being done by parents and the telephone companies?

✗ Detail some examples of community action committees for the homeless.

✔ If your community's schools are involved in busing students from one district to another, detail what the results have been for the students, schools, and the community.

✔ Is there gang activity in your locality? If so, detail how it has affected the community as a whole.

✔ Levels of violence in your city or town. Has it increased? Why? Who is responsible?

✔ Are illegal immigrants on welfare in various communities? In yours? Why?

Key to Symbols

●	average difficulty	◆	narrow down topic
§	substitutes possible	▲	large public or college library required
★	ample information in most libraries	✔	local option topic
○	specialized knowledge required	✗	examples and supporting evidence needed

Compare and Contrast

butterfly : moth
sex : love
ant : termite
high school : college
Greek olympics : modern olympics
letters : telephones
personality : character
walking : jogging
football : soccer
acoustic guitar : electric guitar
watercolor techniques : oil paint-
    ing techniques
Hillary Clinton : Eleanor Roosevelt
blimp : hot air balloon
Napoleon : Alexander the Great
Catholic : Protestant
crocodile : alligator
Pacific Ocean : Atlantic Ocean
water skiing : snow skiing
microwave oven : conventional
    oven
Mayans : Aztecs
Vietnam War : Persian Gulf War
Greeks : Romans (ancient)
luxury : necessity

New York City: San Francisco
upper class : underclass
evolution : creationism
HIV : AIDS
bird : airplane
Buddhism : Hinduism
Robert E. Lee : Ulysses S. Grant
BMW : Lexus
atheism : agnosticism
chiropractors : osteopaths
Claude Monet : Auguste Renoir
propaganda : advertising
Arctic : Antarctic
chimpanzee : gorilla
Mars : Venus
bacteria : virus
ballet : modern dance
heaven : hell
jazz : rock
piano : harpsichord
Democrat : Republican
Johann Sebastian Bach : George
    F. Handel
direct evidence : circumstantial evi-
    dence

Computers

See also Business and Industry; Contemporary Issues — Internet; Mathematics

○ The computer as a medium of cultural change

● How the computer has been used to uncover secrets of the past — for example, Stonehenge and the reconstruction of Akhenaton's temples

☛ Discuss some of the potentials and projections for future computer technology and the ways in which it will affect American life.

● What are the regulations governing computers and privacy? Include both national and international standards. Be sure to use current data.

● How electronic criminals operate

○ Discuss this statement: There is no such thing as a totally secure computer system.

● The "hacker" in the world of computers

▲ Survey any new laws and regulations that will curtail or eliminate electronic crime.

○ Fiber optic technology: how it was developed, what it is, and what it's going to do for us.

● Should computer logic be taught in elementary schools?

✕ Uses for a home computer

§ Computers in the supermarket

● Compare the investment possibilities in four microcomputer companies.

○ Using the computer for simulation

☛ Data bases and their applications

● Compare and contrast the newest microcomputers.

★ The rise and fall of the Apple computer company

☛ Computers in the classroom: an industry hard sell or true learning tool?

● Telecommuting has changed people's lives and their job environments. Explain this development and give relevant examples.

★ Are computers addictive?

● Many suffer from what could be called "computer phobia." What is it and what are the causes and solutions?

● Can others easily access all of your computerized information? Consider health, banks, credit cards, etc.

✕ How computers are changing the lives of persons with disabilities

○ Are flowcharts out as a design tool?

○ Compare and contrast text editing programs.

○ Compare and contrast currently marketed computer education programs from the major computer companies. Focus on elementary, secondary, college, or vocational programs.

★ ENIAC (electronic integrator and calculator), the world's first all-electronic digital computer

● The analytical engine of Charles Babbage

● Public safeguards against unauthorized use of data bank material

● How to select a computer for a small business

● Turn-of-the-century uses for the punched card

● The technology of the IBM Harvard Mark I mechanical computer (1944)

§ How the XYZ Company uses its computer

➥ Current research in artificial intelligence

▲ Management information systems and the computer

○ Compare the computer and the human brain.

● Compare and contrast computers of today and those of twenty-five years ago.

● What are the essential differences between American and Japanese-made computers?

● Why are there so many computer languages? Are they necessary?

● Games for the home computer: a survey

○ Top-down programming

➥ A career as a computer programmer (or systems analyst, or computer scientist)

● Computer graphics

● Computer architecture

▲ Employee resistance to computer use

● Video games: Violence or fantasy?

● The computer "whiz kids"

● Video game stores: A sophisticated babysitter?

● How new languages are developed

● Leaders in computer design

● The United States military and the development of new computer languages

● Memory systems

○ Benefits of using an in-house microcomputer instead of a service bureau

★ The functions of a compiler

● The long-range impact of the computer revolution on society. Evaluate the expectations and the possibilities.

✕ Recent advances in computer capabilities

● How good are laptop computers? Investigate the findings on consumer tests.

- How successful is local area networking?
- ○ Advances in voice synthesizers and voice recognition by computers
- × New uses for microcomputers in home appliances
- § Examine the rise and fall of Atari
- ○ How computer viruses work and why they are dangerous
- Examine the increase of fraud and scams on the Internet.
- ★ Why every student today should be computer literate
- ○ Do we need standards for virtual reality simulations? What are the problems that could arise in the near future?
- How organized crime could take advantage of the information superhighway
- How close are computers to becoming true thinking machines?

- ▲ The new interactive fiction and how it works. Is it a new literary medium?
- New legal aspects of computer crime
- Do computers in the classroom improve learning?
- Why every student needs a personal computer
- ★ Computer games have become increasingly violent. Many parents, educators, and users object. Are these objections valid?
- ★ The term "information highway" is often used. What does it mean?
- Future cultural exchanges via global telecommunication infrastructures
- ▲ How to use flow chart technology
- The best ways to teach children to use computers efficiently

Key to Symbols

- average difficulty
- § substitutes possible
- ★ ample information in most libraries
- ○ specialized knowledge required

- narrow down topic
- ▲ large public or college library required
- local option topic
- × examples and supporting evidence needed

Consumerism

See also: Economics; Personal Finance

★ What the Fair Packaging and Labeling Act means to the consumer
▲ Mail-order health frauds
● Product warranties. What do they include? Are they a reliable and realistic consumer benefit?
★ Consumer-wise furniture purchasing
● Advertised brands and private labels in the supermarket and what they mean to the shopper
● Tenant's and landlord's rights
➤ How to bid and buy at an auction. Select a particular type of merchandise.
● How to prepare a case for small claims court
★ How to buy household appliances (reliability, costs, life, efficiency)
● Antidotes and other home safety precautions
★ Buying for infants and toddlers
✕ The pros and cons of planned retirement communities. Make distinctions between the various types available and discuss

costs, social life, conveniences, etc.
★ How to avoid travel rip-offs
★ How to buy tools for the home workshop
● The fire hazards of synthetic fabrics
● The noninsured driver: Who pays?
● How safe is your automobile?
● Survey the successes and failures of Ralph Nader and his consumer group.
● The Consumer Credit Protection Act and how it benefits the buyer
● Goals and impact of the National Consumers League
● How consumers can fight back
● Credit-card abuse affects the economy. Consider the public, businesses, and credit card companies.
● Frauds and deceptions in the used automobile market
★ How to buy the basics: clothing and food
★ What to look for when buying a house

100

- "Creative" financing
- Consumer cooperatives in the United States
- ✕ Dishonest and shady merchandising practices and how to recognize them
- ★ How safe are childrens' toys?
- How to measure the quality of new home construction
- The prepackaging of foods and the consumer. Include discussion of both quality and costs.
- ✔ Visit five meat markets and determine if the meat has had federal and state inspection and has been graded. Your investigation should also include storage facilities, additives, sources, prices, freshness, etc.
- ✔ Compare the prices of twenty standard grocery items at four stores. Account for the differences.
- ★ How to avoid the high cost of funerals
- Consumer-related games for children
- Sales stratagems every consumer should know
- Home ownership: who can afford it?
- ➤ Consumer buying and social status
- Who pays for advertising? What should this tell the thoughtful consumer?
- ▲ How electronic banking will affect the customer
- ▲ Regulatory agencies have been

accused of becoming too friendly with the companies they have been charged to regulate. Is there a factual basis for this charge? What is the evidence?
- Legal strategies for consumer revenge
- ○ Financing abuses. Discuss common instances, current regulations, and techniques for avoiding misleading and dishonest practices.
- Why we select the brands we buy. Construct and conduct a survey using a previously established survey as a model. Compare the results.
- What every consumer should know about the Truth in Lending law.
- Defend or refute: Magazines and newspapers should screen all advertising before publication in order to protect the consumer.
- Legal rights of the consumer
- ★ When to use the Better Business Bureau and other consumer-oriented agencies
- Cosmetics. Consider health hazards, labeling, ingredients, cost factors, and safety regulations.
- ○ Would the consumer benefit from the breakup of large corporations?
- Food additives: Who profits?
- ▲ Which prescription drugs have been involved in major controversies? Why? Were there any

significant changes or aftereffects because of the problems?

▲ Coronary bypass surgery: an expense that may not always be necessary. Survey recent literature.

✔ Evaluate the house and apartment rental market in your area and compare it to the market ten years previously.

● Seances and other mystical scams

● Compare the costs and efficiency of various home heating systems.

✔ Review the health and medical advertising in several turn-of-the-century magazines. Ask a librarian for available titles.

✕ Nineteenth-century health fraud in America

● How to buy stereo equipment for the home

● Consumer protection safeguards in health and medicine

● How Consumer Reports magazine evaluates products. Other publications also perform this service and may be included in this survey.

★ How to hire and work with a lawyer

● The new underground economy and how it works

● Creating an energy-efficient home

● Consumer advocacy and the automotive industry

● Brand name drugs: Are they a consumer rip-off?

○ Manufacturer product liability. Are the regulations too lax? Should federal controls be strengthened or should manufacturers initiate more stringent self-regulation?

● Describe the effects of advertising in consumer product selection. Use statistics and the results of professional surveys and analysis.

● What makes people buy? Discuss various theories.

● The great saccharin controversy

§ The hidden messages in cigarette advertising

★ What the consumer can do about annoying, misleading, and offensive advertising

● Should all consumers have credit? How much?

● Using examples, explain the function of built-in obsolescence in the American consumer market.

✕ How some advertising manipulates consumers to buy against their better judgment

✔ Analyze the prices of basic goods and services in a slum area as compared to those of a middle-class neighborhood. How do social scientists account for the discrepancy? What are the implications?

● Factors and steps of the buying decision process

○ Where does the American consumer get information to make purchase selections? Formulate a survey using a well-known product and query your respondents on their information source.

- What factors account for the recent rapid expansion of the consumer movement?
- × Alternatives to traditional health insurance have increased. Describe several of these plans. Do they cut costs? Provide effective care?
- ★ How the increased cost of liability insurance affects the American consumer
- ★ Plastic money: you and your credit cards
- How shopping malls have changed America's buying habits
- ○ The Internal Revenue Service has been charged with inefficiency and mismanagement. Is this true? Evaluate the issues involved for the last five years.
- Bankruptcy: a second chance or the ultimate cop-out?

- ○ Evaluate real estate as a profitable investment in today's economy.
- ➤ How will proposed tax reforms affect the consumer?
- How telephone carriers are competing for customers. Compare the various companies and services.
- The controversy surrounding Federal Drug Administration drug releases to the public
- × Is food package labeling adequate? If not, what elements should be added?
- ▲ Should all Americans have free emergency health care?
- ★ Fingerprinting children for safety reasons
- Telemarketing has been increasing. Survey the practices and abuses.
- The rise of junk fax
- × How safe are children's toys? Who sets the standards? Are they enforceable?

Key to Symbols

• **average difficulty**	➤ **narrow down topic**
§ **substitutes possible**	▲ **large public or college**
★ **ample information in most**	**library required**
libraries	✔ **local option topic**
○ **specialized knowledge**	× **examples and supporting**
required	**evidence needed**

Contemporary Issues

See also: American Scene; Social Problems; World Scene

- Should wilderness areas be expanded? Decreased?
- Fur trapping: Are humane reforms possible?
- ☛ The politics of oil
- ☛ Will the United States auto industry survive? What changes will be necessary? Could most of the problems have been avoided by earlier adjustments?
- Financing public transportation: Whose responsibility?
- ☛ Social inequalities and legal justice in the American courts
- § The ruin of the Colorado River
- ★ Objections to legalized gambling
- Ozone controversy
- ✕ Has the Central Intelligence Agency abused its power? When and how?
- ★ Is a nuclear freeze a realistic possibility?
- Compare and contrast definitions of the moment of death in law, medicine, and religion. Why are these differences significant?
- Is preferential treatment for veterans justified?

- What would happen if marijuana were made a prescription drug?
- Should parents be allowed to educate their own children?
- Homosexual clergy?
- Female clergy: An idea whose time has come?
- Was corporal punishment in the schools effective?
- ○ How airplane safety can be improved
- The American second-class citizen: Who and why?
- Are the racial problems in America mainly economic?
- ★ World desertification: The way to a dusty death? What have been the changes in climate and environments in the last fifty years?
- ▲ Discuss recent scientific research into the brain hemisphere function theory.
- ▲ Third world attitudes towards foreign missions and missionaries
- Civil disobedience: Is it ever justified?
- ○ Discuss the social implications of recombinant DNA research and

possibilities.

★ The graduated income tax: Who profits?

● What sacrifices would the consumer have to make if the United States were to become energy self-sufficient?

● Should mentally retarded individuals be sterilized?

● Issues involved in compulsory automobile insurance for all drivers

▲ The advantages of fingerprinting all United States citizens

● Should the individual states be given more control of federal lands?

● The Olympic Games: Who is competing, nations or individuals?

● What have been the major causes of coal mine disasters? Could they have been prevented?

★ Support or refute: Inadequate laws and insufficient punishment are directly responsible for the crime increase.

▲ Biological offensive weapons

● The scientific evaluations of microwave dangers

● Should the limits of diplomatic immunity be changed?

● What are the rights of foreign students in the United States?

★ Rights of nonsmokers

▲ Scientific research (or lack of) on reincarnation

✕ Is equal opportunity still available to all in the United States?

● Defend or refute: College athletic programs should be cut and the money reallocated to academics.

★ Health effects of exposure to Agent Orange used in the Vietnam War

★ Compare science and religion's view of the end of the world.

● Defend the need for an Equal Rights Amendment.

○ Proposed solutions for the Israeli-Palestinian conflict

● The pros and cons of national identity cards and why Americans object

● Do we really have "natural rights" as implied by the Declaration of Independence, or are our rights determined by those in power, in particular congressmen and supreme court justices?

★ Immigration from Mexico. What are the scope and consequences of both legal and illegal entry into the United States?

★ Defenses against political kidnapping and hostage situations

▲ Obstacles to a national medical treatment system in the United States

● Does the United States need further civil rights legislation?

● The case for a stronger United Nations

➤ The church and population control

● An evaluation of state lotteries

× Women's rights in other countries: Behind or ahead?

★ The ethics of wiretapping

★ Has the quality of the American
armed forces deteriorated?
Quote appropriate authorities to
answer this question.

● Is holistic healing a contradic-
tion to traditional medicine?

★ Should sex eduction be taught
in public schools?

● Kidney dialysis: Who chooses
the recipient?

★ Puerto Rico: Should it be a
colony, a state, or a nation?

● Should the Eskimos give up
their primitive hunting lifestyle?
Discuss the issues and ramifications of these cultural changes.

➡ Select one endangered animal
and detail how it became rare
and what is being done, if anything, to prevent its extinction.

★ What are human rights?

● The advantages and disadvantages to society of compulsory
retirement at an early age

● Should United States railroads
be nationalized?

➡ The military/industrial complex in
America and how it affects the
economy

○ Is the United States banking
system safe?

○ How price controls could (could
not) stop inflation

● Substantiate or refute: America
recovers from recessions by
waging war.

● Opposition to zero population
growth

● Free trade versus protectionism
for the American automobile industry. Discuss the issues citing
economists, businessmen, foreign
policy spokesmen, etc.

★ The human consequences of nuclear power plant leaks

★ Was President Carter's Panama
Canal decision in America's best
interest?

● National issues and the right to
know

○ Is carcinogenic testing of new
chemical products adequate?

★ Should the United States have
stricter immigration screening
and selection policies?

○ Local self-government, traditional democratic values, and
the urban community: Do they
mix?

● What additional rights should
Americans have in addition to
their rights as United States citizens?

➡ Welfare reforms

● Low income housing, 1960 to the
present

● Why is there general opposition
to the rights of homosexuals?
What vested interest groups are
against gay rights?

★ The myth of the "harmless atom"

● Vivisection: pros and cons

○ How to reverse inflation. Evaluate the evidence which has been
presented to support each major

theory.

▲ Critical issues in nuclear waste transportation

➥ Will science be able to provide new sources of energy, food, and metals in order to support larger and larger populations?

★ Should compensation be awarded for radiation damage from United States nuclear tests?

● Disarmament: problems of inspection and mutual distrust

▲ Theft of classified national security information: How could it be prevented?

★ Defend or refute: The utility companies subsidize high energy use.

● National parks: Playgrounds or paradises?

● Apportionment of Colorado River water

● The relationship between "progressive" education and the American students' educational achievements

★ Should victims of crime be compensated?

★ Does the current rate of world population growth threaten mankind?

✕ Canada's natural resources and the United States' growing needs

★ Is the Alaskan pipeline a failure?

● The use of school busing to achieve racial integration: Success or failure?

● The impact of legal gambling in New Jersey

○ The politics of chemical warfare

★ Handgun controversy: the pros and cons

● Has the Pope lost his power?

➥ Terrorism: prevention and control techniques

★ Opposition to the Equal Rights Amendment

● The Freedom of Information Act and government security

● How can the president be protected from violence?

➥ Critical issues affecting prison reform

● The lesbian mother: legal and social considerations

○ Can democracy survive? Support your stance with selections from a variety of experts' views.

✕ Refute/defend: Free enterprise and environmental issues are incompatible.

● Are the major environmental issues in the national interest?

● Which should be stressed and why: Equality of eductional opportunity or individual excellence? Consider whether these goals are mutually exclusive.

★ Sports and gambling. Is there a close relationship?

● Should wiretapping legislation be reformed?

▲ Defend/refute: Political illiteracy (particularly in foreign affairs) is encouraged among American youth because of in-

adequate instruction in the schools.
- Should animal organs be used for human transplant surgery?
- "Yankee Imperialism': fact or fallacy?
- Vietnam since the war: economics, politics, and the social scene
- United States/Cuba relations today. How have they most recently evolved?
× Instances of the abuse of presidential power
★ The case for (or against) abortion on demand
★ World use of the metric system
- Why gangs fight
- How South Africa is resolving its racial conflicts. Have these measures been successful so far?
★ Should public employees be allowed to strike?
- Uses and abuses of affirmative action
- Laboratory animals: Necessary cruelty? Defend or refute based on the major arguments and claims of the scientific community or those opposed.
▲ Sales of FDA-banned drugs in foreign countries
- Energy for America: How much, at what price, and for how long?
- Has there been a deliberate cover-up of the damage to victims of American nuclear experimentation?
★ Should a criminal corrections sys-tem reform, punish, or isolate?
- Why many rock lyrics have been labeled pornographic
- Public AIDS (Acquired Immune Deficiency Syndrome) testing: precaution or an invasion of privacy?
× Why the United States is losing the drug traffic war
- Is suicide ever justified?
× Recent examples of international terrorism and how they could (or could not) have been either predicted or prevented
× Privatization of public services may be the wave of the future. Good idea?
- When should we (or should we not) be concerned about ozone holes and global warming?
- Will gun control reduce crime?
- Why is there still a battle aver mandatory school prayer?
- Sheep, notably Dolly, have recently been cloned. What next?
- Artificial hearts: a feasible procedure or costly experiments?
O United States oil and gas reserves face future depletion. What then? A projection
× What exactly constitutes sexual harassment?
★ Gun control: restricting rights or protecting people?
✔ The impact of the lottery on a specific state's fiscal system

Contemporary Issues — Internet

See also: Computers

- How to invest with safety using the Net
- How the Internet could bring a sense of community to urban dwellers
- O Examine the pros and cons of push technology.
- Many experts expect the Internet to radically affect both the mail and the phone service. When will these changes occur and what will they be?
- ★ How your identity could be stolen from the Net and assumed by another
- The advantages of the Internet for college students
- Should there be several Internets–for games, business, research, sex, etc.?
- The Internet and "privacy cookies"
- ★ Your personal information on the Net. Analyze the hazards of revealing too much.
- What do we do today in person that we may do faster and easier on the Internet in the future? Consider advantages and disadvantages.
- Should all of the Internet be free? Will it be in the future?
- O Consider the elements involved in Internet copyright problems.
- Many feel the Internet fosters social isolation to a greater degree than is healthy. Evaluate this thesis.
- Is censorship possible or even necessary on the Internet?
- O Evaluate current anti-virus software and compare and contrast utility of each.
- Future global exchange via the Internet
- ★ Why you can't believe everything you read on the Net
- ★ Should access be curtailed for children? Why? How?
- Employee use of the Internet for non-work related activities: examine the scope and complexity of this situation.
- ★ Describe in simple, nontechnical terms how to access the Internet.
- Should you have a home page? Consider cost as well as utility.
- The increase and easy availability of pornography is a concern to many. Are there practical solutions?
- The inherent dangers of chat rooms
- Why "hate" groups are flourishing on the Internet

Crime and Criminal Justice

See also: Community Concerns; Drug Problems; Law; Social Problems; Sociology

- The police on television as stereotypes
- Should "white-collar" criminals go to prison? What are the alternatives?
- ★ Does punishment prevent crime? The pros and cons of this issue.
- How to spot a scam
- Arson detection methods. What is the state of the art? What are some of the major problems?
- ○ Society's changing attitudes toward prisons
- ➤ Methods for rehabilitation of juvenile delinquents
- ○ Ideal detention facilities for the juvenile offender
- Has parole been an effective measure for rehabilitation?
- ★ The trial of Leopold and Loeb (1924)
- Pros/cons of double celling
- ✔ Investigate the major problems in the correction systems in your state.
- § Prisons in Turkey
- ▲ The voiceprint: its technology, use, and validity

- ✕ Examples of recent prison reform
- The role of the probation office in juvenile crime
- ★ Compare handgun regulations in the United States with those in other western countries.
- Modern causes of international terrorism
- ★ The rise of white-collar crime
- Contemporary definitions of the "hardened criminal"
- The increasing problem of CD, tape, and film piracy
- ○ The significance of the theory of tagging and labeling in criminology
- Why crime rates vary in urban centers of equal size. Examples: Chicago, Washington, D.C., Detroit, Houston, Philadelphia, Milwaukee.
- ▲ How banks protect themselves against robbery and holdups
- ★ Compare and contrast crime in Great Britain and the US.
- Organized crime and professional sports. Is there a relationship?

110

- Street crime has radically increased in the last ten years. Investigate who commits this type of crime and why. Describe proposals for the alleviation of street crime.
- The criminal insanity law: Why reform is crucial. Or, why the law should remain unchanged. How has the Hinkley case altered public opinion?
- The origins of the Mafia in America
○ XYZ syndrome theory
- Home security systems. Analyze those currently available in terms of their price, effectiveness, and utility.
▲ The incidence of family-related homicides
★ Do strict gun control laws prevent crime?
- Why computer crime has increased
- Does legalized gambling subsidize organized crime?
- How community organizations and privatized security are becoming the crime prevention solution for many areas
- How DNA played a role in the trial of O.J. Simpson
▲ The Mafia's infiltration into the American business community
- The Manson "family" and the Sharon Tate murders
- Why is the crime rate increasing among women?
- Library security measures and systems

- Some authorities have suggested that the Mafia is disappearing and is being replaced by other crime networks. What evidence is there to support this hypothesis?
- The Lizzie Borden case
- The level and extent of federal tax evasion among American taxpayers
▲ DNA analysis has been the focus of many controversies. Are they valid?
- Recidivism among released criminals. Is rate constant? What factors are most influential?
✕ The use of computers in law enforcement
★ Capital punishment throughout the ages
○ Compare the pros and cons of determinate and indeterminate sentencing
- The Plain View doctrine in criminal investigations
- Community service versus prison for white-collar crime convicts. Discuss the issues and possible results, both socially and economically.
✕ FBI "sting" operations
- What constitutional rights do convicts have while in prison?
★ Capital punishment as a crime deterrent
▲ The police and minorities: Fair and equal treatment?
- Implications of the Miranda Decision on the American justice system

- Enforcement of prohibition: a qualified success
- How polygraph (lie detector) tests are used in law enforcement. Why can't they be used as evidence? How accurate are they?
- × Practices in prisoner rehabilitation
- What has been the traditional role of prisons in American society?
- Does our criminal justice system discriminate against the economically disadvantaged?
- ✔ Compare and contrast minimum prison standards in your state with those in New York or California.
- ➤ Police weaponry
- Detection by fingerprint. Should everyone have his or her fingerprints on file?
- ➤ Techniques of undercover surveillance in criminal detection
- Famous detectives in literature. Compare their character and methods.
- Compare and contrast the legal aspects of robbery, theft, and burglary.
- ✔ Evaluate the facilities of your local jail (city, county) and compare them to national standards.
- ➤ Police training standards
- ▲ Mental illness among law enforcement officers. What have been the results of national surveys?

- Methods of riot and mob control
- ★ Prison riots in America, from 1960 to date. What are the grievances? How have they been similar? Why?
- ▲ The organization and training of bomb squads
- Structure and scope of operations of Interpol (International Criminal Police Organization)
- Prison work-furlough programs
- Advances in international terrorism control
- ▲ Why law enforcement officers say search and seizure requirements need change and reform
- ○ Improper evidence: Should the rules be relaxed?
- How the courts "handcuff" the police
- ★ Is it the function of prisons to reform, correct, or rehabilitate — or punish?
- The British system of criminal injury compensation
- What happens when the police strike?
- Should wiretapping be allowed? If so, when and where?
- Should prison be abolished?
- ○ Why the criminal justice system resists reform
- ★ Do lighter prison sentences affect the rate of crime?
- § The regulation of mail-order fraud
- The use of helicopters in police work

- Political kidnapping. What is the official United States government policy? Is it adequate? Is it responsible?
- Drug smuggling in the United States: a five-year overview
★ Pornography and the post office
- Rising United States crime rates. What should be done? Survey a large sampling of expert opinions and compare and contrast their theories.
▲ Organized crime and auto theft
- How counterfeit money is made
- What are the major safeguards against nuclear theft? Are they adequate?
× The spread of labor union corruption
➡ Forensic medicine
★ Credit card fraud
★ Credit card abuse
- What does shoplifting cost the consumer? Consider current levels and types.
- Would legalized gambling reduce crime?
★ Burglar alarm systems: costs, technology, and their utility for the home
- Women behind the badge
- The stolen property market. What should be done to curtail its growth and operations?
★ The case for (against) abolishing parole
- What to do about overcrowded jails

▲ Drunk drivers: Some states have initiated new stringent regulations and punishments. Compare and contrast them. Have the results been positive?
- Nonincarceration punishment methods of Great Britain
- Compare and contrast federal and state prison systems: an overview
- Child molesters: detection, prevention, and punishment
- Analyze changing crime rates, citing statistics, demography, and socioeconomic factors that are involved.
§ Juvenile crime in Russia
★ Victimless crimes: Crime and punishment at issue?
➡ Welfare fraud
- The relationships between homosexuality and crime
✔ Chart the crime rates in your locality for the last ten years. What were the changes and fluctuations? How can they be explained?
- Crime in the Islamic world. What are the attitudes toward crime, the rates, the types? What are the usual punishments for major and minor transgressions?
★ The correlation between educational levels and crime. Cite studies and surveys to substantiate your statements.
▲ Criminologists look at the effects of pornography

- Insurance fraud
- The Royal Canadian Mounted Police
- The auto theft racket and how it operates in major metropolitan areas
- What has proven to be the relationship between gun availability and violent crime? Cite expert opinion and verifiable research statistics to support your discussion.
- Famous thefts of works of art from museums and private collections
- Gangs in federal and state correctional institutions
- What are the major areas of crime in your area and what local law enforcement measures are being used to combat them? How effective have they been? Interview law enforcement personnel as part of your research.
- The Lindbergh kidnapping
- The Snyder-Gray murder case (1927)
- The St. Valentine's Day Massacre in Chicago
- ★ International measures to prevent skyjacking
- Should victimless crimes be decriminalized? Support your answer with examples from a variety of sources.
- Does the United States criminal justice system favor the offender?
- What are the normal social and psychological pressures on the urban police patrolman?

- Intergroup violence in the United States. Consider the 1992 riots in Los Angeles as an example.
- America has recently had several serious spy cases. Could they have been prevented? How?
- × Accepted and approved alternatives to prison
- Discuss the nature and scope of the abortion clinic bombings in the United States. Has there been a consistent pattern?
- Methods currently employed to prevent international terrorism incidents
- ▲ Cheating on government contracts has been publicized by several recent cases. Compare these occurrences, their causes, and final resolutions.
- ○ Has plea bargaining become a necessity in our court system? Detail the pros and cons.
- ★ What are the rights of the accused? Are they adequate? Too liberal?
- Stun guns and the controversy surrounding their use
- Problems of plastic detection and airport security
- ○ How to protect against computer viruses
- What are the advantages of for-profit prisons?
- × How to stop credit card theft and abuse
- ▲ Examine advances in the field of forensic DNA testing ("DNA fingerprints").

Customs, Traditions, and Folkways

See also: Anthropology; Myth, Symbol, and Folklore

▲ The ancient sorcerers

§ Compare marriage ceremonies in several differing cultures, such as the United States, India, and Morocco.

● Birthday celebrations in other cultures

▲ The pagan origins of Christian holidays

● Why is prostitution an accepted (and legal) part of society in most of the world while in the United States it has traditionally been considered a crime?

● The caste system in India

● Suttee: cremation practices in India

★ The traditional history of Spanish bullfights

● Trends in divorce in Western European countries

× Traditional attitudes towards abortion: a world overview

● Folk medicine in frontier America

● Witchcraft during the Middle Ages

▲ Embalming practices in the ancient world

○ Discuss the functions of marriage as a contractual relationship in many societies around the world

● The rituals of monarchy. Why do many modern societies continue to foster and encourage royal pomp and ceremony?

● The role of oracles and prophecy in ancient societies

➡ How has television affected American mores and customs?

× Horseshoes, four-leaf clovers, and other superstitions of American life

§ Ancient Celtic burial practices

● Birth customs and practices in the medieval world

● How the rituals and traditions of the engagement period and the wedding ceremony function as an aid to the transition into marriage

● Dating as an American institution

★ Animal worship in primitive religions. Select several cultures for comparison.

★ Marriage rites in the Islamic world

● Manners, morality, and sin in

the days of Queen Victoria
- Afterlife in Greek and Roman religion
- The relationship between lunacy, the moon, and the tides. Cite both ancient and modern beliefs.
▲ Funeral flowers, from ancient days to modern times
- Compare and contrast mores and folkways. Use examples.
- The oriental tea ceremony
- Smoking customs in history
▲ Changes in mummification processes and practices throughout the Egyptian dynasties
- The religious, medical, and magical origins of cosmetics
- Historic uses of tattooing
- Cemeteries around the world
- Abortion and infanticide in Ancient Greece
- The social role of the Roman baths
- Ancient methods of population control
- Origins of American marriage customs
★ Cremation rites and beliefs throughout history
- Spectator sport in ancient Greece and Rome

- American courtship attitudes and practices
★ How we treat our dead in contemporary America
▲ Pregnancy rituals and omens in the ancient world
× The role of ritual in social relationships: some modern examples
- The incest taboo as a cultural universal
★ The role of the shaman in primitive societies
× Life cycle rituals in primitive cultures
× Life cycle rituals in modern civilizations
§ The rituals of baseball
- Compare the themes, characters, motifs, and styles of folk tales from one particular country.
★ The uses of amulets and talismans in magic and religion
- Courtship relationships: a cross-cultural comparison. Select at least three divergent societies for this analysis.
- Customs and manners in Renaissance Italy as reflected in contemporaneous books on manners and etiquette

Dance

See also: Sports and Recreation; Theater

- How to teach folk dancing
▲ Costumes and sets for the Ballet Russe. Why were they unique? Discuss some of the most outstanding ones.
- Musical scores used by Sergei Diaghilev and the Ballet Russe
- Pioneers of modern dance in the United States
★ How the teachings of Isadora Duncan revolutionized dance
▲ The place of dance in Greek drama. Include evidence from vases, sculpture, and writers of the period.
- The characteristics of the movements of dance. Are some gestures and postures common to all dance forms?
§ The folk dances of Greece
- Public response to the dancing of Isadora Duncan
★ Compare and contrast modern ballet and classical ballet.
- The influence of Ruth St. Denis on modern dance
○ Compare and contrast the Bensh and Labanok methods of dance notation.
- Toe dancing: its origins and evolution to contemporary ballet techniques
- The dance paintings of Edgar Degas and Henri de Toulouse-Lautrec
- The choreographic contributions of Marius Petipa to Russian ballet
- Compare and contrast contemporary training techniques and procedures for classical ballet in the United States and Russia.
- Detail the long-range influence of some of the earlier modern dance innovators.
- Trace the history of the revolt of modern dance from classical ballet.
- Primitive hypnotic dances. What have been their religious and social functions?
○ The American Ballet Theater. Discuss innovations in repertory, style, music, dancers.
- Definitions of "modern dance." Survey a number of influential critics and compare and contrast their conclusions.
§ Gesture and symbol in the traditional dances of India

117

★ Compare and contrast dances of the Western world with those of the Orient in terms of gestures, body movement, symbols, and origins.

● The use of Death and the Devil as characters and symbols, from antiquity throughout the Middle Ages

▲ The policy of the early Christian Church towards the dance and the subsequent effects of these attitudes throughout the Middle Ages

● The "magic circle" of primitive and archaic dance

● Ritual dancing and early Christianity

● The function of funeral dances in early culture. Discuss the similarities and differences in a selection of disparate societies.

● The motivations for dance in primitive societies: Religious, social, political, or economic?

● Ring dances throughout the centuries

● Early methods of dance notation

● How the ideas of courtly love and chivalry revolutionized dancing in the twelfth through fourteenth centuries

▲ The Renaissance origins of ballet

● The role of the male dancer in romantic ballet. Has his role changed significantly?

★ Fundamentals and benefits of aerobic dancing

● The Dance Theater of Harlem

§ Pueblo Indian ceremonial dances

➨ Notable contributions of the New York City Ballet to dance in America

● The story of the Arthur Murray Dance Studios: a commercial and social success story

● Hopi Snake Dance

● Teaching ballet to children

● Training for the ballet in the United States today

● Compare folk dances from several adjacent countries. Account for the differences.

● Discuss the historical relationship between popular music and popular dance in America.

★ The origins of American folk dances

● The influence of Agnes de Mille on American dance

● Styles of dance during the Renaissance

● The African origins of the rhumba, conga, and tango

➨ Dance in the American musical comedy. Analyze several outstanding examples.

➨ Small dance companies in the United States. Select one company and investigate its structure, organization, dancers, repertory, contributions, etc.

● The Bolshoi Ballet

★ Simple and easy dances for young children

● The Middle East origins of belly

dancing

▲ Maria Tallchief and the Chicago City Ballet

★ Elements of cowboy and western square dances

● Combining dance and poetry

for young children

● Social dancing during the Renaissance (or Middle Ages). Patterns, styles, and social contexts.

● Dance in the movies

Key to Symbols

● average difficulty
§ substitutes possible
★ ample information in most libraries
○ specialized knowledge required

☛ narrow down topic
▲ large public or college library required
✔ local option topic
✗ examples and supporting evidence needed

Deaths — Famous and Unusual

Listed below are persons whose deaths were significant or memorable. Some were famous personalities or, in some cases, became so because of unique and unusual deaths. Some of these deaths were surrounded by controversy or mystery; some were highly publicized; some changed the course of history. Select one name and focus on the important details in their historical contexts.

Captain James Cook, explorer (1728–1779)
General George Custer, American general at Little Bighorn (1839–1876)
Diana, Princess of Wales, 1961–1997
John Dillinger, bank robber (1902–1934)
Amelia Earhart, American aviatrix (1898–1937?)
Pablo Escobar, Medellin drug lord, 1993
Archduke Francis Ferdinand, heir apparent to the Hapsburg monarchy (1863–1914)
Ambrose Bierce, American author and journalist (1842–1914)
Julius Caesar, Roman general and statesman (100 B.C.–44 B.C.)
Dian Fossey, primatologist (1932–1985)
Indira Gandhi, Indian leader (1917–1984)
Mohandas Karamchand Gandhi, Indian pacifist leader (1869–1948)
General Charles George Gordon, British general (1833–1885)
Ernesto "Che" Guevara, Cuban revolutionary leader (1928–1967)
Alexander Hamilton, American statesman (c. 1755–1804)
Warren G. Harding, United States president (1865–1923)
Adolf Hitler, Chancellor of Nazi Germany (1889–1945)
Harry Houdini, magician (1874–1926)
Howard Hughes, aviator and industrialist (1905–1976)
Thomas "Stonewall" Jackson, Confederate general (1824–1863)
Alfred Jarry, French author (1873–1907)
Jesus Christ, religious leader (c. 4 B.C.–29 A D.?)
Joan d'Arc, French saint and national heroine (1412–1431)
Janis Joplin, singer (1943–1970)
Robert F. Kennedy, lawyer and senator (1925–1968)
Martin Luther King, Jr., American civil rights leader (1929–1968)

John Lennon, musician (1940–1980)

Huey P. Long, Louisiana politician and governor (1893–1935)

Louis XVI, King of France (1754–1793)

Patrice Emergy Lumumba, Congolese premier (1925–1961)

Malcolm X (Malcolm Little), civil rights activist (1925–1965)

Marie Antoinette, Queen of France and wife of Louis XVI (1755–1793)

Christopher Marlowe, English poet and dramatist (1564–1593)

Mary Queen of Scots (Mary Stuart) (1542–1587)

Jan Masaryk, Czechoslovakian patriot (1886–1948)

Maximilian of Hapsburg, Emperor of Mexico (1832–1867)

William McKinley, United States president (1843 – 1901)

Valeria Messalina, Roman empress and third wife of Claudius (d. 48 A D)

Jim Morrison, musician (1943–1971)

Lord Louis Mountbatten, British World War II hero and statesman (1900–1979)

Wolfgang Amadeus Mozart, composer (1756–1791)

Benito Mussolini, Italian dictator (1883–1945)

Nicholas II and family, last czar of Russia (1868–1918)

Sylvia Plath, American poet (1932–1963)

Elvis Presley, rock singer (1935–1977)

Grigori Rasputin, politically powerful Russian monk (1872–1916)

Jack Ruby, Lee Harvey Oswald's murderer (1911–1967)

Nicola Sacco (b. 1891) and Bartolomeo Vanzetti (b. 1888), Italian anarchists (both died 1927)

Anwar Sadat, Egyptian statesman (1918–1981)

Girolamo Savonarola, Florentine priest and dictator (1452–1498)

Robert Falcon Scott, Antarctic explorer (1868–1912)

Karen Silkwood, nuclear industry laboratory worker (1946–1974)

Nicole Brown Simpson, wife of O.J. Simpson 1947–1994

Bessie Smith, American singer (1894–1937)

Socrates, Greek philosopher (469–399 B.C.)

Anastasia Somoza, Nicaraguan leader (1896–1956)

Sharon Tate, American actress (1943–1969)

Gianni Versace, fashion designer 1946–1997

Francisco "Pancho" Villa, Mexican revolutionary leader (1878–1923)

Stanford White, American architect (1853–1906)

Virginia Woolf, English novelist and essayist (1882–1941)

Emiliano Zapata, Mexican revolutionary leader (1879–1919)

Disasters — Man-Made

Many of the following incidents were surrounded by controversy. Evaluate these controversies in terms of the sequence of events, any possible errors in judgment, and the final consequences. What has been the consensus of historians and other authorities? Include any procedure or design changes that resulted from the occurrence. Consult local news sources if available.

London fire, 1666
Sultana steamboat explosion on the Mississippi River, 1865
Peshitigo (Wisconsin) forest fire, 1871
Chicago fire, 1871
Iroquois Theater (Chicago) fire, 1903
Triangle Shirtwaist Company (New York City) fire, 1911
Titanic sinking, 1912
Eastland excursion boat capsizes (Chicago), 1915
Lusitania sinking, 1915
ZR-2 dirigible breakup (Hull, England), 1921
Shenandoah dirigible breakup (Caldwell, Ohio), 1925
St. Francis Dam (Santa Paula, California) failure, 1928
Ohio State Penitentiary (Columbus) fire, 1930
Schoolhouse explosion (New London, Texas), 1937
Hindenburg zeppelin explosion (Lakehurst, New Jersey), 1937
Cocoanut Grove Nightclub (Boston) fire, 1942
Balvino Limited trainwreck (Italy), 1944
Fort Stikine ship explosion (Bombay, India), 1944
Ringling Brothers Circus fire (Hartford, Connecticut), 1944
Plane crash into the Empire State Building (New York), 1945
Bombing of Dresden, 1945
Bombing of Hiroshima, 1945
Grand Prix racing car crash (Le Mans, France), 1955
Grand Canyon (Arizona) airline collision, 1956
Andrea Doria sinking, 1956

Air collision over New York City, 1960
Thresher submarine sinking, 1963
Bangladesh windstorms, 1963 and 1965
Burning of the Apollo I spacecraft, 1967
West Gate Bridge collapse (Melbourne, Australia), 1970
Slymar Tunnel (California) explosion, 1971
Teton Dam (Idaho) collapse, 1976
Nightclub (Southgate, Kentucky) fire, 1977
Pan American KLM aircraft collision (Canary Islands), 1977
Ixtox oil spill (Gulf of Mexico), 1979
MGM Grand Hotel (Las Vegas, Nevada) fire, 1980
Hyatt Regency Hotel suspended walkway collapse (Kansas City, Missouri), 1981
Ocean Ranger oil drilling rig capsizes and sinks off Newfoundland coast, 1982
Bhopal, India chemical accident (1984)
Challenger space vehicle, 1986 explosion
Chernobyl nuclear plant accident, 1986
Challenger Explosion, 1986
Crash of Pan Am flight 103, Lockerbie, Scotland, 1988
Yellowstone forest fire, 1988
Exxon Valdez oil spill, 1989
Windsor Castle fire (England), 1992
Los Angeles riots, 1992
World Trade Center bombing, 1993
Estonia ferry sinking (Baltic Sea), 1994
Oklahoma City federal building bombing, 1995
ValuJet crash in Everglades, May 11, 1996
TWA Boeing 747 (Flight 800) crash off Long Island, July 17, 1996

Disasters — Natural

Describe the course of events for any of the following disasters. What were the consequences? Could the results have been modified or averted? Consult local news sources if available.

Mount Vesuvius eruption burying Pompeii and Herculaneum, 79 A.D.
Black Death, 1348–1351
Shensi earthquake (China), 1556
Chinese floods, 1642, 1887, 1939, 1950
Krakatoa eruption, 1883
Johnstown flood (Pennsylvania), 1889
Galveston storm and tidal wave (Texas), 1900
San Francisco earthquake, 1906
Spanish influenza epidemic, 1918
Japanese earthquake, 1923
Mount Pelèe eruption (Martinique, West Indies), 1932
Ohio-Mississippi River Valleys flood, 1937
The Eastern seaboard hurricane, 1938
Alaskan earthquake, 1964
Pakistan cyclone, 1970
Peruvian earthquake, 1970
Hurricane Agnes (United States east coast), 1972
Big Thompson Canyon flash flood (Loveland, Colorado), 1976
Mount St. Helens eruptions (Washington), 1980–?
Mexico City earthquake, 1985
Colombia volcanic eruption and mudslide, 1985
Armenian earthquake, 1988
Lake Nios, Cameroon, toxic gas, 1986
San Francisco earthquake, 1989
Bangladesh typhoon, 1991
Costa Rica-Panama earthquake, 1991
Mt. Pinatubo volcanic eruption (Philippines), 1991
Hurricane Andrew (Florida), 1992
Hurricane Iniki (Hawaii), 1993
Northridge earthquake (California), 1994
Kobe earthquake (Japan), 1995

Drug Problems

See Also: Health; Medicine

- Drug dealers as role models
- ▲ How drug-related patients have affected American emergency rooms
- Why free syringes are not made widely available to drug users for AIDS prevention
- Behavorial aspects of a heroin user vs. a crack user
- ✕ Are psychoactive drugs permanently harmful?
- The scope of second generation drug dependency
- ✕ Cite examples of successful neighborhood drug eradication and control programs.
- Profile the characteristics of the average crack user.
- It has been suggested that parents should be punished for children's drug use. Is this a valid proposal?
- ✔ Has drug use in your community increased? Have the kinds of drugs used changed?
- Do parents who use harmful drugs encourage recreational drug use by their children?
- ★ Support the view that illegal drugs should be decriminalized.
- ★ The cost of alcohol abuse
- ● Explore the escalating welfare costs to the taxpayer due to illegal drug use.
- ▲ It has been suggested that military camps be used as minimum security prisons for low-level drug dealers. Would this be practical and would it save money?
- What happens when drug gangs move into middle-income areas?
- ○ Drug laws are currently both difficult and expensive to enforce. Consider possible changes.
- Defend or refute: Pregnant women who use drugs should be criminally prosecuted for child abuse.
- Ethnic minorities and the drug trade
- Inner city neighborhoods are the center of drug dealing, drug use and violent behavior. Is there adequate protection for the average citizen in these blighted areas? Describe some possible remedies.
- ▲ The role of INTERPOL in the drug war.
- Who should be subject to random drug testing? Who should make this decision?
- ★ How cocaine becomes an addiction
- Why there is controversy over

125

methadone maintenance programs

- Illicit drug use by young people has been increasing every year. Examine this trend. Is a reversal in sight?
- Why our narcotic laws have failed
- ▲ Explore the incidence of morphine dependence following the Civil War.
- Do persons with addictions have particular personality characteristics? Is their addiction predictable?
- Some critics assert that programs designed to warn young people away from drugs are often failures and may even contribute to the increase in drug use.
- ★ Examine the problems encountered in the care and nuturing of crack babies.
- The pros and cons of drug legalization
- Describe the cocaine trail from the cocoa leaf to the end user.

- If your community has drug prevention and rehabilitation programs, visit these facilities and describe their organization, procedures and results.
- Excessive drinking has recently become less socially acceptable. What accounts for this change?
- Why medical experts no longer believe alcoholism is a single progressive disease with a single cause
- The plight of the inner-city poor and why the drug culture flourishes among them
- ★ The pros and cons of mandatory drug testing
- Drugs in the workforce
- Detail the reasons for the following statement: Crime is most evident among persons who use drugs on a regular basis.
- Was Prohibition a failure?

Ecology

See also: Biology; Environment; The Future; Pollution; Population; Resources

- Compare and contrast a terrestrial and aquatic ecosystem.
- x What are the major components of an ecosystem? Select pertinent examples of each.
- Trace the flow of energy through a food web.
- Heaven or hell: Is technology destroying the environment?
- Research air pollution problems in your state and detail how they have affected the environment. What measures have been instituted or proposed to remedy existing problems?
- Is the California condor doomed?
- Ecological effects of the neutron bomb
- ★ Effects of acid rain
- ★ Amazon deforestation
- Effects of the defoliation program in the Vietnam War, both short-term and long-range
- Prospects for the bald eagle. What has contributed to the decreased populations? Do those factors still exist?
- The survival of the cockroach: its adaption to life in ancient eras and under today's kitchen sinks
- § The ecological niches of herons
- ★ The comeback of the California gray whale
- Aerosols and the ozone layer. What has been the effect thus far of aerosol sprays on the atmosphere? What do scientists project for the future? Is use declining?
- The nature and scope of national wildlife refuges
- § The fate of the alligator
- Acid rain and aquatic ecosystems
- The disappearing jungle. How will this decline affect the total world environment?
- The survival of the whooping crane
- § Should _____ hunting be discontinued? Select a currently hunted animal.
- An ecosystem that doesn't depend on sunlight: the deep vents near the Galapagos
- What happens to the local environments when tropical rain forests are cleared?

- The national damage from man-made forest fires. Compare the trends from 1900 to 1990.
- The consequences to the local environment of increased use of wood as fuel
★ DDT in the food chain, from plankton to waterfowl
- Native Americans as ecologists: historical perspectives
× Methods for the biological control of pests
- Irrigation in arid regions and its long-term implications to the ecosystem
▲ Recycling sewage. Detail successful instances citing costs, utility, and problems.
○ Factors of thermal pollution
▲ Survey and discuss the characteristics of the ecological zones occurring between Palm Springs and the peak of San Jacinto Mountain (California).
× The laws of ecology. Use examples to illustrate each factor.
- Describe in detail an area that has sustained severe environmental damage. Include possible remedies toward a restitution of ecological balance.
- What happens when land is desertified?
➥ How birds help man
- Detail the relationship between plants and animals in a particular ecological system (swamp, desert, meadow).
★ Defend or refute: Bird hunting

should be abolished in the United States.
× Man-made animal extinctions. Detail several case histories.
- Compare and contrast pesticide use versus biological control for insect pests.
× Typical behavioral and physiological reactions of overstressed environmental niches
- Describe the adaptive characteristics of animals capable of existing in fresh, brakish, and in sea water. How do they differ from their more limited relatives?
○ The meadow, the pasture, and grazing livestock. Is balance possible?
× Animal adaptions to extreme cold (or heat)
★ Levels of ozone depletion in the upper stratosphere
○ The relationship of temperature to the development of poikilothermic animals
- The mongoose in Jamaica and the rabbit in Australia as examples of biotopic imbalance
★ The decline of the American buffalo in the nineteenth century
- The ecosystem of a freshwater lake
- Why there is hunger in the third world
- How to teach ecological awareness to children
➥ Select an insect and completely detail all of its environmental

elements.

§ Environmental adaptions among crabs

§ Describe the ecological niche of the _____. Select an organism.

× Discuss the concepts of "niche" and "habitat"; use examples to make the distinctions.

× Compare and contrast mutualism, commensalism, and parasitism among animals.

● Adaptions in ciliate feeding mechanisms

● Ecological awareness and land management by the Southwest Indians today

● Will whales soon be extinct?

● Krakatoa: colonization of a bare land

● Why the burros are bad for the Grand Canyon

● The ecology of a temperate rain forest compared to that of a tropical rain forest

★ Why scientists consider the Aswan Dams an ecological disaster

● Water hyacinths: Pest or water purifier?

§ The food chain of the African elephant

▲ The ecological implications of the Jonglei Canal on the Nile River (Egypt), and on the Sudan

● The deforestation chain of events

○ How much acid rain can an ecosystem withstand?

✔ If you have a mountain nearby, detail the ecological variations of each of its four sides.

× Animal adaptions, both permanent and temporary, to habitats with little or no light

● How the oxygen/carbon dioxide ratio affects animal distribution

● Life in the tidal zones

● Atmospheric carbon dioxide levels in 1900 and in 1990. Discuss reasons for the change and the eventual implications for earth life forms.

● The consequences of excessive noise

× The influence of the moon on marine life reproductive cycles

● The domestication of the reindeer as social parasitism

● The microclimate of cities

● How water purifies itself

● PCB in animals

★ Ecological aspects of pesticides

● Prospects for and examples of integrated pest management

● The status of marine mammal protection

● How the food chain works and what happens when it is disrupted

● Describe in detail a high alpine biotope.

§ Food chains in the Sonoran Desert

§ The fate of Uganda's wildlife

● The impact of Rachel Carson's *Silent Spring*. Survey the reviews of the book at the time of its publication, and comments over the intervening years. Evaluate the book's ecological consciousness-raising contributions.

▲ What happened when the World Health Organization used DDT to eradicate malaria in Borneo? Detail the chain of events.

○ What ecological problems may arise from the effects of DDT on the activity of marine phytoplankton?

● Define human ecology

○ How do archeologists and anthropologists reconstruct past ecological conditions?

▲ Animals that were artificially introduced (deer, opossum, rabbit, goat) into New Zealand caused a vast ecological imbalance. Detail the sequential results.

● What is the significance of the worldwide disappearance of frogs?

▲ Since greenhouse gas pollutants are the most important forces altering the climate, what regulations are in force to curtail the emissions contributing to this condition? Be sure to use up-to-date information.

● Why the tropical forests are endangered ecosystems

● Fire policies of the forest service and their effect on the balance of nature

× The impact of the ecological issue on employment

➥ Tropical rainforests are rapidly disappearing. Examine the consequences—both short and long-term—on wildlife, climate, topography, etc.

★ The Four Corners area: an ecological disgrace

● How the Chernobyl, Ukraine, nuclear plant explosion, fire, and release of radioactive material changed the immediate environment

● How much damage from the Yellowstone fire will be permanent?

● How biomass burning is contributing to global warming

● Russia's ecological nightmare: polluted water, bad air, contaminated soil, and unsafe nuclear plants

★ Many elements have contributed to the return of the bald eagle. Describe them in detail.

● Wolves have been reintroduced to Yellowstone National Park. How are they doing?

Key to Symbols

●	average difficulty	➥	narrow down topic
§	substitutes possible	▲	large public or college
★	ample information in most libraries		library required
		↙	local option topic
○	specialized knowledge required	×	examples and supporting evidence needed

Economics

See also: Business and Industry; Government; Labor; Personal Finance

- The processes used in the compilation of the United States budget
- ○ Can the market system be used to correct environmental problems?
- ✔ Investigate and analyze the services of five local banks (types of services, charges, specialties, and trends).
- How do federal deficits harm (help) the economy?
- ✕ Work enrichment programs
- ★ Do Americans face a permanent decline in national income?
- Problems facing the Federal Reserve system
- ▲ The current stance of the Justice Department concerning antitrust prosecutions
- The role of profit in the allocation of scarce resources
- The possible and probable effects of equal income distribution in the United States
- Henry George and the single-tax movement
- Private ownership of scarce natural resources. What role should the government play?

- Consider the opinions of a selection of economists.
- Is conspicuous consumption necessary to the continuance of the American economic system?
- ★ What has been the traditional impact of immigration on the labor force?
- The computation of the gross national product and why it is a significant indicator
- ✕ How unemployment rates affect the national economy
- Consumer credit: origins, directions, and impact on the economy
- ★ Second homes in America. Has the number increased? The ratio? Who owns them? How are they affected by inflation?
- ★ Can inflation be stopped? What have been some of the principal proposals to alter the price spiral?
- The economics of nuclear power
- ○ How petrodollars have influenced the United States economy
- ▲ Is an international economic order possible?

- Economic aspects of American trade with Russia
- Factors contributing to the United States' recovery from the Great Depression
- How the Arab oil embargo affected United States consumers
○ Effects of regressive taxation. Who is the primary beneficiary?
- American exports and the balance of payments: an overview
- Refute or defend: Automation increases employment.
▲ How the Common Market has influenced the American export trade
✔ How inflation has altered the local job market (in your community)
▲ Why the Brook Farm Community failed
- The Tennessee Valley Authority today. Have the original goals been met? What is its current economic structure?
- The free enterprise system in America. Is it democratic?
- Financial problems of the housing industry
- Trends in consumer buying, from 1975 to date
- The prime interest rate has had wide fluctuations for the last 15 years. Explain the reason(s) for these variations. Include a graph of these changes.
- The effects of gold on the world monetary system

★ The functions of insurance
○ Gold price fluctuations from 1970 to 1990: causes and effects
- Effects of the Vietnam war on the United States economy
- Black Friday (1869)
- The principles of supply-side economics
- Marx's theory of capitalism
- Factors in economic forecasting
★ What banks do with your money
➡ Zero-based budgets
§ The economy of Spain
- American investments in Saudi Arabia
- How OPEC has affected the American economy
- Sum up the results of the 1929 stock market crash
➡ How tariffs have been levied to protect United States trade
- Effectiveness of wage and price controls to diminish inflation. Why the federal government has not instituted such regulations.
★ Pros and cons of the minimum wage. Who benefits? Does it increase employment?
§ Fiscal policies of President Reagan
- Fiscal measures utilized by President Franklin D. Roosevelt's administration to alleviate the Great Depression
○ Economic contributions of the International Monetary Fund
- How inflation has altered home buying patterns since 1970

- The economic impact of oil and gas decontrol
★ The economics of the gold rush in Alaska
○ Should we go back to the gold standard? Cite authorities to justify your answer.
- How Europe's Common Market operates. How have its successes been measured?
- "Creative financing" for home loans. Survey the latest options for the buyer and the seller.
★ The challenge of the Japanese automobile to the American auto industry
★ The electronic games success story
- Tariffs versus free trade
★ The flat tax and how it could function in the United States
- What is the difference between Keynesian economics, monetarism, and supply-side economics? Include attitudes toward inflation.
- Pros and cons of the windfall profits tax
- Uses of the consumer price index
- The rise and fall of the Hunt Brothers
○ Evaluate several current proposals to change the income tax laws.
- Defend or refute: Immigration reform is an economic necessity.
▲ Automated banking in our future

- The international gold and silver markets
▲ Levels of foreign investments in the United States
○ The establishment of foreign markets by United States business and industry
- The bear and bull markets on Wall Street today
- United States balance of payments: the current situation
- Inequitable tax laws and how they should be changed
○ Current conditions affecting the stock market
- American gold reserves yesterday and today
★ The plight of the savings and loan industry
▲ Contemporary bond market determinates
- How the underground economy affects government statistics and why this is significant to the American taxpayer
- People who never pay taxes. Who are they and why aren't they caught?
- Mutual funds: their past performance and possible future
○ This year's five best investments and why
- The role of savings and loans in home mortgages
★ The impact of inflation on retirement income
✔ Visit several local banks and discuss the requirements for a small business loan.

- The rise in the levels of consumer debt. In what ways does this contribute to inflation, lack of investment capital, and other economic ills?
§ Analyze the past performance of <u>Texaco</u> stock and its relation to the industry as a whole. What is its future potential?
- How to read a financial statement
- Starting with a hypothetical $5,000, invest it in several stocks. Research the companies, chart your investments for three months, and explain the results.
★ What events led to the savings and loan disaster? Was it predicted? Could it have been averted?
○ Can wage and price controls assist in solving inflation problems?
- Refute or defend: Advertising increases the cost of all advertised goods.
○ Fluctuations of the dollar on foreign markets. Chart past behavior characteristics and the present status of the American dollar compared to other currencies.
➡ International economic relations: the American role
- The pros and cons of a progressive income tax
✕ Does America have a free market economy?
▲ Origin and history of the consumer price index and other

business indexes
- How the federal government can promote individual savings
- Background of bank insurance
- How should full employment be defined?
★ Explain the decline of savings in America and how it affects the economy.
- How the Federal Reserve system controls the money supply
- How the government measures unemployment rates
- Zero economic growth: Good for the country?
- The functions of the Federal Reserve Board and how they are implemented
➡ Emerging structural changes of financial institutions. Consult current sources for this data.
- Describe the impact of money market accounts on traditional banking.
○ Do large government debts crowd out the public sector?
★ What has caused the growth of the national debt?
- Persuade a developing nation to adopt the market system (capitalism).
- How have changes in the income tax affected income distribution in the United States?
- How the government stabilizes the economy in the short run
○ Should the government prohibit mergers among the Fortune 500 corporations?

- Economic growth versus environmental concerns: the issues
★ The earliest coinage
- Analyze the recovery of the stock market after the Great Crash.
✕ The United States economy is often called a "mixed free enterprise economy." Discuss, using appropriate examples.
- The economic trade-off between unemployment and rising prices
- Compare recent federal attempts to hold down wages and prices. Were they successful?
▲ The nature of surplus accumulation in industrial societies
- The pros and cons of *laissez-faire* capitalism
✕ Functions of the President's Council of Economic Advisers. How much power do they hold to regulate and modify market conditions? Use some recent examples to illustrate your points.
○ How to balance the federal budget—many conflicting solutions have been proposed. Compare and contrast these opinions.
★ Will our children inherit the budget deficit? Our grandchildren?
- How has the World Bank responded to defaults by debtor nations?
- How can developing countries ever repay their national debts? Is it necessary that they do so? Why or why not?
★ A national health program has recently been the center of heated debate. If implemented, how would this plan affect the economic health of our country?
- How a decrease in taxation will (or will not) stimulate employment and production

---

Key to Symbols

•	average difficulty		◂	narrow down topic
§	substitutes possible		▲	large public or college library required
★	ample information in most libraries		↙	local option topic
○	specialized knowledge required		✕	examples and supporting evidence needed

Education

See also: Adolescents; Children

▲ How schools function as vehicles for political and social integration

★ Why high school students drop out

● How aptitude is measured. Is there agreement on methodology?

● Special fields of teaching for the educator

▲ The role of the school counselor in secondary education

● The impact of desegregation on education. For example, was it the same in the North as in the South?

● What to expect from a child's teacher

● A college degree has traditionally been a much desired and valuable attainment. Why has its value declined?

○ Sex differences and learning

▲ The spreading use of vouchers in education

➡ Alternative education programs for the elementary grades

● Correlations between children's television viewing and their reading abilities

○ Teaching music to autistic children

● The use of closed circuit television in the schools

§ Plan a day-school environment for <u>four-year-olds</u> (include playthings, furnishings, and activity centers).

➡ Compare and contrast the learning theories of B.F. Skinner and Jean Piaget.

● The malnourished child in school

● The chronic underachiever. How have educators successfully motivated and changed the behavioral patterns of these consistently bright children?

● Educational possibilities for retarded children. Discuss some of the programs and techniques now widely used.

▲ Teaching language through television

○ How children learn language

★ The adult student in American higher education: a nationwide survey

● Status of parochial school education: how educators evaluate its assets and liabilities

136

○ Problems in evaluating the gifted child

★ What techniques are being employed by schools to avoid violent incidents?

▲ Childhood education in contemporary China

★ The private and public school system of Great Britain

§ Education in <u>Australia</u>

● A characterization of a typical high school drop-out

● Special education as a profession

● South Africa and black education

○ Theories on the teaching of reading to children. Compare and contrast several of them.

● Academic achievement and racial background. Is there a relationship? Cite valid research and supporting evidence.

★ How to study effectively

● The importance of a creative classroom environment

➥ Teaching machines and programmed learning

● Advantages and disadvantages of junior high schools

● Compare and contrast the American high school and European secondary schools.

➥ Learning disabilities

● The Ph.D surplus in education

★ What makes a good teacher?

§ Nature study excursions for <u>fourth</u> graders. Design three, each covering a different subject area. Select any primary grade.

○ The prevention and remediation of reading disabilities

● Compare and explain the three major learning theories

▲ Financing school lunches

● Major causes of stress in the classroom. What can the teacher do to alleviate tension?

➥ Minority education and ethnic cultures

● Socioeconomic aspects of learning disabilities

● The case for the small college versus the large university

● How television has changed the reading and learning abilities of America's children

▲ The value of practice teaching as an adjunct to teacher education

● Changing attitudes toward college fraternities (sororities)

● Dealing with the problem child in the classroom

● Innovations in the education of gifted students

● The advantages of the twelve-month school year

● Effects of poverty and poor nutrition on educational achievements of school children. Cite recent studies and clinical observations.

● The misuse of television education

➥ Education problems in third world countries

§ Design a science unit for the <u>sixth</u> grade (space, earth origins, desert plants, etc.) Include an annotated bibliography.

- The college decision. How to make it sensibly. Include factors such as cost, educational worth, job market, personal goals, etc.

× Uses of computers in secondary education

- Design the layout and equipment for the ideal elementary school gymnasium.

- Causes and remedies for children with dyslexia

- Reading difficulties of black children

§ Adult literacy: Mexico

▲ Perceptual problems in learning-disabled children

- Intelligence tests and their relation to cultural and social backgrounds

- What every teacher should know about group dynamics

- Compare and contrast American and Canadian secondary schools systems.

- Increasing children's attention spans

- Automation in education

- The Kaufman Assessment Battery for Children is a new intelligence test. How does it differ from traditional intelligence tests? Many studies have been completed which measure its effectiveness: What are the results?

- Negative factors involved in the home-education programs for children

- Identify what intelligence tests measure. What does an IQ score mean? How reliable is it as an indicator of achievement?

➥ The mentally retarded child in society

★ The effects of tenure in higher education

§ The education of women in Iran (or select a different Islamic country)

- Higher education in prisons. What are some of the currently used programs? Which seem to be the most successful?

- The perfect high school

★ Successes (or failures) in the busing of school children to achieve integration

- Does the pass/fail grading system affect student achievement?

- Segregated private schools in the South today

- Why all elementary schools should use minimum competency testing

§ Medical education in Mexico

- Do honors programs have a place in American education?

× How magnet schools offer choice and diversity within the public school system

- Should this country have a national or common core curriculum?

Education — Current Issues

See also: Adolescents; Children

- "The elements of instruction . . . should be presented to the mind in childhood, but not with any compulsion." (Plato, *The Republic*) Discuss the implications of this statement in light of contemporary educational theory.
- ▲ The pros/cons of the open classroom system
- Levels of functional illiteracy in the United States. What is the explanation for this figure?
- ★ The "back to basics" movement in education
- The following charge has often been leveled at the American public education system: The pursuit of equality has been at the expense of excellence. Present evidence either supporting or denying this accusation.
- ★ Is bilingual education realistic?
- Mainstreaming the handicapped. How well has this worked? What have been the effects on the impaired student, other students, and teacher efficiency?
- What has been achieved by busing since 1970?
- The pros and cons of government aid to private schools
- Should intellectually gifted children be educated apart from their peers?
- ▲ How to prevent teacher burnout. Include a discussion of the causes of this problem.
- Should able children learn to read before starting school? Justify your stance.
- The case for federal aid to denominational schools
- ▲ The issues involved in awarding college credit for work experiences
- The education major: A worthless degree for teachers?
- Should subject speciality proficiency tests be a standard requirement for teacher certification?
- Do our high schools place too much emphasis on sports?
- Compare and contrast a liberal versus a specialized college education.
- ★ Successfully coping with academic pressures
- Should preschool be public or private?

★ Should the government support the education of gifted children?

★ The case against video games in the school environment

• College tuition costs. Are they too high? Does this often deny the worthy student a college degree?

• The advantages and disadvantages of home education for primary grades

• "The teacher is a guide, not a task-maker." (John Dewey, 1924) Discuss how this statement typifies the split in progressive versus traditional educational theories.

▲ Should some college courses be required for all students? Which ones, and why? Use examples from current college catalogs and from experts in education.

• Should college athletic recruiting practices be changed? In what ways?

▲ Why economically deprived children do poorly in school

• Has the American school system emphasized socialization to the detriment of intellectual education?

• In the view of educational authorities, what is the major deficiency in American public education? Survey a large sample of authoritative opinion.

• "Progressive" education, pros and cons

○ The correlation between educational achievement and family background

★ The relationship between television viewing and reading abilities in children

• The increase of basic skills deficiencies among secondary school students

★ Creation science has a place in the public school biology class. True? What is the educational and scientific justification?

▲ Problems and possible solutions in the education of Native American children

• Private versus public high school education

• The voucher system of public education

○ Discuss both sides of the IQ testing controversy.

▲ The advantages/disadvantages of the secondary education track system which separates students according to ability

• Conflicting concepts of elitism in American education

• Why the Scholastic Assessment Test (S.A.T.) is not an accurate measurement of ability

▲ Should remedial courses be taught in college for college credit?

• Pros and cons of corporal punishment in the schools

• Defend or refute the need for sex education in secondary schools.

• Support or refute: No high

school senior should graduate unless a basic skills competency test is passed.

- Pros/cons of a community college education
- Why many parents and educators support the growing "back to basics" movement
- ○ Why we have more violence in the schools. What reasons for the increase are proposed by educators? By social scientists in general?
- ▲ The rise of the corporate trainee programs. In the opinion of business and industry, why have these programs become critically necessary in many large firms?
- Who should choose school textbooks? What are the major issues of this continuing controversy? What have been some of the most recently disputed instances of textbook selection? Have they been resolved or solved?
- ★ What should be included in sex

education courses for high school students?
- × The implications of California's Proposition 13 for education in the United States
- Examine the pros and cons of mandatory formal education for children aged one to five.
- Special education for the intellectually gifted? Who pays?
- ○ Are standardized tests accurate and fair?
- Recent educational reforms in China
- ★ How should the schools handle AIDS (Acquired Immune Deficiency Syndrome) infected children? Should they be allowed to attend regular classes?
- ▲ How word processors in the schoolroom help teach students to write
- Many educators believe students should have a satisfactory grade average before they are allowed to participate in any extracurricular activities. Comment on this viewpoint.

Key to Symbols

•	average difficulty	◆	narrow down topic
§	substitutes possible	▲	large public or college library required
★	ample information in most libraries	↙	local option topic
○	specialized knowledge required	×	examples and supporting evidence needed

Education — History

See also: Adolescents; Children

- Illiteracy in the United States, yesterday and today
- The education of young men of the upper class in classical Greece
- The academic goals of Summerhill. What was the structure and what were the educational premises presented in *Summerhill: A Radical Approach to Child Rearing* by Alexander Neill?
- The influence of John Dewey on contemporary American education
★ The "open" classroom experiment: Did it work?
- The traditional role of sports in American public education
- The rise of the medieval universities
▲ Medical education in ancient Egypt and Rome
- American primary schools during the colonial period
☛ Education in the Renaissance
- Principles and practices of John Dewey's experimental school
○ Nature and the individual in the educational theories of Jean

Jacques Rousseau
★ The growth of black colleges in America
▲ What changes in education resulted from the student protest movement of the 1960's?
- How education in the United States has been molded and changed by the space age
- What were the educational opportunities for African Americans in the late nineteenth century? How did they affect education in the twentieth century?
☛ Contrast the goals and purposes of education in an ancient culture with those of the modern day.
★ Characterize the British educational system since 1850.
- Federally funded education in nineteenth-century America
- How high schools have changed since 1930
★ College tuition costs: a twenty-year survey
- How coeducational dormitories have changed campus life
- The development and scope of the community college in the

United States: an overview
x Historical roots of academic freedom. Use examples in their historical contexts.
• An analysis of recent teachers' strikes, the demands and negotiations. Evaluate the results.
• Education under the Nazis
• Compare and contrast Aristotle's educational theories with those of John Dewey.
▲ The history of the "initial teaching alphabet"
★ The Head Start Program. What were the necessities which prompted the early efforts? How successful has it been?

★ Maria Montessori: originator of the Montessori method of education for children
• Federal aid to education since 1900
▲ Why did Southern public education lag far behind the rest of the country at the turn of the century? Was segregation a factor?
• Chart the expansion of vocational education in twentieth-century America. What factors supplied the impetus for this change?
• What were the effects of the Great Depression on education in America?

Key to Symbols

•	average difficulty	◆	narrow down topic
§	substitutes possible	▲	large public or college library required
★	ample information in most libraries	✔	local option topic
o	specialized knowledge required	x	examples and supporting evidence needed

Energy

See also: Physics

★ Current levels of the United States' dependence on OPEC fuel sources. What factors have caused these levels to fluctuate?

● Changing consumer attitudes towards energy conservation

● Alternate fuels: How soon and to what degree will they make a difference? Do the experts agree?

▲ How has the energy crisis changed public transportation in the United States?

○ The prospects of ocean thermal energy conversion (OTEC)

● Discuss the security factors involved in future energy supplies for the United States.

● Russia's energy problems

↙ What are the energy policies in your state? What amendments and reforms have been proposed? Initiated?

★ Should the United States use its shale oil reserves?

▲ Practical aspects of energy generation from turbines in the Gulf Stream

● The pros/cons of woodstoves as alternative energy sources

● How to build (or install) a fireplace

● Energy from solar-powered silicone cells

● Does the American oil industry need greater federal regulation?

● Energy sources in the future

● How much of the United States' current energy consumption is generated by nuclear means? What is projected? Are these projections both feasible and realistic?

● Should the utilities be nationalized?

● Solar greenhouses

★ Why environmentalists oppose fast-breeder nuclear reactors

● Pros and cons of nuclear fusion as a long-range energy source

● The future supply of fossil fuels in the United States

● Natural gas resources in the United States

✕ The effects of long-term energy shortages on the economy

● Pedal power: how to produce energy from a stationary bicycle

● Meltdowns and near meltdowns

● Inexpensive energy sources for

the home

▲ Underground villages of the Loire Valley (France): an example of passive energy conservation

● Evaluate the quantity, quality, and accessibility of Russian energy resources.

● How would gas rationing affect the United States' energy supplies?

● Compare and contrast urban and rural utilization of energy resources. How do levels of consumption vary? Why?

★ Is national energy independence a feasible possibility?

● Energy solutions for glass-walled buildings

● Since many experts agree that solar power holds the greatest promise for satisfying future energy requirements, why has the United States not allocated significant funds for its rapid development and expansion?

▲ The potential and the problems of energy-sharing programs with Canada

○ Wind as an energy resource for the individual home

★ How the United States has misused its energy resources

○ Why coal utilization by the process of gasification has not been more universally adopted. What are its advantages and disadvantages?

● Survey and compare to the United States the energy policies, resources, and consumption of several western countries.

☛ The prospects for energy conservation in the United States. Select one subject area.

✕ How the energy shortage has affected American life-styles

☛ Problems of energy transport

▲ Has the increased energy input of high-yield agriculture been justified? Select recent studies and statistical evidence to support your answer.

● Detail how the United States energy problem is directly related to the urbanization/industrialization syndrome.

● The history of United States fuel usage, 1880–1980

★ Energy conservation: what you can do

● Current proposals for a national energy policy

● Land-use strategies for energy conservation. Are these realistically feasible for the United States?

● The charge has often been leveled that United States fuel shortages are artificially engineered. What evidence is there to support this thesis?

● When to convert your home to solar energy

○ How to build a solar water heater

● The fundamentals of passive solar energy design

○ Thermal collection devices for the utilization of solar energy

▲ Problems of utilizing solar power for cooling

● How the discounting of electricity prices to high-volume consumers has contributed to the energy crisis

● Turning waste into energy

▲ Possibilities for the commercial utilization of tidal power

● Refute: Nuclear power is an inexpensive source of energy.

✕ Peacetime uses of atomic energy

● In what ways did the last national election campaign reflect the presence of energy problems and concerns?

§ Atomic power capabilities of <u>India</u>

● How the coal slurry pipeline would alleviate the energy crunch in the next decades

○ What are some of the political ramifications of energy allocation?

● Who really controls energy?

✕ Is the United States properly developing its energy resources?

✕ Examine the response of the oil industry to major/minor oil spills.

★ What have been the long range consequences of the Chernobyl nuclear plant disaster?

★ Nuclear energy as the answer to global warming

● "The unleashed power of the atom has changed everything except our way of thinking." (Albert Einstein) In what ways has this proved to be true?

➡ How artificial sources of energy such a gun powder, steam and electric power, the internal combustion engine, and atomic power have changed our world

▲ How does the nuclear industry propose to prevent the release of radioactive material from burial sites over the next 200,000 years?

● Compare and contrast the environmental effects of consumption of fossil fuels: oil, coal, and gas.

● Investigate the uses of geothermal power in Indonesia, Japan, China, and New Zealand.

● Recent developments in the use of wind energy

● Why bicycles will never replace the automobile on the American Scene

---

Key to Symbols

●	average difficulty	➡	narrow down topic
§	substitutes possible	▲	large public or college library required
★	ample information in most libraries	↙	local option topic
○	specialized knowledge required	✕	examples and supporting evidence

Environment

See also: Ecology; Geography; Pollution; Resources

- Why Theodore Roosevelt's greatest contribution as president was in the field of conservation
- Widespread environmental degradation occurred in Vietnam as an effect of American strategy and weaponry. What were some of the major consequences? Are they still factors in this area?
- ✔ Identify an area of environmental conflict within your locality. What precipitated this conflict? What are the contrasting values held by the opponents? Is a resolution possible?
- ★ What are the major causes of forest fires in the United States? What is the annual toll, both economically and environmentally?
- What do wetlands contribute to the environment?
- How forest fires are controlled
- The Tennessee Valley Authority's Tellico Dam and the controversy surrounding its construction
- What are the basic factors underlying land use conflicts in the United States?
- ★ Bottle laws: pros and cons
- What are the five most critical environmental problems in the United States today? Detail their scope and the ultimate consequences of their unchecked expansion.
- ✕ Examine in detail selected examples of the variety of ways mankind has functioned as a modifer of the environment
- ★ Greenpeace Foundation and whale conservation
- The damage to bird populations from oil spills
- ★ Practical soil erosion controls for farmlands
- Deforestation in the Himalayas
- The environmental impact of Eskimo hunting
- Will zoos be the last wildlife preserves?
- ★ The effects of tanker oil spills on coastal areas
- ▲ Paraquat spraying of marijuana. What have been the environmental consequences?
- Is the Environmental Protection Agency effectively protecting the

environment? Is there agreement on this question?

- Open pit and strip mining: An environmental disaster?
× The failure of technology to serve our environmental interests
- Present the case for wilderness areas
§ The impact of environmental regulation on _____. Select an industry.
- The environmental consequences of the misuse of slash-and-burn agriculture
- What were the goals of the "Green Revolution"? Why have they not been realized? What were the basic contradictions of this philosophy?
§ How the passenger pigeon became extinct
- Wind erosion: Discuss the Dust Bowl of the 1930's and modern instances of this condition as well.
- Clean air in the 1990s: standards, progress, and prospects
← World water shortages
- The burro problem in the Grand Canyon
§ Lead in the environment
- Radioactive fallout. How is it measured? How much has there been? What have been the principal effects?
↙ How effective have the laws and regulations controlling water pollution been in your area? Are they adequate? Should they

be amended, lessened, or increased?

- When overgrazing is allowed, what happens to both the land surfaces and to the naturally occurring grasses?
- Groundwater and what happens to the land when it is all used up
★ The poisoning of Love Canal
- Important activities and achievements of the Sierra Club in the last five years
- Evaluate the predictions of environmentalist Paul Ehrlich
← Levels of pesticide residues in animal populations
- Can Alaska's wilderness be preserved? What are the critical issues?
▲ Land reclamation measures for strip-mined areas. Discuss the most successful projects.
○ Disadvantages of salt water conversion processes. Does technology exist that would make this feasible for large volumes of water?
- Current levels of radioactive waste in the United States
★ Will the Southwest have enough water?
↙ Study the game laws in your state. Discuss essential reforms and changes.
- The consequences of ocean mining on the total environment
← Wilderness areas, government policies, and mineral leasing.

Focus on this relationship and recent instances of conflict and change.

- The facts behind the importation of "exotic" animals
- Survey congressional action on environmental issues over the last five years. Evaluate your findings.
- Wildlife refuges: How effective are they?
- Is the safe disposal of hazardous waste an impossibility?
- The impact of heavy oil mining and/or refining on land, air, and water
- § Major environmental issues in Florida
- § The pollution of Lake Erie
- Refute or defend: Mining oil shale would not be worth the environmental damage to the western United States.
- ★ The effect of off-road vehicles on America's deserts and arid regions
- Why the United States has such poor (or good) environmental legislation. Include quotations from appropriate authorities.
- ▲ Air photography and game management
- Environmental problems of the Industrial Revolution
- ○ Environmental aspects of utilizing the oil from Canada's Athabasca (tar) sands
- × Measures for the preservation of bird life

- The five priorities of environmentalists
- Does the federal government control too much land?
- § Saving the Serengeti or another natural area threatened with destruction
- The long-term effects of pesticide misuse
- Effects of the early widespread use of DDT in the United States
- The Environmental Quality Index and how the measurements are calculated
- The nature and scope of land surface deterioration from overuse in underdeveloped countries. Select a particular area and detail the extent of environmental degradation and depletion.
- ★ Critical issues in radioactive waste disposal
- Nuclear power plant environmental safeguards
- How to survive in the desert
- Mono Lake (California): an ecological battleground
- Limits of recreational use of United States forest lands. What are the current policies? Should they be amended?
- The origin of the Environmental Protection Agency. What are its current goals? Have they changed since the agency was created?
- ○ How the Alaskan pipeline has altered wildlife patterns
- The long-term effects of Agent

Orange on the environment
- ○ Providing habitats for endangered species (select several)
- ★ How the Aswan Dam has affected the Nile Valley
- • Plans to reuse wastewater
- × Measures to prevent noise pollution in urban areas
- ✓ Wildlife conservation measures in your state
- • Western water crisis
- • The scope and goals of the Clean Air Act
- × How man makes a desert
- • Levels of soil erosion in the United States. Compare the current data to that of the era of the Dust Bowl.
- • Why surface mining is responsible for the greatest soil and water loss in the United States today
- § Imperative soil conservation measures for Nepal
- § Environmental issues and the current administration
- ○ Problems in water recovery
- • What have been the environmental consequences of the use of DDT (and related compounds) to date?
- • Public opposition to hazardous waste sites
- • Radioactive waste disposal sites. Who decides?
- ▲ Have the oil-well fires ignited by Iraq in the Persian Gulf War had permanent environmental impact?
- • Detail the effects of a coal slurry pipeline on the environment.
- • How does excess nitrogen affect the environment?
- ★ Nuclear waste management and legislative reform. What measures should be enacted now? In the future?
- ○ What are the purposes of the National Environmental Policy Act? How well have they been realized?
- • What are the major elements of an environmental impact statement? How are they issued? What are the stages of enforcement?
- • The scope and severity of acid rain in the United States in the last three years
- • The 1964 Wilderness Act
- • Fallout during early atomic tests
- • Who should be responsible for pollution control?
- ★ How the Yellowstone wildfire (1988) has affected the park ecosystem
- × The relationship between the profit motive in American industry and the environment
- § Reforestation policies in Oregon
- ▲ A survey of proposed environmental legislation
- • Major sources of water pollution in the United States
- • The costs of air pollution in the United States
- ➜ Current levels of pesticide use in the United States
- § Efforts to save the tiger

✔ If air pollution exists in your locality, what is causing it and what is being done to clean it up?

● Smog: sources, effects, and regulation

● Mediterranean pollution

● How should the release of trace elements into the environment be controlled?

● Life in the jungle canopy

★ The relationship between the Aswan Dam (Egypt) and schistosomiasis

● Organized and mobilized opposition to environmental abuse has been slow to develop in the United States. What are the reasons for this? Is there any recent change?

● Environmental hazards that are of particular danger to children

● The harp seal hunt controversy

▲ The background issues of federal water management, 1900 to date.

● The pros and cons of the Power River Basin controversy

★ The lasting effects of the *Exxon Valdez* oil spill on Prince William Sound (Alaska)

★ The end of whaling. What factors have led to the cessation of large-scale killing on a worldwide basis? Include current and projected future status of whale populations.

● If the Environmental Protection Agency allows the release of an artificially altered bacteria into the external environment, what will be the possible result? What issues are involved in this controversy?

➔ The hazards of toxic wastes

★ Why was the Bhopal chemical disaster so deadly? Could it have been prevented? Could lives have been saved with more stringent safety precautions?

✔ Instances of groundwater pollution in your state

○ Detail the progress since 1970 in cancer prevention through environmental regulation.

✕ A growing number of states have taken the lead in environmental issues. Why? How much is the result of inadequate federal regulation?

★ How acid rain has affected buildings, statues and other man-made structures

● Is the state rather than the federal government in a better position to monitor and control environmental problems?

● What has been the attitude and voting record of the current Congress toward environmental issues? Do they accurately reflect prevailing public opinion?

● The EDB (Ethylene dibromide) contamination of foods

○ The causes and consequences of the Times Beach, Missouri dioxin contamination

▲ What are the environmental and

safety issues involved in natural gas pipelines?

• Are our multinationals exporting environmental hazards to less developed countries? Is there commonly a double standard in operation?

★ The Greenpeace Foundation. What are its philosophy, areas of involvement, tactics and organization?

• The effects of a "nuclear winter" will lead to the starvation of millions. Comment upon this statement.

★ What has been the effect thus far of the Chernobyl nuclear accident on the local environment?

× Some experts maintain that many of the foods we eat are not safe. What is their evidence for this stance?

• Should oil drilling be allowed in Alaska's Arctic National Wildlife Refuge?

• The automobile and the natural environment

× Select several instances of dioxin contamination and examine causes, preventive measures and the result of the contamination.

▲ The growth of the ozone hole over Antarctica. What are the projections for the future of this phenonenon?

× Chart recent changes in climate around the world. Do scientists agree we have a general global warming or greenhouse effect?

▲ Can the ozone layer depletion be halted? How? What measures are currently in force?

★ Recent controversy of grazing on federal lands. Has this privilege been abused? What are the proposed remedies?

Key to Symbols

•	average difficulty	◆	narrow down topic
§	substitutes possible	▲	large public or college library required
★	ample information in most libraries	↙	local option topic
○	specialized knowledge required	×	examples and supporting evidence needed

Essay Suggestions

Essays are best written as an expression of your own experience, values, and background. Rather than being "researched" (expounding on someone else's ideas), your essay should reflect your own thoughts and opinions.

The joys of cooking
Why you should vote for me
How debate fosters learning.
My best year in school
How to tell the difference between good and evil.
The very best way to make a fool of yourself.
Mother's (father's) cooking
A modest proposal
How to teach children manners.
Who needs a college education?
The advantages of honesty
Why I would like to attend this school
What's the matter with being opinionated?
All's fair in love and war.
How to flirt
There is no God.
Why get married nowadays?
What my education lacks
A little learning is a dangerous thing.
Absence makes the heart grow fonder.
The worst experience I ever had
When crime pays
Books that changed my life
Why I'm the best person for this job

Life's most painful lesson(s)
I don't want to have children
How to develop a personal style
Why I love the movies
The perfect relationship between husband and wife (father/son, etc.)
Why I want to be a ___ Select a career
How religion let me down
What I live for
A penny saved is not always a penny earned.
In defense of literacy
How I learned to drive
Can people be judged by their appearance?
The "good old days" weren't so great.
How to keep fit — for life
The art of making and keeping friends
What my friend(s) mean to me
What I want in a wife (husband)
Happiness is a state of mind.
Whatever happened to "America the Beautiful"?
How to get rich
My next house will be an ivory tower.
Lost on the information highway

153

Why I love the movies
The perfect relationship between husband and wife (father/son, etc.)
Why I want to be a _____. Select a career
How religion let me down
What I live for
A penny saved is not always a penny earned.
In defense of literacy
How I learned to drive
Can people be judged by their appearance?
The "good old days" weren't so great.
How to keep fit — for life
The art of making and keeping friends
What my friend(s) mean to me
What I want in a wife (husband)
Happiness is a state of mind.
Whatever happened to "America the Beautiful"?
How to get rich
My next house will be an ivory tower.
Lost on the information highway

Ethical Issues

See also Bioethics; Contemporary Issues; Ethical Business Practices; Humanities; Philosophy; Social Problems; Religion

★ The use of steroids in sports. Besides the medical factors, are there other considerations?

✕ One byproduct of the information explosion is a loss of privacy. Do we need a new code of ethics for information?

● Do political action committees (PACs) have a right to spend unlimited amounts on their candidate?

● Should smoking be banned in all public places?

● What rights do animals have? Should consideration vary by species?

➤ Should the richer nations of the world help poorer countries? Is it an obligation?

★ How children learn responsibility and develop a conscience

● Should everyone take Prozac?

✕ Is wiretapping ever justified?

● The pros and cons of cash incentives for organ donors

★ The ethics of AIDS testing on a non-voluntary (required) basis

★ The homeless constitute on appreciable segment of our population Opinion is divided on whose responsibility it is to care for them. Consider a variety of opinions for your discussion.

● Examine the ethical transgressions of the savings and loan scandals.

● Is Jack Kevorkian (assisted voluntary suicide advocate) to be commended or censured?

● Private and privileged data on individuals is stored in impersonal computers. How can the individual protect this personal information? Where should the line be drawn between the public and the private?

● Should Native Americans be kept on reservations?

★ Is capital punishment a crime deterrent? Cite informed opinion and evidence to support or refute this question.

★ What has been the self-justification of those responsible for abortion clinic bombings and killings?

★ Is assassination ever justified?

● The "ethics" of Watergate

● When is civil disobedience justified?

- The chemical accident in Bhopal, India (Dec., 1984), raised some crucial issues and choices regarding the future of foreign enterprise, chemical manufacturing, and human safety. How has this incident affected these issues?
★ The justification for the use of animals for laboratory experimentation (or the case against)
- Is it fair to cheat?
× There are certain situations in which propaganda is justified. Defend or refute this statement.
- How should governments respond to hostage demands?
✔ When they propose a toxic-waste dump site for your vicinity, who should be responsible for its control?
- Russia's air, soil, and water are now all highly polluted and unsafe, and its nuclear plants are unsound as well. What should surrounding countries be prepared to do?
- Can ethical behavior be taught? Who should teach it — the church, the family, or the school?
☛ Ethics on the Internet
○ The United States suffers a large-scale non-nuclear attack by a foreign country. Is nuclear retaliation then justifiable?
- Are rock music lyrics too suggestive and offensive to the majority? If so, should they be regulated or censored?
- Ethics, AIDS, and the unfaithful mate
- The child who "divorced" his parents: Gregory K. Does this set a poor precedent?
- Should there be rules governing the sterilization of the severely mentally retarded? Who decides?
○ How to combat the piracy of tapes, videos, and fashions
☛ Select a recent breach of ethical behavior by a member of Congress or the executive branch of government. Detail the issues involved and make a final judgment based on these issues.
- Academic research scientists often have a personal financial interest, through corporate connections, in the outcome of their research. Examine this built-in conflict of interest.
- Who owns the ocean (or the moon or space)?

Key to Symbols

•	average difficulty	☛	narrow down topic
§	substitutes possible	▲	large public or college library required
★	ample information in most libraries	✔	local option topic
○	specialized knowledge required	×	examples and supporting evidence needed

Ethnic and Minority Groups

See also: African Americans; Native Americans; Social Problems

- Discuss several race-related riots in American history
- The introduction of slavery into America. What were the first documented instances?
- Self-image and the minority child
- Jewish persecution and the Russian pogroms
- Critical issues affecting minority hiring
- The issues involved in Hawaii's racial conflict or lack thereof
- The new Miami (Florida)
- The 1973 seizure of Wounded Knee: What were the factors leading to this confrontation? Has its aftermath effected any significant change in Anglo-Indian relations?
- § What are the general economic conditions for persons of Spanish origin in the United States? Has their position changed since 1940? Since 1970?
- Unemployment among minority youth and how to alleviate it
- What happened in Little Rock (1957)
- × Racism in children's books

- The learning difficulties of Mexican-American children
- Racism in the military
- Characterize the Chicano gangs of Los Angeles
- The culture of Mexican-American communities in the Southwest
- ★ Stereotypes of the Native American
- Mexican-American crime and juvenile delinquency rates: an overview
- Acculturation problems for Vietnamese refugees in the United States
- ▲ The schooling of native American reservation children. What have been some of the effects on the children and on reservation family life?
- ★ The significance of the Brown v. The Board of Education desegregation decision (1954)
- ★ Cesar Chavez and the California grape growers
- The intelligence tests of Arthur Jensen (1969)
- × Racism in advertising
- § The social system of the Puerto Ricans in New York or of an-

other localized American ethnic group.

- The effects of illegal aliens on the United States labor market. Who is affected and in what ways?
▲ How immigration in the early nineteenth century influenced educational policies in America
- Minority discrimination in the sale and rental of housing. Investigate the progress since 1960 to eliminate unfair practices.
- Are ethnic communities "un-American"?
× Ethnic stereotypes in the American media
★ Migrant workers: their plight and their prospects
➥ Assimilation of ethnic minorities in nineteenth-century America
- Life in a Mexican-American barrio
✔ Describe affirmative action and how it operates in your community. Select several local firms, interview personnel, and compare their efforts to follow the official guidelines.
★ The Scottsboro trials
✔ Important aspects of the Civil Rights movement in your state. In what ways has it changed social, economic, political, and educational structures and organizations?
- Educational attainments of Mex-

ican-Americans today
- Historical characterizations of the Jews
× Instances of anti-Semitism in America, 1900–1950
- The Cajuns
- The first desegregated schools: what happened
▲ Racial tensions in Britain. What have been the contributing factors?
- Should minorities be given preferential employment opportunities?
- How minority groups view affirmative action
- What are the biological perspectives on race and racial differences?
- Group stereotypes: how they originate, are fostered, and flourish
- Common personality dysfunctions of minorities
- Factors influencing skin color. What are the distributive patterns?
▲ What have been the relative gains achieved by African American, Native American, and Hispanic minorities in the United States during the last three decades? Account for any significant differences.
○ It has been suggested that colleges and universities should revise their testing and grading procedures for the benefit of

minority group students. Examine the pros and cons of this proposal.

- Institutional racism: what it is and how to combat it
- Ethnic prejudice is often embedded in the socioeconomic system. How is it perpetuated by the culture?
- What have been the characteristic responses by minority group members to prejudice directed toward them as individuals or as members of the group?
- x While affirmative action is an accepted procedure in our society, many critics charge that its implementation has led to further imbalances and injustices. Evaluate the issues involved in this charge.
- Define the African American "underclass" in the United States today. Examine the causes and the consequences to the individual, to African Americans and to society in general.
- How have race relations in South Africa changed in the last five years?
- Is the United States immigration policy fair? Should existing legislation remain the same or be altered? How?
- ▲ How developments in modern agriculture have affected Mexican-Americans
- Detail the major obstacles normally encountered by recently assimilated Asian-Americans.
- ★ The urban underclass: who they are and how they got that way
- Does most gang activity take place between ethnic minority groups? Why or why not?
- ▲ Federal policy toward and the treatment of Japanese-Americans during World War II. Include a discussion of internment camps
- ★ What role did minorities play in the 1992 Los Angeles riots?
- *The Bell Curve* (Murray and Herrnstein) suggests that different racial groups have different IQs. Discuss the many rebuttals of this book.

Key to Symbols

•	average difficulty	➔	narrow down topic
§	substitutes possible	▲	large public or college
★	ample information in most		library required
	libraries	✔	local option topic
○	specialized knowledge	x	examples and supporting
	required		evidence needed

Evolution

See also: Animal Behavior; Anthropology; Archeology; Biology; Genetics and Heredity; Physiology and Anatomy

- Discuss the relationship between the evolution of the social insects and flowering plants.
§ Given past evolution of the primates, what are some of the future projections?
★ Why has the concept of evolution caused such a great deal of controversy, particularly outside of the scientific community?
- What are the basic assumptions of Darwin's theory?
○ Human sexuality and the evolutionary theory
○ Why was the evolvement of a specialized transport tissue necessary for higher plants to fully utilize the land environment? Use examples to clarify your answer.
★ What are the evolutionary relationships between the major classes of vertebrates?
- What are the various hypotheses to account for the origin of the Protozoa?
➡ What are the problems faced by animals in terrestrial life? What are some of the adapta-

tions that have enabled them to partially solve these problems? Select either terrestrial vertebrates or insects.
- The findings of Louis Leakey. What has been their significance in the further understanding of human evolution?
- Discuss the many ways anthropoids and vertebrates have independently evolved similar adaptive solutions to the problems of reproduction and survival.
- The revisionist theory of evolution
× Effects of regional isolation on evolutionary development
- Brain evolution: from flatworm to human
- Why the Galapagos were uniquely suited to the evolutionary discoveries and theories of Charles Darwin
- The state of the art in biology at the time of Charles Darwin
★ The significance of the opposable thumb to human development

160

- The development of evolutionary theories before Charles Darwin
○ The precepts of macroevolution and their significance to evolutionary knowledge
○ The role of accident in modern evolutionary theory
- What determines the rate of evolution?
- Whatever happened to the remains of the Peking Man? Have any traces of this disappearance been found? Who may have been responsible?
- Compare and contrast individual and group natural selection.
➡ Discuss how mutation, natural selection, and migration affect accurate measurements of evolution.
- Discuss the relative importance of chance and selection.
▲ Select several outstanding examples of genetic drift and relate them to evolutionary theory as a whole.
- Why evolution is not a "theory"
★ Why do species become extinct? Survey the major theories and the most recent evidence supporting them.
× Functions of mutation in nature
× Man-made evolution
- Do organisms evolve in jumps or gradually?
× Convergent evolution
- Evidences of the loss of wings by island birds
- The long road toward upright posture
▲ How the theories of Anaximander (611–547 B.C.) anticipated later theories of evolution
- Examine some of the current discoveries and controversies concerning early man. Evaluate the evidence used to support each issue.
○ What evidence is there to support the hypothesis that hominids evolved from a pre-brachiating ancestry?
- Patterns of cooperation and human evolution
- Compare and contrast the nature of convergent and parallel evolution.
○ Several different taxonomic schemes have been used to classify the australopiths. Explain this variation and the justification and evidence for each.
× By the use of examples, illustrate the process of adaptive radiation.
- Water mammals: how they got there
- How did bacteria evolve?
§ Evolution of the _____. Select an animal. (The horse is particularly suited to this analysis.)
➡ Discuss in detail several of Darwin's discoveries from the Beagle voyage.
- Significance of the bristlecone pine
▲ Pre-Cambrian cell development

- Brain size in early man: facts, estimates, and projections
- The earliest discoveries of human fossils and the theories arising from the finds
★ The Piltdown man hoax
- Compare and contrast Java (*Pithecanthropus*) and Peking (*Sinanthropus*) man.
○ Define the three-race theory.
- Defend the verdict of the 1925 Scopes "Monkey" trial.
- The role of children in human evolution
- Whale evolution
- Man's place in nature at the end of the Ice Age
▲ Theories on animal extinctions during the Cretaceous-Tertiary boundary period
- What happened to the dinosaurs?
× Compare the following, using relevant examples: evolution; natural selection; adaption; and artificial selection.
- Darwin's finches and speciation
- Darwin's debt to Sir Charles Lyell (*Principles of Geology*)
- Punctuated equilibrium: Will it replace the theory of natural selection?
★ The significance of teeth and jaws in fossil remains
- Why *Pithecanthropus erectus* was previously thought to be the "missing link"
★ How birds became airborne and why some birds didn't

- Fossil history of the insect
★ How reptiles evolved from amphibians
▲ Ancient and medieval explanations for fossils
- The significance of recent finds in the Olduvai Gorge (Tanzania)
★ The fossilized remains of the La Brea tar pits (Los Angeles, California)
○ Has human interference with natural selection affected human intelligence?
- Eugene Dubois and the "Java ape man" (*Pithecanthropus erectus*) and its place in evolutionary history
- How the lessening of natural selection has changed man's genetic pool
- Compare and contrast the modern crocodile with dinosaurs of the Cretaceous period.
- Compare multi-character and single-character methods of measuring evolutionary change.
- Opportunism in the evolutionary process
- How does natural selection affect social behavior?
- How did early monkeys develop visually as well as anatomically in order to evolve the capacity to "objectify" their world? What are the implications for Homo sapiens?
○ Was *Ramapithecus* an early hominid? Cite authoritative evi-

dence to support your conclusion.

★ The nature of human mutations

• *Homo erectus* finds show wide variability. What factors may account for this?

• Examine the evidence supporting the relationship between tool-making and brain development among the australopiths.

• Evolution is based upon variation within the habitat and within the population. Discuss the complexities and significance of this statement.

• What are the controversial changes in the theories of human origin brought about by the discovery of "Lucy" (*Australopithecus afarensis*)?

• "Lucy" (*Australopithecus afarensis*) and her "first family." What were their physical characteristics?

★ The controversy surrounding Raymond Dart's "Taung Baby"

• A 225 million year old dinosaur skeleton was excavated in the Petrified Forest National Park. Why was this find newsworthy?

○ Examine the latest data on *Amphipithecus*. Where does this fossil fit into the evolutionary pattern? Why?

Key to Symbols

•	average difficulty	◆	narrow down topic
§	substitutes possible	▲	large public or college
★	ample information in most		library required
	libraries	✔	local option topic
○	specialized knowledge	✕	examples and supporting
	required		evidence needed

Exploration and Discovery

See also: Travel

★ The routes of the Voyageurs. What did they discover?

● Richard Byrd's aerial exploration of the north and south poles

● Why have certain nations always taken the lead in exploration and discovery?

● The feat beyond belief: the first circumnavigation of Africa by the Phoenicians in 600 B.C.

➥ The findings and results of the Lewis and Clark expedition. How did it alter the course of western exploration and settlement?

● Explain: Columbus was one of the world's most successful failures.

➥ John Wesley Powell's Colorado River expeditions

● Early attempts to explore the poles

○ How the first explorers navigated

● Why did the era of New World discovery occur when it did? Why not earlier or later?

● The first attempts to find the source of the Nile. Were any successful?

★ Scurvy, the voyager's disease. Detail the effects, the causes, how it was discovered, and the eventual solution.

➥ The fur trader on the western frontier

● Viking explorations in America. Cite archeological evidence to support your statements.

● The incredible journey of Marco Polo. In what ways did he contribute new knowledge to the western world?

● The mariner's compass: its development and significance to voyage and discovery

● What were the primary problems encountered by the first explorers who attempted expeditions across Australia?

▲ Cold protection procedures on early Arctic and Antarctic explorations

● The earliest western travelers to Tibet

§ Living conditions aboard the ships of Christopher Columbus

● Although attempts to find the Northwest Passage proved to be futile, discuss some of the

164

more notable explorations and explorers. Focus on the significance of the discoveries made enroute.

- How the invention of the astrolabe affected subsequent exploration and trade
- How the development and widespread use of the printing press contributed to exploration and discovery
★ The "Silk Route." What initiatives led to its establishment in the first century? What were the principal trade factors?
✕ Common motives for exploration and colonization by France, Spain, and England in the fifteenth and sixteenth centuries. Use specific instances to illustrate this topic.
★ Compare the early English and Spanish explorers of the New World. Focus on their colonies and the societies they established.
- What were the contributing factors to the Age of Discovery?
- What were the results and prime contributions of the International Geophysical Year (1957–1958)?
- The later voyages of Christopher Columbus
★ Voyager II explorations

Listed are some of the world's most fascinating exploration ventures and discoveries. After selecting one, consider several of the following factors: What were the original goals, financing, and expectations? Before the discovery, what was the extent of knowledge about the area, and what were the myths and stories connected to it? What was the character and personality of the explorer and how did this influence the course of events? What were some of the details of the expedition? Who were the indigenous populations and how were they affected? Was there any controversy surrounding this event? What were the effects on trade, commerce, and colonization? How has man's knowledge been broadened and how has history been changed by this discovery? Be sure to include any relevant and useful maps and diagrams.

Sierra Leone (Hanno) c. 470 B.C.
Punjab, India (Alexander the Great) 327 B.C.
Indian Ocean (Nearchus) 325 B.C.
England (Julius Caesar) 55 B.C.
China (Suliman) 850 A.D.
Greenland (Eric the Red) 985

China (Marco Polo) c. 1272
Tibet (Odoric of Pordenone) c. 1325
Congo River, Africa (Diogo Cão) c. 1484
Cape of Good Hope (Barthelomeu Dias) 1487–1488
West Indies (Christopher Columbus) 1492
India (Cape voyage by Vasco da Gama) 1497–1498
Florida (Ponce de León) 1513
New Guinea (Jorge de Menezes) 1526
South American Coast (Sebastian Cabot) 1526–1530
Peru (Francesco Pizarro) 1532
St. Lawrence River (Jacques Cartier) 1534
Colorado River (Hernando de Alarcón) 1540
Mississippi River (Hernando de Soto) 1541
Maine Cost (Samuel de Champlain) 1604
Hudson Bay (Henry Hudson) 1610
Cape Horn (Wilem Cornelis Schouten) 1615
Baffin Bay (William Baffin) 1616
Tasmania (Abel J. Tasman) 1642
Lake Superior (Daniel Greysolon Duluth) 1678–1687
Alaska (Vitus Bering) 1741
Blue Nile (James Bruce) 1768–1773
South Pacific (James Cook) 1768–1779
Hawaiian Islands (James Cook) 1774–1779
Columbia River (Robert Gray) 1787–1793
Antarctica (Charles Wilkes) 1840
Zambesi River and Victoria Falls (David Livingston) 1851–1856
Lake Tanganyika (Richard Burton and John Speke) 1858
Greenland (Robert E. Peary) 1892
Antarctic (Ernest Shackleton) 1908–1916
North Pole (Robert E. Peary) 1909
South Pole (Roald Amundson) 1911
North Pole, under (Submarine *Nautilus*) 1958
Antarctic (Vivian Fuchs) 1957–1958
Space, first person (Yuri Gagarin) 1961
The moon, first person (Neil Armstrong) 1969

Family Life

See also: Adolescents; Aging; Children; Marriage; Personal Finance; Sex

✕ Describe the ways in which family structure and life styles are affected by social class.

● Black slave family life

● Strategies for the prevention of drug abuse by children

● How children view divorce

● Traditional strengths of African-American family life

○ Does violence run in families? Use authoritative data to support your answer.

★ How families can help disabled children lead normal lives

● The myth of the traditional American family

● Single-parent families: yesterday and today

● Fewer children equals more money: the wave of the future for families

● Adoption opportunities today

✕ Choices in childbirth procedures

▲ Parental attitudes toward children during the Middle Ages

✕ Factors contributing to the disintegration of the American family. Cite and compare the opinions of a variety of authorities.

➥ The year 2050: a projection

● How contested child custody affects children

● First-born children: How do they differ from those who are born later? What are the significant characteristics and the possible reasons for these variations?

● Identify the stereotypes of American family life that are generally portrayed on television. Compare these to actual data and analysis from social scientists.

★ How the parent–child relationship changes during the following periods: infancy, preschool, school-age, adolescence, and adulthood.

● How to deal with Alzheimers in the family

★ Define the ten most important parenting skills

● How children of working parents are adversely affected

✕ Variations in parenting styles as related to class differences

● How families can optimize their child's (children's) cognitive development

● Why sibling rivalry develops and how to cure it

★ How infants change their parents

167

➤ Changes in the American family structure since 1950

• Finances and the single-parent family. In what ways is the budget most affected? Cite successful budgetary practices.

• Sex-role changes in the American family

• Particular problems of the divorced father

✗ How we can prevent instances of elder abuse

• Changes in the traditional role of the father in American family life

• Working parents and the maintenance of family unity. What are some of the practices most likely to help this unity?

★ How to keep your family stress free

○ The extent of rental housing bias against families with children. How has this affected lower-income families? Include methods and practices that would alter and alleviate this situation.

• Since the advent of widespread birth control, the structure of the American family has altered. Examine these particular changes.

★ Describe how children are affected by parents who are alcoholics or drug abusers.

• Would an Equal Rights Amendment be a threat to family life?

• Positive aspects of multigenerational family units

§ Family life in Morocco

• Single parents face many complex problems. Compile a list of books and articles that could aid single parents.

• Infant-care leave should be nationally mandated. Support or refute this statement.

• Family councils: sharing the good and the bad

§ Attitudes toward children in China

• The emotional advantages of tight family structures

✗ Compare the way of life of an inner-city working-class family with that of the suburban middle-class family.

• Maternal employment and child development. Is there a strong relationship? If so, what are the factors?

• The foster parent program. What have been its most successful aspects?

★ Teenage suicide is often associated with family problems. Detail some of the findings from studies in this area.

○ Sociologists refer to the "dysfunctional family." Characterize such a family and justify your points with appropriate sociological data.

★ How much consumer debt should a family incur? Is there a percentage of income to use as a rule?

• How families prosper with two or more incomes. Detail the advantages and disadvantages of this arrangement.

• Why some couples choose to remain childless

★ What family factors may often account for substance abuse by teenage children?

§ The structure of the traditional <u>Japanese</u> family. Include details of mate selection, divorce, economics, and social characteristics of family members, the authority hierarchy, and the status of women.

● What are the particular problems usually encountered in the blending of families through remarriage? How are they best approached and solved?

● Factors influencing gender identity in children

● Theories of child abuse

× Improving speech communication in the family

● What are the costs of child rearing in our society? Include food, clothing, housing, education, etc.

● Legal rights of adoptees when searching for their birthparents

● Family life in ancient Greece and Rome: parallels and contradictions.

★ Books every parent should read

Key to Symbols

● **average difficulty**
§ **substitutes possible**
★ **ample information in most libraries**
○ **specialized knowledge required**

➥ **narrow down topic**
▲ **large public or college library required**
✔ **local option topic**
× **examples and supporting evidence needed**

Fashion

See also: Art; Customs, Traditions, and Folkways

- Dress and fashion as depicted in the Bayeux tapestry
- Helmets: for war and for show. Select a two- or three-century time-span.
▲ Byzantine influences in western dress, from the fifth through the tenth centuries
★ The design of early footwear
- Compare and contrast military costumes of Egypt, Greece, Rome, Persia, and Babylonia.
- Design and structure of early woven garments
- Clerical vestments through the ages
- Traditional dress and jewelry of India
× How class distinctions have traditionally influenced dress and fashion
▲ Costume in Kabuki theater
- The rise and fall of Paris couture
➤ The influence of *Women's Wear Daily* on American fashion and design
➤ Compare and contrast Italian and American designers. Select two from each country.

○ The rise of the boutique and its contribution to fashion
- How the mass production of textiles changed women's clothing design
- Who dictates fashion? Survey a number of authorities in the field and compare their conclusions.
× How the movies change fashion
- An evaluation of children's clothing (1875–1925) in the United States
★ The evolution of denim jeans
- How to be a successful designer
§ Costume in ancient Greece
★ Fashion merchandising as a career
- The properties of linen, polyester, wool, silk, and cotton textiles as garments
○ The "ethics" of fashion piracy
▲ Liturgical garb of the Renaissance
- Important men's accessories: 1890–1990
- Fashions of the "Belle Epoque" period
- Furs as fashion: Should they be banned?

170

↠ The economics of the ready-to-wear industry

● Advances in man-made fabrics. What are the products of the latest research and technology?

● Designing clothes for the theater: some general rules

↠ The social functions of costumes: historical aspects

✕ How the Crusades affected European costume and dress in the twelfth through fourteenth centuries

● The influence of Erté on French design

▲ Costume in early religious dramas. Discuss the symbolism of color, dress, insignia, etc.

● How the French Revolution altered dress in Europe

● Women's undergarments, 1700–1900

★ The clothing of war: ancient and modern

● Early perfumes and their uses

§ The contributions of Elsa Schiaparelli, Italian fashion designer (1890–1973)

● Male hairstyle fads and fashions, ancient and modern

● Military uniforms in the United States and how they have been modified and changed

★ Dress and manners in the court of Louis XIV

● Body coloring among early civilizations. Include materials and designs.

● The attire of Minoan ladies

● Plants and minerals used in early cosmetics

● The netsuke in traditional Japanese attire

▲ Styles and fashions at the court of the Dukes of Burgundy

● Fashions in the antebellum South

● Medical uniforms throughout history

● Basic pattern alteration techniques

★ Furs in dress: a historical overview

▲ American fashion as depicted in the lithographs of Currier and Ives

★ The influence of the American Indian on fashion

● The Chanel suit

● Clothing for the physically handicapped

Film

See also: Media; Photography; Theater

- ● The increase of violence in the movies. Examine the theories explaining this phenomenon.
- ▲ Compare Hollywood's treatment of World War II and the Vietnam War.
- ★ How Alfred Hitchcock achieved suspense
- ● The influence of *The Birth of A Nation* on filmmaking
- ➡ The Academy Awards: from 1927 to the present
- ● The unique appeal of Greta Garbo
- ● Hollywood and Native Americans
- § Common themes in movies of the 1940's
- ▲ The casting of Scarlett O'Hara in *Gone with the Wind*
- ● Describe the first motion picture studio
- ★ The role of the movie director
- ● The impact of Louis Lumière and his cinematography on early movie technology
- ● Why colorization of old movies should be discontinued
- ● The psychology of "disaster" movies. What is their audience appeal?
- ● Andy Warhol's underground films
- ▲ Advances in movie projectors
- ➡ Early movies: making pictures move
- ● The Keystone Cops comedies
- ● Hollywood as depicted in Nathanael West's novel, *The Day of the Locust*
- ● African Americans as depicted in American film from 1900 through World War II
- ● Social comment in movies during the Great Depression
- ● The appeal of Marilyn Monroe: a retrospective analysis
- ○ Documentary films before television
- ● *Star Wars* as a "space western"
- ★ Impact of the teenage market on the movie industry. How has it affected grosses? Quality?
- ● Elements of the Saturday serials, 1930–1940
- § Special effects in *Jurassic Park*
- ○ The French film industry today
- × Stereotypes in the western movie. Include a discussion of

characters, situations, and points of view.

- Compare the novel *The Godfather* (Mario Puzo) with the movie made from it.
- Compare the novel *The French Lieutenant's Woman* with the movie made from it.
§ The movies of <u>Francis Ford Coppola</u>
★ How the motion picture industry changed as a result of talking pictures
☛ Compare four or five critical reviews of a significant movie you have viewed. Do they agree?
- Woody Allen's comedic effects
○ Examine the economic dynamics of the modern movie studio
- Advances in animation techniques
▲ The development of the popular film in the United States in the 1930's: types and trends
- Religious symbolism in Ingmar Bergman's films
- Compare and contrast the facts about the life of T.E. Lawrence to the portrayal of him in the movie *Lawrence of Arabia*.
- Blacklisting in the motion picture industry during the McCarthy era
- The star system in Hollywood and how it operated. What were the effects of it on Hollywood films?
- Film formats and how they affect the final product

- Expressionism in the early movie *The Cabinet of Dr. Caligari*
- The lavish spectacles of Busby Berkeley
- Characteristics of Edith Head's movie costuming
○ Federico Fellini's influence on film technique
- Innovative techniques used in *Citizen Kane* and their effect on later films
★ Why Charlie Chaplin was funny
✕ Compare and contrast remakes of movies (*King Kong, A Star is Born*, etc.) with the originals.
- Compare Joseph Conrad's novel *Heart of Darkness* and the film *Apocalypse Now*
- Compare and contrast the comedic effect of *Animal Crackers* (the Marx brothers) to *Animal House*
▲ The German propaganda films of Leni Riefenstahl
- Humphrey Bogart: the image of a tough hero
- Can the local movie theater survive?
▲ The economics of film distribution in the United States
- The humor of W.C. Fields
★ James Dean as a cult figure
§ The filming of <u>2001: A Space Odyssey</u>
- The lasting appeal of John Wayne and his contemporary prototypes
- A retrospective view of censorship and the motion pictures

- The underground film. Describe typical examples, their quality, content, and contributions to the art.
- From 1975 to 1985 women were featured in several important films. Discuss the roles, themes, and attitudes expressed in several of these films.
- Analyze the social comment in the movie version of *The Grapes of Wrath*.
- Compare the movie and play *The Elephant Man* with the real life of John Merrick.
- Select a film genre (private-eye, western, horror, spy, war, science fiction, etc.) and examine its cyclical variations over a selected time span.
- Film editing: techniques and tricks
- Profile the cowboy stereotype of western films.
○ Elements of the "new wave" in filmmaking, 1959–1975
§ Discuss the role of the police-man in American film. How is he portrayed and what social value does he represent? Is there more than one image?
○ Defend or refute: The "auteur" theory of cinema is better suited to the European filmmaker than to the Hollywood filmmaker.
- Screenwriting techniques
- Thomas Edison's vitascope
★ Making home movies
- The French cinema as an art form
× Special effects and the "disaster" movies
- The magic films of George Méliés (1900's)
▲ The effects on foreign cultures of exported American movies
- How the successful new techniques of *The Great Train Robbery* (1903) influenced early moviemaking
- The optimistic world of Frank Capra
- The prophetic elements of Stanley Kubrick's *A Clockwork Orange*
- Compare the film version of *M*A*S*H* to the television series.
- Luke as a Christ figure in *Cool Hand Luke*
- Character development of politician McKay in *The Candidate*
▲ The relationship of *High Noon* to the McCarthy blacklistings
- The star system of the 1930's and 1940's and how it worked
★ The most expensive film ever produced and why
- Which movies made the most money? Do the experts agree on why?
★ The visionary films of Werner Herzog: What price vision?
- Select a trend in the film industry and evaluate its offerings, past and present. Compare their quality, popularity, critical, and popular receptions.

- Censorship in the movies: self-regulation or governmental intervention?
- Select a movie genre and describe its characteristics, forms, style, and contents. Discuss any variants. (Select, for example, a western, war, disaster, or satanic possession type of movie.)
- Characterize the contemporary movie audience. How has it changed from the movie audience in 1930 and in 1945?

Key to Symbols

- • average difficulty
- § substitutes possible
- ★ ample information in most libraries
- ○ specialized knowledge required

- ◆ narrow down topic
- ▲ large public or college library required
- ↙ local option topic
- ✗ examples and supporting evidence needed

Food and Drink

See also: Health; Nutrition

- Making cheese at home
- § Beer and wine in ancient <u>Egypt</u>
- The folklore of tea customs
- § Myths about <u>apples</u>
- "Nobody advertises asparagus" or how advertising affects what we eat
- How to make your own wine
- ★ Dried foods: how to prepare and use them
- ▲ The wine industry's conquest of the aphid phylloxera
- ○ Recent developments in the California wine industry
- Myths and folklore of wine
- ▲ The first cookbook (Marcus Gavius Apicius, Roman gourmet, Fl. 14–37 A.D.)
- ★ The ancient olive: its origin, uses, and myths
- Early archeological evidence of the culture of fruits and vegetables
- Food for the diabetic
- ▲ Early English cookbooks, including that written by Alexander Neckham (1157–1215). In what ways did they reflect society?
- A comparison of commercial and homemade baby food.

Consider nutritive contents, convenience, additives and appearance.
- ★ Early methods of breadmaking
- ○ Compare and contrast the essentials of classic Chinese and French cooking.
- Foods of the Old Testament
- ★ Consider the various advantages of the convection, microwave, and conventional ovens. What are the principles of operation of each? How do foods cooked in them vary for each type?
- The spice trade and its particular effects on the cuisines of Western Europe
- Cooking with solar energy
- How to plant and maintain a garden of cooking herbs
- Indigenous foods of the New World
- Institutional food: How could it be improved?
- Are fast foods synonymous with junk food? Evaluate them from a nutritional point of view.
- The widespread mechanization of food production has affected food quality. Review some of

these changes, both pro and con.

× Food fads in the twentieth century

• Causes and consequences of the Irish potato famine

• Frozen foods and their effects on American eating habits

§ Gastronomy in Ancient <u>Rome</u>

• The basis of religious dietary restrictions

★ How to cut your food bill and still eat well

▲ Current trends in food service systems

• Early methods of food preservation

• Kitchen efficiency

○ The modern methods for control of food-borne diseases

• The first food additives and how they were used

• The origin of condiments

• Early attempts at federal regulation of the food industry

• Food in the year 2000

★ How salt has affected history

× Examine the many food myths, particularly those ascribing specific and miraculous powers to certain foods.

• Bioengineering and food: what's ahead

• Bread around the world

• How religion has altered the foods that humans eat

▲ Problems in frozen food packaging

• What constitutes a balanced diet? Who decides?

• "You are what you eat." Discuss the varied implications of this statement.

✔ Edible wild foods in your area

• Yogurt benefits: fact and fiction

• The religious basis of vegetarianism

§ The most valued and appreciated foods of _____. (Select a country, preferably non-European.)

• The diet of the astronauts. What were the problems and how were they surmounted?

• Flesh-eating taboos

• The origin and evolution of table manners

▲ How to start and manage a food co-op

• Food additives. Examine those which have caused the most controversy. Present the evidence and discuss the current status of each.

• How to use chemistry in cooking

• The knife, fork, and spoon: the development of eating utensils

× How safe are our foods?

Foreign Policy

See also: Government; World Scene

- Describe President Truman's policy of "containment." How did the following implement this national policy: the Truman Doctrine; the Marshall Plan; the Berlin airlift; and the Point Four program?
- ○ Compare reconstruction policies of the United States in Japan and in Germany after World War II.
- The American image abroad: a composite of characteristics
- How did the Soviet Union's foreign policy change after the death of Stalin?
- ★ "Big stick" diplomacy during Theodore Roosevelt's presidency
- × How internal economic conditions determine foreign policy. Use instances from United States history to support your thesis.
- What were the general trends in American foreign policy in the early 1930's?
- ➤ What were the major goals behind the United States expansion attempts toward Cuba, Panama, Nicaragua, Hawaii,

and Mexico? Select one area and one time period.
- "The more we indulge in uncritical reverences for the supposed wisdom of the American way of life, the more odious we make it in the eyes of the world, and the more we destroy our moral authority . . ." (Reinhold Niebuhr.) Refute or defend this statement.
- ★ Puerto Rico: A new state or a colonial dependency?
- Should the United States change its current Cuban policy? In what ways have relations between these two countries altered in the last ten years? What factors were influential?
- The cold war. What were its origins? In what ways have conditions and attitudes changed since that time? Why?
- ➤ American foreign policy in the South Pacific since World War II
- ▲ How nuclear superiority affects American foreign policy
- Do historians agree on the American response to the Cuban

missile crisis?

- United States' China policy since Mao
- Henry Kissinger's diplomacy. Was it unique? Effective? Why or why not?
- Discuss the pros and cons of several examples of United States intervention in South American political systems.
- Critical issues affecting United States aid to underdeveloped countries
- United States relations with Taiwan. What have been the major issues affecting policy? How do current policies conflict with the United States' China policy?
- Current relations between the United States and Saudi Arabia
- Defend or refute: The United States must share a large part of the responsibility for the fall of the Shah of Iran.
- "Gunboat" diplomacy
- The foreign policy of the current administration
- How global arms sales affect American foreign policy
- Critical issues in Korean–American relations
- American foreign policy and the issue of human rights
- Who determines United States foreign policy, the president or congress?
- The costs to the taxpayer of American arms exports and trade

- Would it be the best interests of the United States to return to its nineteenth-century isolationism stance? Would it be possible?
- Refugees and United States policy. Focus on either the historical or contemporary aspects of this issue.
- Defend or refute: There was no moral or legal justification for the intervention of the United States in Vietnam.
- How America's geographic position has influenced foreign policy
- American/Asian foreign policy, 1950–present
- Aspects of American isolationism in the 1930's
- Examine the relationship (or lack of one) between public sentiment and America's foreign policy.
- What should govern American diplomacy: Expediency or principles?
- Compare and contrast the foreign policy of the last three secretaries of state.
- Levels of United States economic aid to underdeveloped countries: an overview
- What is the current United States policy toward hostage situations? Compare it to that of other Western European nations.
- United States-Canadian rela-

tions, 1940 to date
- Current United States-China trade relations. What is the official policy?
- Historians' review of American military policy in Vietnam
§ The foreign policy of President Richard Nixon
- What was accomplished in the SALT I and II talks?
- The American military presence in Europe
- How has American support of Israel affected United States relations with Arab countries?
★ Is a nuclear test ban realistic?
- OPEC (Organization of Petroleum Exporting Countries) and the coming energy crunch. What should be the United States' response?
- United States-Israeli relations: A status report
○ Can America continue its policy as defender of the Western world? Justify your answer by citing experts from several subject areas.
- Mexico: Potential ally or second-rate neighbor? Discuss the prospects for future relations with the United States.
- What is the relationship between American foreign policy and dwindling world oil supplies?

- Examine American military and economic support of Batista in Cuba and Trujillo in the Dominican Republic in light of the United States' democratic stance.
- Soviet aggression and American policy objectives, 1970–1988
★ Compare and contrast both the military and economic significance of the Panama Canal and Suez Canal to the United States.
- The strategic value of the United States' Pacific possessions and territories. Select several.
○ Why strategic arms limitations have not worked
- Should the United States sell *any* armaments abroad?
- Can American economic aid help emerging nations develop? What types of assistance have proved most successful?
- What are the relevant issues in the diplomatic conflicts between the United States and Mexico since 1975?
★ America and the Philippines: a changing role
- Some would suggest the United States is now a second-rate nation. How has this view affected our foreign policy?

- When and why American foreign policy has supported dictatorships
○ Complexities of American foreign policy in the Middle East
- The role of the Council on Foreign Relations in United States foreign policy
- How does United States foreign policy change as new weapons are developed?
▲ Should morality, idealism, or national interest monitor foreign policy? Each of these stances has been supported by significant critics of America's foreign affairs. Present the case for one using these opinions.
○ The relationship between American ability to protect critical interests abroad and the American public's disinclination to intervene militarily in Third World conflicts. Consider the opinions of a selection of experts in both foreign affairs and in international business.
- American foreign policy as a reflection of United States dependence on critical mineral imports
- Highlights and trends in American foreign policy between World War I and World War II, 1920–1942

- The "balance of power" is often used in reference to the United States' foreign policy. Define this term using historical and contemporary examples.
- What are the implications of Africa's development for United States foreign policy?
× Current controversies surrounding United States foreign aid programs
- What should be the United States' goals for a Middle Eastern foreign policy? Why?
★ What has been the impact of modern communication on the conduct of foreign affairs?
- Declining influence of United States power in Africa and the Middle East since 1960. To what factors do experts attribute this reversal?
○ Should American investments abroad be protected by tax-supported military units in times of unrest and conflict?
- What are the goals of the Caribbean Basin Institute? What is the level of United States involvement?
- Examine the proposed policies for the United States and other nations in their fight to control the AIDS epidemic.

★ What has been the aftermath of the Bhopal, India (1984) chemical leak?

● How the *Achille Lauro* hijacking could have been avoided

O Many experts consider the current conflict in the Middle East a no-win situation. Compare these opinions.

➦ Our new relationship with the former Soviet Union

★ President Carter and the Panama Canal

➦ Should the United States support the emerging democracies of Eastern Europe with massive funding?

O What are the free market policies now in effect? Discuss their usefulness and benefits.

▲ Examine China's policy changes since the Tienanmen Square uprising.

● Should the United States assume a larger role in alleviating world famine?

● What effects — cultural, fiscal, and political — have been seen since Hong Kong reverted to being a Chinese territory?

● Should the United States have intervened in Bosnia? Why or why not?

● United States relations with Iraq: what have been the major issues affecting our policy? Should it change?

Key to Symbols

●	average difficulty	➦	narrow down topic
§	substitutes possible	▲	large public or college library required
★	ample information in most libraries	✔	local option topic
O	specialized knowledge required	×	examples and supporting evidence

The Future

See also: American Scene; Contemporary Issues; Social Problems; World Scene

- The possibilities for a world population decline. What factors might bring this about?
- Organ transplants: Increase or decrease?
★ Defend or refute: Progress will be the downfall of mankind.
○ The prospects for world-wide democracy and for communism in the year 2000. Base your projections on the opinion of informed experts and current political trends.
- New sources of protein
- Steps necessary to provide an adequate food supply for the next century
- Support or refute: The earth is doomed.
- The cost of illness in the future
○ Tomorrow's new medical techniques
✕ The political and economic effects of a climate change on earth
- What are the possibilities for electrical power when the oil supply runs out?
▲ Science looks at the possibility of a man-made disruption of the human genetic code
- Automation tomorrow
- Compare the projections expressed in *The Third Wave* and *Future Shock* (Alvin Toffler) with those in *An Inquiry into the Human Prospect* (Robert L. Heilbroner).
- Is the United States headed for an energy disaster?
★ The kitchen of the future
- Synthetic fuels in the twenty-first century
○ Funding for space research: Necessary or extravagant?
- Prospects for breeding nearly extinct animals in captivity
▲ "Smart" weapons and our military future
- The multifamily house as a possible resolution of the housing shortage
★ Projected uses of artificial satellites
★ The home of tomorrow
- The possibilities for widescale chemical warfare
- Moon stations soon?

- Ground transportation possibilities
○ The potential for genetically engineered growth of new body organs
• Refute or substantiate: "By 2050 the world will consist of two cultures: the permanently poor and the permanently rich."
• Defend: Our world cannot survive the loss of "wild" species of plants and animals.
× Potential energy sources
★ What will be the effects of worldwide overpopulation on the environment?
★ The future prospects for Social Security
• World War III: What could it be like? What is the consensus of informed scientific and military opinion? Do they agree?
• Microcomputers in twenty years
• What is the consensus (if there is one) among authorities relative to Russia's next twenty years?
★ Future of the electric automobile
▲ The possibilities for noncarbon-based life
- The year 2050: a projection. Select one subject and explore in depth the possibilities and implications.
• Life after a nuclear war
• Will the book survive?
• The automobile of the future
• Air transport in thirty years
• Cities of the future: Paradises

or prisons?
★ Overpopulation will affect everyone: How and where?
• The long-range effects of worldwide economic expansion
- Study past forecasts and projections to see which, if any, were accurate.
• Sex roles in the twenty-first century
• Defend or refute: Starvation seems to be the ultimate fate of the human race.
○ Prospects for the United States economy: Growth or stagnation?
• The future of the South Pole (Antarctica)
▲ The possibilities and probabilities of space contamination
• Some experts believe future wars will be fought in space. Is there evidence to support this theory? Are preventative measures possible?
• Genetic engineering: Technology of the future?
- Possible innovations and advances in biomedical engineering
• Robots: the thinking machines of tomorrow
▲ Sociopolitical aspects of Latin America in the next century: trends and perspectives
• The sexual revolution and some of the most significant speculations on its long-range effects on American society
§ Alaska's future development.

What are the potentials and what are the restraints?

- Are resource depletion and pollution of the environment an inevitable and ultimate consequence of America's contemporary life patterns? Survey a variety of authorities and compare opinions.
- Identify and discuss the fundamental problems which will affect urban centers in the next four decades.
▲ The tropical plant Leucoena as a source of food, fertilizer, fuel, paper, and timber. What are the possibilities?
- Is a men's liberation movement likely? What would the issues be?
★ What will be the possible results of the destruction of the earth's stratosphere on the earth and life on it?
O Seafood "greenhouses"?
O Why not energy from the tides?
➡ Information-Age democracy and the changes our country will face
- What are the possibilities of a medical technology which permits parents to select the genetic characteristics of their unborn children? What would be the impact of this process should it become widespread?
- Can humankind be improved through the use of genetic controls? What are some of the possibly dangerous consequences?

- The future course of human evolution. Cite a variety of scientific theories and the supporting evidence for each.
- Extinct species projections for the year 2100 (include man)
- Will Americans continue to be affluent? What factors will precipitate any changes?
- The windships of an energy-poor world
★ Hospitals of tomorrow
★ Arab oil reserves How much is there? How long will it last? What then?
- How to accurately forecast the future. Discuss a particular area of science or the social sciences.
- The future of the videodisk
O Projection for nuclear power in the new century. Include environmental factors.
- The family unit in the next century
O How the space age will affect concepts of private and national property
- Projected uses of the moon
➡ What will be the future impact of the "revolution of rising expectations"?
- Multinational conglomerates in the coming century
- Will birth control technologies ever be universally accepted?

- The multimedia revolution in education
- Is there a "limited nuclear war" in America's future?
○ Possibilities for the electrical control of pain. Include the feasibility of an electronic anesthetic.
- Home services that are possibilities through cable systems
➤ What will be the social effects of the environmental crisis?
- The future of the videotext in United States homes
- Contemporary apocalyptic literature
- How our lifestyles will be affected in the event of a long-lasting energy shortage
➤ How will the United States' vast medical system be funded in the next decades? Will there be a decrease in the quality of health care? How will the consumer be affected?
★ The projections for the disease AIDS (Acquired Immune Deficiency Syndrome) and its widening threat to the public
- Can acts of international terrorism be forecast? How?
★ Tomorrow at Chernobyl (Ukraine)
- Describe the concept of the "nuclear winter"

Key to Symbols

●	average difficulty	➤	narrow down topic
§	substitutes possible	▲	large public or college library required
★	ample information in most libraries	✔	local option topic
○	specialized knowledge required	×	examples and supporting evidence

Gardening

See also: Agriculture

▲ Advances in rare plant conservation
▲ The French Intensive Method for home gardens
★ Organic versus chemical fertilizers for the small garden plot
● The tools and technology of primitive agriculture
● How community gardens are organized and run in various sections of the United States
● The maintenance of the home greenhouse. Discuss the variety of crops that can be successfully grown.
● What is organic gardening?
● How to build a greenhouse. There are many patterns available. Decide which is best for your needs and locality.
★ Natural soil enrichment methods for the home garden
● Principles of hydroponic gardening. Include both the commercial and small-garden applications of this process.
● The nature and philosophy of the Japanese formal garden
☛ Plant propagation techniques

☛ Landscaping your own yard. Select a particular locale and discuss soil, climate, space, annuals versus perennials, appropriate plants, etc.
● Vegetable gardening in arid climates
● The classic English flower garden
§ The _____ in legend and mythology. Select a flower.
● Design a garden/yard with minimal water requirements.
● Design a vegetable garden to feed a family of four.
● What is the philosophy behind composting? How to construct a compost pile and maintain it for maximum efficiency and minimal effort.
● What is biodynamic agriculture?
▲ The story behind the development of the Findhorn gardens
● Companion planting: its development and uses
○ The effects of chemical fertilizers on soil composition
● Planting by the phases of the moon and other early horticul-

ture rules. Are they myths or reality?

- The purpose and development of hybrid plants
- Natural methods of pest control in gardens
- The joys of home gardening. Many have written articles and books on this subject. Select a number of them and compare and contrast them. You may also wish to include your own opinions.
- The aesthetic components of landscape design
- The gardens of Versailles
- Italian gardens in the Middle Ages
- The traditional uses of structures and buildings in designed landscapes
- Gardens of antiquity: their arrangement, components, and functions
★ How to make and use organic composts
- The English influence on European gardens
- The classical Chinese garden. What are its characteristic features? When did it originate?

What are the philosophical guidelines?
§ Kew Gardens, England (or, select another noteworthy botanical garden)
▲ Compare and contrast the Japanese abstract and tea gardens with the classic Chinese garden.
➥ The use of medicinal herbs throughout history
- The reconstructed gardens of Williamsburg, Virginia
✔ Design a small rock garden suitable for your area
- Mechanical aids for the home gardener. What are the latest innovations?
- Plan a scent garden. Include both flowers and plants and include in the design access facilities for a blind person.
- The herbs of American colonial gardens
- Flowers and herbs of the Bible
- Integrating man-made materials into the natural garden
- Safe methods of controlling garden pests
- How Central Park (New York City) was designed and constructed

Gender Issues

See also: Family Life; Marriage; Sex; Women

- Gender stereotyping in the movie western
- Puberty rites in primitive societies. Select several.
- Survey the advertising in several magazines and analyze how it is gender related. Try gender-specific magazines for the most interesting results.
- ★ Are friendships between men different from those between women?
- Pushing children into unisex behavior is stressful and detrimental to their sense of identity. Discuss.
- § Sex roles in the Roman world
- The "glass ceiling" and how it operates for women
- Are single men (women) happier, on the whole, than those married? Is age a factor?
- ★ How gender roles are assigned to children
- Examine the most significant factors in female/male relationships. Do they tend to change over time?
- ★ Anita Hill accused Clarence Thomas, Supreme Court nominee, of sexual harassment. Review both sides of this case.
- Women are and always have been the weaker sex. Defend or refute this statement.
- ✕ Describe the benefits and the disadvantages of male/female roles in society.
- ✕ What constitutes gender-slanted language?
- Gender, affirmative action, and the workplace
- Gender identity and the one-parent family
- Sexual harassment on the job. Describe ideal guidelines.
- Is there really such a phenomenon as male menopause?
- ✕ Sexism on television
- ★ Causes of spousal abuse. Examine current opinions and findings from experts on this subject.
- § Is there a gender bias in professional tennis?
- Is medical care for women different from that given to men?
- ✕ Analyze the advertising for nationally broadcast professional football games in terms of gender. Describe at least ten different ads.
- Do women still need an Equal Rights Amendment?

189

- Sex differences and the learning curve
- PCism. Has political correctness gone too far? Is it really necessary?
- Men and women really are different. Evaluate this statement in light of scientific evidence.
- "Babes in the fox holes." Examine this attitude in the military and elsewhere.
- Why are gender-role changes occurring more rapidly for women than for men? What are the patterns of these changes? When and where are the shifts occurring?
- The Catholic Church has often been criticized for its lack of female clergy. Examine the stance of the Church in today's liberated society.
★ How men can be good "mothers."
○ It has been suggested that most sexual harassment lawsuits have been exaggerated and baseless. True?

Key to Symbols

•	average difficulty	☛	narrow down topic
§	substitutes possible	▲	large public or college library required
★	ample information in most libraries	✔	local option topic
○	specialized knowledge required	x	examples and supporting evidence needed

Genetics and Heredity

See also: Bioethics; Biology; Evolution

○ How does DNA replicate itself?
● Albinism in animals
● Is fetal diagnosis and selective abortion a form of genetic engineering?
○ The genetic bases of aging
★ The peas of Gregor Mendel and what they proved
▲ Current regulations governing genetic alteration experimentation. What is their range? Are they adequate?
○ The white marigold and other hybrids
● Detail the adaptive value of having genetic material packaged in chromosomes
★ Regulation and control of the pharmaceutical industry and recombinant DNA experimentation. What are the possible risks and benefits?
● The genetic factors that cause color blindness
● Select a "genetic" disease and discuss its origin, incidence, control, and effects. Some examples are sickle cell anemia, PKU, Huntington's chorea, and Down's syndrome.

○ Cloning: the scientific advances
● Who owns life? Scientists? Individuals? Society?
● The evolution of genes
● DDT and genetic change
✕ Genetic vulnerability and world food production
➦ The relationship between natural selection and modern genetics
● How much of our behavior is caused by our genes? Cite the major scientific theories and supporting evidence.
✕ How has geographic location affected the genetic structure of different peoples?
▲ Does modern genetic research offer a new chance for a "green revolution"?
▲ Frontiers of genetic research with animals. What is the current state of the art?
○ The economics of the biotechnology industry
○ Industrial applications of genetic research. While this technology is not yet very advanced, what are some of the possibilities, such as oil recovery techniques?
● Instances of naturally occurring

genetic engineering
○ The development of gene splicing
○ Recombinant DNA and the treatment of genetic diseases. What progress has been made in this area?
● The impact of "big money" on recombinant research
★ How the debate among scientists over recombinant DNA safety factors and guidelines changed
● Human genetic engineering: An evolutionary tightrope?
● The advantages of genetic counseling
★ Interferon: Cancer cure or industry hype?
▲ Detail the controversy surrounding Dr. Martin Cline (UCLA) and his use of human subjects for recombinant DNA disease experimentation.
● Japan's giant vegetables
● What are the ethical and economic considerations involved in the following statement: Many geneticists and other scientists in applied areas are involved both with federally and state funded research projects and with the new and highly competitive biotechnology industry.
§ How hemophilia is transmitted
● Ageing and genetics. Survey the newest research.
▲ Our first genetically engineered whole food: the Flavr Savr to-

mato. Chart its progress to the marketplace.
● Apes, man, and genetic patterns
● The mutagenic effects of ionizing radiation
○ How are human mutation rates calculated?
● Some important genetic implications of family planning
● The relationship of DNA to genotypes and phenotypes
▲ Advances in reproductive biology and the applications to livestock production
● What are the possible consequences of using genetically engineered micro-organisms?
× Compare the nature of parallel and convergent evolution. Use significant examples to illustrate these processes.
● What processes affect the gene frequencies of human populations? How do they operate?
○ While gene splicing promises many remarkable breakthroughs, it also has many detractors? Why?
▲ Gene therapy for hereditary disorders: the state of the art
● How current research is aiding the early identification of genetic disorders
▲ Compare the current roles of the government, the universities and the private sector in the development of biotechnology.

☛ Major areas of impact for applied genetics

▲ Scientists are considering genetically altering the coca plant so it will no longer produce cocaine. Detail the ramifications of this proposal.

● Do we all have a fat-regulating gene?

× Designer genes and how we will use them

O The new science of chronogenetics

× Genetically remodeled animals. Describe some recent examples.

● Scientists have recently analyzed DNA extracted from Neanderthal skeletal remains. What did they find?

O Are chimeras, animals customized with genes from different species, a feasible possibility for the future?

● Recent research has enabled geneticists to predict individuals at risk for certain diseases such as breast cancer, Alzheimer's, or Huntington's disease. Should everyone be tested?

★ Scottish geneticists have cloned a sheep, Dolly. Discuss the significance.

● Who supervises biotechnology?

● Has genetic engineering become too commercial? Is there a middle ground or controlling factor?

Key to Symbols

● average difficulty
§ substitutes possible
★ ample information in most libraries
O specialized knowledge required

☛ narrow down topic
▲ large public or college library required
✔ local option topic
× examples and supporting evidence

Geography

See also: Environment; Geology; Population; World Scene

- Unexplored areas of the earth. Select one and present an in-depth study of what is known, what isn't, and what attempts have been made to find out.
- Knowledge of the world in 1500 B.C., 300 B.C., 700 A.D., and 1400 A.D.
▲ The techniques of topographic mapping
- Ancient trade routes
§ Mineral resources of the Ukraine
- The St. Lawrence Seaway and the Canadian economy. Focus on their past and present inter-relationships.
§ Mobility patterns of African Americans in the United States since 1900. (Or, select another ethnic group.) Explain the social, economic, and political factors that influenced these trends.
- Is the earth becoming warmer? Cooler? What is the evidence supporting each?
- China's natural resource potential
- American population levels, past, present, and future. Discuss what experts think would be the optimum population level.
§ The tactical importance of the Suez Canal
- Strip-mining reclamation
§ Effects of deforestation in Brazil
- Discuss the thesis that diffusion of cultural traits has played the principal part in the differentiation of mankind.
- Commercial development in the Amazon Basin
✔ Describe your city in the year 1900 and chart its evolution to the present day.
- Compare and explain the major changes made in the last two United States' censuses.
§ Agricultural products of the state of _____
- Distribution of continental coal fields in the United States
§ Resources of Kuwait (or select another Persian Gulf state)
- What is the degree of the United States' reliance on foreign resources? Describe the amounts and types.
★ Alaskan economic development

194

since 1900

§ Effects of overpopulation on Malaysia (or select a similarly underdeveloped country). Select one country and concentrate on the details of the problem.

● Avalanches: causes, effects, and preventative measures

● Significance of the world grain situation today — and tomorrow

★ Volcanism in the Pacific Northwest

● Logging practices in the United States

● What have been the major problems encountered in the racial classification of mankind?

● The impact of the Pan American highway

★ Potentially destructive forces of the San Andreas Fault (California)

§ Storm patterns in the midwestern United States

● Alaskan oil and what it means to the United States' economy

● Energy consumption in the United States from 1960 to date: a comparison

▲ Early surveying methods in the United States

✕ Instances of ethnic isolation in the United States

● Hurricane patterns on the Atlantic seacoast of the United States

✔ Past population growth rates in your community. What are the projections for the future?

§ Landscape features of Brazil

➤ Map reading and navigation

● Compare and explain levels and the types of agricultural production in the United States in 1890 and in 1990.

● Compare and contrast the native forest of the east and west coasts of the United States.

○ The final results of the Geophysical Year (1957–1958). What has been the significance of the major discoveries and findings?

★ Compare the character of the earth's surface, climate, and vegetation at the North and South Poles.

● Ancient ideas about the earth

● The earth of Ptolemy (second century)

✕ What place names reveal about landscape, environment, history, and culture

● Roman cartography

○ Investigate the truths and myths about the earth in Masudi's Meadows of Gold (950 A.D.).

✔ Discuss and illustrate the varieties of land use in your state (forest, agriculture, urban, etc.).

★ Early trade on the Mississippi River

▲ Continental drift and animal extinction: new theories

✔ Investigate the mineral resources of your state.

● The Alaskan gold rush

● Gold and silver mining in the

United States today
- The economics of oil shale recovery
- Topsoil depletion in the American West: a survey
- Current immigration issues and their possible solutions
- The exploration of Antarctica. Is exploitation next?

★ Growth of the Sun Belt
- Analyze the distribution patterns of Asians in America. What socioeconomic factors in history influenced these patterns?

▲ Birth defects: demographic implications
- Population trends in the United States
- Geographical horizons in the Middle Ages

★ What are some of the relationships between the distribution of language and landforms?
- What was on the first globe of the earth?

▲ The uses of aerial photography in geography and cartography
- Compare and contrast the climate, terrain, and vegetation of the four major American deserts.
- Modern mapmaking methods

× The interrelationship of environment, energy, population, and natural resources in the world. Use one example to illustrate in detail these connections.

☛ Twentieth-century technology and the third world

○ Prehistoric man's effects on the vegetation of northern Europe. Discuss this topic in terms of recent pollen analysis findings.

★ The impact of the transCanadian pipeline on the environment
- Chinook winds, Santa Ana winds, and tornadoes
- The advantages and disadvantages of alternative energy sources
- What are the cultural and economic characteristics of rich nations? Compare to those of poor nations.

○ What broad regional distinctions can be drawn from examination of world patterns of nutritional deficiencies and infectious diseases?

× Native American reservations and cultural isolation
- Remote sensing
- Problems of agricultural development in arid lands
- How has the alteration of natural drainage affected the groundwater system in southern Florida?

★ Irrigation practices from ancient times to the present day
- Water law: arid lands versus humid lands (a priori versus riparian)
- The pros and cons of multiple-use dams
- What has been the effect of landforms on the westward movement? Include railroad

routes, cities, wagon trains, pony express, etc.

• The early cartographers. Select an area of the world and trace its cartographic history.

• The impact of the Quebec separatist movement

• Commercial fishing areas of the United States

• The whaling industry today

• China: A new superpower?

• Global demographic patterns. What changes have taken place in this century?

• Strategic waterways of the world

• Deforestation versus reforestation. Who's winning?

• The impact of populations on tropical soils

★ Levels of urban encroachment on agricultural lands in the United States. Focus on the long-range projections and consequences.

§ The aluminum industry in the United States

★ How will the "Sagebrush Rebellion" affect public lands?

• What have been the most important achievements and contributions of the conservation movement in the United States?

• Examine poverty in the United States in relation to sex, age, family status, and education. Explain the relationships.

• Israel has almost none of the natural resources necessary to industrial development. How has it overcome this obstacle?

▲ The Vinland map forgery. How was it devised? How was the hoax discovered?

• Both New Zealand and Australia have high standards of living. How has this been achieved? Is its continuance probable?

○ Fractals — irregular geometric shapes — are being used as mathematical models for patterns in nature. How are the applications made and used?

• The gap between rich and poor nations is widening. What are future projections, possibilities, and consequences?

▲ Irrigation in the Tigris-Euphrates lowlands: a historical overview and projection for tomorrow

• What are the United States' most vital resource dependencies other than oil? Focus on the sources, supplies, demands, and political ramifications.

• How floods affect the landscape. Use recent catastrophes as examples.

✔ Coastline changes in your area (if applicable)

• What are the major differences between the agricultural economies of northern and southern Europe?

★ What are the geographic dimensions of poverty in the United States? Why?

- What are the most significant economic links between the United States and Canada?
- What have been the fundamental changes in American agriculture since 1950?
- A historical survey of drought in the United States. Describe its scope, causes, and consequences.
- Compare the agricultural resources of Canada, Mexico, and the United States
- ➤ What are the demographics of industrial development in the United States? What factors influenced these patterns?
- Who owns Antarctica?
- ★ The Bering strait: a bridge to the New World
- The English channel as a geographical barrier. How has history been altered by its location and characteristics?

Key to Symbols

•	average difficulty	➤	narrow down topic
§	substitutes possible	▲	large public or college library required
★	ample information in most libraries	↙	local option topic
○	specialized knowledge required	×	examples and supporting evidence needed

Geology

See also: Environment; Geography

- Compare and contrast absolute dating and relative dating.
○ Explain the concept of relative dating. How are fossils and superimposition used in this system?
§ Account for the formation of the Rocky Mountains.
- The geology of thermal energy
← Changes in the ocean floor
§ How the Great Lakes were formed
- The inner layers of the earth. What have been some of the most recent additions to knowledge in this field?
- The physical properties of lunar rocks
★ Why is fresh water a finite resource?
▲ The volcanic actions of ancient Thira (Santorini, Greece). What were the effects on the island's configurations and on its inhabitants?
- Kilauea: Hawaii's major active volcano. Discuss its form and structure, recent and past eruptions, damage to the local area, current status, etc.

- What geologists learn from boreholes. Focus on Project Mohole.
§ The geology of Algeria
- How can the effects of acid rain be reduced?
← Famous gems
§ Commercial minerals of Alaska
§ Geology of the Himalayas. Or, select another mountain range.
- The earth's crust, its composition and variations
○ How the size and weight of the earth is measured
- How soils are classified
§ The geology of Carlsbad Caverns
▲ Geological findings from the Laser Geodynamic Satellite
- Effects of the ice ages on land conformations
★ Geologic past of the Sahara Desert
- Earthquakes in China
§ Major geologic features of Great Britain
- Petroleum resources in the arctic regions
- The San Andreas Fault. How has it recently changed or sug-

gested to scientists that major shifts were imminent?

★ What is the Richter scale and how does it measure earth activity?

● The anatomy of Mount St. Helens' eruptions

○ Advances in earthquake prediction

● Mount St. Helens: What next? Some projections for the future.

● Chinese jade

§ Mineral treasures of Australia

● What activities of man tend to promote the expansion of the world's deserts? What has been the rate of their increase? In what areas is this degradation reaching critical levels?

★ How glaciers move

● The development of Cape Cod as a case study of coastal processes

● Describe the relationship between plate motion and volcanic activity.

○ How the ocean floor is charted. What research equipment is involved?

● Describe the factors involved in the formation of submarine canyons.

▲ What are some of the potential advances possible from the theory of plate tectonics?

● The nature of beaches

★ Careers in geology

● Aeolian soil: formation, structure, and deposits

● Geysers around the world

● How natural deserts are created. Use examples from the past and present.

§ The glaciers of New Zealand

§ The formation of Crater Lake

● The physical characteristics of Death Valley

▲ Loini: Hawaii's newest sea-mounted volcano

● Shrinkage of the Antarctic ice cap

● The morphology of Venus

○ How Mt. St. Helens is monitored

● Prospecting and panning for gold

● The Pacific coastline: evolution and change

▲ Radiometric dating

● Inconsistencies in the theory of continental drift

● Compare and contrast the eruptions of Mt. St. Helens (Washington) and Mt. Pinatubo (Philippines).

☛ Water on earth. Discuss its origin and some of the important changes it has effected on the earth's surface.

● Discuss the relationship between volcanoes and earthquakes.

● How aerial photography is used in geology. Include a discussion of remote sensing.

★ What is the "Ring of Fire"?

● What are the origins and significance of islands and sea-mounts?

▲ What are the predictions of future earthquakes for California? Survey the results of the most recent studies in one general area of the state.

§ What is the life expectancy of Lake Mead (or another man-made lake)?

● Moon geology

★ Western oil shales: problems and prospects

○ Significant data and conclusions from the Joint Oceanographic Institutions for Deep Earth Sampling (JOIDES).

○ Scientific methods for the preservation of the water tables

● The geology of fossil fuels

● Review and compare the evidence for present estimates of the earth's age.

× Examine the relative roles of catastrophic events — such as major storms, earthquakes, volcanic eruptions, and meteorite impacts — in geologic change, as compared with gradual, continuous processes.

○ To what extent do the chemistry compositions of minerals vary? Discuss the range and extent of these variations.

● Why the Kobe, Japan, earthquake (1995) happened.

★ Continental Drift and earthquakes: a lesson in cause and effect

● Differential thermal expansion

● What are the nature and origin of faults?

● What are the earth's significant tectonic features?

● What are the major geologic problems of waste disposal?

● What are the functions of the United States Geological Survey? What have been their past accomplishments?

● How the landscape was changed by the Midwest earthquake of 1911–1912

● How the fossilization process works

● Geologists do not agree on what caused the mass extinctions at the Cretaceous-Tertiary (K-T) boundary. Detail these opposing points of view and include the evidence supporting each.

★ Why Africa has drought

● The Mexico City earthquake (1985) was particularly severe, partially because of geologic conditions. Why?

▲ Detail the most significant findings of the Ocean Drilling Program (ODP).

○ The active geology of the Mid-Atlantic Ocean floor

● Trace the development of the Continental Drift theory. Examine the original premise and final conclusions. Include some of the reasons for early scientific opposition.

Government

See also: Foreign Policy; Politics

- The role of the Central Intelligence Agency in the Watergate scandal
★ The invention of democracy in Ancient Greece
○ The methods of taxation in European countries. Compare and contrast these with United States tax structures.
- Who would benefit from the flat-tax proposal?
- Should the United States give tariff protection and preference to poor countries (the "favored nation" concept)?
➥ Proposals to decrease military spending. Select one and follow it through channels. What was the outcome? What were the obstacles?
➥ Defend or refute: Congress represents the rich and powerful in the United States. Choose a particular period in United States history or analyze the current congress.
- Has the job become too big for Congress? If so, what are some of the possible solutions?
★ Does the government have the

right to conduct mandatory AIDS testing? Is this an invasion of privacy?
- Would the United States be better governed by the parliamentary system?
○ The role of congress in foreign policy. Has it been too little, too much, or the wrong kind?
- Examine The Federalist Papers (Alexander Hamilton, James Madison, John Jay) and discuss their relevance to today's American social system and governmental structure.
○ The congressional seniority system has made the performance of congress less effective in most cases. Discuss this viewpoint, quoting appropriate authorities.
- FDA (Food and Drug Administration) measures to monitor and control carcinogens in human food products
➥ Governmental measures against drug traffic
○ Analyze one or more famous "dissents" in the United States Supreme Court that eventually

became law (i.e., became majority opinions).

- How the Romans governed their empire
- ★ Guarantees of the United States Constitution
- Communism: from Pythagoras to the Kremlin
- How the FDA (Federal Drug Administration) regulates the drug industry
- ▲ Federal aid to cities, 1950 to date. How were appropriations made? Where were monies usually applied? Who benefited?
- × A number of legislators have been recently censured and/or discredited. Select one example and examine the critical issues involved.
- Civil service careers: advantages and disadvantages
- The national interest versus governmental secrecy. Is a middle ground possible? Cite informed opinion to support your answer.
- ★ The significance of the Magna Carta to the modern world
- ★ Compare and contrast governmentally funded health services in the United States and Great Britain.
- How the government combats health fraud and quackery
- ★ Careers in the diplomatic corp
- The fate of public lands in Alaska
- Pesticide regulation: Should federal and state controls be

expanded for the public welfare?

- ▲ Analyze and describe the successes and failures of the last full session of Congress.
- Dimensions of the United States military complex: an overview
- Financial aspects of community health care
- ○ Is the United States' national security adequate?
- Organization and powers of the Bureau of Indian Affairs
- × Relate the merits and problems in several instances of federal regulation of industry.
- ★ Careers in public administration
- Many experts recommend the privatization of government services. Examine the feasibility of some of these suggestions.
- Is American democracy "pure democracy"?
- ➡ Recent abuses of congressional power
- People who don't pay taxes: Who, why, and how?
- Projected and proposed reforms in United States immigration policy
- The case for the nationalization of utilities
- ▲ How legalized gambling has benefited the state of New Jersey
- Federal versus state aid to education. In what ways do these funding sources differ? Are

appropriations variable?

- Defend or refute this statement: The post office should be turned over to private business.
- How should the social security system be altered?
- Should benefits for disabled veterans be increased? Many Vietnam veterans say "yes." Discuss their cause and concerns.
× Problems of diplomatic immunity
- Changes in veterans' benefits, 1960–1990
- Should all federal employees have automatic cost-of-living raises (COLA's)?
- Pros and cons of agricultural price supports
○ Compare and contrast the precepts expressed in *The Prince* (Machiavelli) with those of modern world leaders, including United States presidents.
★ The socialist case against capitalism
- The United States' national debt: 1910, 1930, 1960, 1990
- Compare and contrast the powers of the first president (George Washington) and the current United States president.
▲ Alternatives to the federal tax structure
× What are the qualities of leadership? Use examples such as Hitler, Alexander, Lincoln,

Napoleon, etc.

- The Washington bureaucracy. Has the federal government delegated excessive power to nonelected officials?
○ Trace the evolution of state laws dealing with marijuana.
- The role of Fabians in the formation of the British Labor Party
- Whistle-blowing for the prevention of governmental waste and corruption: the results so far
- Consumer protection agencies. Are they adequately protecting the public sector?
- Refute or defend: The CIA has become too powerful and too secret.
- Legislation regulating smoking areas. Is it adequate? Legal? Too narrow?
- Was President Franklin D. Roosevelt's New Deal democratic or socialistic?
➥ Follow one civil rights issue through the congressional process.
- Historical precedents for increased federalism in government
★ African Americans in Congress
§ Should the federal government sponsor school lunches?
★ What constitutional rights do illegal aliens have in the United States?
§ Compare and contrast the terms of Ronald Reagan and Jerry

Brown as <u>California</u> governors.

☛ States rights versus centralization in the American system. Select one segment of the economy or social structure.

● Was justice done in Watergate? Cite a variety of authorities in government, law, and journalism to substantiate your answer.

★ War powers of the President and congress

● Was the United States Constitution designed to "promote democracy" or to "protect the property of the wealthy"? Compare, substantiate, or refute these opposing theories.

○ The significance of the "Pentagon Papers" today

● President Theodore Roosevelt and environmental protection

★ Compare and contrast the governmental structures of Canada and Great Britain.

○ Strengths and weaknesses of block grant funding

● Proposed postal service reforms and reductions

● What should be the role of the state and/or federal government in long-term nursing care?

▲ The biracial government of the Fiji Islands

● Compare and contrast the office of the British prime minister and the president of the United States.

● The welfare state in America. Are the current criticisms justi-

fied? Quote appropriate authorities to justify your conclusions.

● Major changes in the powers of the presidency since 1950

✔ Detail and analyze the operation of your city's government over the last fifteen years.

✕ The effectiveness of political pressure groups in Washington. Select several for discussion.

○ Are Medicare benefits too costly for the taxpayer?

★ How the system of checks and balances operates in the federal government.

● Compare and contrast private postal systems and the U.S. Postal Service.

● Lotteries in the United States. Who buys, what they win, and where do the profits go?

● Gas taxes and the trucking lobby

★ Changes of the Environmental Protection Agency, 1970 to date

● The problems with the federal Food Stamp Programs

● The extent of welfare fraud and what it costs the taxpayer

● A survey of the amendments to the constitution. Include both those added and those rejected.

▲ Strengths and weaknesses of the selection policies of United States ambassadors and other diplomats

✔ Investigate and analyze the

achievements and failures of the current (or last full-term) governor in your state.

- Bureaucracy in the federal government and what to do about it

○ The president's cabinet and how its powers have changed in each administration

- Function of the Bill of Rights

★ How much do illegal aliens cost the United States (and thus the taxpayers)?

★ Should public transportation be nationalized?

★ Compare and contrast the Teapot Dome Scandal and Watergate.

➤ Some suggested welfare reforms

- Jacksonian democracy

- An overview of social legislation in the United States Congress: 1960–1980

- Corporate power in government

➤ Nepotism, patronage, and the spoils system in the American political system

- Public health care for the aged and the poor

- Present both sides of recent proposals to change the United States Constitution

- Compare and contrast the Roman Senate and the United States Senate.

- Compare the United States' Bill of Rights with those of Canada and England.

- Critical issues affecting ethics in Congress

✔ Investigate the major social (or fiscal) problems faced by your own city government.

➤ Compare and contrast several political systems in the Caribbean Islands.

- Detail the early postal service. Include the pony express, air mail, postage stamps, penny postcards, registered mail, etc.

○ Inequalities, inaccuracies, and irrelevancies in the 1990 census

- Current problems in the Peace Corps

- Long-range effects of the National Labor Relations Act (1935, Wagner Act)

★ Should the electoral college be abolished?

- The possibilities of Social Security bankruptcy

○ Current federal tax inequalities

§ Contributions of Rosalynn Carter to her husband's presidential term

- Defend or refute: American lawmakers are more responsible to special interest groups than to their constituents.

- What are the projections and prospects for federal poverty assistance in the next decade?

- Party government in Great Britain

- What have been the primary criticisms of the operation of the Federal Bureau of Investigation under the leadership of J. Edgar Hoover?

- Compare the democratic governments of France, Great Britain, and the United States.
- ★ What is being done (or not being done) about excessive government waste?
- Examine the Taft-Hartley national emergency strike provisions from 1947 to the present.
- Why we can't afford the Pentagon
- ○ Are federal farm policies fair? To the farmers? Consumers? Bankers?
- ★ The lottery should be abolished. Defend or refute this statement.
- x What recent legislation (both proposed and passed) has affected air pollution and acid rain?
- What are the pros and cons of protectionist trade legislation?
- Has governmental response to the AIDS epidemic been influenced by the fact that most of those originally afflicted were homosexuals and drug addicts?
- x What has been done to tighten United States security since recent espionage cases were disclosed?
- ○ Discuss the release of genetically engineered organisms into the environment. Why have federal agencies approved some experiments and blocked others?
- The voting booth, the tax return and the census form: why citizens aren't cooperating
- Should the FDA change its drug approval systems (including clinical trials)?
- Aldrich H. Ames, employed by the CIA, was a double agent in the service of the Soviet Union. Not only did he compromise U.S. security, but the deaths of a number of agents are attributed to him. How did this situation come about?

Key to Symbols

•	**average difficulty**	✦	**narrow down topic**
§	**substitutes possible**	▲	**large public or college**
★	**ample information in most**		**library required**
	libraries	✔	**local option topic**
○	**specialized knowledge**	x	**examples and supporting**
	required		**evidence needed**

Health

See also: AIDS; Drug Problems; Medicine; Mental Health; Nursing; Nutrition

- The human legacy of the early nuclear tests
- The effects of alcohol consumption on the fetus during pregnancy
- ★ High-altitude health hazards for mountaineers
- Dust pollution as a health factor
- ○ Lead, cadmium, and mercury and their effects on animal systems
- Noise and progressive hearing loss. Survey the scientific data from the last ten years.
- Why women should know more about their own bodies. Include methods for self-knowledge and awareness.
- Mine safety standards and why they are necessary
- ▲ Cholesterol, fats, and heart disease. Check the results of the latest medical studies.
- ➡ The pros and cons of cosmetic surgery
- § The history of <u>cosmetic</u> safety
- How to avoid unnecessary surgery
- When to call a doctor
- ★ Beneficial effects of Hatha Yoga
- How to use exercise equipment

effectively for maximum benefits for both muscular and cardiovascular conditioning
- Senility: the myths and the reality
- The harmless (harmful) effects of marijuana as reported in some clinical reports
- Causes and remedies for acne. Investigate the latest treatments and medications
- ✔ Investigate drinking water safety standards in your community and state.
- Obesity: genetic and physiological aspects
- ★ If your kidneys fail, how do you get new ones?
- Many do not want to know if they have a genetic predisposition for a disease. Others do. Examine both attitudes.
- Examine the cost-benefit analysis of organ transplants.
- Adverse reactions to prescription drugs have increased. Examine causes and possible remedies.
- Collect and analyze evidence

208

proving vitamin E as a medication has no medical value.

- What is included in chiropractic treatment? What is excluded?
▲ Changing approaches to the treatment of pain. Include pain centers.
○ What scientists have discovered about genetic markers and health
★ The relationship between smoking and disease
- Exercise and pregnancy
- Psychological aspects of physical fitness
- Evidence supporting the theory that jogging prevents heart attacks
▲ Problems of health care in rural communities
★ Permanent effects of LSD
★ The dangers of barbiturates
- Emotional stress and the body's reactions
★ Physical and mental results of amphetamine abuse
- Reconstruct the case of "Typhoid Mary." Contrast the events to modern methods of disease control.
- Changing approaches to weight loss. Include diet, behavior modification, and surgery.
- Successful methods for quitting smoking
★ Preventing periodontal disease
- Elements of prenatal care
- Fasting: origins, myths, and consequences

- Asbestos poisoning in industry. Include a definition of the problem and its effects on humans.
★ Alcoholism in Russia today
- Compare birth control methods.
- Body conditioning through weight lifting
- The case for organically grown food
- How violent exercise affects the body. Who should exercise? How and how much?
▲ Injurious effects to humans from the paraquat poisoning of marijuana
★ The use and dangers of nitrates in food
- The multiple benefits of aerobic exercises
- New ways to manage stress
- The common cold: myths and the truth
- The chlorinated water controversy
▲ Is the birth control pill unsafe? What are the latest results from studies and surveys?
- Medical factors about abortion that every woman should know
- The myths about alcohol and the truths behind them
- Preventive measures for common running injuries
- Dangers in your drinking water: a growing national problem
○ Changing concepts of illness and health. Include holistic medicine.
- Who should be immunized and

against what?

- The bilharzia snail and Egyptian public health
- Body building: Ego trip or health boon?
- Teenage eating habits and their relationship to health problems
- Advances in public health facilities in the United States
- Major health problems in third world countries. Select several typical countries.
- The physical fitness boom in the United States. Describe the various directions of the public's interest and how it has altered attitudes towards good health and fitness.
▲ Major elements of naturopathic medicine
- Range and scope of disability from impairments in the United States
- Cardiovascular exercise programs
○ Science looks at the dangers of fad diets
- Accidental poisoning: incidence and preventive measures for both children and adults
★ Menopausal problems and remedies. Discuss both the physical and psychological elements which are often involved.
- How noises affect the body
- Current perspectives on salt consumption
○ Ineffective drugs on the marketplace

★ United States life expectancy rates, 1890–1990
§ Living with heart disease
- Historical treatments for the retarded
- Physical effects of excessive video game usage
- The issues involved in heroin maintenance
- The vitamin oversell
- Programs for drug abuse prevention among young school children
§ How the blind adjust
▲ Scientific advances in the treatment of allergies
- Psychological aspects of the headache, both migraine and other types.
★ Contact lenses. Evaluate the technology, hazards, costs, and advantages.
× Physical exercises for young children
- Effects of color blindness and how the afflicted compensate
- The effects of sleep deprivation
- Saccharin and other artificial sweeteners
▲ Over-the-counter reducing aids. Are they effective, dangerous, or merely another consumer rip-off?
▲ Why is the maternal mortality rate higher in the United States than it is in Sweden or in Scotland?
- How to live with the Herpes virus

- Self-hypnosis techniques for the control of pain and tension
- How the United States controls epidemics
- The effects of fungal toxin weapons
▲ "Miracle" cures for arthritis
- Levels of drug abuse among the elderly and chronically ill
- Would a confiscatory cigarette tax ultimately result in fewer smokers?
▲ The war on health quackery by the Food and Drug Administration
- The rights of patients: what you should expect from your doctor and from a hospital
- Methadone addiction as a cure for the heroin habit
★ Analyze the long-term effects of Agent Orange use in Vietnam
➡ Food additives and their effects and potential dangers
★ Cocaine use in the United States: a growing epidemic
- Exercises for the expectant mother
- Vitamin C and the common cold. Science does not agree on the efficacy of this treatment. Survey a large cross-section of these opinions.
- Health product frauds and why they are still with us
- How carbon monoxide, ozone, and nitric oxides affect the body
- Survey and analyze the mail-order health advertising in ten mass circulation magazines.
○ Why "megavitamin therapy" can be dangerous
★ What is biofeedback?
- Coffee and its effects
- Health problems of heroin addicts
▲ "The drug industry is not in business for your health" is an attitude voiced by many health professionals. Evaluate this statement in light of recent incidents.
○ The dangers of synthetic hormones as medication
- Aids for the deaf and hard-of-hearing
✕ Many health care systems are very impersonal. Can this be avoided? What are the alternatives?
- Lead contamination poisoning and its common causes in home and industry
▲ How to improve the enforcement of the Occupational Safety and Health Act
- Are video display terminals safe? What are the latest findings?
- Nitrates as food additives: pros and cons
- Over half of the antibiotics produced in the United States are used in animal feeds. Why is this considered a dangerous practice by many scientists?
➡ What are the most pressing problems associated with the availability (or quality or costs)

of health care in America?

▲ Current levels of genetic damage from X-rays

○ Disease as a selective element of human evolution

● What factors are associated with extended life expectancies? Refer to evidence from recent studies.

● Why DDT and other chlorinated hydrocarbons are environmental hazards

▲ The federal government has cut its immunization program. Will this lead to more disease? Higher ultimate costs?

● Workplace diseases: Can they be controlled?

★ How can exposure to carcinogens be reduced or eliminated?

● Why the British system of heroin maintenance failed (succeeded)

● Household hallucinogens

● How social drinkers become alcoholics

● Why the contents of alcoholic beverages are not labeled. Should they be?

★ How safe are soft lens contacts?

★ The increase of AIDS (Acquired Immune Deficiency Syndrome). What measures are currently being utilized to curtail the further spread of this disease?

▲ Holistic medicine has recently been popularized by the media. What is it? Is it recognized by the medical community? Who are its practioneers?

○ Should the United States have a permanent bioethics commission?

● What are the medical criteria for In vitro fertilization? Are they adequate?

★ Assisted suicide for terminally or hopelessly ill patients should (or should not) be legally sanctioned.

§ Analyze the cost and benefits of heart transplants.

★ There are many well-publicized and widely believed myths about AIDS. What are they?

★ How to make a living will

★ The dangerous rise of "designer" drugs

● Health Maintenance Organizations (HMOs) are a form of health care that are alternatives to traditional insurance plans. How good are they? How are they viewed by the medical community? What services do they traditionally offer?

▲ Advances in computer-aided communication and electrically stimulated movement for the handicapped

● The food additive sulfite is used to prevent wilting and discoloration and has been linked to the death of several asthmatics. Should this substance be more closely regulated?

● Examine the progress made in asbestos cleanup. Where is this contamination most prevalent and why has it been a problem?

★ How to avoid AIDS

✔ Examine the emergency medical facilities in your area. Are they adequate? Has funding and staffing declined? Who uses them?

★ How the spread of AIDS is tied to the increasing use of crack cocaine

● Detail the advantages and disadvantages of the French abortion pill RU 486. Consider also its new uses in other areas of medicine.

★ Is world famine inevitable?

▲ Are occupation safety/health rules tough enough? Research new rulings on benzene, lead, ethylene oxide, ethylene dibromide and cotton dust.

★ The tragedy of crack babies

Key to Symbols

● average difficulty
§ substitutes possible
★ ample information in most libraries
○ specialized knowledge required

🠶 narrow down topic
▲ large public or college library required
✔ local option topic
✗ examples and supporting evidence needed

History — General

Note: Most subject areas in the book also contain historically oriented topics

• The racial map of the world in 50 A.D., 1500, and 2000

★ The influence of the horse on cultural patterns throughout history

• Compare and contrast the Space Age with the Age of Discovery.

• Patterns of revolution. What are some of the characteristics which are often found in revolutionary movements?

× What are the problems inherent in absolute monarchy? Use historical examples to illustrate each issue.

• Recount steps used to trace a geneology.

• What is the basis for Atlantis theories? Have historians revised their theories in the twentieth century? Why?

★ Gold: the universal prize

• Arab traders: from spices to oil

§ Gore Vidal as historian

• The evolution of surnames

§ The role of monarchy in the Netherlands, past and present

○ The engine of cultural evolution: Hand, brain, or both?

➡ Describe the characteristics of trade between the colonies and mother countries during the era of political colonialism. Do these trade patterns still exist?

× Compare and contrast manifest destiny and imperialism. Use examples from world history as well as from United States history.

➡ Resistance movements that have been successful and have altered history

○ Peter Kropotkin's philosophy of anarchism based on mutual aid

§ Compare and contrast the settlement and development of Australia and New Zealand

• Democracies are never prepared for war. Support or refute this statement with historical evidence and examples.

• In what ways did products and discoveries in the New World enrich the culture and economy of the Old World?

➡ Describe Toynbee's theory of

the inevitable decline of civilization and relate it to our contemporary society.

➥ Political cartoons as a supplement to history. Select one era or one issue and analyze the cartoons associated with it. Did they accurately reflect the facts? Public opinion?

• What factors are involved in the "population explosion" of the last 200 years?

• From the beginnings of civilization, the many have worked on orders from the few. How do historians, anthropologists, psychologists, etc. account for this phenomenon?

✗ What have been the traditional benefits to European society provided by absolute monarchs? Use examples from history.

• Parallels between Pericles's funeral oration and the Gettysburg Address

• Douglas MacArthur and Julius Caesar: some interesting parallels

★ The divine right theory. Why have so many societies been willing to accept this concept? How has it been used by absolute monarchies? Why?

• Long-term effects of the Black Death on medieval Europe and later eras

• Compare America's imperialism with that of ancient Rome.

• What have been the major elements of British-Irish relations in the last 300 years?

• Historical precedents for the death penalty

• Violence in the Vatican: popes who were murdered

Key to Symbols

•	average difficulty	➥	narrow down topic
§	substitutes possible	▲	large public or college
★	ample information in most		library required
	libraries	✓	local option topic
○	specialized knowledge	✗	examples and supporting
	required		evidence needed

History — Ancient

- The importance of stars (astronomy and astrology) to ancient civilizations
- Greek naval tactics at the Battle of Salamis
- ★ Who were the Etruscans? What are some of the theories about their origins?
- Babylonian agriculture: survival in a harsh environment
- ▲ Ancient explanations for eclipses, comets, and other solar phenomena
- × Military combat as depicted in Greek vase paintings
- Roman triumphal architecture: Propaganda tool, monstrous toy, or great art?
- The slave trade of the Greek and Roman states
- Eleusinian mysteries. What were they? Why have they been shrouded in secrecy then and now?
- The Bronze Age copper traders of the Mediterranean
- ★ The Greek Pythian games
- Technology of the lower Paleolithic food gatherers
- ▲ Growth of the temple cities of ancient Sumer
- Preventive war: Rome's third Punic war against Carthage
- ○ How accurate were the predictions of Nostradamus?
- Julius Caesar: Hero or villain?
- The rediscovery of Troy. Did the excavations disprove history? What did they add to our knowledge?
- ▲ The tactics used for the Battle of Thermopylae, 480 B.C.
- The significance of the Battle of Actium (31 B.C.)
- ★ Why language became necessary as civilization evolved
- The trade empire of ancient Greece: policies, routes, and scope
- ▲ The ancient Assyrians as businessmen
- The position and role of "metrics" (resident foreigners) in classical Athens
- ★ The Spartans in war
- The Olympic games: rules and regulations
- ▲ The Greek tholos: an architectural mystery
- ➤ How primitive man hunted:

216

tools, tactics, and traps

⬆ The origin of the Egyptian civilization

● How man develops a written language

★ The building of Hadrian's Wall. Why was it constructed? Did it work?

● Helen of Troy after the Trojan War

● The cult of Isis (Egypt)

● Roman social and political life as detailed in *The Memoirs of Hadrian* (by Marguerite Yourcenar)

● The beliefs of the first Christians. How did this religion change in the first hundred years?

▲ Roman persecutions of Christians: When, why, how. Use evidence from authoritative sources.

● Charlemagne: myths and reality

● How the Romans governed their empire

⬆ Life patterns of the early hunter-gatherers

★ Events leading to the assassination of Julius Caesar

● Constantine and the Christians. In what ways did this relationship influence the course of history?

● Babylonia as a center of trade

⬆ Select one of Alexander's major battles and detail the background of the conflict, his

military tactics, and the outcome.

▲ Burial of Pompeii. Do historians agree? Check finds since 1980.

▲ The health of prehistoric humans. What has science discovered about their levels of infectious disease, chronic disorders, and death rates?

● The Pax Romana as it affected the political, economic, and social structure of Europe

● The Greeks invented democracy but seldom practiced it. Discuss, using relevant examples.

○ Minoan elements in Mycenaean civilization

★ How the gods of antiquity were used to explain natural phenomena

▲ Egypt and Mesopotamia were geographically similar. Why did the cultural and political history of these two regions diverge so markedly?

● Evaluate the Sumerian civilization as a synthesis of developments which occurred in other Persian Gulf regions.

★ What were the major domestic characteristics of Neolithic communities?

✕ How did the invention of the potter's wheel contribute to man's ability to control his environment?

● Discuss those aspects of the art and literature of Mesopotamia and Egypt which show the different attitudes of the peoples in the two regions toward life after death. Evaluate and compare the background of these differences.

- Examine the transition from the late Paleolithic era into the Neolithic era. What were the significant characteristics and innovations?
- ▲ Discuss attempts of Paleolithic man to record the seasonal changes in the environment. What recent discoveries have verified these actions? How did this capacity affect and change primitive man's life patterns?
- The contents of Babylonian cuneiform tablets and their relevance to everyday life
- ★ Man's earliest theories and hypotheses on the formation of the earth and the universe
- ▲ What new advances have been made in the study of the nutrition, eating habits, and health of prehistoric humans? What are some of the analytical methods currently in use?
- ○ Evaluate the various theories which have been proposed to explain the disappearance of the European Neanderthals.
- What theories have been advanced to account for Upper (Late) Paleolithic art? Explain the validity of each.
- ★ Wealth and luxury in the Roman Empire. How much for how

many? What were the economic levels?

- The rise of the Golden Age of Greece — despite the lack of natural resources
- Earliest trade with China. Exports? Imports? What were the major influences on Western Europe?
- ★ The slave rebellion led by Spartacus (73–71 B.C.)
- The causes and the significant effects of the Trojan War, c. 1200 B.C.
- ○ Detail and compare several major theories to explain the decline and fall of the Roman Empire.
- Contrast the conflicting interpretations of Cleopatra. Include discussions of her personality and her influence on history.
- Greek views of the cosmos
- ★ The short, happy career of Caligula
- The tactics of the Greek hoplites versus the Persian mercenaries
- The first female pharaoh: Queen Hatshepsut
- The origin of the ancient Egyptian *Book of the Dead*. What was its social, political, and religious significance?
- ▲ The hidden agenda at the trial of Socrates. What were the unstated issues?
- The influence of the Romans on early Britons

▲ The catastrophic end of the Minoan civilization. In which theories do historians and archeologists place most credence? What new discoveries may have altered these views?

★ The achievements of the Sumerians

● Why the earliest civilizations developed in regional isolation. What were the long-range effects?

★ Silk in its historical contexts

● The role of Alexander the Great in the diffusion of Hellenistic culture

▲ How did geographic location affect the stability, way of life, and ethnic composition of the Yellow River Valley in China?

➼ Commerce in ancient Eurasia. What products were traded? By whom? What were the effects of this trade on indigenous cultures? Were the effects permanent?

● The Bronze Age "Ice Man" found in the Austrian Tyrol (1991) was a remarkable discovery. What did science learn?

▲ New light on the Paleolithic era from the newly discovered cave paintings in the Chauvet Cave (France)

● Detail the origin, growth, and decline of one of these ancient cities. Include building plans and maps, if available. Has the site been excavated? If so, what were the primary discoveries? What is its contemporary condition? Why was this site significant? What was its role in history? What features made it unique?

Antioch	Palmyra
Baalbek	Pergamum
Babylon	Persepolis
Byblos	Pompeii
Carthage	Sardis
Corinth	Sidon
Ephesus	Susa
Gaza	Tarsus
Herculaneum	Thebes (Greece)
Jericho	Thebes (Egypt)
Knossos	Troy
Memphis	Tyre
Mycenae	Ur
Nineveh	

Key to Symbols

●	average difficulty	➼	narrow down topic
§	substitutes possible	▲	large public or college library required
★	ample information in most libraries	✔	local option topic
○	specialized knowledge required	✗	examples and supporting evidence needed

History — Middle Ages

- Early unions: the medieval guilds
- The rules of courtly love in the Middle Ages
- The First Crusade and the fall of Jerusalem
- Events leading to the Saint Bartholomew's Day massacre in 1572. What were the major issues and what was the final result?
- × Medieval heresies and other prophetic revivalist and reform movements
- Masquerades, mummeries, and pageants in the courts of the Middle Ages
- ▲ The function of large fairs in medieval commerce
- The medieval village: layout, size, organization, economy, etc.
- How the Crusades affected the cultural and socioeconomic level of Europe
- ★ Why did feudalism develop? What are its major advantages as a social system?
- Contrast the armies of the crusades with those of the Muslims whose lands they invaded.
- Why the Dark Ages were not so dark

- Medieval courts of love: dialogue and dances
- The Battle of Tours: when the Moslems invaded France (732)
- ○ The course of feudalism after Charles Martel. What factors contributed to the evolution of this social system?
- Charles Martel and the Battle of Poitiers (Tours)
- The Holy Grail: myth and reality
- ➤ Social life and customs in England at the time of King Arthur
- Why was Charlemagne successful? Do historians agree?
- ▲ What were the most significant European population shifts before the Middle Ages?
- Social organization as reflected in the zoning and architecture of medieval cities
- ▲ Protestant revolts before Martin Luther. Did all of them have the same causes? Did any succeed? Which failed? Why?
- How the Ottoman sultan, Muhammad II (1432–1481) conquered Constantinople
- Witches and heretics in the medieval world
- What political, social, and geographical factors led to the Irish

Golden Age, 600–800? What were the major characteristics of this period?

- Forces which contributed to the decline of the medieval church
- ○ How the crusades weakened the powers of the nobility
- ★ Compare life in the medieval city or town with that commonly found in the countryside.
- The role of the monasteries in the Christianizing of medieval Europe
- ★ The founding of the Jesuits by Saint Ignatius of Loyola (1534)
- The contributions of the Hanseatic League to European stability and economic growth
- ★ How William I won the Battle of Hastings. Why was this victory decisive to the course of the Norman conquests?
- ➤ The spread of the art of printing in the Middle Ages. In what way did this alter the course of history?
- The Bayeux tapestry and the Norman conquest
- The religious reforms of Savonarola (1452–1498). Detail how his subsequent fate was the result of his severe attacks on the social and religious community.
- The "People's Crusade"

- The economic effects of the Black Death on Europe
- ★ The Children's Crusade
- The immediate effects of the Reformation on the Christian church
- ▲ Slave trade in Africa before the white man's arrival
- The Jews in the Middle Ages. How were they treated by society? What were their contributions and major problems, status, etc.?
- The dissolution of the monasteries
- ➤ The conquest of the Aztecs in 1521. Discuss Spanish objectives, both official and unofficial, tactics, etc.
- ★ The role of drama and the theater in the Middle Ages
- Compare the Saxon conquest of England with the Frank's subjection of Gaul.
- The Byzantine Empire of Justinian. What was its range, power base, achievements, and influence on Europe?
- Compare the Mongols and Muslims as empire builders.
- Characteristics of medieval centers of learning
- How feudalism restricted and hampered economic growth

History — 15th Through 19th Centuries

§ Was <u>Elizabeth I</u> a "good" queen? Was her reign successful in terms of economic growth and general peace and prosperity? How was she regarded by her contemporaries? How do today's historians view her accomplishments? (Or, select another noteworthy queen or king.)

× How did the rise and spread of humanism affect Western Europe?

• Compare the production and marketing methods of the guilds in the Middle Ages with those commonly employed during the Industrial Revolution.

• Why absolutism failed in England

▲ The rise and fall of Napoleon has been explained and analyzed by many historians. Some do not agree. In what areas?

○ How has the concept of the "Newtonian World Machine" influenced the modern world?

• Causes of the Russo-Japanese War

• Nineteenth-century reactionaries: Napoleon and Metternich. Why did they fail? *Did they fail* in view of the rise of Bismarck, Kaiser Wilhelm, and Hitler?

• Some historians believe the French Revolution occurred not because the French were oppressed, but because they were so advanced. What is the evidence to support this theory?

★ Why the Russians sold Alaska

• How Bismarck planned German unification

➥ The spread of the Industrial Revolution. Examine the rates of industrialization in various European nations, including Great Britain.

• The rise of the merchant class

★ England's trade policies toward the American colonists after 1763. What were the results of these policies?

• How the new technology of the Industrial Revolution contributed to the spread of colonialism

• The effects of the Crimean War on the balance of power in Europe

➥ Select an absolute monarch and investigate how he or she gained, consolidated, and maintained power. Use, for example, Henry VII, Elizabeth I, Henry VIII (England), Philip II

(Spain), Peter the Great (Russia), or Louis XIV (France).

○ How Napoleon advanced the cause of nationalism in Europe

☛ Compare the Spanish and English experience of discovery and colonization. Select, for example, Mexico and Australia.

• How the philosophies of Voltaire, Montesquieu, and Diderot influenced the course of the French Revolution

• The development of the joint-stock trading companies by the English. How did they encourage colonization?

○ Chart the manner in which American democracy has been influenced by developments in France and Britain.

• Domestic reforms of the Napoleonic era

• Political and economic issues of the Reformation. In what ways were they related to the religious issues?

★ Labor problems of the early years in the Industrial Revolution. Include an analysis of hours, wages, working conditions, and child labor.

• How the British government was altered in the seventeenth century. What were the most significant events affecting this change?

§ The colonization and settlement of an African country

☛ The evils of the Industrial Revolution

• What were the factors which directly contributed to the Indian Mutiny of 1856–1858?

• Why was the Reformation successful?

▲ The effects of the Industrial Revolution in Great Britain on rural life. Which changes benefited agrarian society? Which did not?

★ Events leading to the burning of Joan of Arc

• The sinking of the *Medusa*. Who was at fault? What was the aftermath?

× Detail the ways in which the Renaissance differed from the Middle Ages.

★ The fate of the Spanish Armada

• Discuss the radical shifts in French society following the Revolution.

• Political factors in the Reign of Terror (1793). How did they influence the course of French history?

• The Sepoy Rebellion and its influence on the course of British colonialism in India

▲ The state of science in the fifteenth and sixteenth centuries

• Economic effects of the French Revolution

§ British colonialism as exemplified by Singapore

• The long-term results of the

Spanish Inquisition

- ● The ultimate failures of Louis XV and Louis XVI of France
- ★ The far-reaching political consequences of the Dreyfus Affair, 1894
- ● Discuss the reasons for Henry VIII's break from the Church of Rome. What was the impact on English history?
- ● In 1527 Rome was sacked by Charles VIII of France's mercenary troups. What was the extent of the destruction? What were the consequences?
- × The changing role of the artist in the Renaissance
- ▲ How the "Donation of Constantine" was proved a forgery
- ● The impact of the invention of moveable type on the Protestant Reformation
- ○ The invention of capitalism in Renaissance Italy
- ▲ Machiavelli's *Prince*: What was the writer's real intention? What is the status of the current scholarly debate?
- ● The rise and fall of Savonarola
- ● Lucrezia Borgia, villainess or victim?
- ● Events leading to the formation of Prussia
- ● The many talents of Catherine the Great of Russia
- ★ Compare and contrast American slaves and Russian serfs.
- ● England's Irish policies during the potato famine
- ● How England maintained naval supremacy
- ★ Napoleon's retreat from Russia
- ● The origins of the Protestant Reformation
- ▲ Compare contemporaneous accounts of the French Revolution. Explain the differing attitudes of the aristocracy and the common man.
- ○ The revisionist historian and the nineteenth century
- ● The effects of the partition of Poland, 1772–1775
- ● Jesuit advances against the Protestant Revolution
- ● How did the expansion of colonization change Spain?
- ● Napoleon's Egyptian campaign
- ● The Guy Fawkes (Gunpowder) Plot. What were its origins? The consequences?
- ★ The exile and return of Napoleon Bonaparte
- ● Underlying reasons for the Puritan revolt in England
- ● The first settlers of French Polynesia
- ● Oliver Cromwell's religious suppression. What were the results?
- ➡ Building of Versailles
- ● The scope and influence of the Dutch East India Company
- ● What were the conditions, both national and local, which led to the beginnings of the Spanish Civil War?

× The influence of Lorenzo dé Medici on the Renaissance

○ Describe the effects of Luther's translation of the Bible.

● The historical accuracy of the French Revolution as represented in Charles Dickens' *A Tale of Two Cities*

● What was the relationship between the Opium War and the Boxer Rebellion?

● How the British won supremacy in India

★ The Renaissance man as typified by Leonardo da Vinci

★ Compare the life-styles of a wealthy Renaissance landowner with a feudal lord of the Middle Ages.

● What were the deterrents to the spread of the Industrial Revolution in Russia?

○ How the colonial victory in the American Revolution affected the thought and actions of other governments

● The consequences of the fall of Constantinople to the Ottoman Turks in 1453

★ The rise of the middle class in the Industrial Revolution

● Major problems stemming from the growth of cities in the latter half of the 1800's

▲ Compare the achievements of the Utopian socialists with those of the moderate socialists in nineteenth-century Europe.

● Napoleon's unification plans for Europe were a failure because of inadequate transportation and communication technology. Why? Were other factors involved?

▲ Louis XIV's revocation of the Edict of Nantes. How were the French craft industries affected?

● What were the various forms of African political governments which had evolved by 1650?

● "Liberty, equality and fraternity" was the slogan of the French Revolution. To what extent were these principles achieved by this conflict?

★ The origins of the conflict in Northern Ireland

● What were the real achievements of the French Revolution? Cite the opinions of historians and account for their differences.

● Describe Napoleon's reforms. How successful were they? Why?

● The witchcraft fever of the sixteenth and seventeenth centuries. What were its causes and primary manifestations?

History — 20th Century

★ "The German has no idea how much people must be misled if the support of the masses is required." (Adolf Hitler, 1935) What are the implications of this quotation in light of subsequent events?

× The factory system and how it modified or changed employee/employer relations

● The relationship between the Holocaust and the establishment of the state of Israel

▲ Current levels of United States foreign aid. Have the types of assistance changed in the last decade? How and why?

● The issues of the Yom Kippur War (1973)

★ Rules for killing: the Geneva Convention

● What have been the common elements in the following armed conflicts: Congo (1960–1967), Biafra (1967–1970), Malaya (1948–1960), and Cuba (1956–1959)?

▲ Trace the indigenous roots of Vietnamese communism.

● What factors contributed to the ultimate success of Castro's Cuban Revolution?

★ The role of Islam in the Iranian Revolution

● Israel and the Geneva Convention

➥ Peasant wars in the twentieth century: Select one (e.g., Cuba, Algeria, China, Vietnam, etc.) and chart the interrelationships between poverty, politics, colonialism, and revolution.

➥ Nationalism as the disruptive force in twentieth-century Europe. Select one country as a case study.

● How the Ribbentrop-Molotov Pact prepared the way for the invasion of Poland

× Genocide in the twentieth century

▲ The opening of trade with China and Japan changed American trade relations in the Far East. Evaluate both the short- and long-term results of this policy change.

● What have been the most significant problems encountered by the Soviet Union in the implementation of its economic plans?

➥ Origins of the Bolshevik Revolution (1917)

- How the Russians lost the Sino-Japanese War (1905)
- Russian expansionism immediately after World War II. What were the major reasons these maneuvers were successful?
★ The effects of the Iraqui-Iranian war on the economies of both countries
★ Compare and contrast the League of Nations and the United Nations.
- Justifications for apartheid in South Africa
➥ The French in Vietnam. Why were they there originally? Why did they leave?
○ Compare and contrast the rise of the Nazis as reflected in W.L. Shirer's *The Rise and Fall of the Third Reich* and A. Speer's *Inside the Third Reich*.
- Historical background of the Irish Catholic-Protestant conflict
★ The levels and characteristics of nationalism in Nazi Germany
- Cite the evidence of the use of chemical weapons by the Soviets in Afghanistan or in other areas currently engaged in conflict.
- Non-Jewish victims of the Nazi Holocaust
▲ The effect of the Nazi regime on German scholarship
- The origins of the "Iron Curtain"
- The formation of modern Pakistan. What problems did it solve? Create?
- The last years of the reign of Nicholas II of Russia and the start of the Revolution
- The establishment of Israel. Detail the major problems encountered in the early days
- The Russian pogroms against the Jews
○ Great Britain's entry into the Common Market
- Social conditions in Russia before the Revolution of 1917
➥ The destruction of the Third Reich
★ Historians reevaluate Joseph Stalin
- Egyptian seizure of the Suez Canal (1956). What was the justification? Is it still valid?
- Elements of disagreement about the Balfour declaration (1917)
★ Theories on the death of Adolf Hitler. What is the evidence?
- Hermann Goering at Nuremburg: The trial of the second most powerful Nazi
- Why the Swiss have remained neutral in the twentieth century. What has been the advantage to them and to other European nations?
➥ Fascism in Italy, 1930–1945
- Compare and contrast tactics used by Adolf Hitler and Joseph Stalin to gain and maintain political control.
- The formation of the North Atlantic Treaty Organization
- Joseph Stalin: how to purge the opposition

▲ Could the Cold War have been prevented?

☛ The fall of communism

✗ How illegal drugs have changed history

● The Reichstag Fire (1933)

★ The influence of Rasputin on the Russian Court. Include a survey of the economic, political, medical, and psychological factors involved.

● Events leading to the partition of India

● Compare and contrast historical justifications for the founding of the State of Israel and the issues involved in the Arab opposition.

● What are the origins of the Common Market?

○ World War I and World War II were part of the same conflict. Justify or refute this concept.

● Tribal factors influencing the Civil War in Congo Zaire (1960–1965)

★ Trace the history of the Palestinian Liberation Organization.

✗ The effects of Martin Luther King's assassination on the civil rights movement

☛ The Palestinian terrorists' attack at the 1972 Munich Olympics. What did they hope to accomplish? Were their plans successful? Could the deaths have been avoided?

★ Events in the Iranian takeover of the United States Embassy.

Why did the students seem to have more power than the Iranian government?

★ The Berlin Airlift

§ Economy of Germany in the postwar years

● Detail and explain Winston Churchill's 1945 election defeat.

● The Indonesian revolt against the Dutch

★ The Shah of Iran and the United States: where we went wrong

★ The plight of the Boat People (1979–1982)

● Micronesia before and after World War II: a comparison

✗ Chart the course of world overpopulation. What have been the major consequences for the twentieth century?

▲ Advances in arms control since 1970

○ Mexican-United States relations, to date

● Positive aspects of the British rule in India. What were the accomplishments?

● The passive, noncooperation philosophy of Mohandas Gandhi against the British in India

● Idi Amin's reign of terror in Uganda

● The Soviet invasion of Afghanistan. What factors predicated their succcess?

★ Building the Berlin Wall

● Major issues of the Israeli-Arab Six-Day War (1967)

§ The German colonial experience in Samoa

- Lenin's role in the Bolshevik Revolution of 1917. What was that of Plekhanov?
- ↧ German expansionism and the two world wars
- German foreign policy before World War I
- ▲ Historical perspectives on the real T.E. Lawrence (Lawrence of Arabia)
- ★ How Adolf Hitler gained control of Germany
- European student dissent in the 1960's and 1970's
- Mussolini's rise to power in pre-war Italy
- 1956 Hungarian uprising
- Why the League of Nations failed
- Why was the French Resistance so successful in World War II?
- ★ Did the Marshall Plan succeed? What were the original goals and what have been the long-range effects?
- Barrier to freedom: the evolution of the Berlin Wall
- Origins of the myth of the "pure" Aryan race
- The 1968 Soviet invasion of Czechoslovakia
- After Bismarck, who else but Hitler?
- To what degree did the actions of Kaiser William II weaken the position of Germany on the European continent? How did his policies lead to World War I?
- The Hungarian Revolt of 1956. What were the roots of the rebellion and what have been the political consequences?
- What were the critical issues which led to the Armenian Massacre of 1894–1915? What was the Turkish justification?
- ▲ Evaluate the nature of recent criticism of the United Nations.

Key to Symbols

•	average difficulty	↧	narrow down topic
§	substitutes possible	▲	large public or college library required
★	ample information in most libraries	✔	local option topic
○	specialized knowledge required	x	examples and supporting evidence needed

History — Social History

× Islamic contributions to Western culture

• The wall paintings in Pompeii as a depiction of the city's life-styles

▲ Festivities at the opening of the Suez Canal

★ The "self-made man" in nineteenth-century thinking

➡ Everyday life in Elizabethan England. Select one area of society and focus on it in detail.

• Compare and contrast the educational ideals of classical Greece and early China.

▲ Adultery in the ancient and medieval worlds. What was society's attitude? The church's?

★ Knighthood in the British Empire

• "Free love" in the 1920's

• The social role of the troubadour in the medieval court

• The sexual revolution of the 1960's. How revolutionary was it?

§ Life patterns of the lower classes in ancient Egypt (or, in Sumeria, Babylon, Syria, etc.)

§ Domestic life in classical Greece

○ The American character as viewed from nineteenth-century Europe

• A typical day in the Athenian Agora (marketplace)

• The Bedouin: from camels to Cadillacs

• The historic plight of the Gypsies of Europe

§ Social change in Japan, 1960–1990

★ Describe life in a Neolithic clan. Discuss shelter, food, social structure, etc.

• Public reaction to the abdication of the Duke of Windsor

• The danse macabre in the Middle Ages

× The practice of witchcraft during the Reformation

• The "master race" philosophy of Adolf Hitler

• How the Industrial Revolution changed the life of the "common man"

• The plague in London: contemporary accounts

➡ The social role of the eunuch. Select several countries and times when they were prevalent.

• The cultural heritage of the modern Eskimo in a century of rapid change: an analysis

• A medieval romance: Heloise and Abelard

○ Marquis de Sade: Madman or philosopher?

★ Fun and games in the Roman colosseum

● The domestication of cats and dogs as pets

§ Sanitation in ancient <u>Crete</u>

● How chariot racing was part of the social life of Rome

★ The "whole man" concept of Greek education

▲ The life-style in the ancient Greek city of Sybaris

● Social structure of medieval castles

● The survival of modern Greek culture under Turkish rule

★ The role of the juggler in the medieval world

✗ Definitions of love through the ages

● The effects of British colonialism on India's social structure

● Social consequences of the French Revolution

▲ Common uses of Hiberno-Saxon manuscripts

● Uses of the boycott as a lever of social change and reform

● Pomp and splendor in the Byzantine Court

● Utopian socialism as an outgrowth of the Industrial Revolution

● Ways in which World War II permanently altered the social structure of Europe

▲ "Cultural Europeanization." Define and discuss this concept using appropriate contemporary examples.

● The hoax of the Cardiff Giant

§ The social changes brought about by or stemming from the invention of _____.

● Tholos tomb paintings of the Etruscans as reflections of their culture and social life

● Ancient Athens: the first experiment in an open society. Was it a success or a failure?

§ Social system of the <u>Vikings</u>

Key to Symbols

● average difficulty	◄ narrow down topic
§ substitutes possible	▲ large public or college
★ ample information in most	library required
libraries	✔ local option topic
○ specialized knowledge	✗ examples and supporting
required	evidence needed

History — United States

★ An analysis of Lincoln's role as commander-in-chief of the Union forces

↙ The county seat wars. Select one area in Missouri, Kansas, Iowa, Texas, or your own state, if applicable.

▲ The response of the American religious commmunity to the social problems of industrialization in the 1880's and 1890's

● George Washington's foreign policies. Evaluate his successes and weaknesses while president.

● General James Wilkinson's role in the Aaron Burr conspiracy

● The American Protective Association. What were its objectives? In what ways were they realized?

★ The status of former slaves in the South after the Civil War. Include legal, social, and economic factors. In what ways did these elements evolve in the next thirty years?

§ Evaluate the presidency of _____ in terms of campaign promises and their fulfillment.

● Was Benjamin Franklin a typical colonist? In what ways did he also represent the European viewpoint?

★ Detail the economics of the American Revolution.

● What were the major elements in the growth of the populists as a party of protest?

● What factors contributed to economic growth between 1789 and 1815? Include a discussion of both governmental policies and economic developments.

○ How Thomas Jefferson's attitudes towards government changed during his later years

● The United States has never experienced a military coup. Why? Would it be possible?

▲ Why America was unprepared for the war of 1812. How did this alter the course of the conflict?

● In what ways does the United States Constitution remedy the defects of the Articles of Confederation?

● Did the United States win the War of 1812? Historians do not agree. What are the economic and political factors underlying this controversy?

▲ Why the Homestead Act of

232

1862 was a failure

- What factors were involved in the Compromise of 1850? Why did the Democratic party agree to it? What were the results?
- What was the federal government's attitude toward labor in the 1880's and 1890's? When did change occur? Why?
▲ Compare and contrast the English colonies started by corporate ventures to those founded by individuals or a group of partners. Focus on goals and results.
★ Compare the structure of government in England with the structure of government in the individual American colonies.
➥ How did the Civil War affect the United States economy? Include both the Confederacy and the Union.
- What were the long-range effects of John Brown's 1859 raid on Harpers Ferry? Some historians feel it was the direct cause of the Civil War. Support or refute this contention.
★ Compare and contrast the views of Abraham Lincoln and Stephen A. Douglas toward slavery, white supremacy, and governmental power as espoused in the debates of 1858.
▲ The mental disorders of Mary Todd Lincoln and their effect on Abraham Lincoln
★ What was the nature and outcome of the dispute between Abraham Lincoln and congress over the rehabilitation of the defeated South at the end of the Civil War?
- What economic, social, and philosophical factors contributed to the formation of early labor unions in America?
- Social mobility in America: a survey and comparison of the years 1900, 1930, and 1970
- William Randolph Hearst is said to have boasted that it cost him three million dollars to bring on the Spanish-American War. What is the background of this statement? What is the historical evidence?
★ What were the causes of the war with Mexico? Indicate the central cause. Could the war have been avoided?
○ What were the contributing factors that influenced colonial sectional controversies?
- What were the contributory factors that fostered territorial expansion between 1789 and 1867?
- What was the character of American nationalism in the nineteenth century? In what ways was it altered? By what?
- Delineate the common elements in the following government scandals: Credit Mobilier (Ulysses Grant), Teapot Dome (Warren Harding), and Water-

gate (Richard Nixon).

- The lost colony of Roanoke
- Dissent in the American colonies. What were the foremost reasons? Was there a commonality of cause?
- John Winthrop and his leadership of the Massachusetts Bay Company. How do historians now assess his strengths and weaknesses?
- The indentured servant in colonial America
- Why the colonists won the Revolutionary War
- Some historians state that the cause of the Civil War was not slavery but northern industrial imperialism. Discuss the underlying factors of this position.
★ Conflicting views about the impeachment of Andrew Johnson
- Military living conditions during the Revolutionary War
▲ The surveyor: the first land speculator in the United States
- Compare and contrast slaves in the American South with those in ancient Greece and Rome.
○ Social Darwinism and the Industrial Revolution in America
- Economic factors underlying the maintenance of slavery in the antebellum South
- New World discoveries and claims were made by many nations. Discuss and compare the major motivations and advances of Spain, France, England, and

Holland.

- How the Confederates could have won the Civil War
- The expansion of industry in colonial New England
§ The Battle of Yorktown (Revolutionary War)
§ The early days of the textile industry in America
- Could the Civil War have been avoided? What are the views of historians?
- Treatment of prisoners during the Civil War. Did conditions vary geographically between the Confederacy and the Union?
○ The Civil War has often been called the first truly modern war. Substantiate this statement.
★ The carpetbaggers
- Economic factors of the Civil War that influenced the course of history
× Changes in manufacturing technology and products after the Revolutionary War
★ The settlement of Plymouth by the Puritans
- The organization of the underground railway
× Spies in the Revolutionary War
- The origin and significance of the United States Bill of Rights
- The British cause in the American Revolution. Was it justifiable?
× Instances of anarchy in America
- Why the South lost the Civil War

- How Grant captured Vicksburg
- The purchase of Alaska
- The economic aftereffects of the Civil War on the South
- Compare and contrast the military tactics of Civil War generals. Include Robert E. Lee, Ulysses S. Grant, and William T. Sherman.
§ The effects of the cotton gin on the American economy
- The Kansas-Nebraska Act and its effects on slavery
★ Evidence supporting Norse occupation of the New World before Columbus
- The early days of Washington, D.C.
- Benjamin Franklin at the French Court
- Reconstruction policy after the Civil War
★ How history reviews the Boston Tea Party
- Lee's surrender at Appomattox. Why was this Lee's final stand? Should he have surrendered earlier?
- Causes of the Colonial Wars
- The great American "melting pot" and why it proved to be a myth to many nineteenth-century immigrants
- What were the goals of the American Revolution? Were they achieved? Are they still evident in American life?
▲ What was the position of Great Britain and other European countries during the Civil War? Was there a particular bias toward the Confederacy or the Union? Did either side receive aid? In what form?
- Discuss the Boston Tea Party as a modern day event
○ What historical lessons did the founding of Jamestown provide for later colonizers? What were the applications?
- Examine the nature of the struggle for power between President Andrew Johnson and congress. What events led to the House vote to impeach Johnson? What might have been the long-term effect had he been successfully convicted?
§ What were the principal problems confronting William Harrison during his presidency?
○ In what ways did Lincoln's presidency strengthen the powers of the presidency?
- Compare the North and the South at the start of the Civil War in terms of their military preparedness, their attitudes toward war and fighting, and their respective abilities and methods of financing war.
✔ The first thirty years of your state. Cover its original settlers, or its founding as a political entity, its business or agricultural beginnings.

- What were the causes and effects of the slave uprising, called the Southampton Insurrection, led by Nat Turner in 1831?
- Who were the delegates to the Constitutional Convention? Did they represent the country's political attitudes, desires, and needs?
- Living conditions in the American colonies. Select one facet of colonial life, such as medicine, education, housing, etc.
- The fur trade in early America
- Opposition to the Declaration of Independence
× The "robber barons" and *laissez-faire* capitalism
- The basis, scope, and ultimate significance of American nationalism in the nineteenth century
- The final effects of the Monroe Doctrine
- What were the South's arguments in support of slavery?
- American science and scientists in the eighteenth century: the state of the art
- The role of the Jesuit missionaries and fur traders in the development of New France in early America
- Compare the Plymouth and Massachusetts Bay colonies.
▲ Literacy in colonial America. What factors were influential in

raising this rate?
★ Why the Battle of Saratoga was one of the turning points of the American Revolution. Were other incidents equally influential?
- Analyze the Compromise of 1850 and its effects on the South and on slaves' civil rights.
- During the early eighteenth century what were the trends in religious thought that influenced the rise of reform movements in the United States?
○ Compare the basic philosophy of such Republicans as Thomas Jefferson and James Madison to Federalists such as John Hamilton. Include an analysis of the economic, political, and social aspects of their approach.
- Examine and delineate the role of states' rights and the moral issue of slavery as contributing factors of the Civil War.
- The rise of American industrial power and the immigrant work force. What is the interrelationship?
- The original Ku Klux Klan
- The economics of the colonial farm
§ Swedish immigration to the United States
★ What really happened at Wounded Knee?
- The administration of the law in the thirteen colonies

- The press during the Civil War
× The early oil barons
- The origins of the women's suffrage movement in the United States
× The settlement of the United States: for wealth/power or freedom/principles? Contrast several examples.
▲ English restrictions on colonial industry
- The colonies had no newspapers during their early years. Explain the reasons for this condition and describe the character of the first press efforts.
- Detail the effects of the Alien and Sedition Acts of 1798.
- The results of the first United States census, 1790
★ "The American dream" and the nineteenth-century immigrant to the United States. Characterize the dream and the typical immigrant.
- The rise of the big city "boss"
- What was the significance of the Sephardic Jewish community in colonial America?
- Causes of late nineteenth-century urbanization
★ The Haymarket Square riot of 1886
- Labor and manpower organization in the American colonies
- The Dred Scott decision
- Abolitionist activities before the Civil War
★ The day the British burned the White House
▲ Assess the influence of Harriet Beecher Stowe's novel *Uncle Tom's Cabin* on public sentiment and on the abolitionists' cause.
- The Barbary War of 1815
- The establishment of the New England Confederation (1643)
- The Navigation Acts of Charles II and why they contributed to American colonial prosperity
▲ Compare and contrast contemporary accounts of the American Revolution.
★ The Whiskey Rebellion (1794)
➥ The evolvement of an immigration policy in America
- Results of the Mexican-American War, 1846–1848
➥ Evidences of "Yankee imperialism." What was it usually called? What were the reasons for the actions, both official and unofficial? What were the economics of each situation? Select several and compare.
- The super-rich in America, from 1880 to 1920, and how they got that way
- Political, economic, and philosophic arguments advanced by the South to justify the continuation of slavery
- What were the major features of the Jacksonian era? What were their origins and how did they affect the course of history?
- Describe American military de-

feats and victories, as well as the political problems encountered by President Madison during the war of 1812.

- Describe a typical factory town in nineteenth-century America.
○ What have been the contribu-

tions of Roman law and of John Locke to the traditional concepts of equality and freedom in the United States?

- The role of the press in the American Revolution

Key to Symbols

- average difficulty
§ substitutes possible
★ ample information in most libraries
○ specialized knowledge required

☛ narrow down topic
▲ large public or college library required
↙ local option topic
✗ examples and supporting evidence needed

History — United States: The West

- The United States Army often encountered hostility and opposition from settlers on the western frontier. What conflict in aims and purposes precipitated these misunderstandings?
- The impact of the mining "company town" on frontier life
- The first evidences of the labor movement in the West. What were the causal factors that led workers to unite against management?
§ Military campaigns against the Indians in Arizona (or in other western states)
- As the railroads moved west, societal structures were altered in local communities. What were some of these alterations? Did they become permanent changes in society?
★ The impact of the mountain men on westward expansion
- How women's suffrage was established in the Wyoming territory
- The battle of the Alamo in 1836: the Mexican point of view
- What factors encouraged western migration in the nineteenth century? What social classes were involved?
★ The conflict between the farmers and the cattlemen on the frontier West
× How folk ballads reflected the American frontier. Were they accurate representations?
§ How did the United States acquire Oregon? What were the consequences?
- The gold and silver strike of the Comstock Lode in 1859
- Mexicans who fought against Santa Anna in the Mexican Revolution
- Examine the responses of the Sioux and other Western Indians to white civilization during the period between the signing of the Fort Laramie Treaty and the Battle of Little Bighorn.
- How did the various land acts contribute to the economic growth of the West? Were they democratic? Why or why not?
➥ The world of the pulp western: Did it ever exist?
★ How barbed wire changed the life of farmers and the frontier cattlemen
★ The tragic winter of the Donner

Party in the Sierra Nevada
- The effects of the Homestead Act on frontier settlement and expansion
- Transportation and westward expansion
- Homesteading in the nineteenth-century West
§ The first railroad in <u>Wyoming</u>
- The Civil War in the Southwest. What were the major battles and conflicts?
- The Gadsden Purchase
▲ The background of the Mountain Meadows massacre in 1857
✕ Western outlaws and gunfighters: myths and realities
- The successes and failures of the pony express
- The role of religion in westward expansion and settlement
§ <u>Buffalo Bill</u> as a frontier hero
- Kansas and Missouri during the Civil War: the war within the war
§ The <u>California</u> gold rush
- The growth of the Western city in America. What were the major contributing factors?
○ If the outlaw Jesse James were alive today, would society still idolize him as a romantic hero? Have our criteria for heroes changed?
§ <u>Wyatt Earp</u>: the man and the myth (or, Joaquin Marietta, "Pancho" Villa, George A. Custer, Tom Horn)
- How did the Spanish missions change the Native American way of life? How did they change agriculture, education, health? What were the positive factors in this interrelationship?
- Why Denver survived
- Recruitment practices of western mining companies
- How conflicts on the western frontier differed from traditional warfare. What was often the role, for example, of women and children in western warfare?
✕ The single woman of the western frontier who homesteaded, managed ranches, and succeeded in a man's world
- The Chinese immigrant in the American West
- Newspapers in the West: their impact on frontier society
- The westward movement of the Mormons. Why did they migrate? To what extent were they successful in fulfilling their goals and aspirations?
- Select a frontier "boom" town that became a "ghost" town. What were the causes of its growth and decline?
- The facts surrounding the gunfight at the OK Corral
- The Colt revolver and the American frontier. In what ways did its widespread use alter events and change the course of western history?
§ Spanish Missions of <u>California</u> (Or, of Arizona, New Mexico,

or Texas) How were they established? By whom? What was their "mission"?

- The Lost Dutchman Gold Mine: Fact or fiction?
- Democracy, individual freedom, and the politics of the American frontier
- Present evidence to support the following: "American history has been to a rather large degree the history of the

colonization of the great West." (Frederick J. Turner)

§ The route of the Oregon Trail. Discuss its formulation and effects on settlement and trade.

○ Social stratification (or lack of it) in frontier society

➤ The role of the United States Army on the frontier

➤ Manifest Destiny and westward expansion

Key to Symbols

•	average difficulty	➤	narrow down topic
§	substitutes possible	▲	large public or college library required
★	ample information in most libraries	✔	local option topic
○	specialized knowledge required	✕	examples and supporting evidence needed

History — United States: 20th Century

× Has the civil rights movement been a success or a failure?

☛ Wall Street collapse (1929)

● Richard Nixon's last twenty days in the White House

★ President Carter's handling of the Iranian hostage situation has been variously praised and censured. Support one side of the issue.

● The effects of the 1963 Birmingham civil rights demonstrations

● Was the United States' entry into World War I in the national interest?

☛ The American postwar occupation of Japan: problems and achievements

● How did the United States mobilize for war after Pearl Harbor?

★ The Bay of Pigs: historical afterthoughts

● "Brainwashing" of American prisoners of war during the Korean conflict. What techniques were customarily used? What were the results?

● The American bicentennial celebration

● Many historians have named Henry Ford as a symbol of his era. In what ways might this be true? In what ways is it inexact?

● What the New Deal did for the agricultural community. Evaluate both the short- and long-term success of the program.

○ What were the origins and contributing factors of American prosperity in the 1920's? Were they similar to those operant after World War II?

● What has been the human radiation damage from United States nuclear tests? Consult the most recent findings.

○ Levels of United States isolationism and neutrality before entry into World War II

● Nonviolent resistance as social protest in the 1960's civil rights movement

☛ What has been the function of the conglomerate in the American economy since 1950? Select either one industry or a diversified corporation.

☛ Poverty in America in the twentieth century

★ Was the My Lai incident a significant event of the Vietnam War? What were the ethical issues involved?

▲ In what ways was the New

242

Deal a failure? Cite a variety of historians to support your answer.

- What have been the principal causes for the long-term poverty levels in Appalachia? What remedial measures might alleviate the situation?
- → Select a program of rock music of the 1960's whose themes and lyrics reflect and symbolize the prevailing attitudes and critical issues of the era.
- What have been the lasting results of the Cold War? Is it over?
- What has been the impact of the Love Canal on the immediate area and on the nation as a whole? Has it successfully raised the country's consciousness about such dangers?
- ○ Why does Franklin D. Roosevelt remain a figure of controversy? Have the issues changed?
- § Public opinion and the presidency of John F. Kennedy
- Why do historians consider Truman to have been a successful president?
- ○ How Presidents Ford, Carter, and Reagan changed the presidential image created by President Nixon
- § Evaluate Theodore Roosevelt's administration in terms of short-term and long-term results.
- § Analyze the assets and liabilities

of President Wilson's personality in assessing him as president.
- President Wilson's compromises for the establishment of the League of Nations
- ★ Was the United States' participation in World War I justified? To what extent were national interests involved? Could the United States have remained neutral?
- ○ Evaluate Woodrow Wilson's agenda for peace following World War I. Was it realistic in terms of American and European attitudes and goals?
- ★ What military skills and personal attributes contributed to General Douglas MacArthur's military success?
- Native American occupation of Alcatraz Island (San Francisco, 1969). What were the critical issues? Were they resolved by this action?
- ★ Japanese-American internment during World War II
- Who was responsible for the Kent State killings? What has been the basis of the ensuing controversies? How have historians evaluated this event?
- Historians look at Julius and Ethel Rosenberg. Were they guilty? Compare and contrast a variety of informed opinions.
- What happened in Selma, Ala-

bama? Why?

➤ A reassessment of the Pentagon papers case. Has history proved this case for either side? What were the original issues? What would have been the public and political reaction if it had happened yesterday?

★ The first ten years of the Peace Corps, 1961–1971

○ Historians reevaluate the Alger Hiss case. Have modern evidence and events forced historians and political scientists to reexamine the issues?

○ European economic conditions after World War I and the effects they had on the United States economy

● German spies in America in the 1930's

● Federal aid programs during the Great Depression: an evaluative overview

● Why the Vietnam War lasted so long

● Involvement in Vietnam: how it started

★ The United States' withdrawal from Saigon, 1972–1973. What accusations have been made against the United States government's policies and procedures?

★ Conditions in American coal mines before labor unions. In what ways have working situations improved? What regula-

tions fostered these changes?

➤ Events leading to the formation of labor unions in the United States

★ How the United States lost the war in Vietnam

● Tenets of President Franklin D. Roosevelt's "New Deal"

★ The Bonus Army march on Washington (June, 1932)

● How prohibition led to the increased spread and influence of organized crime

● The 1920's: a decade of change. What factors contributed to or caused these shifts in American life?

× Have Eskimo treaties been equitable?

★ Events leading to the decision to drop the atomic bomb on Japan and thus end World War II. What were the issues?

● Kennedy and Khrushchev: a conflict of personality during the Cuban missile crisis

● McCarthyism and American civil liberties

● How we won the Persian Gulf War (1991). Or did we?

➤ Compare and contrast the Korean and Vietnam Wars.

➤ Conspiracy theories about President John F. Kennedy's assassination

● Feminist movements during the 1920's

★ Revisionist historians examine

Pearl Harbor

★ Sacco and Vanzetti: Cruel and unusual punishment?

● Amnesty for Vietnam War evaders

● Discuss the continuing controversy surrounding the Cuban missile crisis.

● Events leading to Watergate

● The Teapot Dome scandal

★ The Truman-MacArthur controversy: the principle of civil control over the military

★ The trial and sentencing of Patricia Hearst. Was justice done?

● Koreagate (1977–1978)

▲ Instances of involuntary sterilization in the United States, 1950–1980

➧ The flavor and context of political and social activism by American youth in the 1960's

● The development of the atomic bomb at Los Alamos, New Mexico

○ What is meant by the "Americanization" of the Vietnam War? What rationales were employed to justify the gradual escalation of the American commitment to Vietnam?

● What were the main reasons for the United States' strong isolationist sentiments in the 1930's? Which major groups were involved? Why?

● Detail the domestic and international factors leading to the rise of McCarthyism and the "red scare" mentality from 1949 through the early 1950's.

● What steps were initiated by President Franklin D. Roosevelt prior to Pearl Harbor and the United States' entry into the war to protect American interests in the Far East? What steps did he take to keep the United States out of armed conflict?

§ Analyze the impact on the economy of President Bush's deference to business interests.

× How television has changed politics since 1960

○ What have been the contributing factors which have led to increasing nationalism in the third world nations? What has been the role of the United States?

● President Gerald Ford's pardon of Richard Nixon: a survey of national attitudes

★ What were the accomplishments of the civil rights movement in the 1960's? In the 1970's?

▲ What was President Johnson's official purpose for American involvement in the Vietnam War? What was the reality of the situation? Compare and contrast these factors.

● Support or refute: American involvement in Vietnam was consistent with its revolutionary heritage.

● The problem of illegal Cuban refugees. Has the United States found a satisfactory solution?

- Lyndon Johnson's "Great Society." Detail its successes in terms of social legislation.
- How did the United States organize and coordinate its manpower needs in World War II?
- What was the genesis of the Cold War?
▲ Would the United States have entered the war in Europe without Pearl Harbor? Consult a variety of authoritative sources and compare their opinions.
➤ The second New Deal and the beginnings of the welfare state
★ The Warren Court. What were some of its most significant and controversial decisions?
★ Were the Los Angeles riots (1992) a unique happening or a look at our future?

- What were, and still are, the major controversies surrounding President Roosevelt's New Deal?
§ How historians have reassessed the strengths and limitations of the presidency of Franklin Roosevelt
○ Examine the factors involved in what historians have called the Second Reconstruction in American history, the two decades since World War II.
§ Compare the leadership qualities of Truman and Eisenhower.
- How did the Progressive movement originate? What factors contributed to its momentum?
▲ Evaluate the "hundred days" of the New Deal in terms of its effect on the economy. Were modifications necessary?

Key to Symbols

•	average difficulty	➤	narrow down topic
§	substitutes possible	▲	large public or college library required
★	ample information in most libraries	✔	local option topic
○	specialized knowledge required	✗	examples and supporting evidence needed

History — United States: Social History

× The cultural impact of the Industrial Revolution in America. In what ways did it influence the arts, education, entertainment, etc.?

• The blue laws and the Puritans

• How the wide use of the telephone changed American life

★ How the Great Depression (1930) affected the working man and his family

• The origins of Alcoholics Anonymous

➡ Trace the influence of Great Britain on American manners and morals.

§ Living conditions in New York City, 1850–1880

§ The integration of Chinese immigrants into American culture

• The Oneida Community: an early commune

• The social and economic structure of the antebellum southern plantation

★ Why the hippie movement was (or was not) unique

• How have attitudes toward prostitution altered in America? Follow the changes from 1600 to the present day.

• Sexual equality: its American roots

➡ The work ethic and the American frontier

• The Western hero: myth and reality

• The frontier as social leveler

• Life on the Erie Canal

§ The early days of the Amana community

• How the social class system in colonial New England affected the course of American history

★ Military posts on the Western frontier. How were they organized and who lived on them? Describe a composite life-style.

• Compare and contrast class structure in America in 1850 and in 1950.

• Civil disobedience in America's past

★ How the automobile changed American society

• Life aboard a Mississippi riverboat

• The influence of the Quakers

▲ Compare and contrast the values of the pre-Civil War Southern slaveholder with those of the Northern abolitionist.

➤ The social consequences of the Vietnam War

▲ Compare newspaper advice columns for the years 1920, 1940, 1960, and 1980.

● Education in one-room country schools

○ The importance of the individual in America has been replaced by an increasing emphasis on collective action. There is historical evidence supporting each side of this issue. Contrast these conflicting views.

○ The negative aftermaths of World War II in the United States socioeconomic system

● The Young Men's Christian Association. What were its original aims and goals? What were the conditions in society that fostered its establishment?

● The impact of the Great Depression was felt on every level of American society. In what ways did it affect and permanently change existing social structures?

★ How have family life-patterns changed since television viewing has increased in most families? What problems has it caused?

★ How was John Steinbeck's novel *The Grapes of Wrath* a mirror for social conditions in the 1930's in America?

§ Popular culture in the <u>1930's</u>

● What inhibited or stopped any significant development of colonial literature, art, and science?

✔ The characteristics and patterns of rural family life on a farm in your locality in the nineteenth century

● Why was Charles Lindbergh a national hero of the 1920's? What aspects of American society did he represent to most Americans?

● The religious camp meetings of the late nineteenth century and early twentieth century

● The role of women in colonial society

● Discuss and compare the distinctive features of social organization in the following colonial living units: the plantation, the farm, the city, and the town.

● The effects of the 1929 stock market crash and the ensuing depression on American attitudes toward government

▲ Drug addiction in nineteenth-century America

● The ingenuity and inventiveness of the Shakers

● The establishment and implementation of early welfare programs in the United States

● Anti-Semitism, fascism, and isolationism: Father Charles Coughlin

▲ Alexander Graham Bell's work with the deaf

★ The abolitionist movement in America

★ Life of the black slave on the

plantation: fact and fiction

- The Women's Christian Temperance Union: the mission and its impact
- Describe the typical United States country store in 1900.
- × Instances of racism in colonial America
- Compare and contrast the cowboy of the movies and western fiction with the American cowboy of the nineteenth century.
- ➡ Radio in the 1930's: the programs and their audiences
- The Puritans: their beliefs, attitudes, and lasting effects on the American character
- ▲ Some social historians assert that ethnic neighborhoods have retarded the assimilation of newer citizens into American culture. Discuss this issue in terms of several communities.
- § How tobacco altered the course of American colonial history
- Compare and contrast the class systems of the North and South before the Civil War in terms of the economic bases on which they rested. How were these systems altered by the war?
- ○ What is the New England "character"? What is the South's? Compare and contrast the two within their social and historical contexts.
- The Puritan influence in America has been more of a bane than a blessing. What are the criteria and the facts supporting this proposition?
- What changes did World War I and its ending bring to American domestic life?
- ➡ Evaluate the "counterculture" of the 1960's. Has it had a lasting effect on American culture? On women? On education?
- § Are the attitudes of American college students in this decade different from those in the last? (or, select another time-span)
- How has the women's liberation movement differed from the women's rights movement?
- ★ Why did Mark Twain call post-Civil War society the "Gilded Age"? What were its characteristics?
- What were the major factors influencing social changes in the last half of the nineteenth century in America?
- ▲ Utopias in America. Why have they had such a relatively small and short-lived impact on American values and living patterns?
- Attitudes toward divorce in America's past
- The 1960's: A decade of social disintegration?
- ○ Historians agree that eighteenth-century America was a society reaching its maturity. What evidence substantiates this opinion?
- What was the most significant social legislation passed in the period 1880–1900? Are the

effects still viable today?

▲ Urban slum reform movements in the late nineteenth century

▲ What was the reception of Sinclair Lewis's novels criticizing the American lifestyle? Were differing views expressed by the professional critics than by the public? How did the press react?

▲ Puritan gravestone images as a reflection of American colonial culture

★ The effects of the Beatles on America's youth

● The American character as viewed by contemporary historian Daniel J. Boorstin

● The witches of Salem and what happened to them

Key to Symbols

● average difficulty
§ substitutes possible
★ ample information in most libraries
○ specialized knowledge required

⬆ narrow down topic
▲ large public or college library required
🗸 local option topic
✗ examples and supporting evidence needed

Hobbies

§ <u>Upholstery</u> techniques for the amateur

§ <u>Home lapidary</u> equipment, its technology, and costs

• Coin collecting as an investment

• The economics of stamp collecting

• The value of hobbies

• Stocking and maintaining a sea-water aquarium

§ How to buy <u>antiques</u>

§ Care and feeding of <u>hamsters</u>. Or, select another pet.

• Model railroads and how they have changed

• Constructive pasttimes for the elderly

• How to make brass rubbings

§ How to collect _____. Select a class of objects, such as United States maps, toy banks, local fossils, etc., and discuss the costs, availability, and historical significance of items in such a collection.

• Papier-mâché projects for children

§ How to breed and raise <u>goats</u>. Or, select another large animal.

• Hobbies of famous people

• Factors to consider when choosing a hobby

• Some hobbies are free. Describe a selection of them.

Key to Symbols

•	average difficulty	↞	narrow down topic
§	substitutes possible	▲	large public or college
★	ample information in most		library required
	libraries	↙	local option topic
o	specialized knowledge	x	examples and supporting
	required		evidence needed

How-To

See also: Essay Suggestions

- become elected
- make money from your invention
- judge character
- change your eating habits for life
- read a financial statement
- retire early and rich
- build a loom
- start your own business
- buy gold and silver
- make maple sugar
- write poetry
- never be lonely
- improve your vocabulary
- overcome any handicap
- produce hybrids
- whistle
- track animals
- improve your community
- read between the lines
- be a vegetarian
- cut food bills
- enjoy old age
- beat insomnia
- be a ventriloquist
- stop smoking
- read navigational charts
- tile a floor
- write a perfect term paper
- uncommercialize Christmas
- win at chess
- train your mind to be creative
- be self-sufficient
- fly a glider
- earthquake-proof a building
- build a low-cost solar collector
- sell your own home
- clean a chimney
- walk on the moon
- bind your own books
- attract birds
- travel cheaply
- be a legend in your own time
- make wine at home
- fight city hall
- refinish furniture
- build a darkroom
- raise llamas
- polish gemstones
- win at poker
- unstop a sink
- make simple repairs on your automobile
- be selected as a game show contestant
- grow vegetables year 'round
- raise and breed parakeets
- build a sandbox
- build a barbeque pit
- please your boss
- kick the television habit
- raise orchids
- discipline children
- sell anything
- save the rainforests

Humanities

See also: Architecture; Art; Film; Literature; Literature — Drama; Music; Philosophy; Photography; Theater

- ○ Form follows function: the development of the sonata allegro form in music
- • Why is no one making Stradivarius violins? What was the secret of making violins in Cremona?
- ◆ Economic and political factors that contributed to the rise of Christianity
- • Getting on in Hollywood. What does it take to write music for films?
- ◆ Satire in the 1980's & 1990's. Survey the levels, variety, and intent of satire directed toward one specific segment of society. Use, for example, college students, bureaucrats, political campaigns, or television.
- × The Faustian legend in art, literature, and music
- • Euripides denounced slavery but Plato, Aristotle, Jesus, and St. Paul accepted it. What were the reasons for their acceptance? What are the implications?
- • Max Reinhardt and the development of the Salzburg Mozart Festival
- • "High-tech" hijinks in contemporary films. Are they a substitute for wit and invention?
- ★ Prehistoric cave paintings: magic, hunting ritual, or art for art's sake?
- • The checkered career of "cultural" channels on television
- § Popular songs in the 1980's. What are the social, ethical, and cultural values they express and promote?
- ▲ Wolfgang Amadeus Mozart was a successful operatic composer but Franz Shubert was not. Why was this so?
- • The relationship between Christian doctrine and contemporary ecological issues and concerns
- • Faith and fanaticism: Savonarola and John Calvin
- • The role of Petrarch as a founder of humanism
- ▲ The influence of nineteenth-

century poetry on romantic opera. Include a discussion of E.T.A. Hoffmann

- Rajput and Mughal (India) miniature paintings as an expression of cultural and social patterns
- The Age of Reason and the perfectability of man. Discuss idealism versus reality.
- Parallels between Noah's flood and the Babylonian *Epic of Gilgamesh*
- Sacred dance during the Middle Ages. Describe the different types with a discussion of their origins and their functions.
- × What have been the problems encountered by the National Endowment for the Arts? Consider several of the issues involved.
- ★ Discuss the Renaissance as a "bridge to the present."
- "Bread and circuses" and the failure of the first public welfare program (Rome)
- ▲ Neoplatonism in Florence and the origins of opera
- ➤ Greek and Roman influences on the Renaissance
- Baroque styles and the design of fountains
- Discuss impressionism in terms of the music of Claude Debussy and the paintings of Claude Monet.
- ➤ Compare the urban design of Williamsburg with that found in English towns of that period.
- ▲ How and why Giovanni Gabrieli

wrote and adapted his music to the design of St. Mark's Cathedral (Venice)

- Macho: Roman chariot drivers compared to American race car drivers
- The development of concert halls in Western culture. Which came first, the hall or the performance? Why?
- Eighteenth-century England and John Gay's *Beggar's Opera*. What factors account for its success?
- × The symbolism of musical instruments in Western art
- § Three-dimensional propaganda: architecture in Nazi Germany. Or, select examples from Stalin's Russia or Mussolini's Italy.
- × The English origins of American folk songs
- Practical and artistic aspects of the performance conventions of Greek tragedies
- ▲ Women composers of the Renaissance. Who were they? What was their role in their contemporary music circles?
- ▲ The influence of Flemish musicians in Italian Renaissance courts. Why were they more influential than native Italians?
- ○ Language and music. Do musical instruments predate language? What are the current theories? What evidence is there in support of each concept?
- The function of the Daily Hours

of Divine Services in medieval monasteries. What were its origins?

- *Choreomania* in the Middle Ages: What was it and why did it happen?
- ▲ The influence of Freudian theories on twentieth-century art in Europe and the United States
- ○ The parallels between literary realism and the realistic style of painting in the nineteenth century
- ★ Compare Greek democratic practices with those practiced by contemporary societies.
- Contrast the cultural growth of classical China with that which developed simultaneously in India.
- Romanticism versus realism in nineteenth-century literature. Which was the better (more valid) expression of the age or reaction to the age?
- How and why Charlemagne encouraged the arts
- Why some cultures never become civilizations
- Richard Wagner and Friedrich Nietzsche: the philosophy of imperial power
- ➤ The impact of Muslim culture on world history
- ✕ Ancient coins as a reflection of cultural values
- § The writings of Charles Dickens as a mirror of his times
- ➤ Byzantine achievements in art, architecture, and science (select one)
- ➤ How the arts have reflected major twentieth-century political changes in Europe. Focus on one art form.
- ✕ A comparison of the love poetry of Ovid with that of the medieval troubadours, with that of contemporary popular music
- The opposing forces in the premiere of Igor Stravinsky's *Rite of Spring*. What were the issues?
- The social status of high Renaissance artists. What was their role? How were they funded?
- Sculptural versions of the Last Judgment
- A comparison of the Renaissance style in the music of Palestrina with the paintings of Raphael
- ✕ Images and symbols in The Book of Revelation
- Artist Ben Shahn's involvement in the Sacco-Vanzetti case
- § Federal support of the arts in the United States compared to artistic subsidies in France (or Austria or Denmark). What are the reasons for the difference?
- ○ Aristotle's *Poetics* applied to *Oedipus Rex* and *Death of a Salesman*
- Refute or support: Culture only flourishes when there is a wealthy segment of society to support it.

Interior Design

See also: Architecture; Art

- ● The effects of color in work environments
- ▲ Problems with current flammability standards for interiors
- ★ Select a furniture style and describe its characteristics, origins, functions, and variations.
- ● Egyptian contributions to, and influence on, world furniture design
- ★ Tomorrow's homes: How different will they be?
- ● Furnishing the one-room apartment. What are the particular considerations for this specialized environment?
- ● Designing and decorating the office environment: some basic considerations
- ● Furniture from the Bauhaus school
- × The functional aspects of American colonial furniture design
- ▲ The influence of Danish modern design on contemporary interiors
- ● How to judge the quality of new furniture
- ● Art nouveau furniture design
- ○ Design concepts and innovations in the houses of Le Corbusier
- ● Fabrics of the future
- ● Bentwood furniture and how its technology led to mass production. Include the work of Thonet.
- ● Barrier-free interiors for the handicapped
- ➧ Essential factors in the design of functional rooms for young children. Select an age range.
- ● How to individualize a room using "ready mades"
- ▲ The significant home design concepts of Bernard Maybeck (1862–1957)
- ● Survey current area rug imports. Include design, quality, price, availability.
- ★ The interior design features of the White House
- ➧ How synthetic fibers have changed the textile industry. Select either the period from 1930 to 1960, or from 1960 to the present.
- ○ Plan the furnishing of a new three-bedroom home on a budget of $15,000.00. Include the number of occupants, decorative style, and potential needs

of the occupants. If possible, interview a real family.

▲ Psychological aspects of space and ergonomics

○ Design and equip the exterior and interior of a hypothetical business. Include costs, equipment, appearance, layout, traffic, pattern considerations, etc.

• How color creates atmosphere in home decoration

• The home interior of the future

☛ Furniture restoration techniques

• Describe the interior of a typical colonial house

• Kitchen workspace design

• How to blend furniture styles

• Carpeting: Wool, acrylics, nylon (all generations), polyester, olefins, or other alternatives.

• Special effects with home lighting

• Treatments of wall surfaces for modern homes. Include product information, as well as a discussion of design possibilities.

★ How to choose a color scheme

• How to make a small room seem large

▲ Trends in contemporary Italian furniture design

○ Ethical considerations and constraints in the home furnishings design industry

• Furniture concepts of Alvar Aalto, Finnish architect and designer

• Compare and contrast the design concepts and motifs of art nouveau, art deco, and the Bauhaus styles.

★ How to create an indoor garden

✓ Interview several interior designers (both independent and those affiliated with retail outlets) and compare and contrast their methods, resources, charges, and availability.

• Design and furnish an artist's studio. Consider lighting, utilities, work areas, conveniences, etc.

• Compare and contrast the qualities of handmade versus machine-made oriental rugs.

• Wallpaper categories

• The contributions of René Lalique and his family to the art of jewelry and glass design

★ Tiffany glass designs

▲ The influence of wallpaper and textile designer William Morris on modern design

§ The functional furniture designs of Charles Eames: an evaluation

• The trend towards ornamentalism in both architecture and interior decoration

Invention and Discovery

See also: Technology

Below is a list of major inventions and discoveries, some simple in concept and application, others complex and with a profound and far-reaching influence. Each innovation has contributed, in a unique way, to technology, science, and society. Some have quite directly changed our lives, while others have remained unrecognized for many years. Select one topic and examine the events that led to its discovery, what processes and technologies were involved, and why its development was singular. What was its reception? How was it used and distributed and what immediate changes did it generate in industry and society? What applications grew out of its development? And, finally, what has been its impact on history?

- Wheel, prehistory
- Fire, 500,000 B.C.
- Cement, 5,000 B.C.
- Chains (cable), 2,500 B.C.
- Gunpowder, 200 B.C.
- Rocket, 1232
- Waterwheel, thirteenth century
- False limbs, 1560
- Knitting machine, 1589
- Microscope, 1590
- Thermometer, 1593
- Telescope, 1608
- Logarithm, 1614
- Rifle, 1620
- Slide rule, 1621
- Adding machine, 1641
- Pendulum clock, 1656
- Velocity of light, 1675

- Piano, 1709
- Steam engine, 1712
- Photography, c. 1727
- Weaving's flying shuttle, 1733
- Sextant and octant, 1750's
- Bifocal lens, c. 1760
- Water-powered loom, 1768
- Hot air balloon, 1783
- Sewing machine, 1790
- Parachute, 1797
- Electric current battery, 1800
- Molecular hypothesis, 1811
- Miner's safety lamp, 1815
- Camera, 1816
- Electric motor, 1822
- Portland cement, 1824
- Matches, 1827
- Braille, 1829

- Reaping machine, 1830
- Dynamo or generator, 1831
- Refrigeration, 1834
- Revolver, 1835
- Steel plow, 1837
- Screw propeller, 1837
- Ozone, 1839
- Bicycle, 1839
- Electric telegraph, 1844
- Nitroglycerine, 1846
- Bullet, 1849
- Ophthalmoscope, 1851
- Gyroscope, 1852
- Aniline dyes, 1856
- Passenger elevator, 1857
- Spectrum analysis, 1859
- Internal combustion engine, c. 1860
- Atlantic cable, 1866
- Typewriter, 1867
- Air brake, 1867
- Torpedo, 1868
- Barbed wire machine, 1874
- Phonograph, 1877
- Cash register, 1879
- Incandescent lamp, 1879
- Artificial languages, 1880
- Machine gun, 1885
- Linotype, 1885
- Automobile, 1887
- Kodak camera, 1888
- Combined harvester and thresher, 1888
- Diphtheria antitoxin, 1890
- Diesel engine, 1893
- Zipper, 1893
- Radio, 1896
- Radioactivity, 1896
- Wireless telegraph, 1897
- Tape recorder, 1898
- Quantum theory, 1901
- Isolation of adrenaline, 1901
- Depth bomb, 1903
- Intelligence testing, 1905
- Theories of relativity, 1905–53
- Wassermann test for syphilis, 1906
- Helicopter, 1909
- Wilson cloud chamber, 1911
- Lewis gun, 1912
- Military tank, 1914
- Insulin, 1922
- Television, 1925
- Quantum mechanics, 1925
- Cyclotron, 1931
- Atom smashing with slow neutrons, 1934
- Radar, 1935
- Jet engine, 1939
- Aerosol spray, 1941
- The structure of DNA, 1953
- Lasers, 1960
- Communications satellite, 1962
- Hubble Space Telescope, 1990

Journalism

See also: Language; Media; Photography; Speech Communication; Television and Radio

- The muckrakers were a good (bad) influence
- Interview a local celebrity and write an article which covers his or her background, accomplishments, and personality.
- The use of business-supplied publicity for news coverage by the journalistic community. Why is this practice criticized by media experts?
- Has the press overextended its role as public watchdog?
- Compare and contrast sensational and yellow journalism with the techniques of straight news reporting. What elements are unique to each?
- The colonial newspapers of James Franklin
- Compare one week of front pages from your local newspaper with _____. Select a large metropolitan daily. Compare the differences in coverage.
- Compare and contrast the public relations specialist and the news reporter.

- Compare an editorial and a straight news story, using significant examples.
- How the presidents have used the media. Start with the term of Franklin D. Roosevelt.
- The era of yellow journalism under Pulitzer and Hearst
- The *Time* v. *Firestone* libel case and the right to privacy issue
- Compare cold type and hot type printing methods.
- What is the law related to the censorship of school newspapers? Include court cases.
- The role of the newspaper during the Revolutionary War
- The influence of advertisers on the news content or editorial policy of a newspaper. Discuss the issues, pressure tactics, journalistic standards, political and social demands, etc.
- The *New York Times* exposed the corrupt Tweed ring in 1871. Discuss its coverage of this event in light of historical evidence.
- John Reed and his coverage of

the Russian Revolution in his book *Ten Days That Shook the World*

x Significant turn-of-the-century newspaper crusades. Include the background, reporting, and final effects of these militant causes.

★ How journalists can slant the news

★ The case of *Progressive* magazine and the hydrogen bomb

○ The outer limits of a free press in the United States

● Can the small newspaper survive?

● How did the Hearst newspaper empire become so powerful and rich?

● Interviewing techniques

● *Life* magazine and photo-journalism

★ How to organize and produce a school newspaper

● A profile of the *Christian Science Monitor* newspaper

● The Pentagon Papers, the *Washington Post*, and journalistic ethics

● News coverage in *Pravda* (Russia)

● The scope and distribution of specialized newsletters in the United States

★ Careers in journalism today

§ Press coverage of a recent international crisis. Compare several papers and magazines.

● The journalistic interview

● Compare local newspaper coverage of an important international event with that of *The New York Times*.

➤ The use of computers in newspaper production

★ A free press versus the right to an impartial trial

➤ The historical role of American newspapers in society

● How to evaluate a newspaper

● The issues of privilege and the press

x Discuss the tenents of the "new journalism" and analyze three examples.

● Financial problems of daily newspapers

● Photojournalism as a profession

★ Essential factors in writing news stories

● Functions of the copy editor on a large city newspaper

● Survey the major changes in newspaper printing processes.

● The "Gonzo" journalist, Hunter S. Thompson

● The presidential press conference. What are its functions?

● Is the role of a reporter always adversarial? Investigate the parameters of this position.

➤ Early American newspapers. Select one that is available for study.

▲ Compare the coverage given to the John Kennedy assassination by three metropolitan newspapers.

○ The effects of televised news on newspaper news contents and readership

✕ What constitutes irresponsible journalism?

● Newspaper editorial policies

● Press bureaus. Examine their functions, economics, and utility.

● Foreign correspondents: training, responsibilities, and life-styles.

✔ Analyze the editorials appearing in your local newspaper for one month and compare them to those for the same period in *The New York Times*. Analyze both content and point of view.

● Compare and contrast journalism and literature.

✕ Using examples, discuss the differences and similarities of factual reporting and interpretive reporting.

● War correspondents during World War II

● Television coverage of the Vietnam War. Was it realistic, factual, and objective?

● Electronic newspapers

★ How to be an editor

● For a one-week period, compare the scope and depth of news coverage on the three early-morning national news programs.

▲ Recent court decisions affecting the press

● William Paley and the formation of CBS

▲ The sensationalized journalistic techniques of James G. Bennett, Jr.'s *New York Herald* in the nineteenth century

✔ Compare news coverage on local television station(s) with the coverage in local newspaper(s).

○ How the mass circulation of newspapers influenced American public opinion in the late nineteenth century

● The "penny press" of the 1830's

● The founding of *The New York Times*

● Political and mercantile newspapers in the early nineteenth century

● The trial of John Peter Zenger and its effects on the restriction of the press

● The tabloid newspaper today

● Evaluate the southern press during the Civil War and during Reconstruction.

● The evening news: Too long? Too short? Superficial? What do journalists advise?

✕ Analyze recent press coverage of AIDS (Acquired Immune Deficiency Syndrome) in several newspapers and magazines, both local and national.

● Consider the ethics involved in protecting the anonymity of news sources.

Labor

See also: Business and Industry; Working World

- How the increasing role of minorities and women in the business community has changed the personnel and human relations policies of business organizations
- ★ The industrial worker in modern Japan. Consider working conditions, wages, job security, and motivation.
- Fluctuations in the composition of the labor force: 1930, 1950, and 1990. Discuss classes of workers, ages, sex, proportions, locations, unemployment, education, and any other relevant elements.
- ➡ The role of Mexican labor in the American economy. Focus, for example, on agriculture in the Southwest.
- § Grievance procedures in the steel industry
- Affirmative action in theory and practice
- ▲ Child labor in the ancient and medieval world
- ★ Conditions and safety regulations for coal miners. How has unionization alleviated previous working conditions which were often unsafe and arduous?
- ○ Growth and change in the Teamster's union
- Federal manpower programs during the Depression
- ▲ The role of women in labor unions
- How labor arbitration is conducted
- § Unionization in the teaching profession
- ✕ Has the right to strike been abused?
- ★ Labor problems in Russia today
- Job factors influencing high productivity
- What are the prospects for white collar unionism during the next few decades in the United States?
- Job satisfaction based on Studs Terkel's book Working and other similar studies
- ○ Collective bargaining for public employees: policies and practices
- ➡ Living conditions of migrant farm workers. Select an area,

such as the South or the South-west.

↩ Trade unions and corruption

▲ Federal efforts to regulate union irregularities and corruption

• A number of powerful factors united to make the 1920's a time of general failure for the labor movement in America. Would it be possible for these same factors to unite again, causing a failure of unionism?

• The 1947 Taft-Hartley Labor Act and its consequences for American labor

★ Historical aspects of child labor in the United States

↩ Current perspectives and prospects for retraining the unemployed. Select one segment of the labor market which is currently stressed by unemployment.

• Unemployment in the last decade. Who, where, and why?

★ Pros and cons of mandatory retirement

• The effects on the labor market of the increased number of illegal aliens in the United States

○ Trends in the area of management prerogatives

○ Have labor unions proved to be in the public interest?

★ The issues involved in the PATCO (Professional Air Traffic Controllers Organization) strike (1981)

• Should public employees be allowed to strike?

× Work-related diseases

▲ The increasing liberalization of economic supplemental benefits appears to be advantageous to the worker. What are some of the possible problems for the future if the trend continues to expand?

• Characteristics of the hard-core unemployed

• The occupational possibilities for unemployed minority teenagers in large cities. What have been the characteristics of some of the more successful programs?

• How the Wagner Act (National Labor Relations Act) affected the development of trade unions

• The effects of organized labor on the nonunion worker

• Labor unions and the individual American worker: A change for better or worse?

○ What are typical features of private pension plans? What are some of the current problems of these plans?

• Examine the role violence has played in American labor union history.

• Support or refute: American labor unions have been largely responsible for inflation.

↩ Drug testing and the workplace

★ The plight of migrant workers during the Depression

▲ Production standards under collective bargaining contracts

- Women as clerical workers: wages, conditions, mobility, benefits, etc.
- ✔ Investigate the levels and causes of unemployment in your state.
- The incidence and nature of industrial accidents
- Closed shops and union shops and how they have influenced wages and working conditions
- Why the labor unions flourished under Franklin D. Roosevelt's presidency
- ★ Cesar Chavez and the United Farm Workers
- Pros/cons of the guaranteed annual wage
- Typical working conditions during the Industrial Revolution in England
- The indentured servant in early America
- ➥ Hiring the "unemployable"
- ▲ Arbitration and the right of management to discharge. What are the primary issues and their consequences?
- Labor arbitration in the 1970's
- The power to strike as a force in collective bargaining
- ★ "Flextime" and productivity
- ➥ Successful incentive systems for factory workers
- § The labor costs in the steel industry, 1950–1990
- ➥ Migrant labor in western Europe today
- Manpower problems in the Arab Gulf states

- The Congress of Industrial Organizations (CIO) and the American Federation of Labor (AFL) merged in 1955. What finally brought this combination about? How did it change the course of labor history in the United States?
- ★ Why do strikes occur? Should measures be instituted to prevent them? If so, what measures?
- Describe the campaign of Mary Harris Jones ("Mother Jones," 1830–1930) in her fight against low pay.
- ➥ Examine unemployment by economic sector, 1970–present
- Voluntary and mandatory wage and price controls. What are the advantages and disadvantages of each?
- Why has the number of strikes declined in the United States in recent years?
- ▲ What has been the reaction of the labor market to the four-day work week and "flexitime" scheduling?
- What circumstances and personal attributes account for the success of John L. Lewis as a labor organizer and leader?
- The development and changes in child labor laws in nineteenth-century America
- ✕ Strike-breaking methods
- ✕ Select several instances of governmental intervention in labor

relations and justify (or criticize) these acts.

- The essential components of modern labor negotiations
- ▲ Seniority has been part of the collective bargaining process. In what ways does it operate? What are the problems typically encountered? Are there exceptions and limitations?
- How the assembly line has affected the labor force
- Working conditions in the gold mines of South Africa
- How the Pullman strike (1894) could have been avoided
- The wage gap for women's earnings: a national survey
- Are the right-to-work laws desirable public policy?
- Proposals to lower the rate of unemployment
- ▲ Future directions of the American labor movement
- Alternatives to the assembly line in factory production
- ➥ Select a famous labor strike, such as the Philadelphia printers' strike in 1786, and recount its origins, scope, important details, and impact on future labor conflicts and negotiations.
- Advances in Workers' Compensation laws
- ✕ Sexual and racial wage disparities in the modern marketplace
- Scope and range of employment

of the handicapped
- Refute: Productivity has declined in proportion to the rise of unionization.
- § The plight of the urban migrant in Mexico City
- ▲ Levels and measures of technological unemployment: a national survey
- ✓ What programs and incentives have been instituted in your area to alleviate unemployment? Is retraining involved or are most of the programs make-work?
- The four-day work week: current practices
- § Automobile unions, past and present
- The division of labor in primitive cultures
- The Teamsters union and organized crime
- ▲ Current federal job training programs: an analysis of their range and impact
- How the Civil War affected labor unions
- Conflicts in labor relations in the United States have often been successfully settled by arbitration. In what ways has this system been effective? Are there problems?
- Automation: A curse or a blessing for the worker?
- The role of the strikebreaker. What have been the traditional

attitudes of unions toward them? Of companies?

- How the labor market has been influenced and changed by affirmative action
- x Explain the decrease of skilled labor in the United States.

- O Discuss current instances of the use by management of the Federal Bankruptcy Act to nullify union contracts.
- Illegal aliens are only taking jobs no one else wants. Is this statement true? Justify with both facts and figures.

Key to Symbols

- • average difficulty
- § substitutes possible
- ★ ample information in most libraries
- o specialized knowledge required

- ☛ narrow down topic
- ▲ large public or college library required
- ↙ local option topic
- x examples and supporting evidence needed

Language

See also: Journalism; Libraries, Books, and Publishing; Literature; Speech Communication

○ Describe the language system used in the novel *Riddley Walker* by Russell Hoban (1980).

● The language of Holden Caulfield (*Catcher in the Rye* by J.D. Salinger) as a reflection of his character and his times

● Analyze the potential for the development of a common world language

● Verner's law

▲ How to read hieroglyphics

○ An analysis of linguists' attitudes toward slang

★ Sequoyah's alphabet

● The language of advertising: an in-depth study. Select one medium (television, magazines, newspapers) and one product area (breakfast cereal, women's lingerie, automobiles) and compare and contrast the words used to describe these similar products.

● Pidgin English: a modern anomaly

★ How are modern English language dictionaries compiled?

What are inclusion and definition parameters? Who decides? Compare and contrast several unabridged dictionaries, considering the number of words, proper nouns, added features in each definition, order of meanings, etc.

✕ Sexism in language

● The earliest dictionaries. Why were they compiled?

§ The language of Afrikaans: its origins, structure, and range

● Dolphin communications. Survey the range of experimentation over the last ten years and discuss the most important advances and discoveries.

▲ The influence of the media on American vocabulary and grammar. The charge has been leveled that it is contributing to a lower level of complexity and nuance. Support or defend this charge with expert opinion.

§ Military euphemisms

● The language of the Spanish and French Basques

● The influence of language on

perceptions of reality. Can we think and perceive without words?

- ○ The brain and its relationship to language
- • Compare and contrast the second and third editions of *Webster's New International Dictionary*.
- × The influence of Latin on the English language
- ○ Methodology for teaching a foreign language
- ○ The roots of the Navajo language. What are the implications?
- ◆ Similarities and differences of the French and English languages
- ▲ The compilation of the *Oxford English Dictionary*, the world's most complex index of words
- • Cryptography: the science of ciphers and codes
- ★ Ways to improve your spelling and vocabulary
- • Distinctive features of Old English
- • Theories on the origin of language. Compare several of the most significant.
- • Language games for children
- • Is language losing its meaning?
- ▲ The case against (for) bilingual education
- × Language and social class in the United States
- • The development of speech in the young child
- • How children learn a second language
- ○ Psycholinguistics
- • Shakespeare's puns
- ◆ Discuss some of the many English words that are borrowed from other languages. Select a subject field or kind of word.
- ○ How speech evolves in a society
- • Is our language male-oriented?
- • Describe and compare the elements of several artificial languages.
- ★ The background and current uses of the Morse code
- × A history of graffiti
- • Contemporary problems with English as a universal language
- • Esperanto: its history, influence, and structure
- • The finger alphabet for the deaf
- × Origins of "black" English and some examples of its vocabulary and syntax
- × Doublespeak
- • There is a growing trend for "political correctness" in our language. Has it already gone too far? Or is it a necessary culture correction?
- • The social implications of the advent of writing
- • The components of man's earliest speech: some scientific conjectures
- • Language from the sports page: a vocabulary unto itself

- Nazi propaganda: an analysis of its vernacular and how it worked
- Grimm's law
★ How the braille system of lettering for the blind was developed and its uses today
- The deciphering of the Rosetta stone by Champollion. In what ways did this add to the body of linguistic knowledge?
- The language of cartoons
§ Analyze the language of an industry, such as the funeral business.
- The language of insults, taunts, and jeers
○ Examine several ways in which scientists propose that language affected the course of biological and cultural evolution.
- Definitions of pornography
○ Collect fifty pieces of "junk" mail. Analyze the language used. How is it suited to its target audiences? How well does the language portray the product?
- Compare the military slang of World War I, World War II, and the Vietnam War.
- How does the human language differ from other animal communication systems?
- What design features of the human language are similar to that learned by the primates Washoe and Sarah? Which are

different?
○ The linguistic contributions of Noam Chomsky
▲ How language reinforces group solidarity
○ The value of nonhuman primate communication models in the study of the evolution of language
- Ancient Greek words in common English usage
- Compare and contrast the cuneiform writing methods of the Egyptians with those of Mayan and Aztec pictographs.
- Read thoroughly the advertisements in a city newspaper and collect all of the grammatical errors. Do the same for television commercials. Discuss the results.
× The language of political propaganda. Use some of the classic examples to exemplify your conclusions.
★ The origins of alphabets
- The Egyptian invention of papyrus. Cite the technology involved and the ultimate significance of this new source of writing material.
➔ How the invention of writing changed the course of human cultural history
- Which was more important to the history of civilization: The invention of writing or the invention of printing?

Latin America

See also: Foreign Policy; World Scene

- The Spanish-American War, freedom of the press, and the Hearst newspapers
- × Describe President Franklin D. Roosevelt's "good neighbor" policy. What was involved? How was it implemented? Was it successful? What were some of the applications in Latin America, in particular Cuba, El Salvador, and Mexico?
- ▲ Latin America and the Monroe Doctrine: the first years
- Why the Panama Canal was not constructed in Nicaragua. Should it have been? Why?
- ○ An overview of political conditions in the Caribbean in the current year
- ★ How Pizarro conquered the Incas
- The United States' Cuban immigration policies and problems since 1975
- ➤ Sports in Latin America. Select either one particular sport and discuss it in terms of several countries, or select one nation's sport scene.
- § Poverty and the culture of poverty in Mexico City
- Has the Free Trade Agreement been successful? If so, for whom?
- ➤ Characterize the agrarian reform movement in Latin America. What are the underlying causes of this movement? Select a specific country.
- How the modern Inca Indians of Peru have maintained ancient traditions, both religious and social, while surrounded by Western traditions.
- Critical issues affecting South American political stability. Are these issues unique to each particular country? Are there common issues?
- Discuss education, literacy, and the cultural achievements of Peru.
- The aims and campaigns of Simón Bolívar
- ★ Can the Amazon rainforest be saved?
- Compare the population demographics of Latin American countries. Why is there such diversity?

- The controversy surrounding the regime of Salvador Allende of Chile
- Discuss the politics and government of a Latin American country from 1940 until now. Of particular interest are those countries which have undergone radical political changes.
- The founding of Brasilia, Brazil and why it failed (succeeded)
- The social organization of the Mayans
- Mexico and OPEC (Organization of Petroleum Exporting Countries)
- Mexico's political structure
- The Aztecs after the Spanish conquest
- The revolutionary platform of Fidel Castro
- The naval blockade of Cuba during the Cuban missile crisis
- Cuba under Castro: economic and educational advances and problems
- Mexican silver industry and its relationship to the international money market
- Should the United States have kept the Panama Canal?
- Contributing factors of the Mexican-American War (1846–48)
- Mexican oil and the United States. What is the current rate of importation? What agreements are in effect? What is the potential?
- The impact of the multinationals on Latin American culture
- Conditions in Cuba under Batista (pre-Castro)
- The conquest of New Spain
- South America has frequently been compared to Africa. Discuss the geographical and human similarities and differences. Account for each of them on the basis of historical and contemporary evidence.
- What are the obstacles to parliamentary democracy or socialism in Latin America?
- How the political philosophy of Fidel Castro has altered and evolved
- The ethnic makeup and backgrounds of modern Mexicans
- Why Argentina was a haven for Nazi war criminals
- How will the huge debts owed by many Latin-American countries be repaid?
- The influence of Nazi Germany on the political thinking of Juan Perón of Argentina
- Civilization and the Indians of Patagonia. How were they affected?
- Major achievements of the Mayan civilization
- The social implications of the Indian in contemporary Mexican culture
- Contemporary Latin American popular music. What are the traditional forms? Are they indigenous?
- The Cuban presence in South America, 1950–1980
- Political activism by the Catholic church in Latin American coun-

tries

× Democracy and dictatorship in Latin America. Use examples from the recent past to illustrate this relationship.

● United States business investments in Latin America: an overview for the year

§ Industrialization in Brazil

§ Economic conditions in Ecuador

● The Aztecs before the conquistadors. Consider their origins, social structure, religion, economy, and geographical distribution.

● Population control in South American countries. What has been the rate of growth? Are control measures adequate? What have been some recent attempts to institute broad measures of birth control?

● The early influences of the Catholic church in Latin America

§ What are the major problems that hinder economic prosperity in _____? Select a Latin American country.

§ What have been the implications of the rural-to-urban population shifts in Mexico?

● The cultural roots of machismo in Latin America

● Bolivia's bleak future

➥ The urban guerrillas of South America

● What is the "boom" in Spanish-American literature and who are its main representatives? How does it differ from previous literary genres?

● Brazil's national debt. How has it affected business and industry? Exports and imports? Living standards?

● What are some of the effects of inflation and unemployment in Mexico?

● Compare our intervention policies in Central America with those employed during the United States' involvement in Vietnam.

● Why Mexico City may never recover from the 1985 earthquake

★ The Colombian drug cartel has committed acts of violence on judges, journalists, industrialists and law enforcement officers. Describe how this has affected law enforcement.

● The destruction of Central and South American habitats and how it has affected North American bird populations

● Peru's Shining Path faction: its origins, progress and goals

● Is Marxism the best kind of government for some Latin American countries?

★ How Manuel Noriega maintained power in Panama

× Human rights in Latin America

● How the United States military presence in various Latin American countries hindered or fostered their development

○ Should the United States aid Latin America's debt repayment?

★ The powers of the Medellin drug cartel

Law

See also: Crime and Criminal Justice; Government

- Who should pay for Three Mile Island? What are the legal factors involved?
- Are "cut-rate" lawyers a threat to the legal profession?
★ Who owns the oceans?
✔ Attend a trial at your local court. Document and detail the process.
★ The advantages (or disadvantages) of no-fault divorce
○ Should the "exclusionary rule" be amended?
★ The issues involved regarding prayer in public school
- Objections to the legalization of prostitution
✗ Supreme Court decision reversals
- What are considered to be the major professional and personal qualifications for Supreme Court justices?
○ Have advances in forensic technology changed court procedures?
○ New uses for computers in court
★ When you should use the small claims court
✗ Current major problems in legal

medicine
- Child custody and the courts: Justice for the child?
➥ Environmental laws around the world. Focus on one type of law or one particular country or geographical area.
▲ The rights of American students abroad
- Legal contracts for unmarried couples
○ Current bail practices. What are the reforms that have been suggested by the legal profession?
- Impartial peers or community prejudice? Have American juries helped or hurt the cause of equality before the law?
✔ Legal services for the indigent. What is ordinarily available? Does variation exist in different areas? Compare to your locality.
- Paternity and the law
★ Should television be allowed in the courtroom?
- Should bankruptcy laws be changed? Cite the views of authorities in several areas, such

274

as law, economics, and business.

§ What are the legal rights and liabilities of <u>health</u> facilities?

● Aspects of confidentiality in the legal profession

● The legal aspects of "palimony" and its prospects in tomorrow's courtrooms

● The impact of abortion laws and legislation

➥ Corrective measures needed in the juvenile justice system

● Laws relating to rape. Are they adequate? If not, in what ways?

● The legal rights of the retarded and mentally ill

✗ How have the bankruptcy laws been abused?

§ Supreme Court decisions on <u>wiretapping</u>

● Plea bargaining: what it is and how it is used

● What constitutes malpractice?

● Fair trials and the press: some issues

● Role of the public defender

➥ How court processes could be made more efficient

○ How the legal community views the death penalty

● What every juror should know

● Military court martials and how they differ from other court proceedings

★ What the new law school graduate can expect in terms of placement, salary, advancement, etc.

✔ Jury selection techniques. Include interviews with several lawyers.

● Legal remedies against sex-bias discrimination

★ The powers of the Supreme Court

● Historical perspectives on trial by jury

● The marijuana legalization controversy: pros and cons

● Laws governing freedom of speech

➥ Select a recent Supreme Court decision and discuss the background of the case and significance of the decision.

● Search and seizure legislation

● Defend: The poor are discriminated against by the United States' legal system.

● Legal gun control solutions

● Legal definitions of death. Compare them to the religious and medical definitions.

✗ Reforms needed in the juvenile court system

● The selection of Supreme Court justices

● The legal rights of students

§ Laws relating to <u>espionage</u>

○ Discriminatory sentencing practices in United States courts

○ The issues involved with insanity as a defense. Discuss the Hinkley case among others.

➥ Sex crimes and the law (federal, state, local)

● Courtroom uses of hypnotism

● Abuses in the practice of plea

bargaining
- How copyright laws should be amended. Select one type of medium.
- What are the rights of private property?
- Homosexual legal rights
- Compare and contrast the legal definitions of the different degrees of murder.
- The court reporter
- Recent "mercy killing" decisions and their possible impact on future court cases
- Compare and contrast trials by jury and by judge.
- Functions of the state bar associations
- Compare and contrast the legal definitions of the different degrees of murder in your state.
- What constitutes an "act of God" in the law?
- Kangaroo courts
- Murder laws and manslaughter
- Court rulings on freedom of speech
- Cite evidence supporting the accusation that the courts have become too lenient
- Capital punishment in the Islamic world
- Pornography: the issues. What is the current legal stance?
- When the jury system fails
- Capital punishment in the United States today
- Are our immigration laws discriminatory? Should American

immigration laws be reformed?
- Trace the legal cases related to the student's right to challenge grades given in school.
- Abortion: laws and legislation, 1940 to date
- Legal rights of children
- Legal aspects of euthanasia
- What the public defender costs the taxpayer
- Many authorities feel that the state and federal regulations of fraudulent advertising should be strengthened. Present their case.
- Recent laws affecting the privacy of the individual
- The enforcement of affirmative action
- Proposed remedies for chronic court backlogs
- Copyright laws and the copy machine
- DNA evidence and the law
- The costs of lawsuits
- International laws controlling the illegal drug trade. Are they adequate?
- Should judges have life-time tenure? What are the advantages and disadvantages?
- Proposals for restructuring the bankruptcy courts
- Living wills and natural death laws
- The computer criminal, electronic thievery, and the law
- Who owns the patents on genetically engineered products?
- Progress in gay rights legislation

▲ Was the Agent Orange decision just? Evaluate the opinions of appropriate authorities.

• Can legislation prevent terrorism?

• New interpretations of the First Amendment to the United States Constitution, 1980 to date.

○ How does the Fourth Amendment's protection against unwarranted search and seizure apply to body fluids and tissue samples now used in forensic DNA testing?

Key to Symbols

• **average difficulty**
§ **substitutes possible**
★ **ample information in most libraries**
○ **specialized knowledge required**

↽ **narrow down topic**
▲ **large public or college library required**
↙ **local option topic**
× **examples and supporting evidence needed**

Law — History

- Legal systems of colonial America
- A review of significant cases, 1950–present, dealing with the proper relationship between schools and religion
- Past and present roles of the grand jury in the American system. Has the system changed?
- ★ The significance of the reverse discrimination case of *Allan Bakke v. University of California Regents* (1978). What have been some of the long-term effects since that decision?
- ★ Pros and cons of the *Escobedo v. Illinois* (1964) decision
- Background of the amendments to the United States Constitution
- Compare and contrast Greek and Roman law (select only one area).
- Social and historical aspects of community blue laws. Are there any in force in your area?
- How prohibition encouraged graft and crime
- × The use of martial law. Include both lawful and unlawful instances of its use.
- × Famous lawyers in literature
- Abuse of the Fifth Amendment

in the courtroom
- The legal evolution of civil rights in the United States
- ★ The witch trials in Salem, Massachusetts (1692). What was the basis of the prosecution? What was the outcome?
- The implications of the Miranda decision on court procedures and law enforcement
- § Have the killers in the <u>Sharon Tate</u> murders been properly punished? Or, select some other well-publicized murder trial and evaluate the court's decisions.
- Recent state laws (of the last ten years) relating to medical malpractice
- The Hammurabi Code of the eighteenth-century B.C. In what ways do elements of this code survive today?
- Discuss the convictions and sentences in the Nuremberg war crimes trials. Was justice served?
- The Scopes trial. Characterize the prosecution and the defense. Define the issues and discuss the consequences of the decision.
- The libel laws: some historic cases

278

- Significant rulings of the Warren Court
★ The development of Roman law
✕ Attempts to define obscenity
- The My Lai massacre and the trial of Lieutenant William Calley
- Significant interpretations of the U.S. Constitution: broad versus strict
- Historic instances of dissent in the Supreme Court
- Detail the *Ulysses* (James Joyce) Supreme Court obscenity decision and its consequences on later similar censorship issues.
○ Analyze Watergate from the perspective of civil rights' double standards, i.e., violations of court procedures which would have invalidated cases against "common criminals."

Key to Symbols

- average difficulty
§ substitutes possible
★ ample information in most libraries
○ specialized knowledge required

↞ narrow down topic
▲ large public or college library required
↗ local option topic
✕ examples and supporting evidence needed

Libraries, Books, and Publishing

See also: Language; Literature

× How the magazine industry has evolved in response to social change and technological development

● Book piracy in nineteenth-century America

★ The future for public library service

● The development of the early copyright laws and regulations

➤ Plan and describe the elements involved in the publication of a new magazine. Include finances, personnel, equipment, editorial content, advertising revenues, printing, distribution, readership potential, etc. You may want to concentrate on one area of publication.

● What was in the library at Alexandria?

▲ The rise of library networks

● How magazines make money

● "Talking books" for the blind: their range, quality, and availability

● The type designs of Frederic Goudy

★ America's first libraries

● Special collections in the Library of Congress

★ What you need to know to efficiently utilize a library's resources

● Information retrieval services and what they can do for the user

● Facilities and resources of the National Library of Medicine

● How to research your family tree

➤ Applications of the computer in publishing

● Should people pay to use a public library?

★ The term paper: efficient research tactics

● The founding of the Library of Congress

● Copyright infringement

○ Microcomputers for smaller libraries

● Theft protection for libraries

● The role of libraries in life-long learning

● The best seller: from 1900 to 1990. What were their characteristics? Were there noticeable trends?

- How libraries serve the special patron
- The art of bookbinding
- How the invention of printing transformed the possibilities for the written word.
▲ Renaissance libraries
- How libraries are coping with the information explosion
- Online search techniques for information retrieval systems
- What makes a book rare?
★ The effects of the Supreme Court Thor Power Tool ruling on the publishing industry
★ Too many librarians?
- The economics of the American book publishing business
- How libraries combat the censor and why they often lose
▲ How libraries and other archives preserve and protect paper and film from deterioration.
- The establishment, funding, contents, and uses of presidential libraries
- Describe a reference collection for the home library. Include an annotated bibliography and set a price limitation for individual

volumes. Outline and justify the total budget.
★ Compare and contrast the Dewey decimal and the Library of Congress classification systems.
○ How to review books
- The printing presses of William Caxton in fifteenth-century England
★ The role of the elementary school librarian
- Do librarians practice preselection censorship?
- The rise of the subscription library in early America
- American book reading habits. Consult some of the studies that have been conducted over the last fifteen years.
★ The influence of Andrew Carnegie on public libraries in the United States
- Computerized research and retrieval
- Is everyone equal in the Information Age?
- The spread of desk top publishing and how it has changed the publishing industry

---

Key to Symbols

•	average difficulty	⬧	narrow down topic
§	substitutes possible	▲	large public or college library required
★	ample information in most libraries	✔	local option topic
○	specialized knowledge required	×	examples and supporting evidence needed

Literature

See also: Humanities; Language; Libraries, Books, and Publishing

▲ Levels of meaning in Dante's In-
ferno
● The role of the clergy in Sten-
dahl's *The Red and the Black*
● Compare and contrast T.S.
Eliot's *Murder in the Cathedral*
and Jean Anouilh's *Becket.*
★ Franz Kafka's world of isolation, guilt, alienation, and
punishment
● Mark Twain has been accused
of racism in his novel *Huckleberry Finn.* Analyze these
charges and consider the advis-
ability of its inclusion for study
in a high school literature class.
★ Central themes in *One Flew
Over the Cuckoo's Nest* (Ken
Kesey). Explain how irony,
humor, and paradox illuminate
these themes.
● Compare and contrast the "heroes" in a selection of detective
fiction (Agatha Christie,
Georges Simenon, Dorothy
Sayers, Ross Macdonald, etc.).
○ What are the common themes
in the novels of Joseph Heller,
Kurt Vonnegut, Jr., John Barth,
and Thomas Pynchon?

○ Through the writings that appeared in the first half of the
nineteenth-century, trace the
gradual emergence of a dis-
tinctively American literature.
● A character analysis of Pangloss
in Voltaire's *Candide*
➤ Analyze the main character in
any of the following novels by
Thomas Wolfe: *You Can't Go
Home Again; Of Time and the
River; Look Homeward, Angel;*
and *The Web and the Rock.*
● The role of guilt in *The Rime of
the Ancient Mariner* (Samuel
Taylor Coleridge)
§ The function of setting in the
novels of Charles Dickens
§ Stylistic devices of Kurt Von-
negut
§ Narrative techniques of Edgar
Allan Poe
● Blues as literature
● The Oedipus theme in literature
● How Thackeray uses the novel
for social criticism
★ Trace the interrelationship of the
Glass family as depicted in the
fiction of J.D. Salinger.
● Analyze the structure of

Faulkner's *The Sound and the Fury*.

- Compare Boccaccio's tales from *The Decameron* and Chaucer's *Canterbury Tales*.
- ▲ The popularity of William Faulkner in Europe during the early stages of his career
- ○ Novelistic elements in *Pilgrim's Progress*
- Common themes in the short stories of James Joyce
- ○ Methodism as reflected in *Adam Bede* (George Eliot)
- Samuel Butler's revolt against authority, the establishment, and his parents as depicted in *The Way of All Flesh*
- The use of irony in Jonathan Swift's *A Modest Proposal*
- ○ Didacticism in the poetry of John Dryden
- Kurt Vonnegut's war experiences as reflected in *Slaughterhouse-Five* and other fiction
- ★ Tone, style, and narrative effects in "The Lottery" by Shirley Jackson
- William Golding's *Lord of the Flies* as allegory
- ★ The "upper class" as portrayed in *The Great Gatsby* (F. Scott Fitzgerald)
- Important retellings in English of the Arthurian legends after Malory's *Morte D'Arthur*
- Flower imagery in the fiction of D.H. Lawrence
- The devil and witchcraft in the fiction of Isaac Bashevis Singer
- ○ Compare and contrast the mystery fiction of Agatha Christie, Margery Allingham, and Dorothy L. Sayers
- The elements of haiku poetry
- ★ The stream of consciousness style in *Ulysses* (James Joyce)
- Existential influences in the novels of Ernest Hemingway
- War and death in *The Red Badge of Courage* (Stephen Crane)
- ➡ Contemporary Russian poetry. Concentrate on several outstanding poets.
- ▲ The influence of Henry Miller on the "beat generation" writers
- ✕ Characterize the Byronic hero and give examples from various literary works.
- The connection of *Book of the Dead* to the religion of ancient Egypt
- ○ The common theme of motherhood in the works of Doris Lessing, Toni Morrison, and Margaret Drabble
- ★ The Agatha Christie mystery: plot, style, character, and structure
- Norman Mailer and the female image
- American family life in the novels of John Updike
- Critical evaluations of recent novels by Kurt Vonnegut. Compare and contrast the differing critical receptions they received

to those of some of his earlier works.

- ● Jack Kerouac's *On the Road* as a forerunner of the hippie movement
- § Autobiographical elements in the novels of F. Scott Fitzgerald
- ● Central themes in the novels of William Faulkner
- ★ *Animal Farm* (George Orwell) as an allegory of the USSR
- ★ *The Great Gatsby* (F. Scott Fitzgerald) as a symbol of the "American Dream"
- ★ Compare the novel *1984* (George Orwell) to contemporary culture.
- ● The journalistic techniques of Stendhal (Marie Henri Beyle)
- ● A character analysis of Aschenbach in *Death in Venice* (Thomas Mann)
- ➧ The gothic in the short fiction of Flannery O'Connor
- ● Joan Didion's alienated heroines
- ● Career or motherhood: role conflict in the poetry of Adrienne Rich
- ● Satire of the academic world in Bernard Malamud's novel *A New Life*
- ● The portrayal of poor whites in the fiction of William Faulkner
- ▲ The literary reputation of Sinclair Lewis, past and present. How has it changed?
- ● Compare a variety of literary appraisals of the works of Ernest Hemingway.
- ● Satire and irony in John Irving's *The World According to Garp*
- × Black humor in contemporary literature
- ★ Sylvia Plath: the last year
- ○ American naturalism in the novels of Frank Norris. What was the extent of his debt to Emile Zola?
- ● Compare and contrast the early writings of Truman Capote with those more recently published. Include style, tone, content, characterization, etc.
- § The literary style of Ernest Hemingway
- ▲ The contribution of Thomas Wolfe's editor Maxwell Perkins to Wolfe's novels
- ● Color imagery in Dylan Thomas's poetry
- × The catholicism of Graham Greene. Use examples from his fiction.
- ★ The novel *Cry, the Beloved Country* (Alan Paton) as political propaganda
- ➧ The Oedipus myth in modern literature
- ● Nathanael West's grim view of the world in *The Day of the Locust*
- ★ Joseph Heller's use of paradox in *Catch 22*
- ● Existentialism as expressed in *The Stranger* (Albert Camus)
- ○ Montage in T.S. Eliot's *The Waste Land*
- ● Aldous Huxley's drug experi-

ences and their relation to his writings

§ Critical appraisals of the poetry of James Dickey

• Loneliness as a major theme in the writings of Carson McCullers

★ The black experience in America as viewed in the following: *Native Son* (Richard Wright), *Blues for Mr. Charlie* (James Baldwin), and *The Invisible Man* (Ralph Ellison).

• Discuss metaphor and symbol in the poem "Stopping by Woods on a Snowy Evening" by Robert Frost

○ *The Grapes of Wrath* (John Steinbeck) as a quest novel

• Novels of political protest in America. Select several from the same general time period.

• Religious themes in Dostoevski's fiction

▲ The meaning of catharsis in Aristotle's *Poetics*

• *Dr. Zhivago* (Boris Pasternak) as social commentary

▲ Alexander Pope's concept of nature

• Social commentary in *The Grapes of Wrath* (John Steinbeck). Is it still relevant today?

• Elements of the Greek epic tradition

○ Compare the sonnet structure and common themes of Petrarch, Shakespeare, John Donne, and John Milton.

§ Social criticism in the works of

Henry Fielding

★ How to evelute a novel

• The Irish nationalism of William Butler Yeats

• The personalized religion and mythology of William Blake

○ Compare the use of stream of consciousness techniques in the works of James Joyce, Virginia Woolf, and John Dos Passos.

• Sinclair Lewis as critic of American values

★ The code of Hemingway's heroes

➡ The Vietnam War as reflected in contemporary fiction. Select several novels published since the end of the war.

• Compare and contrast the poetry of Carl Sandburg and Robert Frost.

• The effects of the Spanish Civil War on the literary works of Ernest Hemingway

• Varying interpretations of *Don Quixote* (Miguel Cervantes). Choose literary analyses by several critics and compare their evaluations.

• Guilt and damnation in the stories of Kafka

○ Common elements in the poetry of Coleridge and Wordsworth

× Techniques of characterization in the novels of Charles Dickens. For example, detail the unique mannerisms of his characters.

• Compare the final episodes of Sir Thomas Malory's *Morte*

D'Arthur and Alfred, Lord Ten-
nyson's "Morte D'Arthur" (from
Idylls of the King).

○ The satiric thrust of Voltaire's
Candide. Include a discussion of
the work's historical connotations.

● How is aristocratic society portrayed in The Americans (Henry
James)?

● Sentimentalism and sentiment in
the short stories of Bret Harte

● Social and political propaganda
in Upton Sinclair's The Jungle

● New York society as portrayed
in Edith Wharton's The Age of
Innocence

○ Different views of the nature of
evil as expressed in the Book of
Job (Bible)

▲ Aspects of feminism in the novels of Charlotte Brontë. Were
these attitudes a reflection of
the times? What was the critical
reception upon publication?

✕ The pessimism of Mark Twain's
later works

● The visionary hero: William
Blake

● Compare and contrast the attitudes towards nature and
society in Henry David Thoreau's Walden and Walt Whit-
man's Leaves of Grass.

★ Detail the use of symbol and
metaphor in Herman Melville's
Moby Dick.

● The allegorical nature of good
and evil in Herman Melville's

Moby Dick

★ Discuss the nature and forms of
sin in The Scarlet Letter
(Nathaniel Hawthorne). How is
this a reflection of Puritan society?

● The character of Pip in Great
Expectations (Charles Dickens)

● American mores and values as
reflected in the novel Sister Car-
rie (Theodore Dreiser)

● Nature and country life in the
short stories of Colette

● The Mississippi River as a symbol in Huckleberry Finn (Mark
Twain)

✕ The Jew as portrayed in the
modern novel: an overview

★ Allegory and symbolism in Lewis
Carroll's Alice in Wonderland

○ Herman Melville's religious
doubts as revealed in Moby
Dick

● The role of chance in Thomas
Hardy's Return of the Native

● Southern attitudes toward African
Americans in the fiction of William Faulkner

✕ Civil War fiction: common
themes

○ Stylistic devices in the fiction of
James Joyce

★ The World According to Garp
(John Irving) as a portrait of
the individual in an alien world

§ Metaphor and symbol in the
poetry of Wallace Stevens

● Themes and values of Beat writers: Allen Ginsberg, Lawrence

Ferlinghetti, Michael McClure, Jack Kerouac, and Gregory Corso

- Honoré de Balzac's portrait of French society as depicted in *Le Père Goriot*

★ The sardonic wit and common sense of Dorothy Parker's poetry

▲ The reactions of clergymen to Sinclair Lewis's novel *Elmer Gantry*, a satire on corruption among the clergy

- The nature of man as expressed in the poetry of Robinson Jeffers

- Compare the heroines in Willa Cather's *O Pioneers!* and Thomas Hardy's *Tess of the D'Urbervilles*.

- The black humor of William Burroughs

- T.S. Eliot's *The Waste Land*: Masterpiece or hoax?

- Compare and contrast themes of death in the poetry of Emily Dickinson and A.E. Housman.

- Hemingway's conception of the nature of love as evidenced in *To Have and Have Not*

➥ Russian literature since 1917

- Alienation in the novels of Saul Bellow

- Views of nature: Thoreau's *Walden* and Annie Dillard's *Pilgrim at Tinker Creek*

★ Differing views of morality in Chaucer's *Canterbury Tales*

★ The satire of *Gulliver's Travels* (Jonathan Swift)

- The theme of death in the works of Edgar Allan Poe

- A character analysis of Henderson in *Henderson, the Rain King* (Saul Bellow)

- The character Meursault's philosophy of life in Camus's *The Stranger*

★ The fate of Oscar Wilde

✕ The rise of the anti-hero in modern fiction

▲ The influence of Edgar Allan Poe on European writers

➥ Compare the differing types of early science fiction.

➥ The origin and development of the detective story

○ Religious argument in Victorian literature

★ Good and evil as depicted in *Heart of Darkness* (Joseph Conrad)

- Themes in the acceptance speeches of Nobel Prize winners for literature

▲ The disillusionment of war as reflected in the poetry and fiction of World War I

- Mark Twain's attitude toward Christianity

- The beginnings of the Russian Revolution as depicted in *Mother* (Maxim Gorky)

➥ Elements of Mark Twain's humor

✕ Gold as a symbol in literature

★ The element of horror in Poe's short stories

★ Compare and contrast plot,

structure, or point of view in *The Adventures of Tom Sawyer* and *Huckleberry Finn* (Mark Twain).

➥ The analysis of a character in Chaucer's *Canterbury Tales*

✕ The characterization of Native Americans in American fiction

● The satire of Ambrose Bierce

● The depiction of women in the novels of Emily Brontë and Jane Austen

▲ Short stories from Egypt's Middle Kingdom papyrus manuscripts

○ Compare and contrast Zeus, as presented in Homer's *Iliad*, to the god of John Milton's *Paradise Lost.*

● Boswell's *Life of Johnson* remains significant because of Boswell. What is the basis for this statement?

● The poetry of the blues

● Compare and contrast Robert Penn Warren's *The Cave* to "The Allegory of the Cave" in Plato's *Republic*.

● Central themes in Sherwood Anderson's *Winesburg, Ohio*

● Dostoevski's concept of freedom

● Felix Krull's approach to life and love in *Confessions of Felix Krull* (Thomas Mann)

● Compare the Louisiana politician Huey Long and the central character Willie Stark of *All the King's Men* (Robert Penn Warren).

● Two views of mental illness: *The Bell Jar* (Sylvia Plath) and *I Never Promised You a Rose Garden* (Hannah Green)

★ Themes and symbols of Ernest Hemingway's *The Old Man and the Sea*

➥ The somber world of Joyce Carol Oates. How does the tone of several of her major works reflect this outlook on life?

★ Analyze the character of Holden Caulfield in J.D. Salinger's *Catcher in the Rye.*

● Racial tragedy in William Faulkner's *Light in August*

● Existential elements in the stories of Franz Kafka

○ Formula fiction and how it works (choose from science fiction, gothic, romance, western, mystery, detective, etc.)

● Why F. Scott Fitzgerald became a "spokesman for the jazz age"

○ Read several of William Faulkner's works (*Absalom, Absalom!*, *The Hamlet*, etc.) and discuss Faulkner's attitudes and feelings about the South.

● William Faulkner's Snopes family as a symbol of social change

● The moral convictions of Leo Tolstoy. How are they reflected in his fiction?

● Portraits of hell in the works of both Dante and Milton

○ Émile Zola as the principal

spokesman for naturalism
- Realistic elements in Gustav Flaubert's *Madame Bovary*
- The dark side of the human spirit as depicted in *Crime and Punishment* or other works by Dostoevski
▲ Aleksandr Pushkin's indebtedness to Lord Byron
- Keats's view of poetry as explained in his letters
- Explain the reasons for using fantasy. Use as examples *Gulliver's Travels, Alice in Wonderland,* and *A Midsummer Night's Dream* among others.
○ The use of the triangle in D.H. Lawrence's fiction (two females and one male)
▲ Yeats's use of Byzantium as the final resting place
○ Unconventional use of religious symbolism in Dylan Thomas's poetry
- Attitudes toward death in *The Iliad* compared to those expressed in *The Odyssey*
✕ Contemporary literary genres in America: a survey

- Love and death in the poetry of Edna St. Vincent Millay
○ American idiom in the poetry of William Carlos Williams
- Robert Browning as champion of the dramatic monologue
- How are the ideas in the fiction of Henry James reflected in his style?
★ Trace the roots of the American transcendental movement.
- The importance of locality in the fiction of Jane Austen
○ Samuel Johnson as a literary critic
- Gothic elements in the fiction of Washington Irving
○ The use of time by John Fowles in *The French Lieutenant's Woman*
○ The journalistic techniques of Daniel Defoe in either *Moll Flanders* or *Robinson Crusoe*
▲ Was *Pamela* (Samuel Richardson) the first novel?
- Calvinistic attitudes in early American literature, such as that of Jonathan Edwards, Cotton Mather, etc.

Key to Symbols

•	average difficulty	◄	narrow down topic
§	substitutes possible	▲	large public or college
★	ample information in most libraries		library required
		✔	local option topic
○	specialized knowledge required	✕	examples and supporting evidence needed

Literature — Drama

See also: Film; Humanities; Theater

- How not to write a play
- ✕ The classical conventions of tragedy
- ➔ Select several works by the same playwright and discuss the uses of parody, irony, didacticism, imagery, and other literary and dramatic techniques.
- ➔ Choose a major character in a well-known play and trace his or her development in four ways: appearance, speech, external actions, what others say about the character.
- ➔ Discuss the use and function of symbolism in a play of your choice.
- ➔ Contrast and compare two characters' motivations in a play. Choose one of the following motivations: hope for reward, love, fear of failure, religious aspirations, revenge, greed, jealousy, hate.
- ➔ Choose a particular type of play (tragedy, comedy, tragicomedy). How does the play conform to the traditional genre? How does it deviate?

- ➔ Discuss the conflict of a play. How do the characters relate to the conflict? How is it resolved? Is it resolvable?
- ▲ Why was Euripides adversely criticized by his contemporaries? In light of current knowledge, was this criticism justified?
- Describe the structure of a selected play in relation to traditional plot development: exposition, rising action, climax, dénouement, conclusion.
- ✕ The isolation of the individual as a theme in contemporary drama
- King Lear as a tragic hero
- ★ Restoration comedy as typified by William Congreve's *The Way of the World*
- Characteristics of the Theater of the Absurd. Use as examples Samuel Beckett's *Waiting for Godot* and Eugène Ionesco's *Rhinoceros* among others.
- Varying interpretations of theme and meaning in the plays of Samuel Beckett
- ○ Compare Eugene O'Neill's *Mourning Becomes Electra* with

the Greek tragedies of Euripides, focusing on *Electra*.

§ Explore the autobiographical elements of a drama by Eugene O'Neill.

• Shakespeare's strong women

○ Shakespeare's use of comic relief in his tragedies

★ The motives and character of Shakespeare's *Hamlet* have been analyzed by many critics. Present a selection of these views. Try to account for the varying opinions.

• Refute or support: The play *Death of a Salesman* (Arthur Miller) is a tragedy in the classic sense.

• Compare and contrast the use of asides and soliloquies in two of Shakespeare's plays.

• Brecht's *Mother Courage and Her Children* as a statement against the capitalistic aspects of war

• Homosexual themes in the dramatic works of Tennessee Williams

• How *Everyman*, the best known of the fifteenth-century morality plays, universalizes man's life. Discuss this concept in terms of its contemporary relevancy, as well as its historical context.

★ Shakespeare's use of more than one plot in a single drama

▲ The origins of naturalism in European drama

• Investigate the wide variety of sources used by Shakespeare, such as history, mythology, and legend, and other literary works.

• What and who were the targets of George Bernard Shaw's satire?

• How the content of drama changed from religious in the Middle Ages to secular in the Renaissance

• Compare the commonalities found in the classical Greek dramas of Aeschylus, Sophocles, and Euripides.

★ Oedipus, a tragic hero

• Social criticism in *The Crucible* (Arthur Miller)

○ Father and son relationships in the dramas of Arthur Miller

○ Compare and contrast the satire of Moliere and Congreve.

▲ Biblical allusion in *Waiting for Godot* (Samuel Beckett)

• British middle-class life as represented in John Osborne's *Look Back in Anger*

★ The issues involved in the controversy surrounding Rolf Hochhuth's play, *The Deputy*

○ Discuss free will versus determinism in classical Greek tragedy.

○ A review of the Oresteia theme throughout the history of drama: Aeschylus, *The Oresteia*; Sophocles, *Electra*; Euripides, *Electra*; Sartre, *The Flies*; O'Neill, *Mourning Becomes Electra*; and Ronconi,

Oresteia

✕ The women of Greek tragedy

● Chance as portrayed in Shakespeare's *Romeo and Juliet*

● Ibsen's view on love and marriage as dramatized in *A Doll's House* and *Ghosts*

● Satire in Sheridan's *School for Scandal*

● Compare and contrast the Antigone of Sophocles with that of Jean Anouilh's *Antigone*.

★ Evidences of hubris in the plays of Sophocles

● Compare and contrast Shaw's play *Pygmalian* to Lerner and Loewe's musical version, *My Fair Lady*.

● Analyze Pirandello's views of reality and illusion.

✕ Common themes of modern African-American playwrights

▲ The impact of the unities on French drama

● Was Hamlet insane?

● Compare and contrast the behavior of the characters in Samuel Beckett's *Endgame* and John Webster's *The White Devil*.

● Word play in Shakespearean drama

● Elements of humor in George Bernard Shaw's *Caesar and Cleopatra*

● The characters in the medieval farce

● Analyze the concept of justice as presented in Aeschylus's trilogy *Oresteia*.

● The broad comedy of Aristophanes

○ Existentialism in the plays of Shakespeare

★ Oscar Wilde's use of parody

● Sexual politics in August Strindberg's *The Father* and *Miss Julie*

○ Likenesses and differences between the seventeenth-century dramatists Corneille, Racine, and Moliere

● Compare the realism of Henrik Ibsen and Anton Chekhov.

○ Analyze Shakespeare's use of prose and poetry as a device for characterization.

● Social satire in Edward Albee's plays *The Sandbox* or *The American Dream*

● Henrik Ibsen's conception of social responsibility as evidenced in *An Enemy of the People*

● Sir Toby Belch of Shakespeare's *Twelfth Night*: An individual or a stereotype?

● Analyze Tennessee Williams's unique ability to create interesting characters who are caught in critical or violent situations.

○ Jean Genet's use of the theme that nothing has meaning without its opposite: law and crime, religion and sin, love and hate

▲ Existentialism in the dramas of Jean-Paul Sartre

● Jean Cocteau's use of the Oedipus legend in *The Infernal Machine*, as compared to its

use by Sophocles
- Archibald MacLeish's *J.B.*, compared to its source, The Book of Job from the Bible
- Eugene O'Neill's experimentation with theatrical devices and dramatic techniques (i.e., *The Great God Brown, Lazarus Laughed,* and *Days without End*)
- The documentary dramas of Peter Weiss
- Molière's *Tartuffe* (or, don't criticize religion)
- How to read a play

Key to Symbols

- average difficulty
- § substitutes possible
- ★ ample information in most libraries
- ○ specialized knowledge required

- ➤ narrow down topic
- ▲ large public or college library required
- ✓ local option topic
- ✗ examples and supporting evidence needed

Literature for Children

See also: Adolescents; Children; Education

- Jules Verne's science fiction and fact. Discuss several of his books in light of current scientific invention and discovery.
- The funniest books for children. Why?
- Plan a poetry reading program for children. Select an age group. Justify each poem selected.
- Interview several children about their reading habits. Tabulate the reading levels, their likes, and dislikes. What is the relation to the home environment?
★ What are some of the guides for evaluating children's literature?
★ The enduring qualities of the "Little House" books by Laura Ingalls Wilder
- How to motivate children to read good literature
- Compare four biographies of the same person. Include an analysis of each one's scope, accuracy, format, and style.
- Discuss character, plot, theme, and style of several titles from a children's series, such as the Nancy Drew books.
- Compare a number of folk tales from several countries which are based on similar or identical themes.
○ Compare and contrast the illustrations from five different Caldecott Medal winners to those illustrations found in a comic book, a grade school text, a picture book from the grocery store, etc.
✕ The classic villains of children's literature
§ Prepare an annotated bibliography of books designed to increase the social awareness of fourth and fifth graders. Include fiction as well.
- Magazines for children: what they offer and how well they do it
- Compare the Pueblo myths with Christian thought in Gerald McDermott's Arrow to the Sun.
- Compare and contrast the fables of Aesop and La Fontaine.
- Tall tales: Compare and contrast the stories about Mike Fink, Paul Bunyan, John Henry,

and Pecos Bill.

★ Examine and compare at least ten different counting books for the very young child.

• Anthropomorphism in children's animal stories

• Black magic, witches, and evil in children's literature

• Read and critique several different books which involve the juvenile reader in such concepts as honesty, courage, pride, etc.

★ What makes a book a good one for young children: a survey of criteria

§ Describe Africans (or, Jews, Puerto Ricans, Mexicans) as depicted in books for juveniles that have been published in the past and in some current books.

• Compare and contrast children's books which examine and teach about death.

☛ Teaching biology to children through the use of animal stories. Analyze elements that are necessary to teach essential scientific concepts. Select a grade level.

• Sexism in juvenile literature: a historical survey

✗ Stereotyping in picture books

• Prepare an annotated list of not more than twenty-five books for a child's home library (cover ages four through ten).

§ Criteria for the evaluation of social studies textbooks for the primary grades

✔ Prepare for young people an annotated bibliography of materials written about your local city, county, or state.

• Compare and contrast the early editions of Mother Goose stories with recent examples.

○ Compare and contrast translations for children of the Greek myths by Nathaniel Hawthorne and Charles Kingsley.

• The world according to Pilgrim's Progress by John Bunyan

• The characteristics of early American primers for children, such as The New England Primer (1691), Spiritual Milk for Boston Babes (1646), Divine and Moral Songs for Children (1775), and other similar titles

✗ What are the criteria for the perfect juvenile science book? Include content, illustration, timeliness, printing, etc. Mention some examples.

○ Compare and contrast the changes from 1930 to 1990 in the structure and style of biography for young people.

• Dime novels and chapbooks as the precursors of the comic book

• Illustrate the steps toward responsibility a child must take, as represented in several novels such as Island of the Blue Dolphin and Summer of the Swans.

• Trace the characterization and description of the cowboy and the West from Ned Buntline (E.Z.C. Judson) to Louis L'Amour.

× The hero in classics of children's literature

§ Horse stories for children. Examine their plots, style, and appeal.

○ Elements of formula fiction for children

• Trends in children's literature, 1970–1990

• Compare and contrast family life as depicted in Louisa May Alcott's *Little Women* and in Judy Blume's *Are You There God? It's Me, Margaret.*

× The advent of realistic themes and attitudes in children's literature. Cite and detail some of the earliest examples.

§ The illustrations of Beatrix Potter

• The fantasy world of Alice in *Alice in Wonderland* and *Through the Looking-Glass* (Lewis Carroll)

• The make-believe world of the Hobbits (J.R.R. Tolkien)

• Compare and contrast animal stories for 3- to 8-year-olds. Particularly suggested for comparison are the "animals as humans" genre.

• Select three children's classics (for example, *Charlotte's Web, Black Beauty, Mary Poppins, Robinson Crusoe*) and evaluate their appeal, theme, style, characters, and history since publication.

★ Reading aloud to children

• Techniques for encouraging reading in young children

• Handbooks, chapbooks, Puritan literature: early English books for young people

• How to select books for children

• Compare and contrast the tone and narrative style of *The Wind in the Willows* (Kenneth Grahame) and *Winnie-the-Pooh* (A.A. Milne).

• The illustrations of Maurice Sendak. Why are they unique?

Key to Symbols

- • average difficulty
- § substitutes possible
- ★ ample information in most libraries
- ○ specialized knowledge required
- ☛ narrow down topic
- ▲ large public or college library required
- ⌐ local option topic
- × examples and supporting evidence needed

Marriage

See also: Adolescents; Aging; Children; Consumerism; Family Life; Gender Issues; Personal Finance; Sex

- Do alternative life-styles pose a threat to the present system of marriage? Justify your answer with appropriate evidence and statistics.
- Cohabitation in the United States: past and present
- Mate selection patterns and mores have changed. Compare the traditional practices of the past with those of our contemporary society.
- Should United States marriage and divorce laws be consistent? What are the barriers to their enactment?
- ★ How to deal positively with divorce
- ★ Common problems of interracial marriages
- The economics of marriage today
- ▲ Attitudes toward premarital sex. Compare and contrast the differing views by age groups or socioeconomic levels.
- Polygamy among the early Mormons
- ★ The problems of the working wife
- Two-career marriages and the traditional family structure
- New attitudes toward marriage in America
- ✔ Compare and contrast the marriage laws and regulations in your state with several surrounding states.
- Why is the divorce rate rising in the United States? Do experts agree on the causes?
- Alternatives to the single-family dwelling
- Should divorce laws be made more stringent? What would be the advantages? Would other problems arise?
- How to learn from quarrels in a marriage
- The economics of the childless marriage
- Socioeconomic aspects of family planning in the Western world
- What are the typical patterns of family violence? What are the reasons for these consistencies?
- ▲ How the Catholic and Protestant churches view interfaith marriages
- Why some couples choose to remain childless

× Typical life-styles of two-career couples

★ How to write a marriage contract

● Changing attitudes towards alimony

➥ Social change in the American marriage

○ Is motherhood instinctive? Consult experts in a variety of disciplines, such as biology, psychology, sociology, etc.

▲ Mate selection: a survey of current research literature

● Books that every couple should read: an annotated bibliography

× Adjustment problems in youthful marriages

● The "open marriage" (or "open family") as an alternative to traditional marriage and family patterns

● In what ways has money been shown to affect marriages? What are the particular problem areas? Consult a variety of authoritative sources for supporting information.

● Examine the various reasons why people enter into group marriage. Is there a basic uniformity of goals? Why?

➥ The functions of dating (courtship) in modern societies

● Family planning: contemporary options

▲ How the blue-collar wife views love and marriage. Discuss the results of several recent sociological and psychological studies

★ Society's changing views of adultery

● Defend or refute: Abortion laws should not be changed.

● Wife abuse. How common is it? What seem to be the major contributory factors?

● The role of the wife in the blue-collar marriage

● Compare and contrast changing attitudes toward divorce: 1920, 1950, and 1990

▲ Historic prohibitions against incest

● The advantages of living together before marriage

★ Legal, social, and religious aspects of artificial insemination by donor (AID)

○ New treatments for infertility

● Should homemakers have Social Security, worker's compensation, and health insurance?

● The case for therapeutic abortions

● The economic aspects of divorce (alimony, child-support, assets, etc.)

● Living together: Is it fair to the woman and/or to the man?

● Does marriage still have its previous social and personal advantages?

★ What are the special problems of widowhood? How are they best resolved?

★ The "empty nest" syndrome: its prevalence, causes, and consequences

▲ Social researchers have studied the underlying factors in extramarital relationships. What are the major issues? Do these researchers agree?

- Problems associated with the transition into parenthood
★ Long-term marriage partners often evidence a high degree of marital satisfaction. What are the major reasons for this success?
▲ Explore the correlation between life satisfaction and marriage satisfaction.
- Defend or refute: The common-law marriage should be abolished.
- Maternal employment and child development. Is there a strong relationship? If so, what are the factors?
▲ The effects of women's changing status in divorce laws in various world areas
- What are the various methods of sterilization? Discuss the advantages and disadvantages of each in terms of the latest medical research.
- The effects of alcoholism and/or drug abuse on marital stability and on divorce. Detail some of the findings from studies in this area.
✔ Interview a selection of (10–20) couples regarding their attitudes toward and their use of credit. When, how, and how much is it

used? How has it affected their marriage? What have been the resultant problems?
- The ingredients of a stable marriage
- The advantages of a second marriage
- Emotional reactions to divorce
- Cohabitation as an alternative to marriage: How well does it work?
▲ Nonverbal communication in marriage. Review some of the recent studies in this area.
- Is there such a thing as an "equal marriage"?
× Some rules for overcoming unhealthy codependence
× Recent public awareness of domestic violence has helped focus on some remedies. Discuss some of the most promising.
- How to get along with your in-laws
○ Role-identification patterns in contemporary marriages
➥ Compare the "ideal" relationship between a man and a woman in several cultures (Eskimo, middle-class American, Iranian, Chinese)
- How the spread of AIDS has changed patterns of infidelity in America

---

Key to Symbols

- **average difficulty**
§ **substitutes possible**
★ **ample information in most libraries**
○ **specialized knowledge required**

➥ **narrow down topic**
▲ **large public or college library required**
✔ **local option topic**
× **examples and supporting evidence needed**

Mathematics

See also: Computers

- Problems that mathematicians have never been able to solve
- × Discuss and illustrate new applications of old mathematical principles.
- Forces of civilization which fostered the development of mathematics
- ★ The Aztec calendar stone
- Compare and contrast Gregorian, Mayan, and Julian calendars
- ★ Mathematical probabilities and the game of poker
- Greek mathematics: How much did they know? What were some of the applications?
- Quantum mathematics
- The source and historic applications of numerology
- ➥ Methods of teaching arithmetic
- ★ Careers in mathematics
- How does an abacus work?
- Methods of calculating: Napier's rods, finger reckoning, and sand calculators
- The slide rule versus the abacus
- Magic squares
- ▲ Number sense in animals and insects

- Ancient and modern measurements
- Perfect numbers
- ○ The relationship between mathematics and music
- ★ Sun dials: their history and technology
- The mathematical basis of commonly used codes
- Tessellations
- Conic sections
- ▲ How changes in sunrise and sunset are computed
- Primitive systems of mathematics
- How logarithms work
- The case for metrics
- Egyptian mathematical advances
- ★ Math games for children
- The mathematical contributions of the Babylonians. Which were the most consequential in terms of later developments?
- ▲ The Rhind Papyrus (copied by Ahmes, c. 2000–1800 B.C.): the oldest known mathematical treatise
- ▲ Do all societies add, subtract, multiply and divide numbers? Consider past cultures as well as contemporary ones.

300

Media

See also: Advertising; Computers; Journalism; Language; Television and Radio

- What is the obligation of newspapers and other media in a democracy with regard to incendiary diplomatic incidents? Cite examples from history.
- ★ Will newspapers be replaced by electronic media? What is the opinion of journalists and other media and technology experts?
- ▲ What was the media characterization of the Germans and Japanese in World War II? Was it realistic? What was the purpose?
- Standards for the media: Censorship or regulation?
- Defend or refute: Many experts accuse the media of influencing current events by their presence, coverage, and, at times, their involvement.
- ➥ Election campaigns and the media: a survey of the last twenty years
- Mass media and the role model. Select one role (hero, mother, macho man, etc.) and analyze the treatment in several media.
- ★ The uncertain future of public broadcasting
- The American comic book as a reflection of social problems. Select either one time frame, one or two titles, or a particular problem.
- Mass media in Russia
- Censorship: Who decides?
- ▲ Propaganda and the war in Vietnam
- The impact of video cassette use on movie attendance
- ✕ How advertisers select appropriate media
- § The appeal of the comic strip "Peanuts" (Charles M. Schulz)
- Should the government regulate the broadcasting industry?
- Compare ten days of television news to your local newspaper's coverage of the same national events.
- What parents can do about violence in the media
- Evidence linking television and motion picture violence and crime rates
- ★ Immediate effects of Gutenberg's invention of moveable type
- ✕ Communication media and gov-

ernment security. When have serious conflicts of interest occurred? Detail the critical issues affecting several.

○ Media responsibility and the people's right to know

● Defend or refute: Great novels make great films.

● The character and basis of relations between the federal government and the national media, 1970–1980 (or select another time span)

● What were the major criticisms leveled against the role of the media in the Vietnam War?

★ Home video and the copyright laws: Is there an equitable solution?

▲ Should the print media be required to screen their advertisers? If so, how? If not, why not?

● Comic book heroes, past and present

● New media outlets: the growth of advertising

● The media forecasts and predictions of Marshall McLuhan in *The Medium is the Message* (1967) and how they have or have not been realized today

✕ Bias in the media

▲ What has been the effect of national television on newspaper sales?

➤ American values and the mass media

● The African-American image as reflected in the media: positive or negative?

○ Does the media have a bias toward negative news? Support your answer with authoritative data and opinion.

➤ Discuss the problems of the relationship between business and the media.

● Who reads newspapers? Are there fewer readers than in the past? What are the demographic variants, educational, cultural, and economic factors involved?

✕ The "typical" American family in the media. Examine television shows, magazine advertising, and articles, etc., for characteristics of this stereotyped ideal.

● What are the characteristics of advertising in the following media: newspapers, television, radio, and magazines?

● Is cigarette or liquor advertising ethical? Should harmful products be advertised? Justify your answer with authoritative opinions.

○ How modern media influence diplomatic relations

○ The media and the political process: a look ahead

✕ What are the most common portrayals of women in the media?

✕ Modern mass communication will radically change all world cultures. Defend or refute.

● Some critics suggest the entertainment media does not accurately reflect American society. Survey the opinions of some of these critics.

Medicine

See also: AIDS; Bioethics; Health; Nursing; Nutrition

- The incidence of prescription drug dependency: an overview
- Medical aspects of euthanasia
- ▲ The relationship between cancer and diet. Survey recent research
- ➡ The computer in the medical world
- The right to refuse medical treatment
- ★ Kidney dialysis: its economics and potentials. Who should be selected for treatment and how should funding be divided?
- Advances in the technology and uses of artificial skin
- The prefrontal lobotomy: medical reevaluations of a radical technique
- What are the major medical drawbacks to national health care?
- Life and death medical situations What are the doctor's legal and ethical obligations?
- Views of the medical community toward a national health plan
- ▲ The cancer research dollar: Who benefits?
- ★ How to get into medical school
- O What are some of the most signifi-

cant medical consequences of the misuse of antibiotics?
- The claim has often been made that unnecessary surgery is increasing. Investigate these accusations.
- What have been the effects of the increase of malpractice suits on the medical profession?
- Implications of the medical definitions of death
- ▲ What are the current guidelines for organ transplants from anencephalic infants? Do they meet all essential criteria?
- What are the ethical and legal issues involved in informed consent?
- ▲ Are the current guidelines for clinical experimentation sufficient? Describe them.
- What are the potential applications for the use of fetal brain tissue?
- Outline the distinctions between brain death and persistent vegetative state.
- × Discuss the recent advances in spinal cord injury repair.
- Advances in the prenatal diag-

nosis of birth defects

➥ Medical scams and quackery

▲ The recent establishment of test-tube baby clinics in the United States. Discuss their operations, guidelines, clientele, and results.

● The long search for artificial blood

★ Many doctors, especially obstetricians, are leaving their professions because of escalating insurance rates. Examine some solutions.

▲ The crisis of trauma care

↙ Health maintenance organizations: Evaluate and compare several of them available in your locality. Consider their facilities, services, staff, costs, etc.

✕ The new medical technology and its high cost to the patient

✕ Waste in hospitals

★ Is Medicare meeting the needs of the aged?

● Analyze the advantages and problems of socialized medicine in Sweden or Great Britain.

★ Should doctors advertise?

➥ Rising hospital costs: Are there solutions? Do they compromise adequate medical care?

▲ Health care for women in a male-dominated medical world: Questions women have asked and some of the answers.

▲ Research in hyperthermic (heat) cancer therapy

● The vitamin E megadose controversy: the medical view

● Why the American Medical Association does not recognize chiropractors

● Cholesterol and heart disease: continuing controversy and continuing discoveries

● Are yearly physicals necessary? Cite informed medical opinion to justify your answer.

● Why doctors are not moving to rural areas of the United States

● Holistic medicine: A new fad or an old remedy?

★ Midwives and the medical profession

● How inflation affects health care prices

○ The politics of national health insurance

● Has health insurance contributed to rising medical costs?

● How should life-sustaining machinery be allocated in society?

§ The changing role of respiration therapy in the medical world

● Why does the United States lag behind other nations in life expectancy and infant mortality?

▲ Snake bite treatments. Include the most recent research findings in your discussion. Why is there still controversy in this area?

● Health care delivery systems in countries with socialized medicine. Select one and identify their system's strengths and weaknesses.

● The dangers of medical x-radiation

○ The uses of optical fibers in medicine

○ Common drugs used during

pregnancy and birth. What are their uses and what is the possible effect on the infant?

• Why the poor more commonly have work-related illnesses and injuries than the affluent. Which workers and which industries are most usually involved?

• What are the consequences of the increase in medical malpractice suits? Consider insurance rates, health care costs, case loads, taxes, and levels of "defensive" medical practices.

• Faith healers in a scientific world

▲ Do medical advances ultimately lead to genetic deterioration?

★ The future of the artificial heart

• Salt and good health: What are the results and conclusions from the most recent studies?

✕ Should patients treat themselves? When? Is it safe?

• Multihospital chains are experiencing rapid growth and expansion. How will this change American health care?

★ Legionnaires' disease: modern medical detection

• The perils of cosmetic surgery

○ How harmful is radiation?

§ Technological breakthroughs in the field of radiology

• Medical costs are rapidly increasing, while funding sources may be less able to afford this rise. Project what the possible results may be.

• The Karen Ann Quinlan case and the euthanasia issues it raised

▲ The growth of pain clinics

§ Advances in kidney transplants

• What are the physiological aspects of abortion which contribute to the ethical and moral controversy?

○ Compare and contrast the advantages of the X-ray, CAT (computerized axial tomography) and the MRI (magnetic resonance imaging) in diagnostic medicine.

• Is a cure in sight for genital herpes? What is the current status of research in this area?

○ Will medicine find a cure for AIDS? Evaluate the current possibilities.

• How organ and tissue donations are obtained

○ Are artificial hearts a viable alternative to human transplants?

▲ How gene therapy is being used to treat HIV and AIDS

★ Liability insurance and the medical profession

✕ Flu epidemics: their causes, courses, and cures

★ How the drug AZT is used for AIDS victims. What are the advantages and disadvantages?

○ Discuss immunotherapy technique in cancer treatment

• Should doctors be able to refuse to treat AIDS patients? Or any patient?

• Does the financial goal of for-profit hospitals conflict with quality medical care?

Medicine — History

See also: Health; Nursing; Nutrition

- Safety problems with anesthesia: a historical overview
- ○ Disease as a selective agent in human evolution
- Historical treatment of leprosy compared to current standards and remedies
- § The treatment of epilepsy before modern medicine
- Syphilis: incidence and treatment throughout the ages
- America's first medical schools
- The evolution of surgical anesthesia
- The medical consequences of the Hiroshima bombing
- ★ Effects of the bubonic plague on Europe in the fourteenth century
- How Hippocrates changed the practice of medicine
- ➥ Ancient theories of disease
- The temples and cult of Asclepius
- Contemporary evaluations of Paracelsus (Philippus Aureolus Theophrastus Bombastus von Hohenheim, 1493–1541)
- ★ Historic treatments of the mentally ill

- The campaign to eradicate hookworm disease in the southern states
- The 1981 influenza epidemic
- ★ The ancient practice of bloodletting
- Describe in detail the dental office of 1900.
- The origins of birth control in America
- ○ Ancient and modern methods of cesarean section births
- ○ Early discoveries which related pathologic anatomy to the diagnosis of disease
- ▲ The long-term significance of Rudolf Virchow's discoveries in cellular pathology
- The first uses of X-rays
- Medicine as practiced in colonial America
- × Epidemics in the medieval world
- Historic theories about brain function
- ★ Cholera incidence and control, 1920–present
- The effects of cholera on the history of humanity
- Phrenology
- ▲ Compare and contrast the dis-

eases treated and medicines used in Egypt and Babylon.

● The relationship between religion and medical practice throughout the ages

● Medieval hospitals

○ The impact of Arab science on medieval medicine

✕ Medical fads: past and present

☛ Famous doctors in literature

§ Early practices in gynecology

● Ancient and modern theories of heart disease

☛ Select a Nobel Prize winner in medicine such as James D. Watson and detail the significant factors leading to his/her award.

☛ The folk origins of medicine. Select an illness, disease, or type of injury and follow its treatment throughout history.

▲ The medical cases described in the Edwin Smith Papyrus

§ The development of the stethoscope and how it changed medical practice (or, select some other significant invention)

● Monastic medicine and the 1130 decree by the Council of Clermont

§ Elements of ancient Greek medicine

● Historical uses of artificial limbs

● Surgical techniques of the Renaissance

▲ Early examples of plastic surgery, particularly in India

● The first heart transplants

● The swine flu immunization program, 1975–1976

§ Early antiseptics

● The founding of the American Medical Association

● The incidence and causes of puerperal (childbed) fever in the nineteenth century

● The discovery and development of antibiotics

☛ The history of innoculation as a disease preventative

★ The traditional uses of native plants in the treatment of injuries

● The development of dental plates

● The conquest of polio

★ Trepanning in ancient cultures

● The significance to medicine of the Code of Hammurabi (Mesopotamia, c. 2000 B.C.)

✕ The first medical schools

Mental Health

See also: Health; Medicine; Psychology

- Historical treatments of schizophrenia
▲ Current uses of antipsychotic drugs on mental patients
- When should the mentally ill be hospitalized or institutionalized? Consider the opinions of a number of experts.
○ Drug therapy for depression
★ How to recognize when a family member needs professional help
↢ Compare and contrast treatment methods in United States mental institutions, past and present.
- Guilt: the great American pastime. Discuss this statement in terms of the psychological and sociological evidence available.
★ What mentally deficient children can be taught
- The interrelationships of genius and mental health. Are people with high IQ's more emotionally stable, satisfied, and productive, than people with lower IQ's? Consult several research studies.
- Treatment of the mentally ill in the medieval world
- The effects of institutionalization on mentally handicapped children
- Electroshock therapy for the mentally ill. What is its status today?
↢ Genetic factors in mental illness
★ The correlations and implications of suicide rates by occupation
○ The psychological basis of music therapy
- Is the price of private practice therapy too high?
★ The possible function of dreams in maintaining daily mental health
- There has been a plethora of books on psychological self-help. Discuss the possible reasons for this development in terms of mental health in the United States.
↢ Common personality disorders
§ Symptoms of paranoia
- Chronic brain syndromes
- Care of mental patients as pictured in One Flew Over the Cuckoo's Nest (Ken Kesey). Is

the portrayal accurate?

★ Is homosexuality a mental illness?

▲ Senile psychosis

● Ancient treatments of mental illness (Greek, Egyptian, Roman)

● Physical and mental characteristics of drug dependence

● Common deviant behavior in prison inmates

● What to do about a phobia

○ Physical causes of psychosis

★ Living with the chronically mentally ill: some guidelines

➥ Residential facilities for the mentally retarded child

● Mental problems of physically disabled children

★ Psychological elements of alcoholism (or drug addiction)

★ Effects of emotional deprivation on the normal adult

✕ How to help the chronically ill child maintain a good mental outlook

● Treating drug addiction as a mental illness

➥ Psychosomatic illness

● The relationship between mental illness and marital status. Cite some recent studies.

● Support or refute: Mental patients should be treated for their symptoms rather than the causes of the illness.

● Federal assistance programs for mental health: a survey

● Twentieth-century changes in the

public's attitude toward the treatment of mental illness

✕ Public education and mental illness. What have been the components of the most successful programs?

● Disturbed children — disturbed parents?

○ The treatment of manic-depressives with lithium

● Biological origins of mental dysfunctions

▲ Differing perspectives on the causes of childhood autism

● Mental difficulties often encountered in adopted children

★ Mental dysfunctions of Vietnam veterans

● Philippe Pinel's reforms in the treatment of the mentally ill

○ The biochemistry of schizophrenia

● Mentally retarded children: home care versus institutionalization

● Personal methods for combating depression. What do doctors advise?

▲ The controversy and facts surrounding the administration of drugs to hyperkinetic children.

↙ Survey and evaluate mental health funding programs and services in your state.

● What changes in the American economic system have contributed to the growth of personal insecurity?

▲ Do modern mental hospitals provide a proper therapeutic climate for patients? Support your answer with relevant evidence.

✔ Survey your own community for mental health agencies or groups. Who is eligible for assistance? How are the public

and private groups funded? Is the assistance adequate for the needs of the community?

• Many doctors believe that hospitalization for mental disorders is often detrimental to the patient. Why? What approaches might be more successful?

○ Has the administration of Prozac (and other similar drugs) changed the mental-health treatment picture?

Key to Symbols

•	average difficulty	↬	narrow down topic
§	substitutes possible	▲	large public or college library required
★	ample information in most libraries	✔	local option topic
○	specialized knowledge required	✗	examples and supporting evidence needed

Military

See also: Foreign Policy; Government

- The military justice system
- ★ What are the possibilities for an accidental nuclear war?
- ★ Have the problems of Vietnam veterans differed significantly from those experienced by veterans of World Wars I and II?
- Changing American attitudes towards military service, 1940 and today
- ▲ Bombing ranges: What should be done for the communities near them?
- The modern Chinese army
- ★ What are the pros and cons of the national conscription of women for military duty?
- Psychological problems of combat
- Levels of censorship in times of war
- What would happen in a biological war?
- Compare and contrast compulsory military service in other countries. Use, for example, Russia, Israel, Germany, China, and Pakistan.
- Current issues of military discipline

- ○ Basic training in the United States military — is it adequate?
- § Recent tank design innovations and improvements
- ▲ Retention problems in the peacetime military
- Military camouflage
- The weapons of the next war
- The weapon technology of the 1990–91 Persian Gulf War
- ○ The American missile arsenal
- § Basic training in the marines
- The nature and scope of morale problems in the United States military establishment
- ○ Strategies for a limited nuclear war
- The role of the mercenary soldier in armed conflicts
- ▲ Compare and contrast military training methods in modern Switzerland, Israel, Great Britain, and the United States.
- Aerial intelligence photography
- ★ The volunteer army versus the draft
- ○ Binary weapons
- × Psychological weapons of war
- ★ Why was Star Wars unsuccessful?

- Can modern nations still wage a "just war"?
§ Plan a military assault on <u>an island</u>
- Tactical uses of the helicopter
- Tactics of fleet actions in naval combat (choose either offensive or defensive)
- The defense of naval shipping in wartime
○ The technology and uses of high energy laser weapons
- Military tactics of the Roman legions
★ Is the navy obsolete?
- Essentials of desert warfare
▲ The myths and realities of the French Foreign Legion
- The technology of the sword
- Warfare and the Geneva Convention
- Critical issues in arms control
- Chemical warfare
- Submarine strategy
- Women in the Israeli army
- The frogmen: underwater strategy during wartime
- Antitank warfare
- Battle fatigue and other war-related mental illnesses
- Life in a United States military academy
- Would the United States military needs be better served by the combination of all services into one unit?
○ The design of the *Nautilus*, the first atomic submarine
- Dalton Trumbo's view of war in

Johnny Got His Gun
★ American military bases in the Persian Gulf: the strategic importance
- How reduced military expenditures affect the United States' economy
▲ Male attitudes toward women in the military
- Should the United States sell military hardware to Middle Eastern countries?
★ Careers in the United States military establishment
- Compare and contrast one element of the Korean and Vietnam wars.
- The elements of surprise in military strategy
- Techniques of modern guerrilla warfare
- Satellites as defense strategies
- The United States Rapid Deployment Force. What were the purposes of its original formation? How has it been utilized?
- The military balance of the future: the experts predict
- Military uses of dogs and other animals
- Are current levels of United States military forces adequate? Compare and contrast the opinions of appropriate authorities.
○ Compare and contrast long-range and medium-range ballistic weapons.
▲ Weapon and military equipment sales to China: who is selling

what?

O Computer designed military exercises

★ Why United States military bases around the world are in jeopardy. Do we still need them? Does their expense justify their existence?

● The armed forces routinely use polygraph (lie-detector) examinations on high security clearance personnel. How is this justified?

★ Did we win the Gulf War?

● Describe and evaluate any new military equipment and/or techniques used in the Gulf War or in other recent conflicts.

● How did the American presence in Bosnia change the character of that conflict?

★ What happened in Rwanda?

Key to Symbols

●   **average difficulty**
§   **substitutes possible**
★   **ample information in most libraries**
○   **specialized knowledge required**

➤   **narrow down topic**
▲   **large public or college library required**
↙   **local option topic**
×   **examples and supporting evidence**

Music

See also: Humanities

- New Orleans jazz funerals
- Barbershop quartets in America
- ○ The tradition of sacred harp singing in American folk music
- ★ Rock recordings are big business
- × Primitive musical instruments
- ▲ The role of Masonic ideology in the music of Mozart
- What are some of the contemporary uses of electronic music?
- What has been the influence of Latin American music on modern jazz?
- ○ Musical notation of electronic music
- Innovations in the musical uses of technology by composer Karlheinz Stockhausen
- Compare and contrast the compositional practices of Mozart and Beethoven.
- Recent conductors of the New York Philharmonic
- Beverly Sills and the New York City Opera
- How to write popular songs
- § Japanese musical instruments
- Orchestral tone color in the music of Debussy

- The technology of valved brass instruments
- Homemade musical instruments
- Unusual, unique, and bizarre musical instruments
- The alp horn in Swiss culture
- ○ Ten thousand trumpets from a mountain top: the orchestration of Hector Berlioz
- Opera: Original language or language of the audience?
- § Popular music in South America
- ★ Impact on the music industry of recording piracy
- ▲ Women instrumentalists in jazz
- Innovations in modern music: Charles Ives
- Merle Haggard's song lyrics
- ➥ American musical theater: from minstrel shows to "My Fair Lady"
- The shofar in Hebrew culture
- The talking drum in African tribal life
- The marketing of rock music
- ➥ The influence of religious music on jazz
- × Social commentary in the lyrics of rock music of the 1960's

314

- Opera as musical theater
- Are rock stars born or made? Cite a variety of musical authorities to justify your answers.
- The humor of the Beatles
- The demise of disco
- "The Merry Widow": the world's most popular operetta
- African origins of modern percussion instruments
★ John Denver's multitalents
- Compare and contrast bluegrass and country and western music.
▲ English folk music in the Appalachians
★ How rock concerts make money
- The President's Marine Corps Band
- The goals and achievements of the Federal Music Project during the Depression
○ The bel canto style in opera
- Ragtime's influence on popular music
- How to get into the song writing business
▲ Music therapy in mental hospitals
★ Compare and contrast folk and country music.
- Compile an annotated bibliography of fifty best recordings for a classical music library. Explain the reason for your selections.
- The influence of John Lennon on contemporary music
★ The instruments of the orchestra: how the components have

changed and evolved
✕ Musical child prodigies
- Disc jockeys and their relationship to the record industry
- The rock opera
- Bach in the twentieth century: adoptions and adaptions
➤ The worldwide influence of American popular music
○ Latest advances in electronic musical instruments
- A reevaluation of the music of Scott Joplin: popular music, classical music — or what?
➤ Modern jazz: the bop revolution and beyond
★ The return of big band jazz: Nostalgia or a revival of high quality popular music?
- How to encourage a child's interest in and enjoyment of music
○ How to make perfect tape recordings
- Compare soft rock, rock, punk rock, and disco. What are the origins of each? Are they ethnic? Geographic?
★ Rock music and the recording industry. Where do we go from here?
- The concerto grosso as a performance style. Where were its origins?
○ A through G: the evolution, peculiarities, and limitations of traditional music notation
- What is musical talent? What have been some of the theories and experimental efforts used to

explain this phenomenon?

○ Recording medieval music. What are the authentic instruments and how should they be played?

○ Elizabethan life and manners as

replicated in English madrigals

• Why rock lyrics have gone too far

• The Live Aid concert: how was it organized, who participated and benefited?

Key to Symbols

•	average difficulty	⌐	narrow down topic
§	substitutes possible	▲	large public or college
★	ample information in most		library required
	libraries	↙	local option topic
○	specialized knowledge	×	examples and supporting
	required		evidence needed

Music — History

See also: Humanities

- Frédéric Chopin and his stormy love affair with George Sand
- ★ The invention of opera: early form and structure
- ▲ Technology and craftsmanship of eighteenth-century pipe organs
- Romantic love and the medieval troubadour-trouvère tradition
- ▲ Music competition at the ancient Greek games
- The American reception of the Beatles (1964)
- Max Reinhardt and the genesis of the Mozart Festival (Salzburg, Austria)
- Richard and Cosima Wagner and the mystique of Bayreuth
- ▲ The Paris premiere of Stravinsky's *The Rite of Spring* (1913)
- ★ Evolution of the symphony orchestra, from Beethoven to Berlioz
- ○ Gothic music in the Cathedral School of Paris
- ▲ Guido d'Arezzo and the development of musical notation
- Warfare and the use of trumpets
- Drummers in eighteenth-century warfare
- The development of military bugle calls
- ▲ "Childe Harold," Louis-Hector Berlioz, and Lord Byron
- Richard Wagner's exploitation of King Ludwig II of Bavaria
- ★ Virtuosos of the Romantic Age: Franz Liszt and Niccolò Paganini
- ▲ Music performance in Greek tragedies
- § The history of the bagpipes
- × African origins of black American folk music
- Pythagoras and the "music of the spheres"
- Beethoven's reactions to his loss of hearing. How was his music affected?
- Martin Luther and German chorales
- Origins of the Viennese waltz
- The technology of the Cremona violin makers
- × The English folk song tradition in the southern United States
- ▲ Rhythm and blues on "race records"
- ★ Scott Joplin and the develop-

317

ment of ragtime

● Origins of the American minstrel show

○ Liturgical music at Charlemagne's court

● Words and music: evolution of the English madrigal

○ The piano etudes of the nineteenth century: Chopin and Liszt

● The collaboration of Igor Stravinsky and Sergei Diaghilev

★ The story of the Grand Ole Opry

▲ Karlheinz Stockhausen and the studio for electronic music of the Cologne Radio Station

● Castrati in seventeenth- and eighteenth-century opera

● Richard Wagner and the quest for the Holy Grail

★ Compare the play *Amadeus* with the facts in Mozart's life.

▲ Johann Sebastian Bach as viewed by his contemporaries

○ Bach's contribution to modern music

▲ Musical genius: What about Mozart's sister?

▲ Music in Biblical times

● The economic and musical reasons for George Frederick Handel's failure as a composer of Italian operas

▲ Pope Gregory the Great and Gregorian chant. What is the true story of Gregorian chant?

● The "eighty-eight": How many strings have pianos had?

➥ Instruments of war. What musical instruments have been used on the field of battle to signal commands and bolster morale?

● Origins and development of the art of conducting symphony orchestras. In what ways has this changed in the twentieth century?

● The origin of Italian tempo indications for music

★ In the beginning: What are the oldest musical instruments?

▲ The development of musical notation since the Middle Ages

● Compare and contrast John Gay's *Beggar's Opera* and Bertolt Brecht's *The Threepenny Opera*. Consider text, music, and the societies being satirized.

▲ Medieval musical instruments

● The incredible career of Jean Baptiste Lully, court musician for Louis XIV

§ Technological development of the flute

➥ Styles of film scores: from the 1950's to the 1990's

▲ Music in medieval courts of love. What kinds of music, and for what purpose?

● King Henry VIII of England as musician and composer

Myth, Symbol, and Folklore

See also: Anthropology; Customs, Traditions, and Folkways

- ★ Huckleberry Finn as outlaw hero
- • Compare Mount Olympus and Valhalla as dwelling places of the gods.
- ▲ The Abominable Snowman. What have been the results of valid scientific research?
- • National flags as metaphors
- ○ Supermen throughout history. Select several figures from history who have had an extraordinary effect on the society of their period and on the course of history. What were the elements of their personality which enabled them to excel, influence change, or accomplish the unusual? Why were they unique?
- ✔ Does your local area have any particular myths and legends? Are they unique to the area or are they adaptions of other mythologies? Focus on their themes, characters, and incidents. Is there a basis of truth to any of them?
- • Military women and female armies in myth and legend
- ➨ The origins of contemporary superstitions
- • Universal symbols for the source of life
- • The Greek myths: What is myth and what is truth?
- • Mythology as depicted in Greek vase paintings
- • The function of the western movie in American mythology
- ★ The symbol of the cross from prehistory to the present
- • The myth of Atlantis versus historical fact. Consult current sources for an archeological and geological overview.
- ▲ Survey and compare the many stories about Prester John, legendary Christian monarch.
- • Fire in myth and symbol
- • Mythology of George Washington. How much is based on fact?
- • The dream in mythology
- • The Greeks as seen through their myths and legends
- ★ The Irish "little people"
- § The moon in mythology
- ▲ Historical perspective on Robin Hood
- • Reincarnation in myth and fable
- ○ Myth and religion: the histor-

ical and semantic discriminations
- The historical context of the Arthurian legends
- Theseus, the Minotaur, and the Minoans
- Myths about the Amazons
- The legend of Bluebeard in myth, story, and song
- Compare the mythology of the Plains and the Pueblo Indians
- The curse of the House of Atreus
- The fairy in folklore
○ King Arthur as archetypal hero
- Hercule Poirot's (Agatha Christie's fictional detective) twelve labors of Heracles. Compare this to the original version depicting Heracles' journey.
- The eternal search for the fountain of youth
▲ Art works depicting the judgment of Paris
- The Fates as they appear in lore and legends of several different cultures
▲ Sources of the fairy tales of the Grimm Brothers
- Freudian complexes and their relation to Greek myths (Oedipus, Electra)
- Discuss how monsters in many myths were used to explain natural geologic disasters and the forces of nature.
- When and where was Troy destroyed? A study of Heinrich Schliemann's excavations.
★ Apollo: how his complex na-

ture is indicated in the many myths about him
- The association of animals with gods and goddesses has taken on characteristics which we still recognize today. Isolate and discuss at least fifteen.
- Myths and folklore of flowers and herbs
- Common themes in mythology
§ Characteristics of Irish mythology
- Origins of the Greek Pantheon
- Compare and contrast three different stories of creation.
- Animism in primitive religions and mythology
- Myths about virgin birth
- Aztec mythology
§ The month of May in mythology and folklore
- Compare and contrast Aphrodite (Greek) and Venus (Roman).
- Characteristics and significance of the phoenix bird in mythology
★ The unicorn as a myth and symbol
- The Norse god of flame, Loki. Consider his characteristics, powers, and similarities to other dieties (Greek, etc.) and possible contributions to the devil image.
★ The lore of witches
- Vampire legends
○ The personality of the Norse god Odin as he gradually

evolves in sophistication

▲ Theories on the actual return route of Odysseus

○ Compare and contrast the folk mythology of William Faulkner with that of the Latin American writer Gabriel Garcia Marquez.

● Aesculapius: the man and the legend

● What have been the functions of myth in society? Why is it found, in one form or another, in every culture?

☛ Myths of the American frontier. Select a particular area and time period.

● The journey motif in mythological history

★ Symbols of female fertility in primitive and ancient cultures

● The western pioneer as folk hero

● The swastika as decoration, symbol, and metaphor

● Why society needs heroes

Key to Symbols

● average difficulty
§ substitutes possible
★ ample information in most libraries
○ specialized knowledge required

☛ narrow down topic
▲ large public or college library required
↙ local option topic
✗ examples and supporting evidence needed

Native Americans

See also: Anthropology; Archeology; Ethnic and Minority Groups

✔ What happened to the original Native Americans in your locality?

● What cultural adjustment problems are common among Native Americans still living on reservations?

✔ Life on a modern reservation. Select several and visit them if possible.

★ Native Americans and alcohol: an overview

● Individual identity in tribal religions

★ What was the importance of the buffalo to the Plains Indians?

▲ The use of dogs by the Native American

● Apache skin paintings: their design, symbols, and significance in the religious system

▲ United States official Indian policy in the nineteenth century: the realities of white/Indian relations. Focus on treaties, acts and accords.

✗ Why the reservations have never been successful

● What were the life patterns of Plains tribes, such as the Sioux, before and after the advent of the white man?

● Discuss the parallels between the Sioux land restitution demands made in 1980 and those made by Red Cloud and Little Bear in 1875.

● What were the new Native American attitudes in the 1990's? What problems generated these changes? What was the response of the federal government?

● Compare and contrast the Spanish and the English treatment of Native Americans.

● The Dawes Act of 1887 and Indian autonomy

★ What was the chain of events that led to the Wounded Knee massacre?

● What were the advantages and disadvantages of the nomadic lifestyle for the Native American?

➤ By what means did settlers and the United States government eliminate opposition from the Native Americans in the West? Consider cultural, military, political, and economic factors.

● Navajo rugs: their dyes and patterns

● Compare and contrast Navajo and Hopi religions

- Can Native American cultural values survive the twentieth century?
- The Four Corners Power Plant and the Navajo
- ▲ Social problems of relocated (from reservation to city) Native Americans
- ▲ The ongoing Navajo-Hopi land controversy
- Organization and utility of the Bureau of Indian Affairs
- Should Native American educators teach tribal culture?
- The location and numbers of indigenous populations in the United States before Columbus
- § Pottery of the <u>Pueblo</u>
- Origin myths of the Navajo
- ✔ Indian treaties: Protection or United States paternalism?
- The potential mineral resources on Southwestern reservations and their significance to Native American independence
- ➡ Incidence, causes, and nature of broken treaties with the Native Americans
- § Burial customs of _____.
- Why the original Americans are poor
- Hunting techniques of the North American Paleo-Indians
- Self-concept among contemporary male Native Americans
- § Prehistoric inhabitants of the American West. Select one tribe, such as the <u>Mogollon</u>, and describe their life, appearance, and

- habitat based on cultural artifacts.
- How to curtail the looting of historical native sites
- ★ Native American pottery today: the state of the art
- ▲ Symbolism of Mimbres pottery design
- ✔ Research the causes, nature, and outcome of an incident involving Indian warfare in your locality.
- ➡ Major social, economic, and political issues of the Native American. Concentrate on one issue.
- The true story of Pocahontas
- The annual cycle of Hopi ceremonies and their basis in the natural world
- Traditional tribal medicine
- § <u>Chippewa</u> myths
- The Southwest's earliest natives — the Hohokam
- Native Americans are fighting a battle with the federal government, museums and anthropologists over the skeletal remains of their ancestors. What are the conflicting values of the controversy?
- ★ How legal gambling on many reservations has changed the tribes' economies
- The Hopi: The end of a culture?
- Socioeconomic aspects of the urban Native American
- Alcoholism among the Navajos
- ★ Effects of the Spanish missions on Native American cultures
- Traditional Native American attitudes towards the environment

Nuclear Power

See also: Energy; Physics

- Are nuclear power plants safe from terrorists?
- Projections for nuclear power plants in the year 2000. How will this affect the environment?
▲ Are the emergency core cooling systems of nuclear power plants adequate?
☛ Critical issues in nuclear waste transportation
★ The inherent dangers of nuclear power
✕ Meltdowns and near meltdowns
- What will happen when nuclear plants wear out?
▲ The cost of decommissioning nuclear power plants
- Determine the adequacy of the standards to safeguard worker health in nuclear power plants.
- Latent effects of radiation
▲ The use of temporary employees ("jumpers") in nuclear power facilities
- Nuclear shutdowns since 1970. Consider this topic on a worldwide basis.
- How much of the United States' current energy consumption is generated by nuclear means?

What is projected? Are these projections both feasible and realistic?
- How does the nuclear industry propose to prevent the release of radioactive material from burial sites over the next 200,000 years?
☛ Nonmilitary applications of nuclear energy
- Who profits from nuclear power?
★ Nuclear war?   a scenario
- The effects of radiation on plant life
○ Earthquakes and nuclear power plants: an analysis of potential hazards
§ Atomic power capabilities of India
- The world's only naturally occurring nuclear reactor
- What were the factors involved in the emergency shutdown of the Robert E. Ginna reactor (New York) in January 1982? Was the handling of this incident an indication of the safety of reactors?
- Could the earth survive a nu-

324

clear war?

★ President Truman's decision to drop the bomb on Japan: pros and cons

● What are the primary arguments against nuclear power as an energy source?

● The breeder-reactor controversy surrounding the Clinch River reactor: What were the issues? Were they resolved?

● Emergency planning for reactor accidents

● Could the incident at Three Mile Island have been prevented?

○ Problems in the decommissioning of radioactive residues in closed or contaminated nuclear facilities

● "The unleashed power of the atom has changed everything except our way of thinking" (Albert Einstein). In what ways

has this proved to be true?

● Will a freeze stop the nuclear arms race?

★ Describe the concept of the "nuclear winter"

● Is nuclear war justifiable? When?

★ Do nuclear weapons provide security in today's world?

▲ What is the level of nuclear expertise in China?

✔ Select a nuclear power plant in your area. Discuss financing, costs, utility, emergency preparedness, past and current problems.

★ To what shortcomings do experts ascribe the Chernobyl nuclear power plant explosion & fire? Could it have been avoided?

● Radiation levels from the Chernobyl nuclear accident. Detail the effects on the European & world community.

Key to Symbols

● **average difficulty**	✦ **narrow down topic**
§ **substitutes possible**	▲ **large public or college**
★ **ample information in most**	**library required**
libraries	✔ **local option topic**
○ **specialized knowledge**	✗ **examples and supporting**
required	**evidence needed**

Nursing

See also: Health; Medicine; Mental Health; Nutrition

- Problems of nursing in the home environment
- Visiting nurse programs in the United States. What changes and improvements have been instituted?
- Major shifts in hospital care, from 1930 to the present
- Nursing the person with loss of intellectual abilities
- The changing role of the operating room nurse
- What is good nursing care? Compare a variety of experts' opinions.
- Caring for the very aged
- The coma victim's special problems
- Caring for the terminally ill
- Working in the hospice situation
- Nursing techniques for premature babies
- Battlefield nursing. Include a discussion of the military's C-4 course
- Home care for the chronically ill
- Nursing careers in the military
- What nurses should know about computer technology
- Caring for the institutionalized mental patient

- Trauma nursing: its pitfalls and rewards
- Emergency cardiac care: what the nurse should and should not do
- Emotional adjustments involved while nursing the dying patient
- Compare and contrast the registered nurse and the licensed practical nurse
- Nursing patients with respiratory problems
- The care of the quadriplegic
- New advances in operating room procedures
- Factors in postoperative care
- The school nurse. Consider training, duties, career opportunities, etc.
- Administrative problems in nursing homes for the aged and the infirm
- Private versus public nursing
- Nursing in modern hospitals. Select one area and detail the changes, advances, and current technology.
- Nursing care for the mentally retarded
- Emergency childbirth procedures
- The increasing use of mid-

wives: pros and cons
- How nurses can improve their sensitivity to patient needs
- Characteristics of the aged patient
- Medical advances in "intensive care" nursing
- Exercises for cardiovascular patients
▲ The male nurse and the hospital situation
○ Psychological problems of institutionalized patients
- Physical fitness programs for the bedridden patient
★ Nonverbal communication and the patient
§ Nursing the long-term diabetic
○ Recent advances in the care of the burned patient
- Therapeutic patient communication
- The importance of touch in the nursing process
- What are the legal rights of patients?
✕ The use of closed circuit television in hospitals
- Qualifications for the emergency room nurse. Include education requirements and the necessary physical and emotional elements
- Feeding the aged patient. Summarize typical nutritional needs and common physical liabilities.
○ Caring for the patient in isolation
- Legal aspects of nursing negligence
★ Preparing children for operations and other hospital proce-

dures. How nurses can help children deal with the experience.
- Nursing burnout: what it is and why it occurs
○ Hospital procedures for rape victims. Include psychological elements.
- Malpractice problems for nurses
- Ethical considerations in nursing care
- Home care for the disabled
- How to sharpen your patient observational skills
★ What is the scope of traditional nursing practice? How has it changed in the last twenty years?
- The role of the visiting nurse in the medical profession
- How to create and maintain a proper psychological atmosphere in the sickroom
- The examination of the newborn
★ The role and functions of modern nurse practitioners
- Legal rights and liabilities of nurses
▲ Varying attitudes towards male and female patients
★ Colleges report a steady decline in the number of students majoring in nursing. Discuss factors involved.
✕ Why are many nurses quitting their profession?
- Contrast the incentives offered to medical and nursing students by U.S. military recruiters.
★ The impact of the feminist movement on the nursing profession

Nutrition

See also: Food and Drink; Health; Medicine

- Compare the nutrient requirements of animals and green plants. Are they mutually dependent? In what significant ways do they differ?
- ○ Teratogenic effects of malnutrition
- ★ The demographics of kwashiorkor, a protein deficiency disease of young children
- ▲ Compare the nutritional content of fresh, frozen, canned, and dehydrated foods. Select several foods as examples.
- Synthetic foods may become a necessary reality in many diets. What are some of the practical possibilities? Is technology currently available?
- The relationship between malnutrition and early childhood physical development.
- The scientific realities of honey and other "miracle" foods
- ★ The dangers of the high protein diet
- ★ Alcohol and mental ability. How does a heavy intake over many years affect the brain? Short-term overindulgence?

- Meat protein substitutes for the daily diet
- The effects of caffeine on body organs
- ➡ Results of steroid use on livestock
- ➡ Food advertising and good nutrition
- Problems in defining "health" foods
- Vitamin E therapy: the medical view
- ★ Junk food in schools. Should it be removed?
- Nutrition against disease. What are several of the more significant discoveries from nutritional studies and surveys?
- ▲ Are commercially used food preservatives safe? Cite informed nutritional opinion to support or refute the question.
- ★ Causes of obesity
- How to evaluate a diet
- Malnutrition among the poor. What successful measures have been instituted in the United States to alleviate this chronic situation?
- World protein resources: a

survey
* ★ Sugar: Eat it now, pay later?
* ● Nutritional aspects of diabetes
* ○ Nutritional aspects of hypertension
* ● The elements of the salt-free diet
* ● The diet of the average American teenager
* ★ Sugar in the American diet: an overview
* ○ Detail and describe a healthy diet for an elderly person with a limited income.
* ▲ How big business has joined the "health food" movement
* ● Pregnancy and nutrition: some guidelines
* ★ Health considerations for crash dieters
* ● American food habits in 1900 and now
* ● The food value of school lunches: what nutritionists say
* ★ Science looks at nutritional supplements
* ➤ Nutritional content of convenience foods: a survey
* ● The correct diet for the nursing mother
* ● Inflation, food costs, and proper nutrition
* ● Controlling hypoglycemia through diet
* ● Evaluate the merits of several currently popular food fads.
* ★ Teaching children the basics of sound nutrition
* ● Minimal dietary requirements.

How are they measured? What are the areas of nutritional controversy?
* ➤ Drugs and nutrition
* ● The soybean solution to world food shortages and famine
* ● Vegetable protein versus meat protein: costs and benefits
* ● Do malnourished infants have diminished mental abilities?
* ➤ Problems with nutrition and the elderly
* ★ The pros and cons of water fluoridation
* ○ The relationship between diet and hyperactivity in children
* ▲ Nutrition problems of the Native American
* ● The pitfalls of vegetarianism
* § Survey the nutritional resources of <u>Haiti</u> (crops, animal, production, etc.).
* ✔ Detail the edible wild plants in your area.
* ● How to have a balanced and interesting diet at a minimum cost. Plan a month's menus following stated guidelines.
* ● Is food that has been grown organically better for you? The nutritional point of view.
* ● Food additives that have been proved to be harmful. Are they still in use?
* ★ How vitamin deficiencies affect behavior
* ➤ Nutritional aspects of protein
* ★ The dangers of "vitamin therapy." How many vitamins

should humans have? What are the potential hazards of over-doses?

- Behavior modification and diet
- When are "health foods" not healthy?
- Sugar versus NutriSweet™ use
- The effects of high sugar consumption by children
★ Breast feeding versus the bottle in relation to infant health and nutrition
▲ The story behind "natural" vitamins
★ The addition of nitrates to foods
- Monosodium glutamate (MSG). How is it commonly used? What are some of its side effects?
- Bread in the United States. How nutritious is it? How nutritious is the bread consumed by the rest of the world?
- The truth about lecithin
- Why hospital food is bad for you
★ The proper diet for a domestic cat or dog

- Poverty and nutrition: What are the main factors in this interrelationship?
- Spaceflight nutrition
- The interrelationship between malnutrition and body size
○ How the levels and kinds of malnutrition and undernourishment found today differ from those found in past famines throughout history
▲ The marketing practices of baby formula manufacturers in underdeveloped countries. Has this controversy been resolved?
- Factors contributing to patient stress
★ What everyone should know about junk food
- Sulfites are often used on food to preserve freshness. Existing evidence indicates that many persons suffer allergic reactions. Should the use of sulfites be curtailed or banned?
- How new government labeling standards have assisted the consumer in food selection

Oceans and Seas

See also: Biology; Boats and Boating; Exploration and Discovery; Geography

× How marine organisms are part of the food webs that sustain higher life forms on earth

● Examine and evaluate the latest innovations in small undersea craft.

➥ Recent proposals to prevent ocean pollution and contamination

★ Trace the evolution of diving hardware

● The search for a shark repellent. What advances have been made in the last twenty years?

★ The formation of ocean atolls from coral reefs

● The biological basis of red tides and bioluminescence

● Coral reef destruction by the crown of thorns starfish. Is this a natural cycle or a permanent imbalance? Cite current remedies being implemented.

● What effect will possible global warming have on the oceans?

★ The permanent result of oil spills

● Life on and in an ocean vent

▲ What has the deep-sea research submarine *Alvin* discovered?

○ The commercial aspects of hot brines

★ The strange Sargasso Sea

● Ocean currents and their effects on land masses

➥ International law and ocean resources

● Farming the ocean: the potential for tomorrow's food supply

○ Frontiers of marine biology. Select an area of significant potential and detail its problems and prospects.

● Tidal waves: how they develop and what some have done

▲ Submarine volcanoes. Consult current research for the newest findings.

● Desalination of ocean water and its practical applications. What have been past obstacles to utilization? How have innovations advanced the technology?

● Buried treasure and the economics of marine salvage

➥ What lives in the oceans'

depths? Include a review of recent literature. Select either plant or animal life.

• The first transatlantic crossing by the *Eagle*

★ How did the invention of the mariner's compass change sea voyages?

○ Practical designs for ocean thermal energy conservation systems

★ The ocean's manganese nodules, their formation, mining potential, and ownership

• Prospects for the commercial fishing of krill

• Ocean rift life

○ Traditional techniques of Pacific navigation

• Seabed mining: prospects and problems

• Properties, distribution, and behavior of icebergs

• The physiology of waves

§ Life forms of the Great Barrier Reef (Australia)

➤ Theories and evidence of transoceanic travel by primitive societies

▲ Current levels of ocean pollution

× How to protect coastlines

• Protecting the world's oceans' ecosystems

○ The uses of radar in oceanography

★ Ocean survival procedures

• Primary features of the ocean floor. Through what processes were they formed?

• The food chain of the coral reef

○ The chemical evolution of the oceans

• How ancient and medieval scientists explained the tides and other ocean phenomena

• What will happen when the ocean is polluted: a scenario for the future

▲ Salmon hatcheries of the Northwest

• Freedom of the seas: international policies

× Adaptions to life in the tidal zone

• Historic fluctuations of sea levels

▲ The first Aqua-lungs and how they were used

○ Modern seafloor maps. How were they charted? How accurate are they?

★ The influence of sea power in history: an overview

• The oceanic observations of Arab historian-geographer Masudi

○ Lavoisier's chemical studies of sea water

• The long-range effects of the *Exxon Valdez* oil spill in Alaska's Prince William Sound

• The first great scientific voyage (Pytheas, 335 – 300 B.C.), where they went, and what they discovered

➤ What have been some of the most recent proposals for ocean shipping reform?

○ The Titanic was located in 1985. How will the equipment used in this discovery revolutionize future exploration of oceans and seafloors?

▲ Animals at underwater hydrothermal vents are unique. Describe them. What is their range in the oceans?

○ The prospects for ocean-wave power plants

● The international Ocean Drilling Program (ODP) has recently started operations. What are the goals of this project? Where will they oper-ate? Who is involved?

× Recent satellite measurements have detected a rapid rise in global sea levels. What will be the result if this trend continues?

§ Can depleted <u>salmon</u> populations ever regain their previous numbers?

● Project the consequences of a large meteor's impacting an ocean.

★ Explore the possible (probable?) results of global warming on ocean levels.

★ What effects did El Niño have on ocean ecosystems?

Key to Symbols

●	average difficulty	➤	narrow down topic
§	substitutes possible	▲	large public or college library required
★	ample information in most libraries	↙	local option topic
○	specialized knowledge required	×	examples and supporting evidence

Personal Finance

See also: Consumerism; Economics; Marriage and Family

○ The best investments for the next ten years. Analyze the trends and possibilities in a variety of investment areas to justify your choices.

★ How to calculate monthly housing costs. Consider mortgage, insurance, utilities, and maintenance.

● How to read a real estate contract

● What are the rights of the mortgager and those of the mortgagee (the lender and the borrower)?

● Survey several medical and hospital plans and choose the best. Justify your personal choice.

★ The return of barter to the American scene

▲ Are medical insurance rates equitable?

§ How to deal in commodities

● Effectively using the small claims court

➡ How to pick the best small business possibility

● Considerations and prerequisites for starting your own business

● The economics of divorce

★ How to teach children about money

§ Detail a budget for a family of four with a $45,000 yearly income.

§ Describe a sensible budget for a young single person with a yearly income of $25,000.

✕ Living well on less

● How to establish and maintain a financial plan for personal income

● How to invest in the stock market and make a profit

§ Art as an investment

★ How to access your net worth. Why is this data essential?

★ Borrowing money: what you should find out before applying for credit

✔ Where to get financial advice. Evaluate these sources. If possible, interview financial advisers.

✔ Select five sources for checking accounts in your locality. Evaluate and compare their costs and services. Include a credit union, if possible.

§ You are married, twenty-five years old, and have one child.

Project and evaluate all life insurance possibilities. (You may change the conditions.)

- Pension problems for new retirees
- How to select "medigap" insurance to cover what Medicare doesn't
★ How to maintain a good credit rating
- Annuity plans: techniques for evaluation
- How to build retirement income
- How to choose and invest in an IRA (Individual Retirement Account)
★ Survival strategies during a recession
➤ Buying land as an investment
- Analyze your family's budgetary allocations (food, housing, taxes, etc.) and suggest ways in which these percentages could (or should) be altered.
○ Marketing your own business
- How to file for personal bankruptcy
- Problems with "creative" home financing
- How to start a home business
- How to sell your home yourself
- How to protect yourself against consumer fraud
★ Planning ahead for a college education: costs, methods, and alternatives
○ Finding and utilizing tax shelters
✔ You want to borrow $10,000. Survey and compare loan sources, interest rates, and repayment schedules.

★ How to evaluate your individual debt level, get out of debt, and stay solvent
- Avoiding bankruptcy
- The advantages and disadvantages of variable interest in home mortgages
➤ Survey differing insurance needs
- Estate planning for future security
- What it takes to become a self-sufficient family in today's world. Consider finances, locations, food, shelter, education, medical expenses, etc.
§ Audio equipment: how to evaluate it before buying
★ How to get the most for your money at the grocery store
★ Food co-ops: Do they save the consumer dollars?
○ Real estate as a tax shelter
- The proper use of credit cards
§ The economics of buying antiques
§ Rules for buying a secondhand car
○ The perils and pitfalls of investing in foreign currency
▲ Investing in precious metals. Survey this market over the last fifteen years.
- Is it more economical to rent or buy a place to live?
- How to avoid an Internal Revenue audit
- The pros and cons of self-

employment
★ Elements of a personal budget
● Saving tax money with trusts
● Is it advisable for sellers to personally finance the sale of their homes? Examine some of the advantages and also detail possible problems and pitfalls.
○ How programmed or computerized stock trading affects the individual investor
● The specter of long-term medical care and the average family's finances
● The advantages of the 401(k), and similar, savings programs
● Why future generations of Ameri-

cans may not live as affluently as the current ones
● What are the advantages/disadvantages of affinity cards, those credit cards offered by various organizations?
★ Why it is unsafe to depend on Social Security for retirement security
● The best way to select a financial advisor
● Why so many homeless Americans lack affordable housing
● How easy is it for others to access personal computerized information? List ways to safeguard this privacy.

Key to Symbols

●   **average difficulty**
§   **substitutes possible**
★   **ample information in most libraries**
○   **specialized knowledge required**

↤   **narrow down topic**
▲   **large public or college library required**
↳   **local option topic**
×   **examples and supporting evidence**

Philosophy

See also: Ethical Issues; Humanities; Religion

× When is propaganda justified?
● Compare and contrast the "this worldliness" of Harvey Cox's *Secular City* with the other-worldliness of Saint Augustine's *City of God.*
★ What is (or has been) "the American dream"?
● The humanism of Erasmus of Rotterdam
● Many believe morality is subjective, based on religion and culture, while others find it an absolute. Discuss this dichotomy.
● Compare and contrast the political philosophies of James Madison and Thomas Jefferson.
● The ethics of wiretapping
○ Compare the dualism of Plato and Descartes.
★ Hiroshima: ethical considerations
● B.F. Skinner's conception of the perfectibility of people as expressed in *Walden II*
➤ War, ethics, and the Geneva Convention
★ Arguments against capital punishment

● The historical roots of pacifism in America
▲ Contemporary definitions of political conservatism, radicalism, liberalism
§ Varying definitions of <u>love</u>
● Theories of the Fabians
● Karl Marx as humanitarian
● The effect of Mohandas K. Gandhi's nonviolent resistance on political movements
● Hitler and the "master race" theory
● Compare and contrast the Socratic method with the process of deductive reasoning.
○ Nietzsche's artist as superman
○ Origins of existentialism
● John Stuart Mill and the equality of women
● Heliocentric theories, from the Greeks to the Renaissance
● Should science be monitored?
● If Lenin were alive today, would his communist philosophy be in accordance with recent Soviet political philosophy?
● Compare atheists and agnostics
● The ethical issues of the Viet-

nam War. Were these concerns different from those in other armed conflicts?

- What are the rights of the unborn child?
- Philosophical definitions of immortality
- Present the issues involved in this stance: Extremism in the defense of liberty is no vice.
- Who should punish the criminal, society or the aggrieved?
★ Compare and contrast the political philosophies of Karl Marx and V.I. Lenin.
- Compare and contrast Stoicism and Epicureanism.
- Wartime atrocities: Who is responsible?
○ The essential differences between theistic and atheistic existentialists
- Is technology progress?
- The philosophic point of view of a comic strip ("Peanuts," "Ziggy," "Pogo," "Doonesbury," etc.)
- Philosophical approaches to the "evil" in man's nature
- Compare and contrast fascist and communist dictatorships.
- Varying concepts of utopia
- Contemporary attitudes towards good and evil
○ The "leap of faith" in the philosophy of Kierkegaard
- What is mysticism? Explore Bertrand Russell, William James, and the Eastern philosophers.

- Does the ultimate source of political power reside in the individual or in society? Support your answer with historical examples and evidence.
✕ Justifications of civil disobedience: a historical survey
- The nature of Thomas Paine's philosophy as expressed in *The Age of Reason*
- Compare Thomas More's *Utopia* with Marxism
○ The "God is dead" thesis (Nietzsche). Describe the movement which grew out of this thesis.
▲ The relationship between John Locke's philosophy and the development of American constitutional democracy
★ Considerations and motives of conscientious objectors
- Pragmaticism: an American philosophy
- Euthanasia: contemporary philosophical perspectives
- Trotsky's theories of revolution
★ Philosophical origins of yoga
- Greek views of liberty and justice
○ Philosophical proofs for the existence of God
- Mark Twain's philosophy in his old age
- The ethical and religious aspects of hunting and killing
- The Renaissance view of man
- Is the Protestant ethic obsolete?
- Pacifism and its applications

- Machiavelli: Political philosopher or psychologist?
- × Practical applications of utopian theories
- Variations on a theme: democracy throughout history
- Investigate Thomas Jefferson's attitudes towards liberty and those towards his own slaves.
- Compare the ideas expressed in the United States Declaration of Independence with those of several newly independent nations of today.
- ○ Jean-Paul Sartre's views on Marxism
- The transcendentalism of Henry David Thoreau
- ★ Moral and ethical issues in population control
- ★ Pornography and public morality. Should pornography be censored for the public good? Should it be eliminated? Include a definition of pornography.
- Compare and contrast hedonism, Epicureanism, and the Sybarites.
- Survey and compare major historical definitions of beauty.
- × Instances of civil disobedience in contemporary society
- "Progress" versus the quality of life. What is the conflict?
- Defend or refute: The Ten Commandments are a life ethic.
- ★ Compare and contrast the theories of socialism and communism.
- Is terrorism revolutionary?
- Refute or defend: Capital punishment fosters a respect for life.
- Philosophical approaches to the problem of free will
- Nonhuman rights: opposing views
- Support or refute: Traditional Christian ethics are no longer valid.
- Compare the world view of the traditional hero in ancient Greece with the modern American hero.
- Ethical considerations in genetic engineering. Why are these problems unique?
- Controlling the autonomic nervous system through yoga
- Can war be eliminated?
- ★ Moral and ethical considerations in the abortion controversy
- Can ethical behavior be taught? Who should teach it, the family, the church or the school?

Photography

See also: Art; Film; Humanities

○ Photo production complexities in filming home video movies

★ The invention of the halftone plate in 1880 and its effects on newspaper coverage

○ How to design and construct your own enlarger

☛ Cinematography, from silent films to cinemascope (or 3–D)

● How good are instant cameras? Have they been improved? How?

● Survey miniature cameras and rank them by price, complexity, and performance.

● The glass plate

● Development and design of the camera obscura

▲ New techniques in film editing

★ Edwin H. Land and his Polaroid camera

○ Camera work as a function of moviemaking

● Camera equipment for filming 35 mm movies

● Techniques of underwater photography

● Laser photography

★ Louis Daguerre and the Daguerreotype

○ Tools, materials, and techniques of photographic retouching

● Compare and contrast color photography and painting.

§ Fashion photography. What special knowledge and techniques are essential?

● Is the portable camcorder making home movies obsolete?

☛ How to learn photocomposition

● Techniques for controlling exposure

★ The technology of light meters and how it has evolved to the present day

★ Cel animation

● Creating a movie sequence

● Using natural lights in moviemaking

● Compare and contrast still and movie photocomposition techniques.

● Special lenses and attachments for movie cameras

★ Filters for special effects

● Recent equipment for close-up photography

● Build and equip your own darkroom

★ How to select a camera for the

340

beginning photographer. Include an appraisal of current models.

▲ The outer reaches of film: photography from space vehicles

● Lighting in portrait photography

● The uses of artificial light for indoor color photography

● The ethics of photojournalism

● Special equipment for the photojournalist

★ Education and training of the photojournalist

● Is color always best? Discuss the special properties of black-and-white.

● Advances in air photography technology

▲ The early efforts of air photographers

● Who really invented photography?

● The pinhole camera: how to teach children to make and use it

● The 3-D process (Eastman Kodak and others)

● Techniques for feature photo sequences

★ The perfect news photograph

● The Associated Press wirephoto network: what it does and how it operates

● The creative esthetics of Alfred Stieglitz

▲ The range, quality, and social impact of the photography collection of the Farm Security Administration, 1935–1942. (The collection is now in the Library of Congress.)

● How interchangeable filters and lenses can expand a photographer's visual range

● Fox Talbot and the calotype

● Stroboscopic lighting (electronic flash). Examine and discuss both professional and amateur equipment.

● The aerial photographs of William A. Garnett

★ George Eastman and the development of the Kodak camera and the Kodak Company

➥ How photography is used in medicine, the law, anthropology, archeology, and the social sciences. Select one area.

● Problems with artificial light and how to conquer them

★ Photography as art: Ansel Adams

● How to think photographically

● After 73 years the *Titanic* was discovered and photographed. What camera was used? Describe the problems encountered in this venture.

Physics

See also: Astronomy; Chemistry; Space

- The physics of tornadoes
- Detail the physical laws involved in the technology of the pipe organ.
- ○ The physical concept of the neutron bomb compared to other nuclear weapons
- ○ The technology and uses of holography
- Theories of propulsion and some advanced applications
- ○ Survey the methods necessary in order to determine temperatures on other planets, stars, etc.
- ○ Compare and contrast the physics of reproducing sounds and images on magnetic tape, records, and laser discs.
- ★ The "science" of physics in the medieval world
- ▲ Frontiers of laser research
- Why a nuclear war will destroy the world
- Radioactivity and time
- Applications of Ohm's law
- ➡ Newtonian mechanics and quantum theory
- Detail the five most significant discoveries in physics, from 1970 to date.

- Volta's work on electric cells
- The discovery and earliest applications of the laser beam
- The origin and composition of quarks
- ▲ Efficient methods of converting sunlight to electricity
- ★ The first gyroscopes
- Modern pendulums
- Do magnetic monopoles exist?
- ★ The search for perpetual motion. What have been some of the more impressive attempts?
- The sun's energy
- New techniques of energy conversion
- ➡ The history of quantum mechanics
- ○ The discovery of negative feedback has long-range significance. Detail some of the changes it may effect.
- Generating electricity from atomic power: basic problems
- The dynamics of waves
- Compare fusion and fission energy.
- The structure of the atom as seen by Niels Bohr
- How the physicist's view of na-

342

ture has evolved
§ Advances in <u>optics</u>
- Does antimatter exist?
- The principles of the quantum theory
- How relativity has been proved or disproved
○ Applications of the thermo-electric effect
- Physics during the Middle Ages
- Physics during the Renaissance
- Ancient and modern theories of matter

○ Theories of curved space
- Einstein and the theory of rela-tivity — right or wrong?
- Solar radiation
- The world inside the atom
○ The controversy surrounding cold fusion
○ Using computers and computer-generated pictures, scientists have discovered hidden patterns within disorder. Discuss the ramifications of the Chaos Theory.

Key to Symbols

•	average difficulty	◆	narrow down topic
§	substitutes possible	▲	large public or college
★	ample information in most libraries		library required
		✓	local option topic
○	specialized knowledge required	✗	examples and supporting evidence needed

Physiology and Anatomy

See also: Biology

- Aging: Delineate and discuss the differences between environmental and hereditary causes.
- ★ What are the general structure and functions of the human cerebral cortex?
- × Compare an open and closed circulatory system. Include detailed examples of each.
- What is the role of the kidneys in maintaining homeostasis?
- × How have lifetime residents of higher mountainous altitudes acclimatized themselves to the lack of oxygen? How has it changed their body chemistry?
- ▲ Are there limits to human physical performances?
- The body's natural opiates. Consult recent sources for data on this subject.
- ★ How we fall asleep: psychological and physiological factors
- The consequences of left handedness
- Long-distance running and the heart
- Compare and contrast the embryonic development of the cat, chicken, and lizard.

- Many very small animals do not have a specialized circulatory system. Why do most higher animals need them?
- ★ Long-term effects on humans of the bombing of Hiroshima
- Compare and contrast the vertebrae of snakes, orangutans, lizards, and humans.
- Primate sense organs
- Compare the fetal development of the respiratory systems of dogs, fish, and humans.
- ○ Cyclic AMP: the second messenger
- How injury can affect the nervous system
- ▲ Muscular atrophy: causes and treatments
- ➡ Human sensory adaptions
- ★ Compare the muscular structure of the primates with that of Homo sapiens.
- ★ Endorphins: the body's own painkilling system
- ★ Effects of cold on humans
- Physical effects of zero gravity
- How the body's immunological system operates
- § The digestion system in <u>cows</u>.

▲ How our senses monitor food preferences. Include recent scientific research.

★ Long-term effects of high decibel noise

● What happens to the body during sleep

● The effects of radiation on animals

● Evolution of the human brain

● Steroids have often been administered to athletes. What have been the results? Consider both short- and long-term effects.

● Physiological factors in menopause

★ High-level alcohol intake and its effects on the body (both short- and long-term)

○ The role of hormones in human development

● What science knows about the pineal gland function

● The physiological effects of sugar

★ Feline vision

● The body's reaction to anxiety and stress

● Man's inner clock

● Fetal brain development

▲ Recent brain function research results

▲ Bodily reactions to the drug PCB

● Compare and contrast the digestive systems of insects, amphibians, and mammals.

○ Discuss the major variances in vertebrate brain structure.

● Physical aspects of hibernation

§ Physiology of the kidney and common misfunctions

● What are the principal anatomical evidences of man's relationship to the primates?

● Human adaptions to erect posture

● Examine the commonalities of primate and human brain morphology, dentition, hand and locomotive structures. Account for the differences.

Key to Symbols

● average difficulty
§ substitutes possible
★ ample information in most libraries
○ specialized knowledge required

↞ narrow down topic
▲ large public or college library required
↙ local option topic
× examples and supporting evidence needed

Politics

See also: Foreign Policy; Government

➥ Discuss the principles of Machiavelli in relation to the philosophy, practices, and accomplishments of any recent American president.

➥ Television images of recent presidential candidates. Compare and contrast the myths and the realities.

★ The goals and achievements of the SDS (Students for a Democratic Society) in the 1960's

× Political pacificism in the twentieth-century

● What it takes to run for political office

● Fascism in Italy: 1930–1945

§ Political parties in France

➥ Factors influencing votes in national elections

● Why communism has failed in the United States

➥ The strengths and weaknesses of the Democratic (Republican) party in Congress, a 20 year survey

● The black vote in American national politics from the Civil War to today

★ The origin and rise of the Nazi Party

➥ Women governors. How many have there been and how were they elected? Select several and compare their backgrounds and achievements.

● The strategy and tactics of political terrorism

● Populism in the United States: an historical overview

§ The early political history of California

● The political satire of Thomas Nast, cartoonist

▲ The effects of paid political advertising on voter beliefs and choices

§ The politics of El Salvador

➥ Revolutions in the modern world. What have been the major precipitating elements? What has been their size, distribution, and social, political, or economic consequences? Select several for comparison.

§ Why did Nixon win in 1968?

× The language of political "double-speak"

● Trace the popularity of several recent presidents as reflected by

346

national opinion polls. What factors influence a rise or fall in credibility and confidence? Are these factors consistent?

★ Abortion as a political issue

● Compare the career of Cicero with a politician of your choice.

§ What were the issues dividing the Democratic party in 1992?

● "Local government is more democratic because it is closer to the people" is an often quoted phrase with which many political scientists disagree. Analyze this thesis.

✗ Sources of political power in the United States. Use contemporary political figures as examples.

✗ The political cartoon both as a reflection of public opinion and as an influence for change in public opinion

§ Why President Woodrow Wilson was a radical, a conservative, a middle-of-the-roader, or a liberal. Support your thesis with adequate evidence.

§ What were the paramount issues in the presidential campaign of _____?

● What effect did the slavery issue have on national politics between 1848 and 1860?

○ To what extent are people's political opinions determined by television news, television shows, the content of public school text-

books, family influences, or other factors?

● The American political system as viewed by Alexis de Tocqueville in *Democracy in America* (1835)

○ Why the United States needs a major third political party

● The politics of world hunger

★ Corruption in the administration of Warren Harding

● Declining voter participation in national elections: causes and effects

★ The goals and political influence of the John Birch Society

○ To what extent do newspaper advertisers adjust their ads to current political opinion?

● The American pork barrel system and Congress

● Compare and contrast the platforms of the major parties in the past presidential election.

★ The American Nazi movement, from 1950 to date

➡ Significant national voting trends and what they signify

▲ Politics and the Bureau of Indian Affairs

➡ The marketing of presidential candidates

● The weaknesses of the two-party system in America

● Origins and highlights of the American Labor Party

● Compare turn-of-the-century politics in America's urban centers (New York, Chicago, Detroit, etc.).

§ <u>Ronald Reagan's</u> early political career

➤ Political rebellion throughout history

○ Examine the dynamics of minority voting behavior

● Voter registration in the South: a historical survey and a current analysis

✔ Analyze your state's presidential voting patterns, 1900 to present, explaining trends, changes, and other significant patterns

● Is the presidency too big a job?

● Boss (William Marcy) Tweed and his "Tweed Ring"

● Political assassination in the early twentieth century

▲ Richard Nixon's California campaign

○ How to use the media in an election campaign

§ The <u>Carter</u> presidency evaluated

● What factors contributed to the political success of Eva Perón in Argentina?

✔ Analyze the performance of your state's two senators during their last full terms in office. Include campaign promises, attendance, voting records, etc.

● Evaluate the current president's policies and actions in light of campaign platforms and campaign speeches.

★ Third world nations as a United Nations voting bloc

● The role the Socialist Party has played in the United States' political system

● Nationalism and how it grew in Africa

● Compare and contrast the "old" and "new" left in American politics.

○ The new role played by campaign management firms in the election process

● How politics would change if the public were levied for campaign expenses

✕ The relationship between the American political system and the socioeconomic elite

● What should be the policy of political candidates regarding advertising?

○ Analyze the "political" language of television news broadcasts. What terms are used to influence the public's reactions to issues?

★ The use of public opinion polls in elections

➤ Volunteers and political campaigns

● The "image makers" in recent presidential elections

● Proposed reforms in political funding

● Discuss the "religious right," with respect to its rapid rise to political prominence and power.

● What would be the political implications of the discovery of intelligent extraterrestrial life?

§ What special interest groups will benefit most from _____

(Use a proposed project such as a dam, canal, pipeline, etc.).

• What is the American fascination with opinion polls? Are the polls worthwhile? Should policy decisions be based on their results?

▲ Are "border studies" a useful new form of political analysis or merely another publishing fad?

• What elements of Karl Marx's theory are part of American democratic theory?

• The Bull Moose Progressive Party. What were its objectives? Were they realized? How did they affect other political parties?

• Watergate: Was justice done?

• Could Abraham Lincoln be elected today?

• How and why the National Rifle Association became powerful

➥ African-American municipal politics in urban America

➥ The profit factor of war

• The function of political parties in nineteenth-century America

○ The antiurban bias of American politics

• Abuses of the spoils systems and the effect on governmental structure and operation

• The role of political consultants in contemporary national campaigns

§ Compare the speeches of Presidents <u>Richard Nixon</u> and <u>John F. Kennedy</u>.

✕ The personal costs of the presidency: pressures and responsibilities

✕ Politicians' wives: their role and its toll

• Political debates: A fair test for candidates?

• The poll tax

✕ Philosophical and historical precedents for civil disobedience in America

• The Whig Party

• Should literacy be a voting requirement?

○ The political implications of the Arab stake in the American economic system

• Presidential abuses of power, 1940–1990

✕ Political language. Select examples from the past or those commonly used today.

✔ Examine and discuss the major pressure and lobbying groups in your state legislature.

• How presidential candidates are selected

• Third-party politics and how they affect national elections

• Functions of the primary election process

➥ The effectiveness of grass roots politics in America today

§ An analysis of the presidential campaign of _____: why he lost

▲ Uses of direct mail in political campaigns

• What is happening to the constitutionally established "wall of sepa-

ration between church and state"?
Consider recent court decisions
concerning prayer and use of
school facilities.

★ Why campaign spending should
be restricted

★ The timely political humor of
Will Rogers

× How religion affects contemporary presidential elections

● The aims and accomplishments
of Common Cause

● Gerrymandering in the United
States

➥ Compare how different societies
solve persistent political issues.
How are honest leaders selected, corruption avoided,
equal justice given for all, etc.?
Select several contemporary
governments or compare an ancient to a modern one.

§ Evaluate the lasting contributions
of the Truman presidency.

● The political structure of Poland, from 1970 to the present

● Financing political campaigns today: how this affects the
selection and political behavior
of the candidate

○ How the implications of the
Watergate tapes changed Americans' perception of the presidency

● Dreyfus Affair (1894) and its political overtones

● The establishment of the Republican (or Democratic) Party

★ The virtues of the two-party system

● Is political apathy the result of
dissatisfaction with government,
or the result of being completely satisfied with the politics
of both major parties? Or are
there other pervasive influences?

○ The hows and whys of political
platforms

× Women in politics, 1960 to present.

▲ Can political behavior be reduced to mathematical represen-
tation/notation? Substantiate
your position with valid examples.

● Should reapportionment be
taken away from state legislators and given to a nonpolitical
commission? How would this
change political tactics and
structure?

➥ Are newspapers biased more in
favor of Republicans or Demo-
crats?

× The uses and abuses of the patronage system: past and present examples

○ Why have empirical political researchers failed to derive a
general theory to explain human
political behavior?

● Gay politics

➥ The political and spiritual power
of the popes. Select an era.

§ Critical issues affecting the campaign of Jesse Jackson

● The soaring costs of running for
office raise questions about the
increasing influence of political
action committees (PACS).
Examine this issue.

Pollution

See also: Ecology; Environment; Resources

- How plants are indicators of pollution
- Current levels of ground water contamination in the United States
- ★ Describe temperature inversions and their relationship to pollution.
- American workers are being exposed to an increasing number of cancer-causing materials. Discuss the primary carcinogens and industries involved in their use.
- ★ The Love Canal time bomb
- Asbestos contamination and its effects on humans
- The Environmental Protection Agency and Clean Air Standards. Evaluate those that are currently being enforced. Should they be broadened and strengthened?
- How the safe disposal of toxic chemical waste is currently controlled by industry and government
- What have been the major legislative attempts to control water pollution? Evaluate their success or failure.
- ★ Evaluate the role of oxygen in water pollution
- ✕ How water pollution has adversely affected wildlife populations
- ○ What are the environmental impacts from the circulation of large volumes of cooled water through natural water systems?
- What are waterborne infectious agents? How are they controlled?
- ✔ Noise control problems and regulations in your state
- Hazardous waste disposal: Whose responsibility?
- ✔ What are the pollution problems in your local community? How are they being controlled or regulated?
- ★ Trace the dysfunctions in the ozone hole over the Antarctic.
- ★ Was the cleanup from the Exxon *Valdez* oil spill adequate?
- What our use of chemicals is doing to the atmosphere and how the weather will change
- § How dioxin contamination can be prevented

§ <u>Hudson River</u> pollution: sources and controls

➡ Problems in the prevention of air pollution. Select an industry.

✔ Discuss air pollution and current regulations now in effect in your state.

○ How is water pollution measured and monitored?

● Is the Environmental Protection Agency tough enough?

★ Smog and what it is doing to American cities

➡ Current measures to control ocean pollution. Include an analysis of their effectiveness.

★ The basis of opposition to stricter water and air pollution control

● London smog: then and now

§ Pollution of the <u>North Sea</u>

● Noise pollution by aircraft in urban areas

§ Oil well pollution in the <u>Santa Barbara</u> area

● Compare and contrast pollution control measures for phosphorus and carbon cycles.

★ Nuclear waste and pollution. What is the current scope and nature of this problem?

● The possibilities of underground storage of radioactive wastes

▲ The use of floating suction pumps for oil slick dispersal

● Sewer sludge compost: how it is processed and used

○ The effects of sulfur dioxide on vegetation

● Advances in sewage treatment and recycling

● Compare and contrast the detrimental effects of DDT and PCB on both animals and humans.

✔ Investigate levels of groundwater purity and safeguards in your local area.

★ Noise and human well-being: test results

● Mercury poisoning

★ The aftermath of the Chernobyl nuclear power plant accident (1986)

● Carbon dioxide and the "greenhouse" effect

● Technical solutions to pollution from auto emissions

● Biological effects of urban air pollution

● Detergent pollutants

● The nature of atmospheric pollution

● How the British cleaned up the Thames River

➡ Water pollution problems from mineral development (for example, uranium, copper, iron ore).

● Lake Erie contamination: Then, now—and tomorrow?

★ Will the United States run out of clean water? Survey a variety of informed opinions and present a composite of their views.

● Oil pollution of rivers and harbors by ocean vessels

▲ Contingency plans for major oil spills

★ The effects of oil spills on ocean birds and fishes

● Countermeasures for acid rain pollution. What is the state of development of technology to combat this problem?

§ How clean are the Great Lakes?

➥ Antipollution technology: Is it adequate?

● How air pollution affects farm crops

○ Quality control measures for safe drinking water

● Hazardous cargos: a growing peril

★ Levels of acid rain pollution in the United States

● Garbage disposal in metropolitan areas

✕ Reversing water pollution. Select some successful examples and detail the measures used to achieve the cleanup.

✔ Describe in detail an example of industrial pollution in your locality. Trace both the history of the problem and any remedial measures used.

● How man's activities have contributed to air pollution in the atmosphere

▲ Scientists are now finding pollutants that are feminizing males (both animal and human) and thus impairing reproduction. Consider the implications of this trend.

✔ What factors have a bearing on air pollution in your locality? Discuss sources, varieties, and levels of pollution.

● Can the Mediterranean be cleaned? Why or why not?

▲ The potential for large-scale tertiary sewage treatment

● Current levels of DDT in the environment

§ Governmental response to _____ pollution, from 1970 to date

● The response of business and industry to pollution control measures. Have attitudes altered in the last ten years? In what ways? Why?

➥ Levels of mercury contamination

✕ How pollution control laws should be refined and amended

● What are the different elements involved in indoor pollution?

★ Are toxic waste sites adequately controlled and monitored?

● How much pollution regulation is acceptable?

● Evidence is mounting, say authorities, that false signals from synthetic chemicals are harming reproduction, immunity, and behavior in wildlife. Are humans next?

Population

See also: Geography; Resources

× Discuss the relationship between the distribution of population and climatic patterns.

• How have the population patterns of African Americans changed since 1900? What social changes have these shifts influenced?

• What have been the major criticisms of the Malthusian theory?

• Can the world's population problems be solved by greater agricultural productivity?

✔ Examine the patterns of population distribution in your local area. What elements in the biophysical environment have affected that distribution?

○ What will be the political impact on the United States of Mexico's population doubling during the next twenty-four years?

➡ What we learned from the 1990 census

★ The long-term effects of zero population growth

• Rural migration trends in the United States

★ Birth control and planned population growth in China. Discuss the period since 1950 and the changes during that era.

• Can the United States feed the world? Should it?

▲ The relationship between overcrowding and violence. Many studies have been conducted in this field; analyze and compare the findings of several.

• World population projections for the years 2000, 2050, and 2100. Include demographics.

× Forced sterilization as a means of population control: instances and ethics

• Why birth control programs have often failed in the third world countries

★ The economics of the large family group in impoverished nations (for example, India)

➡ Worldwide use of the birth control pill. Consider various aspects, including marketing, education, results, scope, and possible side effects.

• Beliefs and practices contributing to birth rate increases in underdeveloped countries

- The male contraceptive pill
○ Discuss exponential growth and its relationship to resource usage, population, and pollution.
- Examine the dynamics of institutional family planning programs in underdeveloped nations.
- The Catholic Church and world population
- What life on earth would be like with one-half the current world population
✔ Population demographics in your state: past, present, and future
- Compare and contrast world population changes and shifts from 1900 to present.
▲ The demographics of American populations for the years 1670 to 1760
★ Causes of infant mortality in third world countries
➥ Many countries have experienced major population shifts from rural to urban centers. What have been the socioeconomic implications of this pattern? Select a country—for example, Greece, Mexico, Spain, etc.
○ Examine the Marxist viewpoint of population in relation to present demographic patterns.
▲ The European attitude toward population growth and change
- What was the earth's population prior to the development of agriculture? Did overcrowding

exist? Was there population deprivation?
- Since the United States government allows a tax exemption for each dependent, it is essentially subsidizing population growth. Is this in the country's best interest? Should it be eliminated? Should refunds be awarded to those not having children?
- The "life boat" ethic and other recent proposals for world population control
- How do birth rates, death rates, and net migrations interact to affect population growth?
x What has happened to the development process in emerging nations with rapidly expanding populations?
- The interrelationship of population density and deviant behaviors
○ How migrations have affected human population genetics
- India's efforts at birth control: Examine the methods used, education, and the current situation. What are future projections?
- Should a limit be placed on the number of people who can live within a stated area? In what instances has this practice been tried in the past?
✔ Analyze your local community in terms of population densities. What dysfunctions and problems

have resulted from crowding? How has it affected the character of the neighborhood(s)?

★ Compare the types of information requested in the census surveys in 1830, 1880, 1920, and 1990.

• What are the major reasons for the increase in population mobility in the United States?

• What have been the major factors in the population redistribution in the United States since 1900?

× How have population pressures changed America's living patterns?

➤ Western Europe's population shifts. Select a five-hundred-year time span and explain in detail both the causes and the consequences of these changes in one area.

• Evaluate the currently feasible birth control measures in terms of safety, expense, convenience, and effectiveness. Include an analysis of their various compatibilities with cultural and religious systems.

★ What are the predominant factors which have traditionally limited population growth?

○ Compare the Malthusian, neo-Malthusian, and technocratic theories of population growth.

○ Food production, disease, and population growth. Discuss these concepts in terms of their contemporary relevances, as well as in terms of their historical context.

• Rapid population growth is a consequence as well as a cause of poverty. Discuss the ramifications of this statement.

• Population control measures have been significantly successful in Hong Kong, China, Singapore, and Taiwan. What were the program details which may account for this reduction in birth rates?

★ The governments of India and China initiated large population control programs. Compare the results of each.

• What are the attitudes toward population control in Latin America and sub-Saharan Africa? Do these countries consider large increasing populations a burden?

• The Catholic Church opposes the use of contraceptives. What have studies shown to be the actual birth control practices of Catholic men and women?

➤ The territorial imperative, overcrowding, and human populations

× Current population policies in a selection of developing countries

× Effects of immigration on population

Pro and Con

- Euthanasia on demand
- Animal experimentation
- Universal abortions
- Capital punishment
- Affirmative action
- Foreign aid
- Fetal tissue transplant and research
- Surrogate motherhood for commercial purposes
- Transfer of body parts for money
- Limits of confidentiality
- Health-care limits for the aged
- Amniocentesis for every fetus
- Government-funded medicine
- Sex education in school
- Ethics in advertising
- Televised executions
- Media violence
- Women's liberation
- Equal Rights Amendment
- Prayer in schools
- United States military intervention in other nations' wars
- Flat-rate income tax

- Cigarette advertising
- Free drugs for addicts
- Free needles for addicts
- Animal rights
- National registration and identity cards
- Foreign sales of United States arms
- Fluoridation of drinking water
- Term limits for elected officials
- Insanity defense
- Immigration law reform
- Gun control
- Gay rights
- Nuclear waste sites
- Global warming
- Limits on pornography
- Genetic testing
- Privatization of the public sector
- Drug testing
- Plea bargaining
- Caller IDs
- Homosexual parents
- Food labeling
- Legalized gambling

Key to Symbols

- • average difficulty
- § substitutes possible
- ★ ample information in most libraries
- ○ specialized knowledge required
- ▾ narrow down topic
- ▲ large public or college library required
- ✓ local option topic
- x examples and supporting evidence needed

357

Psychology

See also: Mental Health

- Select a major personality theory. Describe the basic assumptions of the theory, its origins, strengths, and weaknesses.
○ How personality is assessed. Discuss several measurement modes.
- Compare Freud's psychoanalytic theory to various neoFreudian psychoanalytic theories.
▲ What do modern psychologists feel are the major weaknesses of Freud's psychoanalytic theory?
○ Explore the differences in areas of emphasis between more traditional forms of therapy such as psychoanalysis, and the recently evolved approaches such as Gestalt therapy and rational-emotive therapy.
● Discuss the psychological and physical benefits of laughter.
- The role of the mind in healing the body: some contemporary approaches
★ What is REM (Rapid Eye Movement) sleep? Discuss its discov-

ery and implications in dream research.
● The nightly dream cycle
● Some of the possible meanings of common types of dreams, such as flying, being chased, falling, finding money, etc.
● Report in detail one of your recent dreams and its possible meaning as related to the most important dream theories.
● Subliminal messages and how they can be used to influence thought and behavior
● The benefits of psychoanalysis
★ Genius: criteria, characteristics, and types
○ The outer reaches of human instinct
● Views of Freud by contemporary psychologists
▲ Current experiments in thought control
✕ Mass hysteria: a definition and some famous examples
● Freud's lasting influence on sociology, anthropology, and literature
§ Is Christianity (or another major

religion) based on guilt?

↦ How valid are psychological tests?

● Compare and contrast the behavioral theories of Carl Rogers and B.F. Skinner.

● How constant and severe overcrowding affects people

✕ The uses of propaganda during war

★ Significant findings from recent research with identical twins who were reared apart

● Does birth order affect personality?

↦ Nonverbal communication

● The psychology of the Jonestown mass suicides

○ Is the insanity plea a reasonable defense from a psychological point of view? What are its possible flaws?

● Trace the development of humanistic psychology, from 1950 to the present

● Abraham Maslov used the term self-actualization. What does it mean and how has this concept affected psychology?

○ Freud proposed the libido as the energy force within the personality. What was this theory?

● How trauma affects children's development

✕ Discuss the defense mechanism of repression. Use relevant examples to illustrate this process.

● The so-called "fourth force" in psychology involves an area known as transpersonal psychol-

ogy. What is this and how has it developed out of humanistic psychology?

● Race and intelligence: the scientific view

● Discuss the relationship of the id, ego, and superego as proposed by Freud.

↦ Compare and contrast the learning theories of B.F. Skinner and Jean Piaget.

▲ Possible causes of childhood autism

★ The nature of sleep

▲ Hypnosis in the ancient and medieval worlds

● B.F. Skinner's theories of behavioral conditioning: an overview

§ Elvis Presley as a modern surrogate deity. Focus on the psychological patterns of hero worship, etc.

● How is intelligence measured? Compare a variety of standard testing procedures.

§ Psychology of beer advertising

○ Overachievers and intelligence

§ Clinical uses of hypnotism in dentistry

↦ Discuss the dual roles of heredity and environment in intelligence

● Children react to violence: the cartoons versus real life

✕ Current applications of biofeedback

● A psychological profile of the compulsive gambler

● Violence in the news: Are we

becoming immune to it? If so, what psychological processes are operant?

- Memory storage in the human brain
▲ Advances in pain therapy. What have been some of the most successful applications?
★ How fear is used as a selling mechanism
○ Can autism be cured? To what degree?
- Sleepwalking
★ Psychological factors of faith healing
★ The psychological development of twins who are reared together
- A profile of Joan of Arc
★ Extrasensory experiments of Joseph Banks Rhine: pros and cons
- The hypnotic cures of Franz Mesmer
➥ Common phobias and how to control them. Select one and discuss its origins and the techniques which have proved helpful.
○ The methods of psychodrama in psychotherapy
➥ Compare and contrast the basic theories of Sigmund Freud and Carl Jung.
✕ Environmental aspects of personality development
- How to motivate children to achieve
○ Detail recent sleep experiments

which support the theory of the cyclical or circadian nature of human metabolism.

- Historical perspectives on the psychology of the hippies
▲ Is depression inherited? Cite recent studies and scientific evidence to support your answer.
- Psychological factors in competition
- The pressures of success: how to eliminate counterproductive reactions
✕ Sleep learning theories. What have been some of the most successful applications?
- The origin of Gestalt psychology
➥ The behavioral view of human aggression
- The stages of grief according to Elizabeth Kubler-Ross
- Compare and contrast intelligence and creativity
▲ Psychological problems of paraplegics
★ The emotional effects of solitary confinement
§ A psychological profile of the mercenary soldier
★ How to motivate people
- The outer limits of transcendental meditation: a scientific consideration
✕ New methods of stress management
★ Functions of play
▲ Tenets of Reality Therapy
- The benefits of pets

- Is human aggression inherent?
- Castration: psychological and physical consequences
- The "macho man": Nature or nurture?
- ★ Several significant studies have been completed on the short-term and long-range effects of marijuana on human thought processes. What have been the major conclusions?
- ★ Compare and contrast the training, scope, and functions of psychiatrists and psychologists.
- Psychological aspects in the practices of shamans and witch doctors
- Habits: how they are formed and how they can be changed
- ➥ Thought control and television in America
- Managing interpersonal conflicts
- Time perception in children
- ★ A psychological profile of Napoleon
- ○ The unconscious as proposed by Sigmund Freud
- The Esalin Institute has been highly praised and scorned. Appraise and compare these evaluations.
- Behavior patterns of hyperactive children
- ▲ The effects of color on mental states
- The normal functions of fantasy and daydreams. Investigate the results of some recent studies in these areas.

- ▲ Neurolinguistic programming (NLP)
- ➥ Psychologists look at parapsychology: Discuss and compare some of their evaluations.
- ★ The phenomenon of speaking in tongues (glossolalia)
- Critical views of B.F. Skinner's Walden Two
- Hypnosis and learning
- ✕ Subconscious mechanisms for dealing with mental conflict
- Successful methods to stop smoking
- ○ The idiot savant
- The psychology of magic and conjuring
- Teenagers often identify with a role model, often a celebrity. Is this phenomenon a natural stage of maturation, or a particular manifestation of the twentieth century? What are the psychological factors involved?
- Compare and contrast the extrovert and the introvert
- Why we dream
- ○ Symptoms and causes of exhibitionism
- The limits of artificial intelligence
- ★ "Brainwashing" in the Korean War
- Evaluate the Ik tribe (The Mountain People by Colin Turnbull) in terms of human value norms and deviations.
- ★ Left-handedness
- ○ "Mental cruelty" in psychology

and in the law
- Typical mother-daughter conflicts in modern America
▲ Placebos and pain control: psychological aspects
§ Discuss the televised <u>auto</u> advertisements of three major manufacturers in terms of image-making and emotional appeal.
- The Rorschach test. How is it administered and evaluated?
★ Psychological factors in divorce
- Principles of Primal Therapy
- How normal thought processes work. Compare several of the most important theories.
- Characteristics of the manic-depressive personality
➥ Imprinting in animals and humans
- Psychological aspects of obesity
- Child abusers: a profile
○ Freud's theories of death
- Modern alternatives to psychoanalysis
- Carl Jung and the "collective unconsciousness"
★ Psychological factors in the

death of John Lennon
- Stress and the alcoholic
➥ Compare and contrast Rogerian and Freudian personality theories
- Self-hypnotism and the control of pain
▲ The psychology of helping. Include studies of bystander apathy.
○ How television fosters cooperative behaviors in children
○ The psychology of social class
- How children develop gender identification
- The psychology of the comic strip
- How Prozac (and similar compounds) allows us to change our personalities.
○ The psychological costs of organ transplant surgery
★ Psychological problems of the homeless
- The rise in AIDS victims has resulted in what many term a "plague mentality." Discuss the historical context of this statement and its current ramifications.

Religion

See also: Bioethics; Ethical Issues; Philosophy

- Why there have not been women priests in the Catholic Church
- Compare the attitudes of various religions toward suicide. Where do parallels exist?
- ★ Compare religious conceptions of the afterlife (Hindu, Christian, ancient Egyptian, for example).
- The moral and religious aspects of abortion according to Christian theological tenets
- ★ Mother Teresa's work with India's poor and dying
- What is the status of Christianity in Russia today?
- Zen Buddhism and the tea ceremony
- Compare the tenets of Buddhism and Christianity.
- ★ How popes are selected
- Compare and contrast the Douay and the King James Versions of the Bible.
- Deities of the Incas
- § Baptist foreign missions, past and present
- ▲ The contents of a number of ancient biblical scrolls have never been published. Why?
- The critical reception of the Reader's Digest Bible (1982)
- Compare the inclusions and exclusions of the Reader's Digest Bible with older, more accepted versions of the Bible.
- The concepts of transmigration and reincarnation in the Hindu religion
- ○ What are the similarities and differences in the tenets and organizational structures of Roman Catholicism and Eastern Orthodoxy?
- ★ Jewish basis and justification for the settlement of the West Bank
- The basic concept of Taoism
- Discuss the bases of this statement: "The last Christian died on the cross" (Nietzsche).
- Describe the differences between Islam's sects, the Shiites and the Sunni.
- ▲ Twentieth-century versions of the Bible: an overview
- The Fundamentalist movement in Islam
- ○ Describe the different types of

363

church governmental organization which are functional today.

- Jewish views toward abortion,
  divorce, and infidelity
- Compare and contrast doctrines
  and attitudes of the major religions toward divorce.
- The symbolism of Hopi Indian
  kachina dolls
- Attitudes towards fertility among
  the world's large religions
- Should religion and the political
  system mix? What are the
  moral and ethical considerations?
- How do the Jesuits and the Do-
  minicans differ? In what ways
  are they similar?
★ Symbols of the Christian religion
- Compare Christian and Islamic
  perceptions of ethics and morality.
- Why celibacy for the Catholic
  clergy? The origins of this prac-
  tice and the possibilities for
  future changes.
▲ Economic plight of Catholic religious orders
▲ Compare and contrast Roman
  Catholicism as practiced in the
  United States, Latin America,
  and Italy.
§ Burial rites of the Hindu religion
- Conscientious objectors, loyalty,
  and religious faith
- The social function of voodoo
- Christianity in Islamic countries.
  Discuss this subject historically
  or on a contemporary basis.
§ Choose a cult: Moon, Hari

Krishna, or other. Describe and
explain.

- Changing attitudes towards the
  Ten Commandments
- The traditional Catholic stance
  on birth control and common
  Catholic practice
- Christian ethics in theory and in
  practice
★ Catholic orders in the United
  States
§ Compare and contrast beliefs
  and practices of the Baptists
  and the Presbyterians.
§ The Lutheran Church in the
  United States today
- Death as viewed by Christianity,
  Buddhism, Islam, and Hinduism
- Mayan religion
- Theories of reincarnation
▲ Why missionaries are no longer
  welcome in Africa
§ Varieties of Baptist beliefs
- The role of Mecca in the Muslim
  world
★ Hinduism and nonviolence
- The Black Muslim religion
  today. Contrast it to its goals
  and practice in its earlier his-
  tory.
- The unique religion of Bali,
  Indonesia
▲ Proofs of Jesus as a historical
  reality
- "Original sin" and the Christian
  religion
- The Brahman caste system
★ Profile of a Zen monk
- How major religions view homo-

sexuality

★ In what ways is atheism similar to a religion?

➤ Recent advances in biblical archeology

○ Compare the King James and the Revised Standard Versions of the Bible.

§ The Catholic Church in <u>Mexico</u> (or another South American country)

● The effects on neighborhood churches of the televised evangelical movement

● The cult phenomenon: recruitment, retention, and lifestyle. Account for its successes.

★ Describe the religious and social significance of the bar mitzvah

➤ Precepts of contemporary Jewish religion

● Fire as a symbol in the world's religions

✔ Investigate the organized religions represented in your local community (numbers, origins, types, members).

● Predestination in religious thought

● Compare the concept of sin in the Christian and Islamic religions.

▲ Who should interpret the Bible? Examine a range of theological views.

● Pantheism

● Precepts, goals, and practices of the Salvation Army

● The theological aspects of infallibility

● Careers in religion

● Judaic dietary laws

▲ Interpretations of the Islamic jihad (holy war)

★ Compare atheism and agnosticism

● Parallels between the Old Testament and the Koran

● The Jonestown deaths: why they happened

● The modern Pentecostal movement in America

○ Are we living in a postChristian world? Cite informed opinion and evidence to support or refute this question.

✕ The uses of ritual in religious worship

● Religious opposition to genetic engineering. What beliefs and practices contribute to this controversy?

● The role of the clergy in the abortion issue

● How have the recent scandals (Swaggert, Bakker, etc.) in television evangelism affected the ministry as a whole?

● Rastafarian religion — a new force in the Caribbean?

● Hindu gurus

● The economics of televised religion: Big business or big charity?

● Religious issues in contemporary public education

● Hopi views of the natural world

○ Why is American society becoming increasingly secular?

- What are the similarities between Hebrew, Egyptian, and Christian religious beliefs?
- What are the personal functions of religion? What are its functions to society? Support your answers with informed opinions.
- ▲ How modern religious systems have changed with the growth of technological complexity
- ○ The United States has experienced an increasing interest in the occult. To what factors do social scientists attribute this

growth?

- ★ The plot to assassinate Pope John Paul II (1981) has been variously explained. Examine the hypotheses. Compare and contrast their validity.
- ✕ How science affects religion
- Historically, has organized religion harmed or helped society?
- Why the religious right is opposed to the gay movement
- What is China's current policy toward religion?
- ★ Politics in the pulpit: an objective review

Key to Symbols

•	average difficulty	☛	narrow down topic
§	substitutes possible	▲	large public or college
★	ample information in most		library required
	libraries	✔	local option topic
○	specialized knowledge	✕	examples and supporting
	required		evidence needed

Religion — History

See also: Anthropology; Philosophy

- Why the early Christians condemned idolatry
▲ Heretics in the medieval world. What were their beliefs, role in the religious and social world, and what was public reaction to their doctrine?
- Why the Mormons practiced polygamy. What is the modern attitude toward this practice?
○ The Christian roots of Islam
- Why Islam spread. Examine the range and rates of conversion. How has this changed over the centuries?
★ The influence of the Quakers in American history
★ The causes and consequences of Martin Luther's break from the church
- Excommunication: past and present
- The establishment and functions of Vatican City
○ Historical perspectives on the Christian church as a social unit
- The fate of the Huguenots
- Religious freedom during the Thirty Years War
▲ The reactions of Protestant churches to the Supreme Court ruling barring prayer in the schools
★ Compare Mohammed and Jesus Christ.
- The ecumenical movement
- The Maccabean revolt
- Compare the kingship of Saul and David.
- What is the historical basis for the religion/science conflict?
○ Trace the concept of the "remnant"
○ Compare the political prophecies of Isaiah, Amos, and Jeremiah.
- The reason for the spread of the teachings of Islam, 632–750, 1000–1500, and in the twentieth century
★ What was the religious composition of the American colonies? What circumstances account for the diversity?
- "An eye for an eye; a tooth for a tooth" was an advanced, humane concept for its time. Explain.
▲ Compare the Essene teachings with the Gospel accounts of Jesus' life.

- Compare Christianity and Mithraism. Why did one succeed and the other one fail?
- Donation of Pepin and the rise of the Papal States
- Methods of modern Biblical research
- Historical perspectives on the effects of the Crusades on European economic and social life
- ○ The impact on church theology of Saint Augustine
- The Shakers, yesterday and today
- The Catholic Church and the Spanish Inquisition
- Fiction — and the facts — about the druids
- The papacy at Avignon
- The influence of the Abbey of Cluny on medieval life
- ○ Augustine and the beginnings of Christianity in Britain
- Christian art and worship in the catacombs of Rome
- ★ Egyptian attitudes toward death
- The Church of Rome versus the Albigensian heresy
- Causes and effects of the First Council of Nicaea (325 A.D.)
- Compare the earliest Christian theology with that which was practiced in Europe in 800 A.D.
- ✕ The "value" of the religious war. Use historical and contemporary examples.
- The origin and historical significance of baptism
- Why did the Jews reject Jesus

as the Messiah?
- § The snake in myth and religion
- ➡ The implications to Christian theology of the Gnostic Gospels
- Biblical agriculture
- The role of music, art, and literature in early Christianity
- Compare and contrast the story of creation in Genesis, Chapter One to that of Genesis, Chapter Two.
- ○ Trace a concept (fidelity, justice, peace, retribution) through Old Testament prophets into the New Testament.
- ➡ Evolution and change in American churches (1940–1980). Compare several denominations or select one and present a detailed analysis.
- ★ Compare and contrast the goals and achievements of Martin Luther and John Calvin.
- ★ The theological significance of the Dead Sea Scrolls. What have they added to Christian knowledge?
- Origins of Christian religious holidays
- Which of Martin Luther's Ninety-five Theses are relevant to the contemporary Christian church?
- Consequences of the Albigensian Crusade
- The religious and magic background of Egyptian mummification practices
- ▲ The relationship of the early

Christian Church to late Judaism

- The consequences of the Second Vatican Council (1962)
- The anti-Semitism of Martin Luther
- ▲ The sybaritic life-styles of Renaissance popes
- The persistent legend of Pope Joan
- Who were the victims of the Spanish Inquisition? How did it affect the course of religion? Of science?
- ★ Daily life in a medieval monastery
- ○ Bernadette and the doctrine of the Immaculate Conception

- Sectarian division after Mohammed
- ✕ "Mystery cults" of the ancient world
- The status of religion in the Roman Empire at the beginning of the Christian era
- Life in an early Benedictine monastery
- ○ Doctrinal heresies in early Christianity
- Relationship between the early Church and the monastic movement
- How Constantine's conversion to Christianity changed the course of history

---

Key to Symbols

•	average difficulty	◆	narrow down topic
§	substitutes possible	▲	large public or college library required
★	ample information in most libraries	✔	local option topic
○	specialized knowledge required	✕	examples and supporting evidence needed

Resources

See also: Ecology; Environment; Pollution; Population

★ The Florida Everglades are experiencing problems. What are the causes?

✕ Are we running out of land in the United States?

☛ Evaluate the success or failure of the Environmental Protection Agency in several recent rulings.

★ Present the case for or against the hunting and trapping of wild animals.

● The mature forests of the Pacific Northwest are rapidly being harvested. Should the government immediately curtail or stop this cutting?

● Why diamond prices remain fairly constant

✔ Evaluate the water resources in an area. Consider both current and potential problems, water tables, usage rates and allotment ratios.

● Rainforests are being burned and destroyed all over the world. How has this affected world climates? What are future projections?

● Could the United States be energy self-sufficient?

● Defend or refute: Nuclear power is a failure in the United States.

○ What is the technology necessary for seabed mining? Detail the environmental impact as well.

§ Deforestation in ———

★ Examine current United States dependence on foreign oil and consider the prospects for the future.

● Children are a national resource. Are we educating them adequately?

★ The return of the coyote

● Many scientists think famine will always occur in poor countries in the future. Examine the reasons for these negative predictions.

○ Should the United Nations establish a world seed bank to conserve and preserve plant species?

★ How wetlands affect the wild bird population

● Why are dolphins disappearing?

● Catfish farms have proved both practical and economical in the Southern United States. Examine the economics and the ecology of this trend.

✕ How newer methods of conservation have alleviated topsoil erosion in the United States

§ Acid rain and the forests of Western Europe. Consider the sources, effects and remedies.

★ Current perspectives on whale populations. Include a discussion of recent bans on whale hunting.

§ Detail the food chain of the <u>wolf</u>.

● How Hawaiian rainforests are threatened by feral animals

● Evaluate the arguments for and against widespread utilization of solar energy.

● Why the United States has not tapped into its shale oil resources

★ How recycling saves resources

○ Will salt water conservation technologies be feasible on a broad scale?

➤ Why commercial fishing in the United States is less productive and more costly than in other countries. Select a specific area.

● It has been suggested the United States needs more trees. Why?

● The Nature Conservancy is an American success story. Detail this organization's methods, funding and accomplishments.

★ Fossil fuels are being rapidly depleted. What other sources of energy will replace them?

● United States' agricultural surpluses are often dumped. Why are these products not given to those in need?

Key to Symbols

●	average difficulty	➤	narrow down topic
§	substitutes possible	▲	large public or college library required
★	ample information in most libraries	↙	local option topic
○	specialized knowledge required	✕	examples and supporting evidence needed

Science

See also: individual sciences listed as subject headings

× What are the limitations of the scientific method?

○ Compare and contrast the light microscope, transmission electron microscope, and the scanning electron microscope.

● Does the Scopes trial represent the basic schism between science and religion? Detail the issues which are representative.

§ What was Benjamin Franklin's contribution to scientific knowledge?

● Does the United States have a science policy? If not, why? If so, what is it?

★ The Smithsonian Institution Center for Short-Lived Phenomena. What are its objectives? What have been some of the most unusual and important findings?

● How does the scientific method attempt to minimize personal bias? Error? Give some examples of possible dysfunctions.

★ Scientific theories, or why there are no absolutes in science

☛ The Protestant Reformation and the rise of science: cause and effect

○ Why guidelines for recombinant DNA experiments are necessary

● The perpetual search for perpetual motion

○ What are the theories for a flat-space or curved-space universe?

● The contributions of radio astronomy to cosmology

● The scientific truth about poltergeists

● The outer limits of artificial intelligence

★ The atom: Gateway to the stars or trapdoor to hell?

● Can/should the scientific method be applied to the social sciences?

● The effects on Western civilization of Newton's discovery of gravity

▲ The rise and fall of the Ionian school of science

○ What methods have been used in calculating the age of the universe? Why do the conclusions differ?

● How the ancients viewed the cosmos

× Recurrent patterns and forms in

nature (spiral, bilateral, symmetry, etc.)

● The effects of the Renaissance on science

▲ How science has discredited the popular theories of Immanuel Velikovsky

★ The International Geophysical Year: discoveries and contributions

● Describe the "scientific method" using examples of its use and misuse.

○ New areas of psychogenic research

● The influence of the discovery of radium on both science and industry

▲ How honest can scientists be when they have a personal financial interest through corporate connections in the outcome of their research? Is this a built-in conflict of interest? Do scientists agree on a middle ground?

○ Discuss, compare, and evaluate current theories about the origins of the solar system.

● Historical perceptions of spontaneous generation

● How does nature utilize solar energy?

▲ Discuss the criteria for the selection of high school science textbooks.

✕ Detail the process of radio-carbon dating. What has science learned from its applications? Select several differing subject areas.

● What are the arguments for and against sociobiology (Darwin's theories applied to behavior)?

● Refute or defend: Great scientific discoveries are usually made by the young.

○ How is the universe held together? Discuss some of the current theories which attempt to answer this question.

● Discuss the "visitors from outer space" theories of Erich Von Daniken from the point of view of the scientific community.

✕ Are new scientific theories rejected more for political or religious reasons than for scientific ones? For example, ERA advocates' opposition to sociobiology because of its sexist connotations rather than its faulty data. Use Darwin also as another instance.

➥ What science has learned from space exploration and how it has been applied to the body of knowledge in a variety of disciplines

★ Current speculations about time travel

● The scientific methodology of Leonardo da Vinci

● Science and religion: The eternal conflict?

➥ Is science improving society? Select an area of scientific research and discovery and analyze its benefits or the negative factors.

- The origin of the "scientific method"
- ▲ The teaching of science in colonial America
- ○ Antiscientific aspects of Pierre Teilhard de Chardin's *The Phenomenon of Man*
- Scientific findings from the Landsat Satellite data
- Microbes and the electron microscope
- ★ Refute or defend: Creationism is religion, not science, and belongs in church, not in school.
- The origin of the universe: current theories
- Should scientists have policy-making roles in government?
- Scientists look at astral projection
- ★ Medieval alchemy: its goals, practitioners, and accomplishments
- The long-range scientific ramifications of recombinant DNA methodology are crucial. Review the most important ones, considering their significance and potential hazards.
- How the Spanish Inquisition and the conviction of Galileo changed the course of scientific inquiry and knowledge
- How did scientific thought of the Enlightenment era conflict with existing institutions and traditional concepts?

- ○ The proper use of laboratory animals
- ✕ The significance of conflict and debate in science. Use examples to illustrate your points.
- ★ What have been the major elements in the historic conflict between science and religion?
- ✕ Using significant examples, define the differences between a hypothesis, a theory, and a law.
- How scientists construct research designs. Use several prominent and successful studies as examples.
- Many antievolutionists believe that since science does not have answers for every question, scientific conclusions are not necessarily correct. Explain why this failure to understand the nature of science is so widespread and firmly espoused. Survey writings in this area since 1975.
- Contrast the theory of taxonomy of the eighteenth century with its modern counterpart.
- What major concepts about the nature of mankind and the cosmos had to be altered before an evolutionary concept could be developed?
- ▲ Problems in industry-supported academic research
- Astrology as a pseudoscience. Review scientific opinion.
- Science versus creationism is not

a new battle. Discuss the issues in their historical perspectives.

★ Detail the growth of man's concept of time. What methods were developed to measure it?

§ Galileo's contributions to science

▲ There have been several recent experiments in cryogenics (suspending life in low temperatures). Review the results of this testing.

● What controls are used to prevent fraud in scientific experiments on extrasensory perception?

★ What did the discovery of relativity mean to the scientific community?

○ Current origin-of-life theories

● The contributions of Democritus to Greek science

➥ Detail the ten most important scientific discoveries in history. Justify and substantiate your choices.

➥ Detail ten scientific discoveries that man could have done without. Justify and substantiate your choices.

● Can man travel faster than the speed of light?: Einstein and the laws of nature.

● What are the basic assumptions underlying science?

○ What we have learned from Halley's Comet

✗ Are science and religion compatible?

✗ The cultural effects of fundamental science

● Show how different statistical methods applied to the same data can distort or reveal reality.

★ What is pseudo science? By what criteria is it discerned? What are its major characteristics?

● The crisis in science education

● How to distinguish bias from reason

Key to Symbols

●	average difficulty	➥	narrow down topic
§	substitutes possible	▲	large public or college library required
★	ample information in most libraries	✓	local option topic
○	specialized knowledge required	✗	examples and supporting evidence needed

Sex

See also: Family Life; Marriage

× Social perceptions of incest
● The male menopause: A medical reality or a media hype?
§ Homosexuals in the <u>sports</u> world
● The legal rights of homosexuals
★ What constitutes sexual harassment?
○ Causes of homosexuality
➡ Treatment programs for the sexually maladjusted
● Dangers of the IUD (intrauterine device) as a contraceptive method
▲ Father-daughter incest. Consult case studies.
● The hetaera in ancient Greece
● Should medical insurance cover sex change operations?
▲ Sexuality and the medieval church
● Sexual patterns of the newly divorced
➡ Homosexuality from ancient to modern times. Select a time period.
× Science views human sexual differences
● Advances in contraception methods for men and women

● Sexual mores in the Islamic world
▲ Incidence and scope of homosexuality in correctional institutions
★ Changing social attitudes toward homosexuality
● The nature and extent of sex-related crime in the United States
● Puritan attitudes towards sex and how they have influenced American sexual mores
● The gay liberation movement: its origins and early years
● Particular problems of lesbian women
● Should homosexuals be allowed to adopt children?
★ Normal sex play of the young child
▲ Ancient attitudes toward incest (Babylonia, Egypt, Greece, etc.)
× Traditional prohibitions against incest in primitive societies
○ The pathology of the habitual sex offender
● Important changes in American

attitudes toward sex between 1950 and 1990
- Adultery in the American marriage: prevalence, causes, and results
- Homosexuality and the Christian religion
★ The healthy development of sexuality in children
➥ The media's influence on sex role determination
- Sexuality in the Victorian era
- Sex roles in the Islamic world
- Sexual deviance: changing definitions from ancient to modern times
- A profile of the male prostitute
- Sexual infidelity and American mores. Is there a double standard?
★ Should American laws against victimless sex acts be abolished?
○ The evolution of human sexuality
✕ What have been the benefits and disadvantages of traditional female and male roles in American society?
- Was there a sexual revolution in the "roaring twenties"? Justify your judgment with authoritative historical evidence.
➥ Major sexual dysfunctions and their causes
- Review several sex manuals published over a forty-year period. What changes have occurred in the content, tone, and attitudes expressed?
○ Compare the biological and so-

cial origins of sexual behavior.
- Successful remedies for male impotence. Sex therapists have developed a variety of treatment formats. Describe those most often employed.
- Controversy over sex education in the public schools. Compare the issues and viewpoints involved.
★ What to tell young children about sex and how to answer their questions
- Compare the attitudes toward sex in several primitive cultures and compare and contrast them to those most commonly held in the United States today.
- The chastity belt during the Middle Ages
- Birth control practices: a chronology
★ Factors involved in vasectomy operations
○ Sexual ethics in modern America. Do we have any?
- Social and historical perspectives on chastity
- Compare and contrast sexual ethics in ancient Greece and Rome with those most prevalent in the western world.
- What happens in sex change operations?
- How revolutionary was the "sexual revolution"?
➥ Sexual myths and misconceptions
○ Sigmund Freud on human sexuality

- The practice of female circumcision or excision in modern times
▲ Drugs and sexual stimulation: the scientific findings
- America's changing views of prostitution
- The relationship between sexual satisfaction and marital satisfaction
- Changing perceptions of virginity
○ Find and compare a number of reviews of the sex research of Masters and Johnson. Do analysts agree? What is the consensus?
× The changing role of the sexes in contemporary America
- Discuss this statement and cite appropriate authorities to substantiate your point of view: Given the biological realities, sexism is inevitable.
- Adultery in Islam: prevalence and punishment
- How the spread of AIDS (Acquired Immune Deficiency Syndrome) influences sexual attitudes

★ Detail the scientific and proven methods available to protect yourself against sexually transmitted diseases.
- Discuss changing homosexual lifestyles since the increase in AIDS victims.
★ How homosexuals are (or are not) overcoming a national bias
▲ Programs designed to protect children from sexual abuse
- Should birth control clinics be established in high schools? Why or why not?
★ Problems associated with the increasing accessibility of "dial-a-porn" pornography via the telephone
▲ Why American pharmaceutical companies are not developing new forms of contraception
★ How AIDS has affected sexual mores in America
★ Discuss the controversy surrounding the development and distribution of the French abortion pill, RU486, and comment upon its current status.

Key to Symbols

•	average difficulty	◆	narrow down topic
§	substitutes possible	▲	large public or college library required
★	ample information in most libraries	↙	local option topic
○	specialized knowledge required	×	examples and supporting evidence needed

Social Problems

See also: Contemporary Issues; Drug Problems; Sociology

▲ Does poverty cause crime? This traditional view may no longer be true. Present a compilation of experts' opinion.

● Defend or refute: By and large, welfare goes to those who really need it.

○ Defend or refute: Violence begets violence in any society.

● Reasons for parental kidnapping. What is the scope of this activity in the United States today?

● The issues involved in "active euthanasia" for deformed infants

★ Defend or refute: The state should fund abortions for women on welfare.

● Tenets of male liberation

● Problems of midlife unemployment

★ Violence on TV and its possible effects on young children

★ The effects on the welfare roles of illegal aliens. Focus on the economic factors involved.

● Why the United States should have zero population growth

➤ The portrayal of women in magazine advertising. Select one product area.

● Book censorship in America—1970 to date

● The use and effects of PCP (angel dust)

★ Effects of long-term marijuana use. What have been the results of recent scientific studies?

★ Pros and cons of the legalization of marijuana

● Self-help organizations for alcoholics

● Methadone treatment for drug addiction. What has been the success rate using this procedure? Have there been auxiliary problems?

✕ Complications of reverse discrimination in contemporary America

▲ Questions have been raised about the fund-raising methods of public charities. What has been the basis of these issues? Have abuses occurred in major charitable campaigns?

§ Evaluate the current birth control programs in India.

➤ Living conditions of migrant agricultural workers in America

● Surrogate mothers: legal aspects

● Can we safeguard against biological warfare?

● Are civil defense measures adequate in the United States?

● What can be done about "kiddie porn"? How widespread is this problem?

★ Noise pollution: What are the levels of toleration, stress, and damage?

● Pros and cons of national health insurance

★ Birth-control pills: current findings on long-term effects

➤ Current perspectives on rehabilitation for the disabled

● Socialized medicine in Great Britain today

○ What are the ethical considerations relating to the use of human subjects in clinical biological and genetic research?

● Independent living for the handicapped: a survey of some successful ways and means.

✕ Changing attitudes in America toward motherhood

★ The ethics of mercy killing

○ How to achieve an equitable distribution of worldwide food supplies

➤ How should society regulate pornography?

● Condominiums are increasing. What has been their effect on low-income and elderly renters?

● Deprogramming religious converts. Do parents have the right to force deprogramming upon adult children?

● Should Indian reservations be maintained or abolished?

● Obscenity, pornography, and cable television

✕ Defend or refute: Affirmative action is often unfair and discriminatory.

● Hunting: Recreation, conservation, or a balance? What changes should be made?

● Brand name versus generic drugs. What are the pros and cons for the consumer?

● Does legalized gambling promote an increase in the number of gamblers?

▲ Discrimination against the obese. Consider both children and adults.

● Overpopulation and the food supply: Who decides who will starve?

★ Why we should have federal gun control

● Should the victims of crime be compensated for their loss?

● Why the United States is losing its war on crime

● Why is there an epidemic of teenage pregnancies?

★ The pros and cons of bilingual education

★ Should adopted children be

able to locate their natural parents?

○ What should be done to aid the victim of incest?

● World hunger: 1970–present

● The age-old case for legalized prostitution

● Strengths and weaknesses of the federal food stamp program

○ Defend or refute: International control of nuclear weapons is no longer possible.

● Defend or refute: State prostitution laws are archaic and should be broadened.

○ Integrating the mentally disabled into the community. Discuss the methods which have proved to be successful.

➤ Housing for low-income families

● Dying with dignity: the ethics involved

✕ The "youth cult" in American life

● Social and religious opposition to voluntary sterilization

● Should we have compulsory retirement?

➤ Hunger in America

● Euthanasia throughout history

● Public opinion and abortion. Investigate a number of public opinion polls and compare and contrast the results. Use at least a twenty-year time-span.

● Analyze the political aspects of national health care

● Investigate why there is a lack of consensus among legal, religious, and medical institutions towards definitions of death.

★ Support or deny: Funeral rituals are not necessary for modern man.

● Does a steady diet of television encourage cheapened human relationships, violence, and general "malnutrition" of values? If so, why? There have been many books and articles which have touched upon this issue. Read several and analyze your findings.

★ The right-to-life point of view

● What are the justifications for the decriminalization of drug use in the United States?

➤ Which of our contemporary social problems would not have been considered critical, or even problems, during earlier periods of American history? Trace the development of several to their current level and status.

▲ The causes for the spread of crack cocaine addiction. Survey several recent studies.

● What are the ethical, legal, and social issues raised by the Karen Ann Quinlan case and the use of life-support systems?

▲ What are the reasons for the inequality of access to health services in the United States?

● The social effects of drug abuse

● What are the leading social

problems in American society? Justify your choices.

☛ Rehabilitation problems of narcotic abusers and addicts

● The continuing plight of the homeless in America. Why have their numbers increased?

★ The pros and cons of mandatory testing for AIDS (Acquired Immune Deficiency Syndrome)

● Is the incidence of sexually transmitted diseases increasing or decreasing? Substantiate your finding with current medical statistics.

✔ What programs are in place or currently being implemented to aid the homeless in your community?

● Alternatives to welfare have recently been proposed. What are some of them? Have they been tested and implemented? Determine their success in terms of both the recipients and the community.

★ The impact of poverty on the elderly

● Many of the measures being considered for the control of AIDs (Acquired Immune Deficiency Syndrome) touch upon the issues of confidentiality, privacy and civil rights. Examine these implications.

★ What ethical problems surround the authorization for the use of embryo tissue in research and transplantation?

● Fertility drugs: a mixed blessing

● Euthanasia in the state of Oregon. Should this be the norm in other states? Is it likely to become more commonly accepted?

● Adults, as well as children, suffer from Attention Deficit Syndrome (ADS). How does it affect their personalities, learning, and occupations?

× Health problems of the homeless

● It has been suggested that cash for voluntary sterilization would decrease the ranks of unwanted babies. True? Possible? Why?

Key to Symbols

●	average difficulty	☛	narrow down topic
§	substitutes possible	▲	large public or college library required
★	ample information in most libraries	✔	local option topic
○	specialized knowledge required	×	examples and supporting evidence

Sociology

See also: Contemporary Issues; Social Problems

- Detail some of the possible effects of automation on society.
- Social change in Sun Belt cities. Select one large metropolitan area as an example and enumerate the alterations in its social demographics over the last decade.
- Discrimination in housing. Detail the changes in its characteristics and scope since 1965.
- Has the American woman changed her aims and goals since 1950? Focus on trends.
- What are the traditional limits and restraints to social mobility in the United States? Have they been recently altered? If so, in what ways?
- Compare marriage relationships in both urban and rural areas of the United States.
- What are some of the strengths and weaknesses of modern courtship customs in America? Do they contribute to successful marriages?
- § Courtship and marriage customs in Russia

- ○ How children develop a self-concept
- Victorian morality codes
- Correlations between over-population and crime. Use examples from contemporary urban environments.
- ★ Drug-related crimes. What is the national incidence and type? What have been the social consequences?
- ★ Boy (Girl) Scouts: What these organizations can do for children
- Is divorce changing the American family?
- ✔ Survey and evaluate the social service organizations in your area in terms of scope and outreach potential.
- The rise of the great American middle class
- The relationship between television habits and delinquent youths
- ★ No-fault divorce
- The social effects of rapid technological change on uneducated populations
- America as a transient society

383

and the effects on family sta-
bility
- Class structure in third world
countries: an overview
§ The Italian family in the United
States: ethnic patterns
× What causes social change in
modern societies? Use examples.
- The ethics of involuntary steril-
ization
§ Compare and contrast the family in Mexico and the United
States.
- Why Alcoholics Anonymous has
been successful
➤ What are the relationships between environment and criminal
behavior?
- The relationship between minor-
ities and poverty in the United
States
○ Structure, accuracy, and uses of
public opinion polls
- Changing attitudes toward di-
vorce, 1920 to present
- Structure a public opinion poll
on a selected social question.
Administer the survey to an appropriate sample and analyze
the results. How accurate are
they? What would you change
were it repeated?
- Alternatives to marriage in contemporary society
× Problems in teenage marriages
○ Who defines culture in America?
- Socioeconomic effects of America's postwar baby boom

- Sociology of retirement communities
- Is there really a generation
gap?
▲ Parent abuse
- New York City: an example of
social disintegration
○ Drug addict rehabilitation practices. Account for the success of
those most often used.
- Large numbers of alien workers
cause social dysfunction in a society. What are some examples?
Include Europe as well as the
United States in your survey.
- Discuss the correlation between
the poverty and congestion of
urban slums and the disease
and death rates in these same
areas.
★ How advertising creates status
symbols
- The values of small town life
- How day-care facilities for the
economically impoverished
should be improved
○ Parent education in child abuse
cases
- Social mobility in America.
What strata of society are most
flexible? Which are least flexible? Why?
★ How social scientists account for
the increasing divorce rate in
America
- What constitutes a social movement? Use a twentieth-century
movement such as women's lib-

eration as a prototype.

- To what factors do social scientists attribute the revival of fundamentalism and the rise of mysticism in our society?
★ How religion functions on the individual level. What are its advantages to the believer?
- American society has traditional sexual stereotypes coexisting with sex roles and patterns. Explain how this is possible.
○ Define cultural universals and detail each by examples from a wide range of cultural contexts.
▲ How do sociologists explain and account for the variance in crime rates in different social classes?
○ Define and select relevant examples of Max Weber's theory of the multidimensional nature of social stratification.
○ Identify the major functions of prisons and evaluate the extent to which prisons are effective in accomplishing those functions.
- Does America have social classes? If so, define and characterize each.
○ Compare the social control mechanisms associated with these organizational units: bands, tribes, chiefdoms, and states.
➥ Select a currently functioning and successful extremist group in the United States. What is

the economic source of their power? How have they gained social control? To what extent have they been successful in fulfilling their goals?
▲ Compare the means and agents of social control in several of the following societies: Bushmen, Amish, IK, Hasidic Jews, Semangs, and Hutterites.
- Compare a socially stratified system based on caste with one based on class. Use examples to illustrate the differences and similarities. Consider social mobility, economic, educational, and political factors.
▲ A shift toward androgyny has been isolated by several studies of social scientists. What do they feel are the primary causes of this change?
★ Legalizing heroin: pros and cons
- Family backgrounds of heroin addicts
- The role of the sociologist in understanding and treating social problems
- Gay liberation as a social reform movement
- What is the basis for the negative stereotype of homosexuality in American society? Quote authoritative sources to support your conclusions.
○ Analyze the social implications of the research conclusions on

television violence and aggression.

- What are the racial, class, and cultural biases which may be involved with the testing of intelligence?
- ▲ How have social scientists defined the nature of maturity? Evaluate a wide range of definitions from a variety of disciplines.
- Drunken driving. The scope of the problem and remediation measures which have had positive effects.
- ★ Compare and contrast the blue-collar and the white-collar worker in terms of jobs, goals, status, education, and attitudes.
- ➤ Corrective measures to aid the chronically unemployed
- Compare the American aristocracy: 1880 and 1990. Describe and justify the alterations.
- Changing attitudes towards infidelity
- ★ Status symbols of middle-class America
- ○ Rock stars as antiheroes. Define the antihero in its historical context.
- Analyze Jack Henry Abbott's *In the Belly of the Beast* (1981) and relate it to Abbott's background and subsequent actions after publication.
- Social order in the barrio
- ★ The hippies as a social phenom-

enon: a look backward

- Sports as a social institution
- ○ Plan in detail the organization of the perfect commune. Why will it be successful?
- Human sacrifice in the ancient and medieval worlds
- ✔ Identify and detail the five major social problems in your community
- ✗ Identify and give examples of the "ghetto mentality."
- ★ Social work today
- ➤ The changing roles of men and women in contemporary marriages. Include a discussion of the social and economic realities contributing to this change.
- According to Alvin Toffler in *Future Shock*, the twentieth century has exposed society to more change than any time in history. What have been the broad-range results of this exposure?
- Nutritional aspects of poverty in the rural South
- ➤ Leisure and culture: cause and effect
- ▲ Socioeconomic stratification of the African-American ghetto
- The use of halfway houses in drug rehabilitation
- Goals and contributions of the Planned Parenthood organization
- Children who have been raised in communes. Several studies have recently been completed. What are the essential conclu-

sions? Was there agreement?

- The Great Depression mentality. What was it and how has it affected the character of American life?
★ The Big Brother program
- Poverty in Appalachia
- Contrast the social and personal functions of religion
- Psychological factors of youthful rebellion
➥ Prostitution: from the Greeks to the present
- The young unwed mother: a scenario for her future
- Fatherless families in the African-American ghetto
▲ Social deprivation of foster family children
✔ Are social services adequate for unmarried mothers in your area?
- The homeless: How did they get there?
✕ Are the underclasses — the homeless, drug addicts, welfare recipients — changing the character of the United States?
- How birth control has changed the American family
★ Class distinction in British society
✔ Does your local community have a class structure? If so, describe and compare it to other similar communities.
- How the "black death" altered society in medieval Europe
- Sociologists look at social caste in America: a survey of current opinion

- Societal attitudes towards drug reliance. Compare the different levels of toleration or condemnation toward a variety of substances, such as hallucinogens, marijuana, alcohol, heroin, and tranquilizers.
- Contrast social revolution and social evolution.
✕ Areas of social conflict in urban America
➥ American reactions to the war in Vietnam: Compare and contrast reactions during the war and after the peace.
- Alienation in modern society as reflected in David Riesman's *Lonely Crowd*
○ Sociology of combat
- Acculturation problems in contemporary Eskimo societies
- Funeral rites in the Islamic world
★ How public opinion surveys are conducted
- The alcoholic teenager
➥ Does American society still have taboos? If so, have they changed during the twentieth century? How do they affect American manners and morals?
- How to solve alien labor problems in the United States
- Successful single-parent families: techniques and innovations
✔ How your local community is combating drug abuse
- Outline the social values con-

veyed by popular song lyrics. Survey each song on one week's top twenty (or fifty, etc.) list.

▲ What is the relationship between heredity and criminal behavior? What have been the results of scientific studies since 1950?

➥ Contemporary status symbols. Focus on a single segment of the class structure.

○ How should poverty be measured? What are the complexities involved?

● What are the implications about the sanity of society as reflected in *One Flew Over the Cuckoo's Nest* (Ken Kesey). How does the author convey these attitudes?

↙ Investigate the level of welfare expenditures in your community. What areas are involved? Who are the recipients? Have the characteristics of any of these changed?

★ The welfare roles and the new dependent class

● Pros and cons of national marriage and divorce laws

↙ Poverty levels in your community or county

➥ The relationship between crime and poverty

§ The plight of the poor in Mexico City (or Lima, Peru; Djakarta, Indonesia, etc.)

● How cultural values have changed as Americans move from an agrarian way of life to urban centers

§ Village life in Greece (in Turkey, Spain, Italy, Portugal)

○ Social change in middle-class America. Select one socioeconomic group or one ten-year time-span.

● Sex roles in America

● Husband/wife relationships in Middle Eastern countries

● India's caste system as it existed in the past and as it exists today

○ Implications of Social Darwinism to modern sociology

● Social change in the San Francisco Chinese community within the last twenty-five years

● Gamblers Anonymous

○ The evolution of sociology from a social philosophy to a social science. Include the contributions of Émile Durkheim and Max Weber.

➥ How social class influences family life

● The establishment of settlement houses in late nineteenth-century America. What were the major accomplishments?

● What factors in the American political and social system have allowed organized crime to flourish?

✗ The use of wealth, power, and prestige as measurements of social class

● American education has been viewed and often used as a vehicle for social mobility. What is the basis for this attitude?

○ The roots of prejudice in American society: psychological, cultural, and structural complexities

• Who drinks? Support your answer with evidence from a selection of research and studies.

• The economic, political, and social organization of the utopian Oneida Colony (Oneida, New York)

Key to Symbols

•	average difficulty	☛	narrow down topic
§	substitutes possible	▲	large public or college library required
★	ample information in most libraries	↙	local option topic
○	specialized knowledge required	×	examples and supporting evidence needed

Space

See also: Astronomy; Aviation

- Has the space program lived up to its original objectives?
★ Is there other intelligent life in the universe? Include a survey of reputable scientific evaluations on this subject.
- Consider the possibilities of bacterial contamination from space exploration.
★ Women astronauts
★ Science looks at flying saucers
- Careers in space technology
- The early space suits
- How the astronauts train for weightlessness
▲ The laser geodynamic satellite
- Compare and contrast United States and Russian space achievements. Cover the entire span of space endeavor.
- Weather satellites: past and present
○ Biosatellites
- Spacecraft design for the space shuttle
★ The phenomenon of weightlessness and its effects on the body. What are the problems in space?
○ Generating electrical power in space
- Satellite communication today and tomorrow
× Ancient and medieval attitudes towards the cosmos
- The Soviet *Venera* spacecraft explorations of Venus, including a description of the spacecraft, the flight, and significant discoveries
- What have been the significant aftereffects of space flight, both mental and physical? What are the implications of these symptoms?
- The flight of Voyager 2
- Future prospects for the National Aeronautics and Space Administration (NASA). Discuss space goals, budget cutbacks, and current technological complications.
- Russian space stations today
▲ The Solar Mesosphere Explorer Satellite (1981)
★ The USSR's Sputnik and how

it affected United States technology and science education
- Are manned space stations a
possibility? Describe some of the
most essential technology involved.
- Interstellar communication. Examine the various possibilities,
either real or proposed by scientists.
- Prospects for interplanetary
travel
○ Spacecraft life-support systems
- Compare the aims or the results
of the Voyager, Mariner, and
Viking unmanned planetary mis-
sions.
- The composition and habits of
asteroids
★ Details of the surface of the
moon as learned from space
flights
○ Beyond our solar system:
recent discoveries
★ The first moon shot: what we
learned about moon walks
- Compare early space science
fiction with actual technologies
and events.
- Astronaut training requirements
- The first manned space flight
- The first unmanned space flights
★ The first jets
- Modern space suit design
★ How the first astronauts trained
- The outer limits of man in space
○ Prospects for construction in
space

- How the astronauts breathe in
flight
- Health hazards of space flight
- Detail the progress of space-
based reconnaissance for intelligence gathering and analysis.
- Examine and compare the experience and educational background of a selection of
astronauts.
★ Occupations in aerospace
✕ Current innovations with nutri-
ents for space flights
- What guidelines have been suggested for the colonization of
space?
- Physical changes to humans in
the spacecraft environment
▲ Will space exploration promote
the "brotherhood of man"?
What has been suggested by a
variety of writers who have considered this subject?
- Space fiction before the twen-
tieth century
§ Inside the Apollo
○ Signals from life in outer space.
What means of communication
would be possible?
- Soviet space disasters
▲ How to attract entrepreneurs to
the space business
★ Examine the cause of the Chal-
lenger space shuttle accident.
Could it have been prevented?
What were its effects on the
space program?

Speech Communication

See also: Advertising; Journalism; Language; Media

★ How to conduct an interview

● How the new feminism has affected communication between men and women

○ Communicating with emotionally disturbed children

● Money as a system of communication

➥ How we communicate with computers

● What are some of the special qualities and aspects of nonverbal group interactions?

● What elements are unique to broadcast speech?

● Factors in audience analysis

○ Analyze the style of the leading anchorman (woman) of a television newscast.

● Select examples of emotional appeals from charity solicitations, television advertising, political campaigns, newspapers, or magazines. What techniques are effective? What is the effect?

● Analyze the interviewing style of a prominent television talk show host

★ How truckers communicate — verbally and nonverbally

➥ Space and distance in interpersonal communication

▲ How public speaking was used by Martin Luther King, Jr. to gain supporters, inspire loyalty, and further the civil rights cause

★ How to plan a successful group presentation. What are the most important considerations?

➥ Identify a specific speech communication problem. Describe the barriers it imposes on giving and receiving information.

✕ Guidelines for using visual aids effectively. Use examples to clarify each guideline.

● Characteristics of aphasia

● How Helen Keller learned to speak

● Elements of public speaking: enunciation, gesture, pitch, inflection, etc.

● How to improve your techniques of verbal persuasion

● Sign languages for the deaf

○ How primates communicate

● Kinesics as a form of communication

★ How to research information for a short speech
• The relationship between aggression and communication among animals
★ Overcoming nervousness in public performance
○ Analyze several of Winston Churchill's wartime speeches and focus on their composition, audience, and psychological appeal.
• Posture as communication
★ Communicating with dolphins: the latest advances
▲ Underwater sounds of marine life: Noise or communication?
• How to overcome communication dysfunctions
▲ The body language of Charlie Chaplin
• Communication through role-playing
• Nonverbal communication in American culture
★ Gesture as communication
• The body language of young children
• The propaganda used by Hitler in World War II
★ Describe the major inventions and achievements in the communications area for the period 1900–1920. Include a discussion of why these discoveries were significant.
➡ Dialects in America
• Twin intercommunication
• Traffic signals: their origins and variety
○ Communication and the dying person
• Stuttering
○ Realistic prospects for interstellar communication
▲ The influence of Cicero on oration
• Analyze the speeches of the current president for style and effective communication.
• Cultural barriers to full communication
○ How speech dysfunctions are measured, audited, and diagnosed
➡ Speech problems in children
★ How whales seem to communicate
• Common causes of defective speech
★ The brain and its relation to speech
• The emotional factor in persuasion
★ What are the fundamental characteristics of logical argument?
• Select a speech from any issue of *Vital Speeches*. Evaluate it in terms of audience, credibility, organization, appeal, etc.
• Describe and use examples of the three kinds of delivery systems in communication.
• What negative habits interfere with a person's ability to listen? How might this affect learning?
• Assertive versus aggressive behavior. Describe the differences

as they are employed in speech.

× How statistics lie

• Select a well-known speech which was based on logical argument. Analyze the arguments and the effectiveness of the reasoning.

★ What are the personal benefits of public speaking?

★ How to prepare for employment interviews

• How the honey bees communicate

× Nonverbal communication in sports

★ How to research debate topics

• We hear what we want to hear. How does this operate in speech communications?

• What are the pros and cons of speaking from a manuscript, from notes, from an outline, or from memory? How do particular situations affect a speaker's choice of delivery modes?

• How to train yourself to be a good listener

• The "media presidency" of John F. Kennedy

• How to use sound recordings to enhance a speech. Include any possible problems and drawbacks.

▲ Abraham Maslov has described five levels of basic needs. How does each relate to the communication process?

• How to develop poise and confidence as a speaker

• Physical properties which detract from effective public speaking. How can they be minimized or avoided?

• How public speakers can recognize, analyze, and utilize feedback

➥ Read a famous speech from the past. What was its impact upon the political, economic, or social scene? In what ways might it have changed the course of history?

• Select five television commercials and analyze the nonverbal elements in each. The results will be more significant if all are for the same products.

○ Select a published speech by a contemporary or historical speaker and prepare an analysis and evaluation based on the Toulmin construct.

• What are the distinctions between an oral and a written style?

○ Analyze five newspapers or magazine advertisements using the Toulmin concept of analysis.

★ Exercise for the improvement of diction

• How the following qualities affect the listener's reaction to a message: pitch, volume, rate articulation, pronunciation, and vocal quality

• The speaker's image

➥ Criteria for persuasive speaking

▲ Review and compare inaugural addresses by several presidents. Identify the theme, tone, style, and language levels. In what ways were these speeches ritualized?

● Analyze the communication techniques employed by Adolf Hitler at the Nuremberg rallies during the early months of the Third Reich.

➤ Music as communication

● The role of speech in interpersonal relations

▲ Select several speeches made by a nationally prominent personality. What do they reveal about the character of the speaker?

Key to Symbols

● average difficulty
§ substitutes possible
★ ample information in most libraries
○ specialized knowledge required

➤ narrow down topic
▲ large public or college library required
✔ local option topic
✗ examples and supporting evidence needed

Sports and Recreation

See also: Dance; Health

- When body-building is harmful
- Horse-racing regulations. What reforms are necessary?
- Athletes continue to set new records in events requiring speed, strength, and endurance. What are the outer limits?
- Free weight exercise systems versus machines
- § Baseball in Japan
- § Basketball in Europe
- Problems of climbing in the Himalayas
- The preparation for, and perils of, long-distance swimming. What particular training is essential?
- ★ The differences between English and American soccer. Include national attitudes.
- The training of greyhounds for racing. What are their natural characteristics?
- § Hiking in the Grand Canyon
- For or against: competitive sports in grade school
- ★ How to select running shoes for maximum comfort, safety, and wear. Compare a number of those available.

- Are amateur sports really amateur? Has this situation altered since 1970?
- ▲ How corporate involvement may change United States Olympic programs
- Compare and contrast games and play in young children (or adults).
- Sports and politics: Do they mix? Consider all of the advantages and disadvantages. What are the international aspects?
- ▲ Compare the professional black and professional white athlete. Consider salary, position in game, injury rates, postcareer benefits, secondary benefits, longevity.
- ○ The function of sports as a social institution
- Early football games and the rules governing them
- ★ Weightlifting for beginners
- § Detail the three best exercise programs for children and explain the particular benefits from each (or for heart patients, runners, etc.).
- ○ Physiological aspects of exercise

and the human body
- Packing to backpack
- The economics of big league baseball
- Prevalence of steroid use in gymnastics or other sports
- The designated hitter: pros and cons
- What all outdoor enthusiasts should know about hypothermia
- Sports' use of computers
- What sports are best for children
- Common athletic injuries and how they can be avoided
§ How to teach elementary gymnastics to young children
★ Defend or refute: Boxing regulations should be made more strict to protect the participants.
- What Americans do with their leisure time: a national overview
- Legalized gambling in the United States
▲ Teaching team sports to children
▲ Outdoor recreation possibilities for the physically handicapped
- What a country must do to prepare for the Olympics. What an individual must do to be accepted for the Olympics.
§ Arnold Palmer as a businessman
- Training and preparation for long-distance bicycling
× Noncompetitive games for adults
- Physical problems of runners
§ The dangers of skating
- Evaluate the arguments against

intercollegiate athletics
- Proposed reforms and changes of the Olympics' rules
- Swimming safety
- Regional aspects of American sports
- Intercollegiate athletics for women
▲ Playground design for the secondary school
- The athlete and coronary disease. What are the long-range consequences of intensive athletic training?
- Sex bias and discrimination in women's athletics
- Mountain climbing: safety techniques
- The pleasures and dangers of skydiving. Include a discussion of necessary safety factors.
- How to coach Little League baseball
- Defend or refute: Steroid use in athletics should be outlawed
★ Defend the accusations that professional sports salaries are too high.
× Tactics for the recruitment of college athletes
- Compare the American attitude towards athletes and athletics with that of ancient Greece and Rome.
- Recreation for everyone: some unique and unusual pastimes
- Who controls sports? Select one major American sport.
§ Compare and contrast the bas-

ketball style and tactics of Anfernee Hardaway and Reggie Miller.

- Are intercollegiate sports an expensive luxury for the few?
- Pros/cons of coeducational physical education activities for children
§ How to teach basketball
- The Boston Marathon
- How safe is hang gliding?
- Special Olympics for the handicapped
- "Amateur" rules in the Olympics
★ Aquatic exercises for total fitness
★ Girls' basketball as played in the United States. What are the reasons for its popularity?
- Is violence in sports part of the game?
- What should a runner eat?
○ Why we have sports heroes
§ Changes in hockey tactics since the early days of the game
- Compare and contrast rugby, soccer, and American football
○ Mountaineering descent techniques
§ Effects of television on both the organization and the playing patterns of professional football
- The relationship of karate to Zen Buddhism
- Compare and contrast karate and judo.
- Exercise systems: Compare and contrast Hatha yoga, Kundalini yoga, Tai Chi, isometrics, and

aerobics.
- Physical fitness sports for senior citizens
- Training for endurance
- Violence in hockey. Is it necessary? What is the audience appeal?
× The unique and colorful language of the sports writer
★ Financial support for amateur athletics: pros and cons
× Recruiting abuses for college athletic programs
- Support or deny: Sports do not build character.
- Is college football too commercial?
- Gymnastics safety rules
- Energy requirements of athletics
- The management of stress through active sports
▲ Recreation for retarded teenagers
- The rise of corporate fitness programs. How do these programs compare with those in Japanese business and industry?
○ How air pollution affects athletic performance
- Distance running for children: pros and cons
- Athletic performance and stress
§ Strategies for competitive runners
- Athletes have recently been using EPO (erythropoietin), a hormone, to greatly increase performance levels. Examine the risks and benefits of this procedure.

★ Should all athletic competitions include pregame drug testing?

● Players' strikes and their effect upon the sport and the fans.

● Cleaning up professional sports. What should the penalties be for convicted drug users?

★ Should eligibility for participation in collegiate sports depend upon academic qualifications and achievements?

● Blood doping in sports and why it is now illegal

★ Olympian Ben Johnson's steroid use

★ How Pete Rose gambled and lost. What were the results?

● European soccer games have had several instances of mob violence. What is the background and solution to this problem?

Key to Symbols

● average difficulty
§ substitutes possible
★ ample information in most libraries
○ specialized knowledge required

☛ narrow down topic
▲ large public or college library required
↙ local option topic
× examples and supporting evidence needed

Sports and Recreation — History

- How football equipment has been improved since the game's beginnings
- National Hockey League, 1925–1980
- ★ The causes of the professional football players' strikes in the 1970's and early 1980's. What were the results?
- Chariot racing in the Roman empire
- The Indianapolis 500: how the race has changed
- What are the forms of juvenile recreation depicted in the painting *Children's Games* (Pieter Bruegel, 1559)?
- ★ Jackie Robinson's contributions to sports
- The first modern Olympics (Athens, Greece, 1896)
- ➥ Recreational activities of the Greeks and Romans
- Games of the Native American
- Sports in colonial America
- The first ascent of Mount Everest. What were the problems encountered? Were they expected? Surmounted?
- ★ Marathons, then and now
- ★ The origin and evolution of the bow and arrow

- ➥ The world's oldest sport: wrestling
- How baseball has changed in America. Has the sport been improved? How? Should other changes be made?
- The history of the Olympic Decathlon contest
- The 1980 American boycott of the Moscow Summer Olympics
- The ancient "sport" of animal baiting
- ▲ Trace today's popular sports as outgrowths of man's oldest imperative: survival against nature
- ▲ The association of early games and sports with religious worship
- ★ Sports of the Bible
- Compare and contrast Roman gladiatorial combat and professional football.
- The evolution of professionalism in the Greek games
- Techniques of the long jump in ancient Greek games
- Contrast the techniques and practices of chariot racing in ancient Greece and Rome.
- ★ The background of weight lifting as a competitive sport

- The importance of swimming in the ancient world
★ The sport of falconry. What were its earliest uses? How were the falcons trained?
▲ Roman attitudes towards Greek athletics
- The Greek Pythian, Memean, and Isthmian games

§ The changes in basketball rules
- Swimmers of the English Channel
- Origins of the World Cup
- The world's first sporting events
§ Ancient Egyptian games and recreations
- The ball: its earliest uses and forms

Key to Symbols

•	average difficulty
§	substitutes possible
★	ample information in most libraries
○	specialized knowledge required

☛	narrow down topic
▲	large public or college library required
✔	local option topic
✗	examples and supporting evidence needed

Technology

See also: Invention and Discovery

○ How bugging devices work

▲ New uses for fiber optics

● The boomerang and other primitive throwing sticks

○ The use of lasers in video reproduction

● How silk is processed

● Compare and contrast the video tape and the video disc.

§ Recent advances in <u>glassmaking</u>

✕ The impact and changes brought about by the invention and widespread use of the plastic container

➥ Appropriate technology for underdeveloped countries. Select a particular area such as agriculture, textiles, mining, etc.

● The holograph and its uses

★ Compare and contrast the crystal and the transistor radio

★ Scientific uses for hot air balloons

● In what industries has automation proved to be most successful? Why?

● Compare and contrast refractor and reflector telescopes.

● Solar energy: practical applications for the home craftsman

● Digital recording technology

➥ Synthetic fuels

➥ Identify a fundamental technological breakthrough of the modern world. What were its origins? How was it set in motion? What technological, intellectual, and social conditions encouraged the breakthrough?

✕ How has technology expanded the agricultural resource base?

● The "smaller is better" trend in technology

● It has been estimated that 25 percent of our national energy consumption is wasted through inefficient processes in industry and domestic buildings. In what ways do the most significant losses occur? What technological aids could remedy them?

★ The computer has touched and altered almost everyone's life. How about yours?

● "Existing technologies are no longer capable of ensuring sufficient growth to maintain present fiscal and social policies" (Francis Kelly). Support or refute this quotation with scientific evidence.

- Each year hundreds of new chemical compounds are marketed. Are they all tested for harmful effects? If not, why not?
★ The new generation of nuclear weapons
- Why astronomers dislike the space shuttle and why the communications industry loves it
▲ Electronic sensors for the blind
§ The future for <u>paper</u>
- The stone buildings and monuments in the world's cities are suffering severe weather and pollution damage. What preventative measures are being used to control this situation?
- Advances in the control of forest fires
- Desalination technology: the state of the art
✗ How new innovations are contributing to airplane safety.
- Development and uses of the Geiger counter
§ The craftsmanship of the <u>Steinway piano</u>
- Military and civilian uses of Hovercraft
- Wheelchair innovation and design
- Shore protection measures. Why are they necessary?
▲ The future role of systems engineering
- Varieties of contemporary

bridge construction. Include detailed examples of each type.
- How to build a tunnel under a river
- The dynamics of the orb weaver's (spider) web
★ Careers for women in engineering: past and future
- Modern aqueducts
- Roman aqueducts
○ Fire control in large buildings
- Elements of the cantilever structure
- The design and construction of ocean oil rigs
- Cyronics
§ How <u>perfumes</u> are developed and produced
- An evaluation of solar hot water kits. Survey the major products on the market. Compare them in terms of price, complexity, size, and durability. Use professional product evaluations if available.
- How communication satellites work
- Modern alternatives to the internal combustion engine
★ The Japanese sword and how it is fabricated. What is its cultural significance?
★ An evaluation of the dangers of microwaves
- Placer mining
§ The preparation of <u>leather</u>
- The story of the silicon chip
- Is there a robot in your future?
- The trend toward miniaturization

§ Geothermal energy in <u>New Zealand</u>

○ How guided missiles work

● Why are European railroads better than those in the United States?

☛ Select one use of the transistor (hearing aids, space instruments, telephone, etc.) and detail its origin, development, and practical applications.

● Sound recording: an overview, from Edison to digital

✗ Electronic warfare and high technology

○ NMR (nuclear magnetic resonance) is used as an imaging device in modern medicine. What are its current uses and advantages?

● Technology and the changing face of war

● Is technology too dominant a factor in our society? Is this trend detrimental? Select a specific area for your discussion.

● The joys of robots

▲ The use of expert systems in business

● Technology and transportation: is it helping?

○ "Hot viruses" and how they work. Do we have the technology to control them, should a serious outbreak arise?

● The risks of gene manipulation

★ Are feasible alternative energy sources being developed? In the United States? World-wide? If not, why not?

● The positron reemission microscope and its technological significance

● New underwater diving technology and the resulting discoveries

✔ If you have a highly automated factory in your area, explore the technologies involved.

● The "smart" car now and in the future.

☛ How genetic engineering has been utilized since 1985.

● Explore the many ways in which telecommunications have changed education.

● "The technological knowledge we use today will represent only 1 percent of the knowledge available in 2050." Examine this statement.

Key to Symbols

●	average difficulty	☛	narrow down topic
§	substitutes possible	▲	large public or college library required
★	ample information in most libraries	✔	local option topic
○	specialized knowledge required	✗	examples and supporting evidence needed

Technology — History

See also: Invention and Discovery

- Man's first tools — their uses and design
- Earliest uses of the potter's wheel, both simple and foot-powered
★ Firemaking methods up to and including the development of the sulfur match
- The earliest applications of rotary motion
- The evolution of fishing technology among primitive peoples
▲ Fireworks and flares: ancient and modern
- Early efforts to use solar energy
- The impact on local economies of the cotton gin
§ Early developments in metallurgy
➥ Locks throughout the ages
- Compare the historical significance of the discovery of electricity with that of steam.
▲ Early innovations in the design of the incandescent lamp
- Camera: an overview from the invention of light-polarizing plastics to the Polaroid camera
§ The first applications of lasers
▲ Cottage industry during the Industrial Revolution
- The realistic inventions of Leonardo da Vinci
★ Ancient and primitive clocks
➥ Select a particular industry and discuss the changes brought to it by the Industrial Revolution.
§ Early uses of glass
- What were the first kinds of paper?
▲ The Qanats, the underground canals of Iran
- Bird and animal traps among primitive cultures
- The development and design of the Gatling gun (machine gun)
▲ The rope bridge of San Luis Rey
➥ Evaluate the steam engine's historical contributions
○ Wind tunnels in the space age
○ The significance of nineteenth-century metallurgical advances
- The logistics of the transatlantic cable (1851)
- Brickmaking: ancient and modern
- Early instances of worked leather
★ Ben Franklin's inventions

405

- Medieval torture devices
- Building the Trans-Siberian railway
- × Historic attempts to harness the ocean's power
- ★ Building the Great Wall of China
- Hydraulic mining in ancient Egypt
- ➥ Irrigation in the ancient world. Compare and contrast the methods, and the extent and success of various cultures (Sumeria, India, Egypt, China, etc.)
- Engineering problems in the building of the Panama Canal
- § Construction of the Roosevelt Dam
- Construction of the Saint Gotthard Tunnel, 1872–1882, Switzerland and Italy
- ★ Logistical and political obstacles to construction of the tunnel under the English Channel; the final product.
- § Construction of the Empire State Building
- ➥ Early projects of the Army engineers
- § Construction of the Alaskan highway
- The Freemason in the medieval world
- Incan engineering of Machu Picchu, Peru
- § The earliest of bells. Who made them? What were the materials employed?

- × Attempts at perpetual motion
- Egyptian stone working techniques
- Early misuses of X-rays, radium, and other radioactive materials
- × Ancient "industrial" uses of cultivated plants
- ★ Henry Ford: mass production techniques for the early automobiles
- Linen, flax, and cotton textiles of early Egypt
- Describe the major advances in military technology between 1900 and 1920. Include a discussion of why each is significant.
- The ancient origins of moveable bridges
- ▲ Military and civilian uses of Hovercraft surface effect vehicles
- How the development and use of gunpowder changed history
- ★ Trace the developments leading to the production of iron tools and weapons in the Iron Age.
- Invention and uses of the Bailey Bridge
- Interest and inventions in the mechanical arts did not flourish until medieval times. What were the reasons for this slow growth?
- × What were the principal technological advances that made mass production possible?
- ➥ New technologies developed rapidly with the advent of do-

mestic agriculture in the Neolithic era. Select several of the most significant and detail their evolution.

- The engineering of the Egyptian pyramids. Discuss some of the theories which have been advanced to account for some of the more puzzling construction details.

- Invention and technology in colonial America

Key to Symbols

- • average difficulty
- § substitutes possible
- ★ ample information in most libraries
- o specialized knowledge required
- ➤ narrow down topic
- ▲ large public or college library required
- ↙ local option topic
- × examples and supporting evidence needed

Television and Radio

See also: Advertising; Journalism; Media; Speech Communication

- ➥ The censorship of television news by sponsors (and others)
- ➥ Radio programs for children: 1930–1945. Analyze in detail one segment or type of program.
- ● Detail the steps necessary to produce a typical TV commercial.
- ★ Should television be allowed in the courtroom?
- ● Sin and the "soaps," or, how times have changed
- ● Network broadcasting and how it affected radio
- ● An analysis of children's programs on commercial television
- ✕ Innovative uses of computer-generated graphics on television
- ➥ Social and cultural change and the radio in America (1920–1940)
- ● Should the United States have nationalized television similar to the BBC (British Broadcasting Corporation)?
- ▲ Innovations in educational television
- ✔ The future of cable television in your area

- ● The public reaction to Orson Welles' "Invasion from Mars" radio broadcast (1938)
- ▲ Compare radio programming in the 1930's to today
- ➥ Television and political conventions
- ▲ Uses of Sesame Street in the classroom
- ▲ How do the results of television polls affect programming?
- ● Sexist stereotyping in television sitcoms
- ➥ Competition in the television industry and how it affects programming
- ● How has the content of television changed since its early days?
- ➥ What has been the impact of television on education?
- ● How Proctor and Gamble's advertising created the "soap opera"
- ● Is the censorship of television commercials a violation of free speech?
- ★ Why some cable TV systems have failed
- ▲ What particular difficulties are

408

inherent in the production of high quality television commercials?

○ What are some of the effects of television on social attitudes?

● The "catharsis" hypothesis of television violence. Cite authoritative sources and the results of valid scientific inquiry.

● People who do not watch television: a profile

● Children's eating preferences as motivated by television advertising

○ Psychologists look at television and its relationship to the cognitive development of children

★ Why M*A*S*H survived

➥ The impact of the television age on American family life

● Television viewing habits of children in lower income families

▲ Compare early radio (1920–1935) in the United States and Great Britain.

➥ The image of women as portrayed on television commercials. Select a specific time-span and monitor the advertising for one week.

● The television ministry, 1960 to date. In what ways has it evolved and expanded?

§ Television in Japan

§ How television has changed the game of baseball

● How television perpetuates sexism

✕ The first radio broadcasts

➥ Television and the presidency

● How television program ratings are compiled

● How has competition from cable, video tape recorders, and satellite technology affected the major networks?

▲ The future for interactive television

● The rise of Court TV. Does it educate the public or is it legal voyeurism?

● How the ratings affect programming

● What have been some of the criticisms of television news coverage? Are they justified? Consult media experts for information to support your answer.

● Discuss the implications of this statement: Television is not an entertainment medium, it is an advertising medium.

● Television violence and children. Since the results are in, why has the violence increased?

★ The effects of extended television viewing on children. Survey the opinions of both educators and psychologists.

★ Compare the violence in television cartoons with that of the classic fairy tales.

● The major elements of the sitcom (situation comedy)

● Portrayal of men in daytime soap operas. What are the stereotypes?

○ Who controls television programming?

- Prospects for public television in the next ten years
- The future of broadcasting: projections by the experts
★ Television in Congress?
- What cable television deregulation will mean
× Ethnic stereotypes on television
- The $64,000 question: the rise and fall of television's specialized game shows
- How the development of children's reading and language skills are affected by television viewing

- Television viewing time in America. What are the variations of age, education, location, income, etc.?
- Examine the growth of cable television's satellite channels
★ How the expansion of VCR usage has affected television programming
- What network news must do to survive
★ Talk shows and what's wrong with them
- Are voters manipulated by presidential television advertisements?
- Television causes illiteracy. Defend or refute this statement.

Key to Symbols

•	average difficulty	➤	narrow down topic
§	substitutes possible	▲	large public or college
★	ample information in most		library required
	libraries	⌐	local option topic
○	specialized knowledge	×	examples and supporting
	required		evidence needed

Theater

See also: Film; Humanities; Literature—Drama; Speech Communication

- How the Great Depression affected American theater
★ The use and effects of the chorus in Greek drama
▲ Broadway: 1940, 1960, and 1990. In which ways was each of these periods unique?
★ Elizabethan theater: design and equipment
- The storyteller in history
- The mime of Marcel Marceau
- Constructing marionettes. What are the traditional materials and techniques? Have there been any novel innovations?
- The medieval mystery play
- Characteristics of Japanese kabuki theater
- The Chautauqua tradition in America
▲ Performance practices of the commedia dell'arte
▲ Early critical reception of theater of the absurd plays and productions
➡ The development of the American musical theater
- Characteristic productions of "off-off-Broadway"

- Plot and character in Japanese Nō theater
○ Select and compare examples of the Greek chorus as used in contemporary drama.
➡ How the theater evolved from ritual to its many contemporary variations
✕ Early theatrical makeup
▲ Describe costumes which were used in Renaissance theater. For example, the attire of: classical figures; fanciful creatures (ghosts, witches, fairies, gods); traditional, national, and racial figures; and the unfashionable garments for parody.
- The stagecraft of flying, from the Italian Renaissance to today's modern theaters
- The value of improvisation training for actors
- Relate and compare the relative importance to the actor of scenic designs, lighting, costume, and stage decoration
- Safety rules for the theater
- Career problems of black actors in a white-oriented business

411

★ How to organize and supervise a properties crew

● Criteria in selecting a play for production by and/or for children

● Methods of theatrical promotion

× Children's theater in the United States: some exemplary programs

● Greek theater architecture. Relate these structural forms to the conventions of classical Greek drama.

▲ How opera has borrowed commedia dell'arte principles

● The origin and use of masks in various forms of drama

▲ The innovative techniques of Giacomo Torelli, Italian Renaissance stage craftsman

● Worship of Dionysus and the annual dramatic festivals of the fifth century B.C. in Greece

● Theater in nineteenth-century America

★ The revolutionary ideas of Konstantin Stanislavsky

● Punch and Judy shows: the plots and the puppets

▲ This season's London theater: the critics' critique. What are the five best? Why?

▲ Sarah Bernhardt's American reception

● Oberammergau's Passion Play (Germany)

● Staging principles and practices of medieval liturgical dramas

➥ Trends in American repertory theater

● Compare and contrast Marcel Marceau's character Bip and Charlie Chaplin's Little Tramp.

➥ Theatrical makeup. Select one type and detail the essential techniques.

➥ Select a major Broadway production from the last ten years and compare and contrast the critical reviews it received. (It is preferable to pick one you have seen.)

● How to block a play

● How the Greeks staged plays. What were the standard conventions?

● How to audition successfully

★ Compare and contrast the proscenium, the theater-in-the-round, and the platform stage, and the ways in which productions must be staged for each.

● The first community theaters in the United States

● Pantomime: old and new

× The use of color in stage design

★ The role of the stage manager

● The first years of Dublin's Abbey Theater

▲ The stereotypical black of the American minstrel show

● How to cast a play

● The practical and aesthetic purposes of stage lighting

● Techniques for special effects through scenery design and painting

× Vaudeville humor

- Both Lee Strasberg and Stella Adler were highly successful acting instructors. What factors account for their success? How were their teaching techniques similar and how did they significantly differ?
§ How the musical Oliver! was made from the Charles Dickens novel (or, select a similar adaptation)
▲ Experimental theater in America, 1965 to present
- Theater in America: first stages
- Getting into television commercials
○ Acting in the Elizabethan theater
▲ Vaudeville and the Palace Theater, 1913–1930
- Productions of the D'Oyly Carte Opera Company

- Comédie Française
★ The architecture of Shakespeare's Globe Theater. Was it typical of theater design? What was its influence on later constructions?
▲ The bizarre theater of Alfred Jarry
- Roman pantomime, the forerunner of modern ballet
- The decline of Roman theater as a result of the rise of Christianity in Rome
- Characteristics of the Ludi Romani, Roman public theatrical festivals (also Ludi publici and Ludi scaenici)
- Directing child actors
- Voice training for the stage
✕ Theater customs and folklore
§ The comedic talents of Jack Benny

Key to Symbols

-   **average difficulty**
§   **substitutes possible**
★   **ample information in most libraries**
○   **specialized knowledge required**

-   **narrow down topic**
▲   **large public or college library required**
↙   **local option topic**
✕   **examples and supporting evidence needed**

Transportation

See also: Automotive; Aviation; Boats and Boating

- How did the issue of the transcontinental railroad contribute to the sectional controversy on the American frontier?
- ▲ Modern monorail design
- ☛ Financial problems of American railroads
- Routes and logistics of the pony express
- ✔ Mass transportation problems in your local community
- ★ The condition of the nation's freeways. Levels of deterioration and maintenance.
- Arguments favoring the nationalization of the railroads
- ★ The dangers of hazardous cargo on airlines, ships, and railroads
- § Highway systems of Germany
- ○ How computers are utilized in large aircraft
- Should the railroad industry be deregulated?
- The economics of the ocean freight industry. What are current problems?
- Conrail: why it failed
- ▲ The building of the Karakorum highway between China and Pakistan

- ☛ Solutions to urban congestion
- The railroads at the time of the Civil War
- Critical issues involved in urban mass transit systems
- Railroad crime prevention measures
- ☛ Discuss the major inventions and achievements in transportation for the period 1900–1920. Include a thorough discussion of the significance of each.
- Barge traffic on the Mississippi River today
- Why the government regulated the railroads in 1887. What changes resulted from this action?
- ★ Does the trucking industry pay its fair share in highway construction and maintenance?
- The design, utility, and range of the prairie schooner
- ▲ Early turnpike design
- § Building the Alaskan Highway
- The Pan American Highway. Evaluate its costs, utility, and routing.
- ✕ Early influences of the railroads on American manufacturing

414

- AMTRAK: Success or failure?
○ The automobile industry's impact on the economy. Include discussion of the industry as an economic indicator.
- Problems in automobile safety
- The future of American railroads: an overview of experts' opinions
★ How will the tunnel between England and France affect either or both countries?
- Should the electric street car be returned to large cities?
- Causes and consequences of railroad featherbedding
- Decide whether automobile emission controls and standards are adequate. If they need to be altered and improved, how?
✔ Evaluate your local mass transit system and detail possible improvements.
- Funding for freeways: Whose responsibility?
- Canal use in the United States
➡ Economic aspects of mass transportation
- The role that the longshoremen's union has played in American shipping
★ What was the nineteenth century's "transportation revolution"?
- The future for human-powered transportation: new designs for bicycles, pedal-driven boats, and airplanes
▲ Why is energy conservation in the transportation sector of the economy a critical issue? What measures are being considered or instituted to alleviate the rates of consumption?
- Select one of the following trains or railways notable for its design and influence on the history of transportation:

The Orient Express
Trans-Siberian Express
The Blue Train
The Twentieth Century Limited
The Overland Limited
Pioneer Zephyr (Burlington Railroad)
City of Portland (Union Pacific)
The Super Chief (Atchinson, Topeka and Santa Fe)
The Alton Limited
The California Limited
The Burlington Zephyr
The Denver and Salt Lake Railway
Union Pacific's No. 4001
Consolidation-type locomotive

- What was the impact of the railroad on Indian/white relations on the American plains during the latter part of the nineteenth century?
▲ How American engineering reshaped British railway design in the nineteenth and twentieth centuries
- A United States transportation agenda for the next century
× Successful mass transit programs (for example, Portland, Oregon; Seattle, Washington; San

Mateo, California; Nashville, Tennessee, etc.)
- No-fare transit: A possibility or a pipedream?
▲ Compare the economics of small commuter airlines and the large airline operations.
- What forms for transportation are the most energy-efficient (per cargo/ton miles)? Which are the least? Why?
★ Why the transportation of radioactive wastes is currently considered to be dangerously

unsafe
- The future of rapid transit
- How safe are the large tractor trailers on our highways?
- The truck of the future
★ How to reduce your highway accident risk
★ Has the 55-mile-an-hour speed limit been successful? What major problems have been encountered?
× Will transportation technology advances alleviate the possibility of national gridlock on both land and air?

Key to Symbols

•	average difficulty	┅	narrow down topic
§	substitutes possible	▲	large public or college
★	ample information in most		library required
	libraries	↙	local option topic
o	specialized knowledge	×	examples and supporting
	required		evidence needed

Travel

See also: Exploration and Discovery; Geography; World Scene

- Plan a two-week history-oriented stay in Washington, D.C. Include some day trips out of the city to what you consider to be the most noteworthy historical sites.
§ Organize a trip centered around the castles of England. Explain why each was included and describe the distinctive features and history of each.
§ Plan a botanical tour of Alaska
- Detail a tour visiting the major Mayan sites, including as many historically significant sites as possible.
- Student travel in Europe: how to beat the high cost
- Traveling on the *Orient Express* in its heyday
- Select three forms of motor vehicles and compare and contrast their values as transportation in a transAmerican tour. Among the factors discussed, include economy, comfort, safety, and accommodations.
- Tourism in ancient Egypt and Greece—by the ancients

§ Plan a detailed bicycle tour of Holland
- How to use the railroads in Europe efficiently and inexpensively
§ How tourism has affected the people of Bali, Indonesia. Or, select another small, underdeveloped country.
- Compare and contrast the Hawaiian Islands and several Caribbean islands as vacation retreats.
- Organize a canoe trip in the Boundary Waters Canoe Area (Minnesota/Canada). Include an itinerary and list of all supplies.
○ Describe all of the necessities for a month's stay in Antarctica.
§ Plan the itinerary for a tour through Japan that will afford the traveler the greatest exposure to traditional Japanese culture.
§ Select the significant architectural structures of Italy and arrange a trip, including a visit to each.

417

- Describe a tour of biblically significant sights in Israel and Middle Eastern countries.
§ How to plan a trip to _____. Select a country or city. Include everything the potential traveler should know: costs, accommodations, schedules, highlights, specialties, etc.
★ Essentials for backpackers
§ How to travel inexpensively in Germany
- The advantages and disadvantages of African tenting safaris
✔ Travel in China: Investigate and evaluate current commercial tours. If possible, interview travel agents and previous visitors to China.
- Geology of the West. Organize a tour including the twenty most significant areas.
- Plan a two-week holiday in London including historical sights, museums, theaters, restaurants, and two trips to the environs.
- Plan a tour of a variety of religious sites in the Middle East— Christian and Islamic, ancient and modern.
○ Plan a trip around the world in eighty days. Include stopovers, fares, prices, routes, baggage, etc. Justify and verify your choices.
- Select five travel books which cover the same area. Compare and contrast their contents, timeliness, accuracy, maps and illustrations, range and price. If possible, select an area which is familiar.
§ Plan the itinerary for a trip to the museums of France. Select a time-frame, budget, and point of view.
- Design a tour of Civil War battlefields
- Travel in the future
- What are the problems involved in traveling in third world countries? Include financial, social, language, accommodations, and transportation aspects.
- Surfing: finding the perfect wave
- Plan the ideal cross-country trip in the United States for a bird-watcher.
★ Traveling with children and how to keep them happy, healthy and interested
- Protecting your health and safety when traveling abroad
★ Careers in the travel industry
▲ The economics of tourism in the United States. Foreign travelers are increasingly touring the United States. Detail the financial aspects of this situation.
- How to plan a cruise. Discuss needs, options, prices, and itineraries.
➡ Changing patterns in world tourism
- French chateaus, vineyards, and

Michelin-starred restaurants: a selective tour

- Plan a trip for a foreign student who has never been in the United States. Select a realistic budget and itinerary. Does your student have some special inter-

ests? Be sure to include them.

§ Caribbean tourism and the local economy

- Government efforts to bolster tourism in Mexico

§ Hotels and other travel amenities in China today

Key to Symbols

- average difficulty
§ substitutes possible
★ ample information in most libraries
o specialized knowledge required

◆ narrow down topic
▲ large public or college library required
↙ local option topic
✗ examples and supporting evidence needed

Urban Affairs

See also: Community Concerns

- How is the federal government alleviating urban blight? Describe some of the most successful programs over a ten-year period.
- ✕ Contrast the effects of governmental planning on the evolution of large metropolitan areas in North America, Western Europe, and Russia.
- Characterize the nature and role of the city in the Islamic world. Discuss its social and economic functions within the culture as well as its traditional form.
- How are the problems of metropolitan areas aggravated by the multiplicity of governmental units?
- Critical issues involved in funding and maintaining the inner city school
- How cities go bankrupt and what happens then
- ○ How the coming energy crisis will affect urban organization and structure
- ★ Why our cities are dying
- ✕ Successful solutions to traffic congestion
- § How New York City is solving its financial problems
- Humanizing the city
- The future for the monorail in American urban centers
- Why freeways are (or are not) the solution to city congestion
- Design problems of urban airports
- ▲ Municipal organization in colonial America
- The possibilities and specifications for self-contained cities
- Levels of federal assistance for urban renewal. Survey and analyze a five-to-ten-year time-span.
- ★ Inner city decay: a typical profile
- ▲ City gardens for the handicapped
- Compare and contrast the modern metropolis or megalopolis and the traditional city.
- ▲ Successful uses of pedestrian malls in downtown redevelopment efforts
- Health problems in slums and ghettos

- What's American about American cities?
- Successful volunteer projects for neighborhood groups
★ Population dislocation and relocation problems in urban renewal
★ Has urbanization lowered the quality of American life? Present the case for either side.
× The planned community in America. Compare and contrast several significant examples.
▲ Successes and failures in urban riverfront redevelopment projects
- Homicide in America's large cities. Cover the causes, types, rates, geographic shifts, etc.
- Is the decline of older neighborhoods within metropolitan areas an inevitable process?
★ Life in the African-American ghetto: myths and realities
- Levels of urban unemployment. What are the socioeconomic issues?
- Brasília: the plan, the execution, and the results
➥ The American city as the new frontier
- Factors that have led to the proliferation of shopping centers and the concurrent decline of central retail areas
★ Compare and contrast mass transit systems in Paris, London, Moscow, and New York.
○ Land values and urban renewal
§ Compare and contrast the life-styles in New York City and Los Angeles.
- The development and economic character of cities along the Mississippi, from 1850 to 1900
✔ Select, describe, and evaluate an urban renewal project in your state.
- Factors affecting the urbanization of America during the Industrial Revolution
▲ A realistic evaluation of Paolo Soleri's urban concepts
- Transportation for the elderly in the inner city
- Why rent control is unfair (or fair)
➥ Select a large foreign city and detail its history, government, geography, businesses, etc.
- Harlem in 1900, 1940, and today
× Successfully recycling old buildings
× Mass transit systems that work
➥ Juvenile gangs in urban areas
- Many experts feel that slum clearance in the inner city does not solve the problem but merely relocates it. Evaluate this thesis.
- Elements necessary for successful urban renewal
★ What factors contributed to the beginnings and spread of urban "sprawl"?
- Many public housing projects have literally turned into public slums. Why has this occurred

with such regularity? Who is responsible? Can a realistic turnaround be effected?

★ Cities of the future. Include the megastructure, the tetrahedral neighborhood, the city in the sea, etc.

• The growth of cities continued from the Middle Ages through the Renaissance. Chart the course of this growth and include the primary technological developments influential in this expansion.

• The growing problems of abandoned buildings in city centers

• Should central cities be financed regionally?

• Levels and effects of the loss of agriculturally productive areas to urban development in the United States

➧ Trace the growth of a megalopolis area, such as San Francisco, Los Angeles, Boston, New York City, or Washington, D.C., and relate it to the growth of the area's business and industry.

▲ Many urban specialists and governmental officials say: "Downtown is back." Discuss this stance in terms of contemporary studies, statistics, and surveys.

• Life in the urban turn-of-the-century slum

• How to live in a city

✔ Detail the changes since 1940 in the old inner city residential areas in your city.

• How topography affects city design. Use your area as an example, if applicable.

• The future of urban areas in developing countries—a projection

★ Pragmatic engineering: city planning in the Roman Empire

➧ Urban law enforcement issues

▲ Maintenance costs in America's older cities. Why are some cities unable to meet these needs while others are more fiscally prepared? How much is required by cities to keep up repairs? What is the percentage of the tax base customarily allocated for maintenance and repair?

• Urban agriculture

• Measures to control urban growth

• Problems in the New York subway system

○ The feasibility of urban renewal: how the experts evaluate an area's potential

▲ The funding crisis of urban transit systems. Is there a solution?

★ Fair housing practices

• Grass roots arts for urban communities

• The urban policies of the current president and administration

× Historical preservation in urban communities

✔ Measures to save old neighborhoods. Select an example of

successful revitalization in urban America. If possible, visit the area.

★ Compare cities before and after the widespread use of the automobile.

• How to organize for cooperative housing

• Define the nuclear civil defense needs of cities. Are they possible to fulfill?

✔ Plan a walking tour of your city, visiting historic, cultural, and scenic sites.

★ What American cities do not provide for their inhabitants

• Are suburban areas in major United States cities facing a transportation mobility crisis?

• Supercities: their growth, problems and future

• The case for privatization of previously public utilities and services

★ The blight of the crack house

★ The plight of homeless families with children

• Lead poisoning in our city soils. Consider both paint and leaded gasoline as sources.

➤ The crisis in waste disposal. What are the environmental hazards? Costs? Technology?

✕ Prison overcrowding is severe in most large cities. What are some possible solutions?

Key to Symbols

• average difficulty	➤ narrow down topic
§ substitutes possible	▲ large public or college library required
★ ample information in most libraries	✔ local option topic
○ specialized knowledge required	✕ examples and supporting evidence needed

War and Peace

See also: Military

▲ The Montgomery/Rommel confrontation in North Africa in WWII. What were the deciding factors that influenced the outcome?

● The logistics of trench warfare in WWI

★ The story behind the bombing of Coventry

★ Profile of a Roman legionary

§ The establishment of the United States Air Force

● What were the major United States air strategies in the Pacific against the Japanese during WWII?

● Napoleon's retreat from Russia. Examine the major and fatal errors of that campaign.

★ Nazi justification for the concentration camps. Detail the official party line.

✕ Problems of troop morale and discipline in the Vietnam War

★ Evaluate George Washington as a general.

○ Do knowledgeable observers see further discord in South Africa even though apartheid has been formally abolished?

● What were the major allied disagreements on military strategy in the campaign against Hitler?

● The Gallipoli campaign of WWI

★ What the Bayeux tapestry tells us about the Norman Conquest

✕ Defend or refute: Motivated nations win wars in spite of the level of armament. Cite historical instances and examples.

● The capture of Fort Ticonderoga during the Revolutionary War

● The German submarine campaign in WWI. In what ways was it successful? Why?

● British strategy in the war in the Falkland Islands

★ A new kind of warfare: the German "blitzkrieg"

● The drummer boys and bands of the Civil War

★ The role of the Gestapo, the secret police force of Nazi Germany

● How Israel won the Six-Day War

▲ Opposition by the scientific community to the use of the atomic bomb in WWII

● Compare the number and causes of battle casualties in WWI, WWII, and the Vietnam War

★ Will there ever be a Palestinian accord? Why or why not?

★ Why the South lost the Civil War

● Could Iran and Iraq resume their armed conflict?

● Experimentation on humans in German prison camps during World War II

● Significant events leading to the Persian Gulf War

✕ Battle tactics of Ulysses S. Grant

● Will the Serbians, Croations, and Muslims in the former Yugoslavia ever find accord? What are the persistent issues that have prevented a peaceful settlement?

● Could the Revolutionary War have been avoided? Why and how? Cite informed opinion and evidence to support your answer.

▲ The justification by the military for the use of Agent Orange in Vietnam

● Why the Germans were defeated in World Wars I and II. Were the causes similar?

▲ The South Pacific Battle of the Coral Sea changed the course of WWII. How?

● The last days of Stalingrad: the death of the German Sixth Army

★ The last days of the Vietnam War. What have been the major criticisms of the role of the United States during this period?

§ Life (and death) in Buchenwald (German concentration camp of WWII)

✕ Military strategies of the battle of Gettysburg, Antietam and other Civil War battles

● The contributions of women to the labor market in the United States during WWII

○ Breaking the Japanese codes in WWII. Discuss either the methodology or how this breakthrough influenced the course of the war.

● The bombing of Dresden during WWII.

● Nuclear war? A scenario

● President Truman's decision to drop the atomic bomb on Japan: pros and cons

● How the air power of the United States ended the Gulf War

● Examine the United States' presence in Bosnia. What were the original issues? Was our presence justified?

Weather and Climate

See also: Geography

- Inside a thunderstorm
★ The dynamics of a tornado
▲ Climatological changes that have been artificially induced by man since 1950
➥ The role of climate in the extinction of species in past evolutionary history
- Climate changes and carbon dioxide increases in the atmosphere
- The effects of nuclear explosions on weather and climate
➥ Weather and military operations
★ Reading weather indications from cloud formations
§ Myths and facts about lightning
- How vegetation affects the climate
○ The possibilities for man-made climates
- Are the polar ice caps melting? Cite meteorological statistics and scientific findings as evidence to support your thesis.
- Scientific evidence supporting a worldwide cold shift
- The radiation balance of the earth, what may happen to it, and what will happen to life on

earth if it does alter
▲ Rainmaking technology and its practical applications
- Elements of high altitude weather
➥ Atmospheric factors in health and disease
- The climatic impact of volcanic activity
★ The "greenhouse" effect in the biosphere
- Weather folklore, ancient and medieval
○ Political implictions of weather control
➥ Follow the path of a "killer" storm (Diane, Blizzard of '88, etc.) and describe its patterns, scope, and impact on the environment.
○ How energy technologies affect weather and climate
▲ Explain the procedure used to obtain "normal" weather statistics. Is this the correct terminology?
- Differentiate between dew, frost, ice, and fog. Explain their effects on vegetation. What other environmental fac-

426

tors are involved?

★ Discuss unique weather phenomena such as halos, sun dogs, glories, rainbows, and *aurora borealis*.

★ Waterspouts and dust devils: their makeup and behavior

● What are the differences between hurricanes, typhoons, and tornados? What are nature's particular distribution patterns?

● The effects of weather on aviation history

● Consequences of a permanent warming climate change. How would it affect human society?

● How weather predictions are made

● Profile of a typical hurricane. Include pattern, duration, and range.

● Causes and results of the 1930's Dust Bowl in the American Midwest. Consider the effects on both the environment and people involved.

○ The uses of artificial satellites in meteorology

● The causes of recent droughts. Approach this subject on a worldwide basis.

▲ Modern advances in hurricane and tornado prediction

● How trade winds affect world climates

★ El Niño weather variations have been increasing. What do climatologists feel is causing this variation?

● How the weather affects humans, physically and psychologically

● Hurricane tracking from space

● How can air pollutants affect weather and climate?

● What are the differences between western Europe's marine and Mediterranean climates? How have these variations affected those peoples living in each area?

○ What are some of the theories explaining the formation of the earth's atmosphere?

★ The folklore of weather prediction

● The energy budget of the atmosphere

× How the study of tree rings (dendrochronology) contributes to scientific knowledge about climates and environments of the past

● How the climate of urban areas differs from those of surrounding countrysides

● Can science predict, control, and harness lightning?

● Discuss the conflicting scientific views on global warming due to "greenhouse" gases accumulating in the atmosphere.

● Why storms regularly kill thousands in Bangladesh

● How the weather has been affected worldwide by the 1991 eruption of Mt. Pinatubo (Philippines)

Women

See also: Family Life; Gender Issues; Marriage; Sex

- Women doctors: their numbers, status, and characteristics
★ Defend or refute this statement: Women should be drafted
- Are there equal opportunities for girls in athletics?
○ Contradictions in Germaine Greer's *The Female Eunuch*
- Why women have not been accepted into the blue-collar trades. Has the trend shifted in terms of numbers and attitudes?
- Child care facilities for the low-salaried working woman
✔ Investigate the treatment of women prisoners in your state as compared to that of men, and also to facilities in other states.
- The midlife crisis of American women (or, what happens when the children leave home)
- Women in Greek drama
- Consumer credit for women
★ Villainous women in the Roman empire
- Effects of steroid use by women in sports
▲ Critical review of *The Woman's Bible* by Elizabeth Cady Stanton. Read the book and survey

and contrast the reviews and other comments.
§ Women in contemporary Iran. Consult the latest information for this survey.
- New federal and state laws resulting from the women's liberation movement
➤ Women in the military during World War II
- Miss America, past and present: some feminist perspectives
- Nancy Drew as American supergirl
- Problems of the "battered" woman. Consult the most current sources for information on this topic.
★ Compare the women's rights movement and the women's liberation movement.
- Menopausal myths and medical realities
- Particular problems of blue-collar wives
▲ The influence of Aspasia on Periclean Athens
★ The traditional attitude of the courts towards rape
- Compare and contrast the reviews of the book *Women and Madness* by Phyllis Chesler.

- John Stuart Mill on women's rights. In what ways were his opinions revolutionary?
- Examine the complexities of the issue of comparable worth
- ▲ The British suffragist movement
- What is a "liberated" male? Is he different in his beliefs and practices from a liberated woman?
- The treatment of women in the criminal justice system
- Negative aspects of the feminist movement
- Early attempts to secure the vote
- ▲ The use and effectiveness of female consciousness-raising groups
- ★ Defense against rape
- × Female genital mutilation is a common practice in many countries. What are the factors involved?
- What women gained from suffrage
- ★ The alcoholic housewife: a hidden horror
- × Expanding career possibilities for women
- ➡ Women in politics
- Does a double standard still exist? What women say about the issue.
- The Victorian female: manners, modesty, and morality
- ▲ Is there sexism in medical care?
- Compare and contrast the role of the housewife to the working woman.

- Compare and contrast the condition of women as characterized in Simone de Beauvoir's *The Second Sex* and Betty Friedan's *The Feminine Mystique*.
- The image of the black woman in American fiction. Select several characterizations, either from current fiction or from the past.
- ★ Women in the military academies. What are their particular problems?
- ▲ Amazons: Legend, myth, or reality?
- ▲ Women in the labor force during World War II when traditional male factory jobs were filled by women.
- § The social status of women in Italy
- Mohammed's views on the role of women. Compare this to the contemporary conventional Islamic attitudes.
- ○ Discrimination against women as evidenced in Christian theology.
- Why women object to the sexual double standard
- ➡ The characteristics of the major women in the Bible
- Why is there a stigma against single woman in most modern societies?
- × Examples of media stereotyping of the image of the American mother. How realistic is this image?
- Image myths of the American

black woman
- Women as depicted in TV commercials. Select for analysis a single time frame or the ads for a particular product type.
- Women's rights in communist countries
- Young prostitutes in America's urban centers
- Women in Congress
- Compare and contrast the traditional conception of womanhood with that espoused by the feminists.
- Refute or support: All women should be entitled to abortion upon demand.
× Sexual stereotyping in language
- Sexism in the world of business
§ Women in the novels of Leo Tolstoy (or D.H. Lawrence, Gustave Flaubert, John Updike, etc.)
- The accomplishments and influence of women film directors
- Major tenets of the women's rights movement
- The early days of "women's lib"
§ The role of women in Greek society
○ The character of Nora in A Doll's House and modern prototypes in contemporary fiction
- How women's attitudes towards marriage in the United States have altered since 1950
- The status of the medieval woman
- Findings of the President's Com-

mission on the Status of Women (1961)
- Self-defense for women
- Assess the effects of the women's movement on politics, education, and the economy.
- The physiological and psychological dimensions of menopause. What physical changes take place? What is the normal psychological response? What are some of the problems most often encountered?
- Select a variety of advertisements (use newspapers and magazines) in which women are depicted as sex objects in unrelated advertisements. Analyze the source, the intended audience, and the validity of each ad.
- The influence of women during the age of chivalry
- Why are gender role changes occurring more rapidly for women than for men? What are the patterns of these changes? Where and when are these shifts occurring?
- Sigmund Freud as a male chauvinist
○ The 1920's were the years of the "roaring twenties," bathtub gin and the flapper. Was this flapper a newly liberated woman with a different role and new freedom, or was she a product of media hype?
× The position of women in poly-

gamous societies. Use examples from several cultures as illustrations.

○ Parents, educators, and psychologists have been increasingly concerned over the rapid social maturation of adolescent American girls. Is this concern justified? Why? What are the personal hazards of "growing up too fast"?

★ The hardest choice for young mothers: staying home or the job career. Discuss choices, options and compromises.

● What role should women have in churches?

● The aims and goals of 9 to 5, National Association of Working Women

● How has feminism affected traditionally female professions (nursing, secretarial)?

Key to Symbols

● **average difficulty**	◆ **narrow down topic**
§ **substitutes possible**	▲ **large public or college**
★ **ample information in most**	**library required**
libraries	✔ **local option topic**
○ **specialized knowledge**	✗ **examples and supporting**
required	**evidence needed**

Working World

See also: Business and Industry; Computers; Labor

→ The ten best and the ten worst careers. Compile this list in terms of economics, educational opportunities, working conditions, etc. Thoroughly investigate each occupation and justify your selection.

• Maintaining creativity on the job

★ How to prepare for your first job

• New careers through technology. What are the possibilities and potentials?

• Career switching: a success story for many

▲ Career patterns of professional women

★ How to find a job you want. What job-hunting techniques have been consistently useful and successful?

• Basic language skills: self-improvement techniques. Include grammar, syntax, writing skills, vocabulary, etc.

• How has organized labor benefited the American economy? Discuss both short- and long-range benefits.

§ Prospects for a career in oceanography

× How automation has affected the American worker

• Describe in detail and justify the choices for a self-improvement reading program in your occupational area or in one you wish to enter.

• Managing effectively in a supervisory position

★ On-the-job stress and how to control and eliminate it

• How to instruct a trainee

× Methods for resolving interpersonal conflicts in the work environment

• How employee attitudes and morale affect productivity

• Underemployment among college graduates. What is the range of this problem? Are some career areas more overpopulated than others? Which are not?

○ Socioeconomic aspects of the robot revolution

○ Buying a word processor. Survey the currently marketed machines and evaluate them by cost, functions, complexity, and the office situation in which they

432

will be used.

- What has been the opposition to academic tenure? What are some of the proposed alternatives?
★ New bonuses for American workers. Consider profit sharing, day care centers, health clubs, home work schedules, etc.
- If you are employed, how would you run your company (or institution, etc.)? Describe your choices and changes and justify them with expert opinions and firm data. Would you get an "A" or an "F" from your boss?
▲ The work ethic and how it has changed in America since 1950 and why. A number of sociologists, psychologists, and social historians have addressed themselves to this issue. Consider and compare their theories.
§ Training <u>retail</u> personnel
✔ Select a <u>local</u> company and analyze employment opportunities, wages, working conditions, and fringe benefits.
- How to evaluate fringe benefits
§ Managing a <u>restaurant kitchen</u>
★ Why many small businesses fail. Are the reasons for current business failures the same as they were in 1930? In 1955?
- Affirmative action evaluated
★ Pros and cons of flexitime work schedules

★ Efficient filing procedures
- Business perks: Income tax dodges or a just compensation?
✕ Businesses you can run from home
- MBA's (Master of Business Administration) and the job market
○ How to evaluate pension plans
- Problems of women reentering the work force
- What are the principle advantages of midlife career changes?
- Psychological factors of unemployment
✕ Problems encountered by women in traditional male professions
- Work schedules. What are some of the newer options? How to determine which type of scheduling will work best for each particular situation.
- Should the United States institute large-scale occupational retraining for the unemployed?
✔ Interview several people engaged in your chosen career. Design your interview carefully.
- Methods of corrective action and discipline in the office or factory environment
- Managerial ethics
▲ The classic theory of motivation holds that money is the sole motivator in the workplace. Discuss this statement. Do authorities other than economists agree?
- Detail the conditions of work which best promote job

satisfaction.

○ How to effectively use the grievance procedure for the settlement of disputes

▲ Compare several of the most widely used methods of job evaluation and describe when and how each is most effective.

● How to motivate your employees

○ Considerations in office forms design

● Environmental factors for office planning. Include lighting, color, air conditioning, and sound.

○ Buying versus leasing word processing equipment

● How to plan space requirements for office workers. Focus on cost, flexibility, taxes, service, and capital investment.

● A positive program for job performance appraisal

★ What are the behavioral characteristics typical of leaders?

● How to improve communication between management and employees

§ A secretary's code of ethics

➥ Analyze the career choices of college graduates. You may wish to select from a particular field. Consider both economic and social status.

● The extent and significance of the underground economy in the United States. This includes illegal work, moonlighting, cheating on taxes, secret wages.

➥ How large companies recruit and select employees

○ Recession/inflation and national employment pattern changes

● Many of the unemployed are between the ages of 45 and 65. What are their particular occupational problems?

§ The training necessary for a veterinarian

● How to be a perfect boss

● Trends in employee education

✕ How group dynamics works in business situations

✔ Interview the personnel representatives of several companies to determine how their personnel policies (hiring, payscale, benefits, advancement potentials) have changed since the advent of affirmative action.

● How and why the employment possibilities for the handicapped have improved and increased

★ How to close a sale

● The ethics of sales work

● Work factors related to heart disease

● How to determine your managerial potential

● Increase your business vocabulary

▲ Ergonomics and the total office plan

● Improving speech communication in the office

● Who should be responsible for worker health and safety? The federal government, the state government, or the industry? Consult qualified experts to justify your answers.

- Brainstorming: What are the uses of this technique in the working world? What are its strengths and weaknesses?
- Holographic filing
- How is office automation altering the workplace?
★ What are the advantages and disadvantages of using polygraphy (lie detectors) for truth verification of employees? On what occasions should these tests be administered?
- The dangers of video terminal radiation
- How the trade deficit has affected the American job market

▲ Many modern offices contain chemical irritants. Discuss the extent of this problem and some of the potential solutions.
- Drug testing in the workplace and why it is increasingly necessary
○ What are the obstacles and objections to the computerized tracking of on-the-job activities?
- Why has union membership been decreasing in the work force over the last decade?
★ Telecommuting, when employees work at home and communicate with their office via computers and other media, has had an increasing impact on the workplace. Discuss the advantages and disadvantages of this arrangement.

Key to Symbols

- average difficulty
§ substitutes possible
★ ample information in most libraries
○ specialized knowledge required

- narrow down topic
▲ large public or college library required
↙ local option topic
× examples and supporting evidence needed

World Scene

See also: Contemporary Issues; Foreign Policy; Social Problems; Travel

★ European reaction to the Chernobyl nuclear accident
● The power of the House of Saud (Saudi Arabia)
★ The Zionist cause
★ The Rwandan genocide
● Has the collapse of the Soviet Union and communism led to democracy and capitalism?
● Why the United States withdrew from the United Nations Educational, Scientific and Cultural Organization (UNESCO).
● The status and strategic importance of Gibraltar. Survey the period from 1945 to date.
● The historic Bedouin lifestyle and how it is changing in the twentieth century
★ Amerasians: children of Americans in Vietnam. What has happened to those left behind?
● Terrorism in Israel
● Refute or support: America is no longer a major world power.
★ The Peace Corps today
● The origins of Africa's movements towards independence
● Terrorism and the I.R.A. (Irish Republican Army)

● The possibilities for international cooperation for future space flights
● Lebanon, Israel, and the Palestinians: Is peace possible?
● Palestinians in Arab lands today
○ The politics of Persian Gulf Oil
● The Israeli occupation of the West Bank and the Gaza Strip: the issues
● Is there a solution to the Israeli/ Arab conflict?
● Sikh violence in India. Describe the contemporary context of this conflict in terms of historical and religious origins.
○ Defend or refute: The third world has come of age.
➤ Human rights violations
● Is a universal language either practical or possible?
● The coal mines and miners in Ireland
● Current Russian relations with formerly Soviet republics
▲ The Flemish-Walloon controversy in Belgium
✗ Environmental management in underdeveloped nations
● The French role in Algeria

436

- The prevention of international kidnapping incidents
- Communism in South America: a current analysis and overview
- Proposed reforms for the United Nations
- × Effects of tourism on third world countries
- ★ Events leading to the death of Anwar Sadat
- What are the major ethical considerations of arms sales to third world countries?
- Gypsy life in modern Europe
- Property ownership in China
- ★ Can Venice be preserved?
- ★ Northern Ireland's new martyrs
- § Namibia's future
- ▲ The significance of the new Karakorum highway between Pakistan and China
- Strengths and weaknesses of socialized medicine as practiced in Sweden and in Great Britain
- The phenomenal growth of Singapore as world trade center
- O Food surpluses and political power
- ★ Should the United States have kept the Panama Canal?
- Pesticide use in developing countries: levels, effects, and controls
- ▲ Nuclear proliferation: Who has what today? Tomorrow?
- § The nature and scope of communism in Italy
- Economical, social, and political problems of the state of Israel
- Background, organization, and current status of the Palestinian Liberation Organization (PLO)
- The major issues in the Arab-Israeli conflict
- ★ Why Quebec wants to secede
- × The social, economic, and political effects of large military budgets in underdeveloped nations.
- O Prospects for stability in the Persian Gulf. What are the issues or powers which may affect and influence this sensitive area?
- Foreign language instruction in Western Europe's schools
- The current status of Iran's petroleum industry
- Why Che Guevara became a hero
- Are the lawsuit settlements in the Bhopal disaster equitable?
- What happened to the Berlin Wall?
- Why does Israel receive more United States assistance than any other nation?
- O What are the social, political and economic consequences of German reunification?
- ▲ Poland and Russia: How their relationship has changed since 1980
- United Nations: peacekeeper or peacemaker?
- § Life in a rural Indian village
- The dynamics of a Kibbutz
- Is the United Nations a failure?
- O The impact of OPEC on world fuel prices: 1972–1986
- Survey and compare the relationship between income and fertility. Include third world countries. What conclusions may be drawn?

- ➤ The roles of third world nations in global politics
- ○ The role of the United Nations in decolonization
- ✕ Ecological values versus economic preferences
- ● The new techniques of urban guerrillas
- ➤ The consequences of nonalignment
- ● Proposals for a world food bank. What are the current prospects?
- ● What are the limits of growth for the world's population?
- ○ How the North Atlantic Treaty Organization (NATO) has contributed to European prosperity
- ✕ Critical issues affecting nuclear diplomacy
- ➤ Did European colonists properly prepare emerging African nations for independence? Select a country.
- ● What are the difficulties encountered by newly independent African countries?
- ● Common themes among Nobel prizewinners
- ▲ Remnants of the Hammurabi code in today's world
- ● Plans to eliminate world poverty: a historical overview
- ➤ Levels of malnutrition in emerging nations
- ● Should the United Nations Charter be reviewed and revised? What have been the major changes proposed in the past?
- ● Some experts predict that the industrialized world may be only

- 10–15 years away from the greatest dependency ever on Mideast oil. Comment.
- ➤ Spain before and after Franco
- ● The American image abroad and its relation to American television exports
- ▲ Examine urbanization as a global phenomenon
- ★ Is Europe (and/or the rest of the world) being "Americanized"?
- ○ Western Europe is becoming "a United States of Europe." Support or refute this statement with appropriate data and evidence.
- ● How has the Common Market modified the traditional national political sovereignty of member countries?
- § Describe the major barriers to economic prosperity in Portugal.
- ● Compare social and economic conditions in Iran as they existed under the rule of the Shah and as they are today.
- ➤ Select one developing nation and investigate its productive potential. What major factors hinder development?
- ▲ What has been the United Nations' disarmament record to date? Do authorities consider this satisfactory?
- ● Compare and contrast Mecca and Medina.
- ● What have been the causes of recent famines?
- ▲ Strengths and weaknesses of the European Common Market

★ World famine: Whose responsibility?

• Should governments agree to terrorist demands in order to save the lives of hostages?

• A goal for the United Nations: international water supply and sanitation codes

• The implications of "brain drain" from underdeveloped countries

▲ A contemporary assessment of guerrilla actions around the world

★ Sources of political unrest in the Caribbean countries

✕ Changing conceptions of nationalism in emerging nations

• Soviet life as depicted in the works of Aleksandr Solzhenitsyn

➥ Military regimes in South America

§ Current economic problems in Great Britain

➥ Levels of soil depletion in underdeveloped countries

• The purposes and effectiveness of OAS (Organization of American States)

▲ The status of the Catholic Church in communist Cuba

★ India's nuclear capabilities

• Political trends in the Middle East

• How the French influence has been retained in its former colonies of French Polynesia, Morocco, and Martinique

▲ The charge has often been made that much of U.S. foreign aid has not benefited those for whom it was originally intended, but, through graft and lack of supervision, was diverted into unauthorized channels. Investigate this accusation.

★ Africa has rising levels of famine. Why are these food problems increasing?

✕ Have recent famine relief projects been successful? Have they had a permanent positive effect?

✕ The "Westernization" of China

• How good are international relief agencies?

★ Have Palestinian rights been ignored in the Middle East?

○ Escalating levels of global debt

★ Is it possible to prevent international terrorism? Consider the opinions of several experts currently studying the problem.

• Unemployment violence in Great Britain

★ The worldwide demographics of AIDS

• The results of the Hungarian Revolution (1956)

• Communist genocide in Cambodia

• The Basque Separatist movement

★ The basis of the Iraq-Iran War

• The origins of the Sino-Soviet split

○ An overview of revolution in South American countries in the twentieth century

• The pros and cons of African federations

• The causes and extent of racial tension in Great Britain

▲ The logistics of world famine relief

★ Compare the governments of Batista and Castro in Cuba.

- Many experts believe that the greatest risk of nuclear war or attack is between (or from) terrorist groups. Why?
- Limitations of the Green Revolution in developing countries
- How the Berbers of Morrocco have survived in the twentieth century
▲ Global corporations and underdeveloped countries: the economics of power
O Proposals have often been made to convert potentially arable lands in South America, Asia, and Africa into agricultural production. What are the possible benefits compared to the problems involved?
- The arms race in the Middle East
★ Islam: Seventh, fourteenth, or twentieth century?
★ Events leading to the Tiananmen Square massacre (1989)
- What factors account for the global increase of tuberculosis?
▲ Current relations between China

and Russia. Consult the most recent sources.
★ Should Northern Ireland be given independence?
- Radiation levels from the Chernobyl nuclear accident. Detail the effects on the European and world communities.
- Support or refute the use of euthanasia in the Netherlands.
★ Is the greenhouse effect a reality?
- Gang violence has increased to dangerous levels in the nations of the former Soviet Union. Describe the current situation and proposed solutions.
- Should the British have relinquished Hong Kong?
★ Evaluate the worldwide production of chlorofluorocarbons (CFCs) and their eventual environmental effects.
★ The stratospheric ozone hole and our future on earth
➤ What are the realistic prospects for peace in the Middle East?

"HOW TO" GUIDES

How to Interpret Poetry

How to Read and Write About Fiction

How to Write Book Reports

How to Write Poetry

How to Write Research Papers

How To Write Short Stories

How to Write Themes and Essays

How to Write a Thesis

MACMILLAN•USA

Other fine references from

Webster's
NewWorld

Webster's New World™
Children's Dictionary

Webster's New World™
Student's Dictionary

Webster's New World™
Compact School and Office Dictionary

Webster's New World™
Pocket Dictionary

Webster's New World™ Thesaurus
New Revised Edition

Webster's New World™
Speller/Divider